ALEXANDER THE GREAT

Museum Capitolinum, Rome

SIX THOUSAND YEARS OF HISTORY

BY

EDGAR SANDERSON, A. M.

AUTHOR "HISTORY OF THE BRITISH EMPIRE"

J. P. LAMBERTON, A. M.

AUTHOR "HISTORIC CHARACTERS AND FAMOUS EVENTS," "LITERATURE OF ALL NATIONS," ETC.

JOHN McGOVERN

AUTHOR "THE GOLDEN LEGACY," "THE TOILERS' DIADEM," "FAMOUS AMERICAN
STATESMAN," ETC.

AND THE FOLLOWING EMINENT AMERICAN EDITORS
AND WRITERS:

JOSEPH M. ROGERS, A. M.; LAURENCE E. GREENE; M. A. LANE;
G. SENECA JONES, A. M.; FREDERICK LOGAN;
WILLIAM MATTHEWS HANDY

INTRODUCTION BY

MARSHALL S. SNOW, A. M.

PROFESSOR OF HISTORY WASHINGTON UNIVERSITY AND DEAN OF THE COLLEGE; AUTHOR
"CITY GOVERNMENT," "POLITICAL STUDIES," ETC., ETC.

TEN VOLUMES

VOL. VI.

FAMOUS WARRIORS

E. R. DuMONT, PUBLISHER

PHILADELPHIA   CHICAGO   ST. LOUIS

1899

ILLUSTRATIONS

WORLD'S FAMOUS WARRIORS

ALEXANDER THE GREAT
B. C. 356-323

HE NEVER KNEW DEFEAT

That the true history of a man so remarkable and a
career so brilliant as that of Alexander the Great should
have become surrounded and obscured by a confusing mass
of tradition and legend, which, even to the present day
leaves in doubt and uncertainty, much of importance regarding his real character and the motives which dominated him, is but natural when contemporary conditions
are taken into consideration. He occupied the center of
the world's arena in an era of superstition and idolatry and
his scenes of action were distributed over so great a territory and among so many nations, differing widely in
religion, thought and manners, that both the written and
unwritten accounts handed down to us, partake of the
prejudices and peculiarities of time and locality. In the
mass of Greek narrative, Oriental hyperbole, Barbaric tradition, Arabic lore, and Egyptian story he has been lauded
and defamed, both to an exaggerated degree. He has been
charged with the most infamous crimes and the justice of
his course as a King and conqueror has been questioned,
but his prowess as a warrior in every acceptance of
the word, neither friend or foe has attempted to deny.
His achievements on the field of battle stand unsurpassed
in the world's history. With his victorious armies he
marched to the confines of the then known earth and never

suffered defeat. During his brief reign he proceeded from one conquest to another, encountering and surmounting the greatest difficulties. His personal bravery and skill was often brought to the test and never failed him. Arrian says of him: "In body he was handsome, most indefatigable, most active; in mind, most manly, most ambitious of glory, most enterprising and most religious. In sensual pleasures he was most temperate and of mental excitements, insatiable of praise alone. In arraying, arming and marshaling armies, most skillful. In raising the soldiers' courage, filling them with hopes of victory and dispelling their fears by his own undaunted bearing, most chivalrous. In doubtful enterprises most daring. In wresting advantages from enemies and anticipating even their suspicions of his measures most successful. In fulfilling his own engagements most faithful, in guarding against being overreached by others, most cautious. In his own personal expenses most frugal, but in munificence to others most unsparing." Alexander became King of Macedonia at the age of twenty years, and died before he reached the age of thirty-three. During those twelve years he demonstrated the supremacy of the Macedonian arms over the most powerful kingdoms of the world. The complex character of the conqueror is shown in many instances of his life. In some cases he exhibited the greatest forbearance and mercy, and in others appeared to delight in cruelty. Thousands of barbarians were unnecessarily put to the sword, and cities were destroyed for revenge. Alexander wept when he parted with his veterans, yet with his own hand in a drunken rage he slew the friend who had saved his life in battle. By some he has been designated a tyrant, by others a deliverer. He died at the height of his success, "and perhaps," says Arrian, "it was better thus to depart, to the extreme regret of all men, while his glory was unstained and before he was overtaken by those calamities to which mortals are exposed and on account of which Solon advised Crœsus to consider the end of life and to pronounce no man happy on this side of the grave."

Alexander's death resulted from fever, although in this as in almost every event of his career the chroniclers of ancient times invented a story to the effect that he was poisoned by a glass of wine. Alexander was also credited with divine origin and some have gone so far as to credit him with miraculous powers. Another instance of exaggeration appears in the stories about the horse Bucephalus, which none but Alexander was said to be able to ride. The animal was also credited with mysterious origin. Arrian says the horse was presented to Alexander early in life by Demaratus, a Corinthian.

Alexander was the third King of Macedonia of that name. He was born at Pella in the year 356 B. C. His father, Philip, was renowned as a monarch of great courage and sound judgment who had made his name feared and respected among the nations and tribes which surrounded his kingdom. His court was one of splendor and he had surrounded himself with many of the ablest minds of that period. It was but natural therefore that Alexander should receive the benefit of the best education that could be procured. While little is known regarding his infancy and the training received by him during early boyhood, it is evident that no time had been lost, for it is recorded that when eleven years of age he was proudly exhibited by King Philip before Demosthenes, Æschines, and eight other leading Athenians who were visiting the court as Ambassadors. The boy then gave specimens of his skill on the harp and in declamations. In his fifteenth year he was placed under the immediate tuition of the great philosopher, Aristotle, who continued to teach and advise his pupil until the invasion of Asia. The scope of his education, according to Plutarch, included moral philosophy, logic, rhetoric, the art of poetry, the theory of practical government and even metaphysics. Among all his studies, Homer delighted him most. Meanwhile it must not be supposed that Aristotle's well-known system of education had permitted the neglect of the physical as well as mental training of his pupil. His studies were diversified at the early age of sixteen by his initiation into the duties of the high station of Regent of Macedonia, to which position he was appointed by his father while the latter was detained at the siege of Byzantium. Two years later he received his first practical experience on the field of battle. It was at the celebrated battle of Chæronea, where he commanded the left wing of the army and defeated the Thebans before his father, who commanded the right wing, had succeeded in gaining the victory over the Athenians, against whom he was pitted.

In the year following, Philip married Cleopatra, the daughter of one of his Generals, and this led to discord in the royal family. He had previously married several wives, daughters or sisters of Thracian, Illyrian, and Thessalian chiefs, but when he accepted as wife the daughter of a Macedonian General and went so far as to change her name to that of his mother, Eurydice, it became apparent to Olympias, the mother of Alexander, that she herself was no longer to be regarded as the legitimate Queen. Alexander also viewed this action with suspicion and the result was that he retired with his mother to Epirus, her native country. Soon afterward a reconciliation was effected and mother and son returned to Macedonia. The re-union was celebrated by the marriage of Alexander, King of Epirus, and brother of Olympias to Philip's daughter, Cleopatra. During the festivities, Philip was assassinated at the door of the temple by Pausanias, an officer of the King's bodyguard. Although various reasons were assigned by the historians of the period as the cause for the crime, there is little doubt but that it was a conspiracy originated in Persia, as Demosthenes, the principal agent of Persia in Greece; announced the death of Philip to the Athenian Assembly, long before the news reached Athens from any other source.

In the tumult following the assassination, the Macedonian Assembly was hastily called together and Alexander was proclaimed King. At the time of his death, Philip was preparing to invade Asia. Alexander announced that the plans of his father would be carried out, that the Government of Macedonia would continue as before, only under another name. Thus, having just passed his twentieth year, Alexander began a reign, the fame of which spread to the ends of the earth. The first step taken by the young King was to avenge the death of his father. He caused the execution of three of the alleged conspirators, so Justin tells us, and one of the Princes supposed to be involved fled to Persia, where he was received with joy by Darius, who later placed him in command of his Greek mercenaries.

Immediately following the death of Philip, Macedonia became beset on all sides with dangers. The Barbarian tribes on the north, east, and west were preparing to renounce their subjection. There was disaffection in some of the states of the Grecian Confederacy. Sparta was ripe for revolt and Athens, as a result of the harangues of Demosthenes and other anti-Macedonian leaders, was ready to renounce her allegiance to the Confederacy. Even Thessaly, which had profited greatly under Macedonian rule, contained a faction which stood out for violent

opposition to the new King. But they did not yet know
Alexander. Within two months after his father's death,
the youth had entered Thessaly with an army of unconquered Macedonians at his back. The Thessalians in
the face of this resolute move did not hesitate, but
promptly decided that their relations should remain the
same with him as they had with his father. He proceeded
to Thermopylæ, where the Council duly recognized him
as his father's successor, and then he hastened to Corinth,
where a Pan-Hellenic Council met. He was appointed
Captain-General of the Greek Confederacy and empowered
to make war upon their common enemy, the Persians. In
these negotiations, Plutarch asserts, Alexander wisely
consulted the two great Ministers and Generals of his
father, Antipater and Parmenio, both of whom he had
retained in their previous positions. Having successfully
concluded his affairs in Southern Greece, Alexander returned to Macedonia to spend the winter in preparation for
the moves against the Northern and Western barbarians,
which he considered necessary before leaving his dominion
to carry out his project against Persia.

Early in the spring, he set out with his army and made
for the southern foot of Mount Hæmus, the modern Balkans. Here his passage through the mountain defiles was
disputed by the fierce mountaineer tribes of Thracians.
They could not long withstand the Macedonian phalanx,
however, and the expedition pushed forward into the vast
plains between the Balkans and the Danube, occupied by
the warlike Triballi, who had only recently become masters
of the country, having driven the Getæ to the northern side
of the Danube. Syrmus, the Triballian chief, retired before the advance of Alexander to a large island in the
Danube, close to the sea. While in rapid pursuit, the
Macedonians received information that a large body of the

Triballi had made a circuit and were posted on a stream which Arrian calls, Lyginus, so as to intercept any communication between Alexander and Macedonia. He marched his army back, found the enemy as indicated, and after a desperate battle, in which 3,000 of the Triballi were slain, resumed his march upon the island, which he reached after three days. A fleet which he had dispatched from Byzantium was already there. He embarked his troops on the ships and attempted to effect a landing, but the failure of the ships to strike the island at the proper points, together with the desperate resistance made by the besieged, made the attempt a failure and the effort was abandoned.

On the opposite bank of the Danube, during this time, had gathered great crowds of the clans of Getæ, making warlike demonstrations. Alexander decided to attack them and during the night, with the aid of his few ships, all the canoes that he could collect and large numbers of hastily constructed rafts, he threw across the river 1,000 cavalry and 4,000 infantry. At dawn, when the surprised Getæ beheld this array of Macedonians, they fled to their city, pursued by Alexander's army. The city was plundered and the booty was considerable, for even at this early day, according to ancient historians, these Scythians were a commercial and agricultural people. For this success Alexander offered up sacrifices to Jupiter, the Preserver, to Hercules, the supposed ancestor of the Scythians and to the river god who had permitted him to cross the mighty river in safety. This practice, here begun by Alexander, of worshiping the gods of every nation, according to the customs of the people among whom he happened to be, was persistently followed by him throughout all of his succeeding campaigns. Invariably his first care after a battle was to repair to the temple and there, under the directions of the priests, offer sacrifices for the victory. The brilliancy of Alexander's exploit against the Getæ made so strong an impression upon the Triballi chief that he renewed without further ado the treaties previously made with Philip, and his action was followed by all the rebellious tribes in the vicinity.

As Alexander was returning from the Danube and had reached Pæonia, situated between the Nestus and Strygmon rivers, intelligence reached him that two Illyrian chiefs, Glaucius and Cleitus had taken up arms and declared their independence. Pæonia had formerly been independent and the race was once, we are informed by Hippocrates, more civilized than the Macedonians. But the Nation had been subdued by Philip and annexed to Macedonia. The Nation was divided into a number of tribes and one of these, the Agrian, was ruled by Langarus, a youthful companion and fast friend of Alexander. He now came to his Sovereign with the information that the tribe called Autariatæ had been persuaded by the rebellious chiefs to invade Macedonia. Langarus offered to invade the territory of this tribe and keep them engaged at home while Alexander dealt with Glaucius and Cleitus, who proposed to invade Macedonia from the West. Alexander marched his troops into Illyricum, where he found Cleitus advantageously situated on the hills above the City of Pellium. Alexander at once prepared to attack the town. With the determination to save the town, the army of Cleitus came down from the hills. Alexander attacked and routed the enemy, of which the majority took refuge in Pellium. The arrival of Glaucius, with a numerous army, compelled Alexander to desist from his efforts against the town and he found himself, moreover, in a perilous position, from which he extricated his army only by the most skillful movements. Having safely crossed the river which flowed at the foot of the hills he found comparative security for his troops and encamped there for two days to rest his army. The Illyrians regarded his retreat as a great victory for them, and instead of attempting to pursue their advantage or preparing defenses, they gave themselves up to feasting and celebration. The opportunity was not allowed to escape by Alexander. During the third night, he suddenly re-crossed the river, attacked the enemy in their camp and put them to complete rout. The blow was so severe that Cleitus, despairing of holding the town against his adversary, set it on fire and retired. Never again during the reign of Alexander did the Illyrians take up arms against him, so wholesome was the defeat administered.

Just at this time events of importance were transpiring in the South, which, when reported to Alexander, made it necessary for him to exercise all haste in conducting his army thither. After the battle of Chæronea, in which Alexander had himself participated nearly three years previous, Philip had placed a Macedonian garrison in the Cadmeia, the citadel of Thebes, after banishing the Theban leaders and appointing Macedonians as Governors of Thebes. But the exiles of Thebes secretly returned, surprised the Macedonian Governors and killed them and by asserting that Alexander had been slain in the Illyrian campaign, caused the Thebans to revolt. The garrison in the citadel held out against the Theban armies, while Antipater, at the head of a Macedonian column, was vainly seeking to relieve it. The news of the revolt of Thebes spread over Greece like wildfire, under the zealous agitation of Demosthenes and other Persian agents in Greece. Athens was on the point of following the example of Thebes, but the Assembly prudently concluded to await further confirmation of the report of Alexander's death.

The Lacedæmonians as usual were ready to aid in the proposed anti-Macedonian move.

In the brief space of thirteen days he marched his army from the mountains of Illyria and reached Thermopylæ. Within a few days later he was encamped on the hills to the north of Thebes. The Thebans were loath to believe that Alexander was approaching. The leaders of the revolt maintained that the troops was but a reinforcement for the column of Antipater. They were soon undeceived, for on the following day Alexander joined forces with Antipater and moved upon the city. He hoped to gain possession by peaceable means, but the leaders in the rebellion knew that no mercy would be shown them and assiduously impressed upon the Thebans that the only chance of safety lay in armed resistence. Alexander had scarcely encamped to the south of the city with the double purpose of cutting off communication with Athens and of being as near as possible to the citadel, when he was attacked by the Thebans and a number of his men slain. The real attack on Thebes, according to Ptolemy, began by accident and not design. Perdiccas, one of Alexander's commanders, had been placed with a brigade close to the circumvallation constructed by the Thebans between the foot of the citadel and Alexander's camp. He saw a favorable opportunity, and, without waiting for orders, furiously attacked and destroyed a part of the defences, gaining entrance to the enclosed space. Other brigades followed him, and Alexander, seeing the advantage gained, brought up a fresh phalanx. In the meantime, the brigade of Perdiccas had surmounted the second line of circumvallation and was fighting in the space between it and the citadel. The Thebans were driven as far as the temple of Hercules, but here they made a stand, charged their pursuers, and drove them back to the breach. Now

Alexander, with the flower of the phalanx, set upon the Thebans and carried all before him and reached the gates of the city simultaneously with the Thebans. Before the gates could be closed the Macedonians had made their ground good within the walls. At the same time others of his troops, joined by the garrison from the citadel, entered the city by way of the Temple of Amphion. The Thebans in despair gave up the contest. In Alexander's army of confederates were several tribes which in the past had suffered great injuries at the hands of the Thebans. These proceeded to take a terrible revenge. "No mercy was shown to age or infancy," says Williams in his narrative, "the distinction of sex was disregarded. The virgin at the foot of the altar met with the same fate as the warrior who refused quarter, and nothing but the active interference of the Macedonians stayed the butchery and saved a part of the inhabitants."

The fate of Thebes was decided by an assembly of the confederacy. The city was leveled to the ground and the captured Thebans with their wives and children were sold into slavery. Priests and priestesses and all friends of Macedonia were excepted. The only house left standing among the ruins was that which had been occupied by the lyric poet Pindarus, and Alexander himself interfered to save the descendants of the poet from injury and loss. Plutarch asserts that Alexander, later in life, regretted his severity against Thebes, but there is no definite evidence that such was the case. Viewed in the light of those times, Thebes suffered a just retribution for the merciless atrocities she had previously perpetrated upon the peoples of Greece.

The fate of Thebes caused Athens, which had shared in a large degree in the conspiracy, to tremble. Demosthenes and his associates, who had openly rejoiced at the

murder of Philip and had mocked Alexander, had cause
to dread his vengeance. To avert the expected blow, the
assembly met and sent a delegation to congratulate the
young conqueror on his successes in Thrace and Illyricum
and on the suppression of the Theban revolt. In return,
Alexander demanded the surrender of Demosthenes and
nine other common disturbers of Grecian tranquillity. The
Athenians beseeched him not to insist upon his demand,
and it was magnanimously withdrawn.

Alexander then returned to Macedonia, having in one
spring, summer and autumn carried to a successful conclusion a campaign unrivaled in Grecian history. He
had invaded Thrace, passed Mount Hæmus, defeated the
Triballi, crossed the Danube, subjugated the Getæ,
marched against and defeated the Illyrians, reduced
Thebes, and satisfactorily settled all dissensions in Southern Greece. "This campaign alone," says Williams, "was
sufficient to prove that no equal military genius had yet
appeared among men."

Alexander spent the winter at Ægæ, the primitive capital of Macedonia, and in the spring of the year 334 B. C.
set out on his first campaign in Asia, to satisfy his cherished design of conquering Persia. He marched to Sestus,
where his fleet, consisting of 160 triremes, had been assembled. With his army he crossed the Hellespont, and,
according to Arrian, was himself the first to set foot on
Asiatic ground. Following his usual custom, Alexander
made it his first duty to offer sacrifices to the gods. He
ascended to the city of Priam and worshipped in the temple of the Ilian Minerva. The army of invasion consisted,
says Williams, who closely follows Arrian and Strabo in
all of the more important events of Alexander's career,
of 30,000 infantry and 4,500 cavalry. The infantry
included 12,000 Macedonians, 7,000 confederates, 5,000

mercenary Greeks, 5,000 Thracians, Triballians and Illyrians and 1,000 Agrians. In the cavalry there were 1,500
Macedonians, a similar number of Thessalians, 900 Thracians and Pænians, and 600 confederates. With this force
Alexander had been able to enter Asia unopposed.
Whether his rapid movements had taken the Persian
satraps by surprise, or whether they were willing that he
should enter their domain, hoping to annihilate his force,
history does not record. At any rate, no attempt was made
to bar his progress until the army had been led to Arisba
by Parmenio, while Alexander lingered to explore the
ruins of Troy. Information then reached him that the
Persians were collecting at Zeleia, and he at once advanced
in that direction. At the River Granicus the enemy was
found drawn up on the opposite bank. On a narrow strip
of level ground, between the river and the foot of a long
line of low hills, was the Persian cavalry, numbering
20,000. The hills in the rear were occupied by a similar
number of Greek mercenaries under the Persian leader,
Omares. The hostile armies faced each other on opposite
banks of the river, and Alexander, after briefly exhorting
his followers to prove themselves good warriors, plunged
into the stream at the head of the right wing and personally led the attack. It was a contest between the Persian
javelins and scimetars and the Macedonian lance, between
the fierce but wild fighting of the Persians and the
discipline and skill of the Macedonians. The conflict
began in the water itself, but gradually the Persians
were driven back from the bank and the Macedonians
gained the level ground between the river and the mountains. Alexander was easily recognized by the white
plume in his helmet, his gorgeous shield and the magnificent equipment of his retinue. Thus marked, he was
instantly attacked by Mithridates, the son-in-law of

Darius, at the head of a troop of horse. Alexander did not
wait for the attack, but spurred his horse forward, and
with one thrust of his lance slew Mithridates. While dis-
engaging his weapon he was assailed by Rhœsaces,
another Persian nobleman, who with his sword struck
off a part of Alexander's plume and helmet. Alexander
pierced the Persian's breast through his corslet and slew
him, also. It was here that Cleitus, captain of the royal
troop of cavalry, known as Companions, saved the life of
his sovereign. While engaged in the combat with Rhœsaces, Alexander was attacked from behind by Spithrid-
ates, the Ionian satrap, whose scimetar was raised to
strike, when Cleitus, with a tremendous stroke, severed
the Persian's arm at the shoulder. No doubt the battle
abounded with incidents of a similar character, but the
above, as affecting the personal bravery and prowess of
the young sovereign, have been thought worthy of record
by nearly all of his historians, from the earliest to the more
modern. During this desperate conflict against the left
wing of the Persian cavalry, the left wing of the Macedonians had put to rout the right wing of the Persians,
and when the left gave way before Alexander, it became
general and the Persian cavalry fled, leaving the Greek
mercenaries to their fate. The defeat of the Persian cavalry had been accomplished by employing only the Macedonian cavalry and the light troops, the Macedonian phalanx having as yet not been engaged in the battle. As the
Greek mercenaries of the Persian army still held their
ground on the hills, however, the phalanx was brought
up to attack them in front, while the two wings of cavalry
under Alexander and Parmenio assailed them on the
flanks. The fate of these professional warriors who
fought under a foreign banner against their own countrymen for hire, was terrible. Omares, their leader, fell

at his post, and all but 2,000 of the 20,000 were slain. The living were sent as prisoners to Macedonia and made slaves. The record of losses on the Macedonian side is given as but twenty-five of the Companion cavalry, sixty other horsemen, and thirty foot soldiers. Williams and other modern historians agree that many more were slain, but that the ancient records of the campaign mentioned the loss of only native born Macedonians. This battle gave Alexander control of the Hellespontian Phrygia. The chief city of the satrapy was Dascylium, and Parmenio was sent there and took possession without resistance. Alexander appointed Calas, a Macedonian, as Governor, and instructed him to exact no greater revenue from the provincials than had previously been payable to Darius.

Alexander's way was now for a time made easy by the fame and terror of his name. As he took up the march into Southern Asia, the cities capitulated without resistance, and when within eight miles of Sardes, the Lydian capital, he was met by a deputation from Mithrenes, the Governor, who surrendered the citadel with all its treasure. This not only furnished Alexander with funds, but gave him possession of the most important fortress in Western Asia. The Lydians had once been a powerful nation, but for 200 years, following their subjugation by Cyrus the Elder, had been tributaries to Persia. Alexander issued a decree, restoring to them all rights and laws as they existed before the Persian conquest, and also proclaimed their nominal independence. From Sardes he marched upon Ephesus. There were two factions in Ephesus, the democratic and the aristocratic, and the latter had recently acquired control of the government through the patronage of Persia. The approach of Alexander was therefore hailed by the democracy, while the Persian garrison, overawed by the news of the victory at Granicus, abandoned the city and retired to Miletus. This restored the supremacy of the democratic faction, and they proceeded to revenge themselves upon the aristocracy. Several of the aristocratic leaders were stoned to death, and only the arrival of Alexander prevented a general massacre. Arrian writes that this act of mercy on Alexander's part gave him more favorable renown than any other of his deeds in Asia Minor. He also gained favor with the Ephesians by showing due honor to their great idol, Diana, in whose worship he caused a grand procession to be given by his troops. Alexander now hastened to Miletus, the Ionian capital. The Governor promised to give up the city without resistance, but the arrival of the Persian fleet caused him to change his mind. Alexander immediately stormed the city and captured it. Previous to the arrival of the Persian fleet, the Macedonian fleet had arrived and occupied the narrow entrance to the Milesian harbor, and while not strong enough to attack the Persian fleet in the open sea, was so situated as to prevent the entrance of the Persians to aid in the defense of the city. Halicarnassus, the capital of Caria, was the next point to which Alexander turned his attention, and here he met with stubborn resistance. Darius, on receiving news of the rapid strides being made by the invader, had given Memnon, who escaped death at the battle of the Granicus by flight, unlimited power in the defense of Lower Asia. The rapidity of Alexander's movements through Ionia had made it impossible to withstand him there, but Memnon had collected at Halicarnassus a fleet of 400 triremes and large bodies of troops, and had carefully fortified and provisioned the city. Two strong citadels guarded the town, and the land side was protected by a ditch thirty cubits in width and fifteen deep. This had to be filled by the Macedonians before they could bring their battering engines to bear upon the walls. Ephialtes, the Athenian, with a chosen body of troops, and supported by Memnon, made a savage attack upon Alexander's troops in an effort to destroy his works and engines, and were prevented only by the implacable bravery of the Macedonians. Finding that they would be unable to withstand further assault by the besiegers, the Persians set fire to the city and retired to the citadels. These appeared impregnable, and a body of troops was left to blockade them, while Parmenio, with the Thessalians, the Greeks of the confederacy, and the more cumbersome baggage, was sent to Sardes to go into quarters for the approaching winter. Alexander also granted permission at this time to all officers and men who had recently been married, to return to Macedonia to spend the winter with their brides. This act, whether from political motives or from pure kindness, redounded greatly to Alexander's fame, for every returned warrior helped to spread among all classes of Greece, accounts of the valor and generosity of the Macedonian sovereign.

Winter did not, however, put a check on the triumphal progress of Alexander. With that part of the army which he had retained, he continued his advance into the enemy's possessions, and city after city through Lycia and Pamphylia opened their gates to the conqueror. The important city of Phaselis sent to him a deputation with a golden crown and offers of submission. On his way thither he took by storm the mountain town of Termissus, and thus conferred a favor upon the dwellers of the lowland towns, who were subject to periodical raids from the bandit tribes which occupied Termissus. It was mid-winter when Alexander reached Phaselis, and in this city of luxury and wealth he remained for a brief period of repose. While here he received a message from Parmenio, informing him that Alexander, the son of Æropus, who had been suspected in connection with the assassination of Philip, but who had later so far ingratiated himself in the good graces of the son, that he had been appointed commander of the Thessalian cavalry; was engaged in a traitorous correspondence with the Persian court. On orders immediately returned by Alexander, the conspirator was taken into custody, before he could accomplish his designs against the King. Alexander now took up the march to Perga, and this march was attended by a rash and dangerous adventure, which is worth relating. He had a choice between two routes, either to cross the precipitous Mount Climax, or go by way of the treacherous road along the sea. Strabo gives a clear idea of the incident in the following words: "Mount Climax overhangs the Pamphylian Sea, but leaves a narrow road upon the beach. This, in calm weather, is dry, and passable by travelers; but when the sea flows, the road, to a great extent, is covered by the waves. The passage over the hills is circuitous and difficult; consequently, in fine weather, the shore road is used. But Alexander, although the weather was boisterous, trusting principally to chance, set out before the swell had ceased, and the soldiers had to march during the whole day up to their middle in water." Inasmuch as it was regarded as miraculous that a south wind did not arise and dash the army to death against the rocks, it gave the royal sycophants opportunity to proclaim that even the sea had retired before the victorious Alexander. He himself made no miracle of the event, and in his letters, quoted by Plutarch, he simply says: "I marched from Phaselis by the way called Climax." After visiting Perga and several other cities, none of which offered any opposition, Alexander proceeded to cross Mount Taurus with the intention of entering Phrygia. His progress was hampered by conflicts with the powerful Pisidian tribes occupying the mountain passes and cities, and it was only after a decisive battle had been fought before Sagalassus, which was taken, that his sovereignty over the whole of Pisidia was acknowledged. Although but meager accounts are given of this mid-winter campaign among the mountain wilds and against the most savage adversaries, it must be recorded as one of the great achievements of Alexander. He now continued to Celænæ, capital of the Greater Phrygia, which surrendered after holding out for a brief season. With the object of concentrating his army for the campaign of the approaching spring, Alexander marched to Gordium, where he was joined by the troops under Parmenio and the bridegrooms who had been allowed to spend the winter in Macedonia. Gordium was the ancient capital of Phrygia during the period of its independence and power, and here was preserved the famous cart of Gordius with the knot which fastened the yoke to the pole, and the tradition which maintained that whoever should succeed in untying the knot was to be the future sovereign of Asia. Alexander ascended to the citadel to examine the knot, and the accounts of the manner in which he solved the difficulty vary. The general acceptation is that he cut the knot with his sword, and this, it is conceded would be most in keeping with his character, but Aristobulus, who is supposed to have been present, writes that Alexander removed the pin which traversed the pole, and was thus enabled to detect the manner in which the mysterious knot could be untied. At any rate, it was agreed by the Phrygians that he had fulfilled the tradition, and he was recognized by them as lord of Asia.

In the spring of the year 333 B. C. Alexander, with his reorganized army, marched from Gordium with the purpose of conquering the two powerful provinces of

Paphlagonia and Cappadocia. On reaching Ancyra, the
modern Angora, he was met by deputies from the Paph-
lagonian chiefs, with professions of submission.   He
granted their prayer not to invade the province with an
armed force and proceeded to Cappadocia. After subduing the whole of this province, he turned southward
into Cilicia, though not without some opposition in the
mountain defiles.   He had scarcely led his army down
upon the plains of Cilicia, when information reached him
that Arsames, the satrap of Tarsus, was about to burn
the town. With his cavalry, Alexander hastened to the
threatened city and saved it from destruction. Here Alexander for the first time gave way to the strain and hardships which he had undergone since the beginning of his
reign, and was stricken with a fever that nearly proved
fatal.   But youth and his vigorous constitution conquered,
and he was soon again at the head of his victorious army.
In the meantime, Memnon, with his Persian fleet, had
been active. Chios had been betrayed into his hands, and
he had induced four of the five cities on the island of Lesbos to renounce the Macedonian alliance. Mitylene, the
chief city, held out against him, and as he was besieging
it, he fell ill and died. This, Arrian says, was the most
severe blow that could have befallen Darius. The hopes
of the anti-Macedonians in Greece had also been raised,
as all the information they received from Persia was partisan, and matters had advanced so far that Agis, the King
of Sparta, was conferring with Pharnabazus, the successor of Memnon, relative to forming an anti-Macedonian
confederacy in Greece; when the news of the defeat of the
Persians at Issus put an end to the negotiations.

Darius had during this time been encamped with his
army on the plains between the Syrian Gates and the modern Aleppo, awaiting the advance of the enemy. But the

illness of Alexander and the expedition into Cilicia had
caused such delay that the Persian monarch began to be
persuaded that Alexander did not mean to attack him. He
therefore marched with his army into Cilicia.   At this
time Alexander, having heard of the advance of the Persian army, was moving toward Castabala, whither also,
Parmenio with his force was moving to meet him.   Parmenio had forced his way over the western ridge of Mount
Amanus, through the pass known as the lower Amanian
Gates, captured Issus and occupied the more eastern passes
into Syria.   Two days after Parmenio joined Alexander,
the combined army encamped at Myriandrus.   That night
a heavy storm confined the Macedonians within their camp
and the following day Alexander learned to his astonishment that Darius was in his rear.   The Persian army had
passed through the upper Amanian Gates into the plain
of Issus, recaptured the city and slain the Macedonian
invalids they found there, then passed on to the Pinarus
River.

Having satisfied himself during the day that his information was correct, Alexander exhorted his men and consulted with his officers, and in the darkness of the ensuing
night the entire army marched to the gates, and at midnight occupied the defile leading down to the plain of
Issus, which was fairly ablaze with the camp-fires of the
Persian hosts.   At dawn the Macedonians moved down
through the narrow pass, deploying into line as it opened,
with the mountain on the right and the sea on the left.
The troops of Darius were of such vast numbers that in
order not to embarrass the movements of the main formation, he ordered his 30,000 cavalry and 20,000 light troops
to cross the Pinarus.   In forming his line, he placed in
the center the heavy armed Greek mercenaries, numbering
30,000. On either side of these he placed a similar number

of equally well armed Cardaces, all Persians, and trained in arms from their youth. To the extreme left, on the side of a hill, so situated as to threaten Alexander's right wing, were placed 20,000 light troops. On the Macedonian side, Alexander, as usual, commanded the right wing and Parmenio the left. His formation was practically as usual, with the Macedonian phalanx facing the Greek mercenaries of the Persians and the cavalry and confederates equally divided between himself and Parmenio. The Agrians, supported by a body of archers and a small body of cavalry, was posted facing the 20,000 light troops on the hill. Alexander determined to test the stability of this portion of the enemy's troops, and ordered the Agrians, archers and cavalry to charge. The Persians precipitously retired from the side to the summit of the hill. Satisfied that there was little danger from that quarter, Alexander added the Agrians and archers to the right wing and left only 300 cavalry to keep the 20,000 in check. As the Macedonians moved forward to the attack, Darius recalled his cavalry and posted it opposite Parmenio's wing. Alexander at once dispatched his Thessalian cavalry to the support of Parmenio. Slowly and majestically the Macedonians advanced while their King rode down the lines, addressing his warriors and inspiring them to heroic action. As soon as the advancing line came within range of the Persian missiles, Alexander led his wing into a furious charge against the Cardaces, who fled at the first onslaught, leaving the 15,000 troops known as Kinsmen and the 10,000 Immortals, posted back of the Cardaces, to battle against Alexander, and although these made a desperate resistance, they were ultimately cut to pieces and scattered. At this time the Macedonian phalanx was being hard pressed by the Greek mercenaries, who as stated, numbered 30,000, while the phalanx in this instance consisted of but five brigades. Having vanquished the foe in his immediate front, Alexander turned to the relief of his phalanx, attacking the mercenaries in the flank and instantly turning the tide of battle. Still the fate of Parmenio's command hung in the balance. The Persian cavalry attacked desperately, and it required all the skill and bravery of Parmenio and his Thessalian horse to maintain their ground. What the result would have been is doubtful, had not the tidings reached the Persians that the rest of the army had been routed and that their king had fled. This filled them with despair and they too fled from the field. Darius in his royal chariot, had taken to flight at the first sign of defeat. When he reached uneven ground he abandoned his chariot, shield, arms and royal robe and continued his flight on horseback and did not stop until he had reached a point beyond the Euphrates. He had made no effort to take with him his wife, son and daughters, who were left in the royal tent to the mercy of the victors. The number slain in battle is given as 10,000 Persian horsemen and 100,000 infantry. The losses of the Macedonians were also large, though not proportionately. The facts in regard to the battle are as recorded by Aristobulus and Ptolemy, who are also followed by Arrian, and, according to their account, the battle lasted from daybreak until dark. From the figures given it is shown that Darius had as formidable an army as ever engaged in battle, and it is inferred by historians generally that he had besides the five great divisions named, multitudes of other troops who took no part in the battle, either through cowardice or lack of proper leadership. The result can be attributed only to the superior skill and valor of the Macedonian troops, so ably exemplified by their leader, who although he had himself received a sword wound in the thigh, on the following day visited the wounded and delivered a funeral oration over the dead. The wife and daughters of Darius were afforded every protection by Alexander, who announced that he had no animosity against Darius and was only engaged in a legitimate struggle for the Empire of Asia.

Before advancing to battle Darius had transferred the court and treasures of Persia to Damascus, where were also the families of the principal Persians and the foreign ambassadors. Parmenio and the Thessalian cavalry was sent to take possession, and although the whole body had left Damascus in an effort to escape, they were overtaken and captured, together with all the rich booty of the Persian treasury. Among the prisoners were envoys from the treacherous Athenians, but Alexander mercifully liberated them.

Alexander himself marched southward along the coast, and the first Phœnician state to submit was the island Aradus with its dependencies. While at Marathus, one of these dependencies, ambassadors from Darius came to Alexander with a message in which the Persian sovereign demanded the restoration to him of his family and possessions, and offered to make a treaty with Alexander, claiming that he had battled only to retain his rightly inherited kingdom. Alexander replied briefly that Darius need have no fear for his personal safety and might freely come to claim his family, but that any further communications to Alexander must be addressed to him as King of Asia. He also accused Darius of conspiring at the murder of Philip and inciting the Greeks against Macedonia, and concluded that if Darius desired to dispute the sovereignty of Asia, to stand his ground and he would attack him wherever he might be.

Alexander then continued his march to the center of Phœnicia, receiving the submission of many cities. Tyre was among the number who sent him the usual crown of gold, but they refused to permit him to enter the city, although he announced it as his purpose to worship in their Temple of Hercules, which Arrian says was not the Grecian Hercules, but another, worshiped many Centuries before. Alexander then determined to lay siege to Tyre. His desire was to gain possession of all Phœnicia, in order to receive the support of the great Phœnician fleet, the most numerous and efficient of the Persian navy. With this addition to the Macedonian fleet, he argued, he could acquire Cyprus and its fleet, and with the three combined he would be enabled to sweep the sea of Persia's maritime superiority. Finally, he hoped to invade and conquer Egypt and thus set at rest all fears for the safety of Greece and Macedonia. Thus, toward the end of the year 333 B. C., began the siege of Tyre. The old town had not been rebuilt, but the new town which had sprung from its ashes occupied an island, according to Pliny, two miles and a half in circumference, and situated from the mainland by an arm of the sea, half a mile in width. The city was extremely populous and its buildings were many-storied. It was surrounded by walls and fortifications of great strength, and would scarcely have been regarded as pregnable even if located in such a position that it could be approached by land. Alexander proposed to capture this stronghold without a single ship, and in the face of a formidable navy. He began to construct a mound through the sea from the shore to the walls of the city, and there, with the aid of battering rams and engines to effect a breach and storm the city. There was plenty of material for the undertaking to be had from the ruins of old Tyre, but as the work progressed it became more and more difficult. His troops while at work were exposed to the missiles thrown from engines planted on the walls of the city and also from attacks on both flanks by armed triremes. Finally the Tyrians made a successful attack, and in a few hours destroyed all that had been accomplished. Nothing daunted, he at once began the construction of a second mound on a larger scale. Winter was now setting in and the fleets of many of the Phœnician cities which had joined him were returning home. Soon he had mustered over 100 of these, and a little later secured the services of an even larger number from the Kings of Cyprus. Various plans of attack were attempted and proved failures, but finally, after seven months, with the aid of rafts carrying battering engines, a breach was made and the city was simultaneously attacked from all sides. In the long siege the Macedonians had lost many men and beside harbored revenge against the Tyrians for one especial act of cruelty practiced by the Tyrians against a number of Macedonians captured by them. The prisoners were murdered in cold blood and thrown into the sea in view of their comrades. When, therefore, the city fell into the hands of the besiegers, 8,000 Tyrians were put to the sword and 30,000 were sold into slavery. But for this blot upon the victory, the capture of Tyre might have been counted as the greatest of Alexander's military exploits. During all the months of the siege no effort had been made, apparently, to relieve the beleaguered city. It is related by Arrian and other historians that shortly before the fall of Tyre, a second deputation came to Alexander from Darius, and with an offer of 10,000 talents, the hand of one of his daughters in marriage, and all that portion of Asia west of the Euphrates. Like all other propositions it was submitted to the Macedonian council, and Parmenio is reported to have said: "Were I Alexander, I should conclude the war on these terms and run no further risk." To this Alexander replied: "So would I, were I Par-

menio, but as I am Alexander, I cannot." Following this
he sent a curt message to Darius, announcing that if he
felt inclined to marry Darius' daughter, he would do so
without asking consent, and also notified Darius that if
he desired any favors, he must come personally and ask
for them. Darius realized that further negotiations would
be fruitless, and began his preparations for the final struggle to retain his kingdom.

Alexander now turned, as he had intended, to Egypt.
Palestine and other districts willingly submitted to the
conqueror. Gaza, governed by a eunuch, alone dared to
resist. The city was built on a mound near the edge of
the desert that separated Syria from Egypt, and was well
fortified. For two months he besieged the city, finally
forced his way in, and, as the garrison refused quarter,
all its defenders were slain. The city was of considerable
importance as a mart for Arabian goods, and had a fine
harbor. A rich booty of aromatics and frankincense fell
into the hands of the victor. Josephus asserts that Alexander marched from Gaza to Jerusalem with hostile intentions, and that he was received by the priests of that city,
and, as was his wont, made acknowledgments to their God.
Having crossed the dangerous desert to Pelusium in seven
days, Alexander was received without resistance, and his
sovereignty accepted with apparent joy. He then
advanced with his army along the eastern branch of the
Nile, he visited Heliopolis and later, Memphis, the capital
of lower Egypt. Here he embarked on the Nile, sailed
down the Canopic branch and into Mareotic Lake, where
he viewed the site upon which Alexandria was afterward
built. Here Hegelochus, his admiral in the Ægean,
brought information of the dissolution of the Persian fleet
and the recovery of Tenedos, Lesbos and Chios. This
resulted from the acquiring of the Phœnician fleet, and

made Macedonia master of the seas. Alexander having concluded to visit and consult the oracle at the shrine of Jupiter Ammon in the Libyan desert, he set out with a small detachment, and, after stopping at Parætonium on the sea shore, plunged southward into the desert and in eleven days reached the Ammonian Oasis. Some historians have ventured to narrate the questions asked by Alexander and the answers given by the oracle, but historians of the period assert that Alexander, who alone was admitted to the innermost shrine, simply stated on coming forth, that the answers had been satisfactory to him. The reported and widely accepted announcement of the oracle was to the effect that Alexander was the son of the god, Zeus.

On his return he joined his army at Memphis, and marching through Phœnicia, he crossed the Euphrates, turned northward and reached the Tigris in the vicinity of Nineveh or Old Mosul. The entrance of the army into Assyria was marked by a total eclipse of the moon. According to the calculations of astronomers, this was on a night in September. Historians fail to record where or how Alexander and his army spent the time from the crossing of the Euphrates in July until the entrance into Assyria in the end of September. For three days the army marched along the bank of the Tigris without any sign of an enemy, but on the morning of the fourth a body of Persian cavalry was discovered on the plain. They attempted to escape by flight, but were pursued, and several captured. From these prisoners, Alexander learned that Darius with his army was encampd near Gaugamela, where he had selected his battle-field and even smoothed down hillocks and removed obstacles that might interfere with the movements of his cavalry. The Macedonians went into camp and remained for four days resting from

the fatigues of the march. On the morning of the fifth
day the advance was taken up, the troops carrying nothing
but their weapons. The day was already far advanced
when Alexander came within sight of the Persian hosts.
A council was held over the question whether it was
advisable to attack at once or wait until the following
morning. The majority of the Generals were for immediate action, but Parmenio expressed the opinion that
various parts of the field had been trenched and that it
would be prudent to first make an examination. This
advice was adopted and the army encamped under arms
and in line of battle, while Alexander, with a strong
detachment, made as close an examination of the field as
circumstances would permit. He returned to encourage
his officers and men and they in turn told him to be of good
cheer. While the Macedonians were catching a few hours
of sleep and rest the army of Darius was kept under arms,
as they had been all of the previous day. Darius, having
chosen his ground, could not change it without throwing
his whole line into confusion. His preparations had been
extensive, his army was composed of warriors of nearly all
the nations of the then known earth, and his order of battle
was as follows: The center, commanded by Darius himself, included the Royal Kinsmen, the Immortals, the Indians, Carians, and Mardian Archers. On the left were the
Bactrians, Dahæ, Persians, Susians, and Cadusians. The
right was composed of Syrians, Mesopotamians, Medes,
Parthians, Sacæ Tapeiri, Hycanians, Albanians, and Saca-
senæ. Behind, a second line was formed of Uxians, Baby-
lonians, Sitacenians, and Carmanians. In front of the
left wing was drawn up all the Scythian cavalry and 1,000
Bactrians, as well as 100 scythe-armed chariots. Fifteen
elephants and 50 war chariots were placed in front of
Darius and facing Alexander and his Companion cav-

alry. In front of the right wing were posted the Armenian and Cappadocian cavalry, and 50 war chariots. The Greek mercenaries were drawn up on either side of Darius to withstand the charge of the Macedonian phalanx. Arrian computed the total number of infantry under Darius at 1,000,000 and the cavalry at 40,000. Alexander's army consisted of 40,000 infantry and 7,000 horse. His formation of the main body was in a general way similar to that at Issus, except that the flanks were better protected by large bodies of Confederates and mercenary cavalry and a second line of infantry was drawn up behind the phalanx with orders to face about in the event of attack from that quarter. These precautions were taken as it was certain that the myriads of the enemy must encircle the Macedonians and attack was expected from every quarter. When the battle opened, Alexander charged obliquely, either to avoid the elephants and the chariots or else to turn the right of the enemy's center. The chariots did little execution, the drivers and horses being easily picked off by the javelin men. None of the historians relate what became of the fifteen elephants and the presumption is that they also failed in their mission. Alexander at the head of the Companion cavalry pierced the Persian line and attacked the left center of Darius in flank, with the object of forcing his way through the Kinsmen and Immortals and reaching Darius. The Persian cavalry soon began to give way and the infantry at various points were unable to withstand the pikes of the phalanx. As on the plain of Issus, Parmenio was sore beset by the Albanians and the multitudes of Parthians and Sacæs, so that Parmenio was forced to send a message for aid. Just before the message reached Alexander, Darius had ingloriously fled from the rout which was gradually surrounding him and Alexander was setting out in pursuit, but the demand from Parmenio caused him to lead his Companions to the relief. However, the tide had already turned in Parmenio's favor and Alexander met the Persian and Parthian cavalry in full retreat. In the conflict which ensued the fugitives fought for life and liberty, not to gain a battle, and in this encounter sixty of the Companion cavalry were slain. The victory was now decisive in all parts of the field and Alexander resumed his pursuit of Darius as far as Arbela, forty miles from the field of battle. But Darius had been too fleet and the troops had to be content with capturing the royal treasure which had been left there and another chariot and spear which the escaping monarch had left behind. Arrian places the number of lives lost in the battle at 300,000, and more than that number of prisoners were taken. From Arbela, Alexander marched in four days through a submissive country to Babylon, where his appearance called forth demonstrations of joy from the crowds that poured forth to greet him as their new master. Having arranged the affairs of Assyria, he proceeded to Susa.

Abulites, the satrap of the Susians, readily surrendered the city and citadel to Alexander. The place had been a favorite seat for Persian monarchs and was used as a treasury. Alexander came into possession here of fifty thousand talents of silver, besides other valuables. He left a Macedonian Governor and garrison in the citadel, but reappointed Abulites to the satrapy. He now set out for Persia proper, or, according to its Greek name, Persis. He entered the territory of the Uxians, and started for Persepolis, the ancient capital of Cyrus. The royal road between Susa and Persepolis ran through a defile in the mountains which was held by a warlike tribe of Uxians, so powerful that they had been in the habit of collecting tribute from the King every time he passed through the

territory. They sent a message to Alexander informing
him that he could not pass unless he consented to paying a
similar tribute. He at once took 8,000 chosen infantry,
and, entering the mountain gorges, reached the chief
Uxian villages by night under the guidance of friendly
Uxians and surprised the inhabitants. Many were slain
and their herds and valuables were seized. He then
hastened to the pass, where the mountaineers had assembled to protest his passage. They were caught
between Alexander's force, which came up from the rear,
and the main body in front, and completely scattered. In
entering Persis, Alexander was met at the strong position
known as the Persian Gates, by Ariobarzanes and a strong
army, numbering 40,000, and was for a time compelled to
retreat, but later carried the pass and moved upon Persepolis. According to Diodorus and Curtius, Alexander
gave over the whole city to his soldiers for plunder, and
they made the destruction complete. The great palace of
Darius, according to Arrian, was deliberately burned.
This unusual course on Alexander's part, the historian
holds was to revenge the destruction of Athens by Xerxes.
The ruins of the once magnificent palace are still to be seen
near Istakar. The winter of the year 331 B. C. was now
setting in, but Alexander, with picked bodies of troops,
attacked and subdued the mountain tribes of the vicinity,
and Pasargada, built by the elder Cyrus, surrendered without a struggle. Here also he secured rich treasures and an
immense train was made up to carry the spoils of Persepolis and Pasargada with the army, as Alexander did not
dare leave this treasure in the province. After remaining
four months in Persis, he once more set out in pursuit of
Darius. This fugitive monarch had taken refuge at Ecbatana, the modern Ispahan, then the capital of Media. It
was reported that Darius was preparing to once more give

battle to the invader, and Alexander hurried forward with his effective force only to learn after entering Media that Darius was on his way to the Upper Provinces. The conqueror entered Ecbatana, which is described by ancient writers as one of the wealthiest and most magnificent capitals in Asia. Six thousand Macedonians and a strong body of cavalry was left to garrison the city and guard the treasures which had been taken, and were now deposited in the citadel of the Median capital. Parmenio was sent by a circuitous route through the territory of the Cadusians into Hyrcania, while Alexander, with the Companion cavalry, the greater portion of the phalanx, the Agrians, and the archers went in pursuit of Darius. His hopes of overtaking Darius were baffled and after having passed the Caspian Gates he received information that several of the satraps who accompanied Darius with their troops in his flight had seized the King and made him a prisoner. Alexander now set out with the utmost haste, accompanied by only the Companion cavalry, with the purpose of rescuing the unhappy monarch from the hands of traitors. The leaders in the treachery against Darius were the satraps, Bessus of Bactria, Barsæntes of the Drangæ, Brazas of the Arachosians, and Satibarzanes of Areia. Nabarzanes, the commander of the royal guards, also aided in the treachery. After several days' pursuit, during which Alexander learned that Darius was being conveyed in a covered wagon, he came within sight of the barbarians and their royal prisoner. For a short time they pressed on, carrying Darius with them, but seeing that they would be overtaken, inflicted a fatal wound on the King and left him dying in the road. By the time Alexander reached him, Darius was dead. This took place, according to Arrian, in July, 330 B. C. After resting his troops at Hecatompylos, Alexander prepared to invade Hyrcania, situated between Mount Taurus and the Caspian Sea. He met with practically no opposition from any of the satraps throughout all this territory. At this time a conspiracy against Alexander was discovered, which resulted in the execution of two of the most powerful men in his army. Alexander had long previously been warned against Philotas, the son of Parmenio, but the suspicion seemed to him incredible, as the closest friendship had always existed between them, and Alexander had shown great honors both to father and son. There are various accounts of this conspiracy, the confession of Philotas and the execution of both Philotas and his father, the great Parmenio, who had aided Alexander to win so many of his battles. The version of the Greek historians, who seized this incident to blacken the name of Alexander, is that Philotas was compelled by torture to confess and implicate his father and that Parmenio was assassinated by the orders of Alexander. Ptolemy, the son of Lagus, writes that Philotas was brought before the assembled Macedonians and convicted on the testimony of witnesses in addition to his own confession that he was aware of a plot against the King, yet had failed to reveal it. It is certain that if Alexander had been slain, the command of the army would naturally have fallen to Philotas, who commanded the Companion cavalry, and with his father, Parmenio, who was at this time in charge of the troops at Ecbatana, they could with little difficulty have claimed and held the Empire. In addition to Parmenio and Philotas, several others of lesser rank were convicted of complicity and also executed. Alexander now marched eastward, receiving as he advanced the submission of the Drangæ, the Drangogæ, and the Arachosians. While he was thus engaged, Satibarzanes, one of the murderers of Darius, led a revolt in Areia. Troops were sent against him, but he stood his ground and was slain in battle. Alexander's main army continued to the eastern part of the Taurus range of mountains and remained during the two worst months of the winter. Early in the spring of 329 B. C. the army crossed the main ridge into Bactria, where the satrap Bessus had prepared to dispute Alexander's advance. He did not remain to give battle, however, but retired across the Oxus into Sogdiana. The Macedonians captured the two chief cities of Bactria, Aornus, and Bactra. The pursuit of Bessus was then taken up. The river Oxus presented a formidable barrier to Alexander's progress northward. Efforts to bridge it proved failures, and finally floats were formed of hides, either inflated or stuffed with hay, and with these he managed to get the army across in five days. Bessus was betrayed by the satrap of Sogdiana, and Alexander sent him in chains to Bactria. All Transoxiana now admitted the authority of Alexander and garrisons were placed in the principal cities. Meanwhile, with the main army, he advanced to the Jaxartes and there learned that the Sogdians had revolted, massacred most of the Macedonian garrisons, and taken up arms. Alexander sent Craterus with a detachment to march against Cyropolis, the chief city, and himself proceeded to Gaza, which, though walled and well defended, was carried by storm the first day. The men of the town were ruthlessly put to the sword. During the two following days, two other towns were similarly treated. The inhabitants of still two other towns abandoned their homes and attempted to escape, but were overtaken and cut to pieces by the cavalry. Alexander then moved against the capital, which was well fortified and garrisoned by 1,800 barbarians. Access to the city was gained by the discovery of an aperture under the wall, where a small stream had run. Alexander himself, with a few others, crept in, and, rushing to the nearest gate, succeeded in opening it for the entrance of the Macedonians before the garrison could prevent them. Many were slain and thousands of prisoners were exiled. He then proceeded again to the Jaxartes, and founded another Alexandria.　During the progress of this work he crossed the river and engaged the Scythians in battle, defeating and putting them to flight.　In the meantime Spitamenes had besieged the Macedonian garrison at Maracanda and Alexander sent 1,500 infantry, 800 cavalry, and 60 Companions to their relief.　Spitamenes retired and was pursued by the Macedonians until the edge of the desert was reached, when battle was given and the Macedonians retreated in disorder.　A massacre followed and but forty of the cavalry and 300 of the infantry returned to Maracanda.　This was revenged by Alexander, who turned his wrath against the inhabitants of the vicinity and laid the country waste.　He retired to Bactra and spent the winter there.　It was during his stay at Bactra that Alexander in a fit of rage killed Cleitus, who had saved his sovereign's life at the battle of Granicus.　The festival of Bacchus was being observed and Alexander as well as his commanders had been drinking heavily.　Alexander was boasting of his great deeds and comparing them to those of his father, when Cleitus took issue with him. The enraged King, who had been disarmed by his friends, who feared his violence, snatched a weapon from one of the guards and slew Cleitus.　For some time he appeared to suffer the greatest remorse, refusing to eat or drink for three days.　Before Alexander's departure from Bactra, he had Bessus, the prisoner, brought before a general council, which ordered that the nose and ears of the traitor be cut off.　After thus being mutilated, he was sent to Ecbatana to be executed by his own countrymen.　As soon as the winter was over, Alexander again entered Sogdiana, divided his army into five sections under separate leaders, and subdued the insurrection, except for a few points, among which was the Sogdian rock, which was held by Oxyartes, a Bactrian chief, who had refused to surrender, but had taken refuge with his family and followers upon this precipitous rock, abundantly well supplied for a long siege. Alexander made overtures for the surrender of the place, but the garrison felt secure. Liberal rewards were then offered to those of his men who would first scale the rock. Of the many that volunteered, 300 were selected, and these, with the aid of iron hooks, used for fastening down tents, and strong cords, spent the night in scaling the cliff and at daybreak all but thirty, who had missed their holds and fell to death, reached the summit. Oxyartes' surrender followed and among the captives was Roxana, his eldest daughter. Her beauty completely captivated Alexander, who at once married her. This was about a year after he entered Sogdiana for the second time, and neither Arrian nor Strabo are very clear in regard to these campaigns. It is agreed, however, that he entered Margiana and there founded a city. As usual, it was named after himself. It soon fell into decay, was later restored by Antiochus, and still exists under the name of Meru Shah-Ian. During this time, it is related Alexander gave considerable of his time to hunting wild beasts in the great parks of the chiefs he had conquered. On one of these occasions a page was punished for an offense and entered into a conspiracy, together with other pages and some of the subdued satraps, to murder Alexander. The conspiracy was revealed and confessions obtained under torture which implicated, among others, Calisthenes, a Grecian philosopher who had attached himself to Alexander's retinue and who had on several occasions shown insolence to the King. Ptolemy and Aristobulus both record that the pages admitted that Calisthenes had incited and encouraged them in their plot. Aristobulus says that Calisthenes died while in custody, but Ptolemy asserts that he was first put to the torture and then hanged. Among his own class in Greece he was regarded as a martyr and the enemies of Alexander made the incident one of the many tales of tyranny and cruelty which they circulated about him.

Alexander was now preparing to invade India, and in the middle of the summer, 327 B. C., he set out from Bactria. His progress into India and along the Indus River met with little real resistence until he came upon a great body of Indians, who had retreated before his advance, but were now encamped and ready to fight. After a desperate battle he gained the victory, took 40,000 prisoners, and 230,000 head of various kind of cattle. Next he advanced upon Massaga, a large and wealthy capital. He succeeded in reducing it by means of a tower and movable bridge similar to that used in the capture of Tyre. The inhabitants of Bezira and Ora being unable to withstand Alexander took refuge on the celebrated rock of Aornos, reputed to have thrice held out against the fabulous Hercules. Arrian describes the rock as about twelve miles in circuit, with its lowest point three quarters of a mile above the plain and its summit a cultivated plateau. The rock was cut by great ravines and abounded with detached summits. It was by gaining one of these, located higher than the position held by the Indians, and thus attacking them from above and below simultaneously, that gained the first strong foothold on the rock. Alexander began the work of building a mound across the ravine, which seperated his army from the enemy, and soon his engines began to play havoc with the Indians and after the garrison in the outworks had deserted under cover of night, the fortress itself was assailed and captured. Alexander found plenty of timber along the Indus and set about constructing a fleet, visiting, in the meantime, the City of Nysa, where the inhabitants received him as their protector and claimed to be the descendents of a part of the victorious host of Dionysus. The whole summer and winter had passed during his march from Bactria, and now with the commencement of the spring of 326 B. C. he crossed the Indus over a bridge constructed by Hephæstion and Perdiccas. The army marched first to Taxila, the capital of a great territory between the Indus and the Hydaspes. Taxiles, the ruler, sent presents to Alexander and welcomed him. Alexander, in turn, is reported to have given Taxiles one thousand talents, but on resuming his march left a garrison at Taxila. When the Hydaspes was reached, the opposite shore was lined with the infantry and cavalry, war chariots and elephants of Porus, chief of the territory east of the Hydaspes, who was prepared to defend his dominion. At this season of the year the river was a mile wide, turbulent and deep. This was not a great obstacle, for Alexander had brought with him his ships, in sections from the Indus. His main concern was that he would on reaching the opposite side of the river be unable to form his cavalry owing to the elephants which lined the banks. He made camp and gave it all the appearance of permanency, as if he intended to wait until later in the season, when the river would fall. At night he marched his cavalry up and down the river and made an uproar which caused Porus to keep his army constantly on the alert and moving. As nothing seemed to come of this, however, Porus was gradually lulled into a feeling of security. Meanwhile Alexander had selected a spot ten miles up stream, where there was a bend in the river and a wooded island in the middle of the channel, as the place

for crossing.   In the night during a storm he crossed the
river at this point and at dawn was on the shore occupied
by Porus.   Alexander's troops numbered 11,000.   The
army which Porus brought up to attack him consisted of
30,000 infantry, 4,000 cavalry, 300 war chariots, and 200
elephants.   The battle ended in a decisive victory for the
Macedonians.   According to Arrian, 20,000 of the Indian
infantry and 3,000 of their cavalry fell and all the chariots
and the surviving elephants were captured.   In this battle,
Alexander's horse, the famed Bucephalus, which had borne
him in all of his great battles, died, not of wounds, but of
age, heat, and over-exertion.   Porus, who had shown
great valor in the battle, won the regard of Alexander, who
restored him to his kingdom and added to it.   The whole
country between the Hydaspes and the Acesines was
reduced and placed under Porus.   Alexander then crossed
the Hydraotes, the modern Ravee, where a warlike Nation,
the Cathaians and two other independent tribes, were in
arms and waiting for the invader at the strong city of
Sangala.   Alexander carried the city by storm, losing
only 100 men, while the enemy had 17,000 slain and 70,000
were taken prisoners.   The Cathaians were armed principally with arrows and hand missiles, which proved of
little effect against the heavy armor of the Macedonians.
Alexander marched southeast to the banks of the Hyph-
asis, the modern Sutlej, and was preparing to cross it in
search of further conquest.   But the Macedonians, fatigued with the rains and sickened by the climate, besides
being disappointed in having found so little booty; de-
murred against going further.   He tried in vain to induce
them to follow him and finally sacrificed to the gods and
found that the signs were ominous, whereupon he
decided to return.   He erected twelve great alters to
mark the limit of his advance and then with his

army retraced his steps to the Hydaspes, where the battle with Porus was fought, and where the cities of Nicæa and Bucephala had been founded, and a force of men had been at work building ships for Alexander. The army was now divided into three divisions, one proceeding down the left bank, another down the right, while Alexander, with the third, embarked aboard the 2,000 river craft and started down stream. In eight days the confluence of the Hydaspes and the Acesines was reached. Alexander received information that two Indian tribes, the Malli and the Oxydracæ, would dispute his passage through their territories. The army was again reformed into three divisions, not including that part which continued down the Acesines. Alexander himself took charge of one division and by making a forced march through twenty-five miles of desert surprised and captured a Mallian city after the inhabitants had made a brave but vain resistence. The next day he marched to the Hydraotes, came up with the rear guard of the fugitive Malli and cut it to pieces, crossed the river and attacked a Brachman (Brahmin) town and slew 5,000 Indians. As Alexander advanced the Malli fled before him, but finally to the number of 50,000, made a stand on the left bank of the Hydraotes. When Alexander crossed the river and attacked with only his cavalry, a severe conflict was carried on until the arrival of the Agrians. Then the Malli retired to a neighboring fortress, which was at once besieged by the Macedonians. Alexander was the first to scale the wall and as the ladders broke under the crowding of his followers, he was left alone to face the missiles of the barbarians inside. Without hesitation he leaped down among them and began a combat single handed against thousands. He was soon joined by a few of his own warriors, but sank from an arrow wound in the breast.

Within a brief space, the Macedonians swarmed into the fortress and in the frenzy of seeing their King, as they supposed dead, put every man, woman, and child within the walls to death. Alexander slowly recovered from his wound, while additions were being made to his fleet. On recovering sufficiently, he sailed down the Acesines to the Indus and proceeded down to the royal palace at Sogdi. Continuing to Pattala, at the head of the delta of the Indus, he ordered a harbor and docks constructed and began building a citadel. Then he followed the Indus to its mouth, and returning to Pattala, made ready for the homeward march. Separate routes were taken by the divisions, Alexander with his troops entering the desert of Gedrosia, the modern Makran. After sixty days of terrible suffering, during which many men died of thirst or fatigue, he arrived at Pura, the capital of Gedrosia. He then proceeded to Kirman and was there joined by the division of his army under Craterus, while the satraps of neighboring provinces came forward with horses, mules, and camels for the use of the army, well knowing what must have been the result of the march through the desert. With the exception of the Bactrian and Sogdian insurrections, none of the many satraps which had submitted to him had rebelled in all that territory from the Hellespont to the banks of the Indus, and from the borders of Scythia to the desert of Æthiopia. On his way to Persis, Alexander gratified his desire to visit the tomb of Cyrus. He found it broken open and despoiled of most of its valuable belongings, even the lid of the golden coffin having been carried away. Alexander ordered the tomb restored to its former magnificence. On arriving at Susa, he decided to draw closer the union he had effected between Persia and Macedonia, and was married amid the greatest pomp and ceremony to Stateira, the daughter of Darius. Eighty of his chief officers followed his example and married women of the Persian nobility. In addition, ten thousand of his soldiers took Persian wives. During his campaign in the upper provinces, Alexander had selected 30,000 boys to be taught the Greek language and armed and equipped like the Macedonian phalanx. This army, composed of the flower of the youth of Persia, was now reviewed by the King. This, however, greatly displeased the Macedonian veterans, and when he proposed to send home the aged and wounded, there were cries of disapprobation and mutinous taunts. Alexander became enraged, and calling upon the guards, he rushed among his warriors and with his own hand seized or pointed out the most mutinous, thirteen in number, and ordered their instant execution. After this he shut himself up in the palace for two days and on the third, when he was preparing to replace his veterans with Persians, the Macedonians implored his mercy and a reconciliation took place, which was celebrated with a great feast. It was now the autumn of the year 324 B. C., and Alexander visited and examined some of the more important cities through Media. It was during this tour that he acted as peacemaker between Hephæstion and Eumenes, who had for some time been at variance. Hephæstion died only a short time after, and apparently Alexander was deeply affected. He is credited by the various writers with having shown his grief in the most extravagant deeds. That he sincerely lamented the loss of his friend is evident. On his way to Babylon from Ecbatana, he found some diversion from his mournful feelings in the effort of a powerful mountain tribe, the Cossæi, to collect tribute as they had done from previous Kings who passed through their domain. With his soldiers, Alexander, although the winter was well advanced, pursued the bold barbarians into their mountain fastnesses and defeated them.　As he advanced toward Babylon, he was waited upon by deputations from every known Nation who sought either alliance or protection.　After he had crossed the Tigris, on his way to Babylon, he was met by a delegation of Chaldean priests, who came to inform him that their god had communicated to them that it would be to Alexander's disadvantage to visit the city at that time. Nevertheless, Alexander entered Babylon and held court with great magnificence, but his mind was busy with further conquest.　He was at this time planning the conquest of Arabia.　The naval preparations were going forward rapidly, and large additions were made to the army.　Before setting out on the expedition, Alexander, as usual, offered sacrifices and feasted and drank with his officers. He was taken with a fever, but continued his preparations for the expedition, giving orders in regard to it and continuing to offer sacrifices for its success even after his illness had assumed such a stage that he had to be carried to the place of worship.　News of his illness threw the army into consternation, and among the troops his death was reported and believed several days before it really happened.　On the ninth day, according to Arrian, who furnished a copy of the royal bulletins, issued for the benefit of the soldiers, Alexander sent for the great Generals, evidently with the intention of giving them his last orders, but when they arrived, nature had given way and the King was unable to make known his wishes.　It was midsummer of the year 323 B. C. when Alexander died, at the age, according to Aristobulus, of thirty-two years and eight months, and after having reigned less than thirteen years.

HANNIBAL
B. C. 247-183

DEFEATED, BUT UNCONQUERED

Hannibal, son of Hamilcar, and hero of the second Punic War, was unquestionably one of the ablest military organizers and greatest tacticians of ancient times, and one of the foremost in the world's history. For fifteen years he menaced the Roman Empire, and ravaged Italy from its most northern provinces to the southern extremities, during which his progress was marked by a series of victories in battle seldom equaled and never excelled by any warrior, ancient or modern.

From childhood on for half a Century he held firmly to a vengeful purpose against the enemies of his land. He defeated the greatest armies of Rome and outgeneraled her most brilliant commanders, this, too, largely with troops recruited in a hostile country, and mercenaries who often could not be depended upon. His efforts ceased only with death. In the career of Hannibal, the genius and power of Carthage, blazed into a flame that lasted throughout his life and then expired with him. He died as he had lived, defiant, unconquered, and unyielding. Fearing the ingratitude of his own countrymen, hunted and persecuted by the Romans, who feared him even after the Nations were at peace, he became a voluntary exile and finally, when about to be surrendered into the power of his enemies by a cowardly ruler, chose death at his own hands rather than yield to the ignominy and humiliation of captivity.

The first Punic War had stripped Carthage of one of her richest colonies, Sicily, and laid the conquered State under a burdensome tribute to the victors. Then Sardinia was wrested from her. It was a bitter blow to the Carthaginian patriots, although a large and powerful party, consisting of the aristocratic and mercantile classes, cared little about these losses, except as they affected trade or reduced the revenues of the wealthy. To these classes it meant a considerable pecuniary loss, for the Sardinian and Sicilian commerce was highly lucrative. Notwithstanding this, they were opposed to another war, whereas the popular and patriotic party felt keenly the loss of the National prestige and the diminution of the ancient power of Carthage.

To this party belonged Hamilcar Barca, the father of Hannibal, and he trained and taught his son, along the lines deeply graven in his own life, hatred of Rome. This was the predominating spirit of the patriot party, of which Hamilcar was a leader, and it became the animating motive of his son.

After the first Punic War Hamilcar had undertaken several expeditions against the rebellious African tributaries of Carthage, and Roman suspicion had become lulled. But Hamilcar had not forgotten his hate nor abandoned his determination to avenge the wrongs of his country. By political intrigue, at which he was a master, he secured the supreme command of the Carthaginian troops for the purpose of a war with the Libyans, and made preparations for the great enterprise of conquering Spain.

At this time Hannibal, who was born, according to the generally accepted authorities, in 247 B. C., was nine years old. Even at this tender age he seemed to realize the destiny that awaited him. He begged his father to be allowed to accompany him to the war. The request was granted, but first the parent took pains to instil into the mind of the child the antagonism of his own nature toward Rome. He caused the boy to take a vow of eternal hatred to the Roman name. Hannibal never forgot the oath of his boyhood. It clung to him through youth and manhood, and years after he had become a homeless wanderer and the cause of Carthage had been lost forever, it continued to be the animating motive of his life.

According to the most authentic record, Hamilcar started from Carthage in the spring of 236 B. C., apparently with the intention of attacking the Libyans. As he proceeded along the coast with his army his son-in-law, Hasdrubal, who commanded the fleet, followed with his ships close to the shore. The next thing the Carthaginians heard of Hamilcar was that he had crossed to Spain with the aid of the fleet and secured a foothold there for his army.

For nine years Hamilcar toiled at the gigantic task he had imposed upon himself and then fell in battle. During eight succeeding years Hasdrubal, to whom the supreme command had fallen, continued the fighting, the cajoling of Celtic chiefs and the formation of alliances which Hamilcar had begun, and among other achievements founded Carthagena, or New Carthage, on a fine harbor on the southern coast.

The complaints of the Conservatives at home were stilled by the results of this activity, for the trade that had been lost in Sardinia and Sicily was, to a large extent, being replaced through Hamilcar's enterprise in the colonization of Spain. Wealth once more flowed into the coffers of the Carthaginian Treasury, and even the Senate willingly accepted the situation.

In 220 B. C., according to the chronology of Mommsen, Hasdrubal fell at the hand of a Celtic assassin. The army as well as the people of Carthage called Hannibal to take the command. According to R. Boswell Smith, he was at this time in his twenty-sixth year, or twenty-five years of age. On this point Smith is quoted by Larned in his "History for Ready Reference." Dr. Thomas Arnold also gives his age as twenty-five, and this seems to accord best with Hannibal's own statement of his age when he took the oath against Rome, and with the periods that followed, but Mommsen says he was in his twenty-ninth year, or twenty-eight years of age. The young commander was a thorough warrior, trained to arms through all his life. His earliest recollections were of the camp, the battle and the siege. He had been present when his father fell. His associates from childhood had been warriors. He had already commanded cavalry under Hasdrubal and had shown unmistakable talents for leadership. He was a skilled horseman, an expert swordsman, and excelled in those feats of physical daring that always excite the admiration of men. His mind was amply endowed with all the cunning and craft of the Orient, and in addition to this he was an accomplished Greek scholar, so that even the learned men of the period whose historical criticisms of him are adverse, found something to admire in him.

As soon as he was appointed to the command of the army Hannibal determined to lose no time in striking at his hereditary enemy, the Romans. His difficulty was to find a pretext. In Carthage the peace party had gained ascendency. The Romans in spite of the menace which the expanding power of Carthage in Spain contained, made no move which would give him cause to attack them. He resolved upon a cunning plan to bring about hostilities.

HANNIBAL
Museum Nazzionale, Naples

The town of Saguntum in Spain, originally a Greek colony, but now tributary to Rome, he selected as the means of provoking the Romans into action. He harassed the territory of the Saguntines and shamefully encroached upon their rights, but instead of making any show of resistence they only complained to Rome and the Romans in turn despatched a commission to Carthage protesting against Hannibal's action. Having thus far been disappointed in his efforts to induce the Romans to declare war, Hannibal falsely reported that the Saguntines were responsible for the trouble, and without waiting for further instructions he began the siege of Saguntum. The town held out for eight months, and when it fell Hannibal had carried out the initial step in his great design against Rome.

At last the Romans were aroused. An embassy was sent to Carthage with the demand that Hannibal be surrendered to them. But the crafty commander had foreseen this very move and had already taken steps to outwit them. He had judiciously sent to Carthage the rich spoils of Saguntum, and its distribution among the people had won favor for the daring General and kindled popular pride in his exploits. The demands of Rome were peremptorily refused.

Then followed a scene thrilling in its intensity and important in its consequences. The Roman embassy was headed by the proud Quintus Fabius. Livy, the Latin historian, tells us that in response to the curt refusal of the Carthaginians, Fabius gathered the folds of his toga about him and spoke in solemn tones: "Here I carry peace and war; say, ye men of Carthage, which you chose." "Give us which ye will," replied the Carthaginians. "Then we give you war," and Fabius spread out his toga. "We accept it, and will support it with the same spirit with which we have accepted it," haughtily replied the Carthaginians.

War had at last been declared. Hannibal's great desire had been gratified. In his prowess as a warrior he had gained his first great victory in the fall of Saguntum, while the Roman declaration of war was a triumph of his intellectual cunning.

After the fall of Saguntum Hannibal retired to Cartagena to pass the winter and reorganize his forces for the attack on Italy. He had about 120,000 infantry, 16,000 cavalry, and 58 elephants. On the sea were 50 quinqueremes. His army consisted of mercenaries, Libyans, and Spanish Celts. As Commander-in-Chief of the Carthaginian armies in Africa as well as Europe he had to provide for the safety of the capital and, moreover, must preserve the Carthaginian Empire in Spain. When he had detached a sufficient number of troops for these purposes he had remaining about 90,000 infantry, 12,000 cavalry, and 37 elephants.

In the spring of 218 B. C., Hannibal had completed every preparation and was ready to move. He made an address to his troops. With perfect frankness he stated to the common soldiers the purposes of his project. He pointed out the peril of Roman aggressiveness and inflamed their hearts with the hatred which he himself bore toward the enemy. No body of troops was ever more eager to follow its leader than were the soldiers of Hannibal after listening to this address.

While Hannibal was acting with decision the Romans apparently were doing nothing. Until he marched into Italy they did not appear to realize the extent of the action which Fabius had precipitated. They raised armies, but moved them slowly, and the advantages gained by Hanni-

bal through this fact were great.   Tiberius Sempronious
Longus commanded one of the consular armies which was
to be sent to Sicily and Africa, while Publius Cornelius
Scipio headed another which was to operate against Hannibal in Spain.   Before Scipio was fairly ready, Hannibal
was already out of Spain and well on his way to Italy.
The Carthaginian General encountered resistence on the
Ebro and sacrificed a quarter of his army in reaching the
Pyrenees.   Here he detached a part of his troops, which
had become dissatisfied, and with 50,000 veteran infantry
and 9,000 cavalry, he ascended the mountains and began
to make his way through the Celtic territory, some of the
inhabitants of which he had previously induced to make
common cause with him against the Romans.

The army of Scipio was now at Massilia, a five days'
march distant, and that General sent word to the Celts to
hold Hannibal in check until he could arrive.   But the
movements of Hannibal were too rapid.   The Carthaginians had no boats, but all the craft on the Rhone in that
vicinity were bought up and rafts were made out of felled
trees to carry the army over.   While this was being done
a strong detachment was dispatched two days' march up
stream to outflank the Gauls.   Three days later the army
of Hannibal began to cross the river.   The Gauls assembled for resistance, but immediately the cry was started
that their camp was in flames and on turning about they
were taken in flank by the detachment previously sent out
and completely routed.   When Scipio, who had been holding counsels of war, learned what had happened, he started
for the locality of Avignon, but arrived too late.   Hannibal had cleverly outgeneraled him and Scipio returned to
Massilia in disgust.   Here he divided his army, sending
part into Spain and leading part to Pisa in order to intercept Hannibal in Cisalpine Gaul.   It was not the intention

of the wary Hannibal to attack Rome directly, but to gain a thorough foothold in Italy that would serve him as a base of operations. After crossing the Rhone, he took up his march toward the Alps. There has been a dispute among historians in regard to which route Hannibal took in crossing the mountains, but Leighton, Mommsen, and the more modern students of history agree that the army used the pass of the Little St. Bernard. The passage of the Alps proved a terrible experience for the Carthaginian army. The season was well advanced. The summits of the passes were covered with snow. The paths were continually blocked by avalanches. The half famished elephants struggled desperately along the icy trails and became a hindrance. Horses and riders frequently disappeared over the edges of precipices and were dashed to death in the chasms. To add to all of these natural disadvantages and difficulties of the passage the army was continually harassed by hostile tribes, which threatened to throw the column into helpless confusion. The suffering of the African soldiers in this frigid climate was terrible, and resulted in disease and death to many.

At the pass over the first range of the Alps the Allobroges in force were waiting for Hannibal, but he had been warned and waited until night, when he seized the pass by a quick move and dispersed the enemy. At the second wall an attempt was made to destroy the Carthaginians by treachery. Hannibal suspected that the protestations of friendship and the effusive welcome accorded him were false, and sent his baggage ahead, thus saving it from falling into the hands of the enemy, and giving his men more freedom to repel the attacks made upon them. The descent was almost as perilous as the upward march had been. It was necessary to cut and build roads through the fields of ice in order to make any progress. After fifteen days of the greatest hardship, during which 50,000 infantry and 9,000 cavalry had been reduced to 20,000 infantry and 6,000 cavalry, the heroic army at last was enabled to go into camp on Italian soil among friendly people, who hailed the Carthaginians as deliverers. In the entire valley of the upper Po the tribe of the Taurini alone opposed Hannibal but he quickly brought them to terms.

Scipio now hastened to take command of the army in northern Italy. Advancing up the left bank of the Po his cavalry encountered the Carthaginian cavalry near the confluence of the Ticinus. The battle, the first in the second Punic war resulted in a rout for the Romans, Scipio himself being among the severely wounded. The Romans now retreated to Placentia and Scipio's force was joined by that under Sempronius. The hostile forces were here separated by the Trebia, a southern affluent of the Po. In numbers the Romans were far superior to the forces of Hannibal, having 40,000 troops, but the latter by his skilful strategy, drew the enemy across the river and in a tremendous battle gained a decided victory. The remnants of the Roman forces retreated to Placentia, the Gauls joined the victorious army and the northern part of Italy was practically in Hannibal's control.

For the next campaign four new legions were raised by the Romans and placed under the command of Servilius and Flaminius, consuls for the year 217 B. C. Once again Hannibal demonstrated his great ability as a strategist. By rapid marches he crossed the Appenines and his army after enduring great suffering in the low grounds along the Arno where the soldiers were compelled to wade in swamps up to their shoulders and where Hannibal himself suffered the loss of an eye from opthalmia, he marched past the camp of Flaminius at Arretium and at Lake Trasimenus prepared an ambuscade that nearly resulted in the annihilation of the consul's army. Part of the Carthaginian forces had been posted on the heights of a narrow defile while the remainder waited in the bottom for the appearance of the Romans. They unsuspectedly followed the Carthaginians into the gorge and as the rear guard entered the defile Hannibal gave the signal to attack. Pressed on all sides and from above the Romans became panic stricken and were literally cut to pieces. Fifteen thousand were killed and as many were taken prisoners. Flaminius was among the slain. Hannibal dismissed the Roman allies without ransom in the hope of gaining their friendship. By this victory Etruria was won and the pathway opened to Rome, but Hannibal knew too well the temper of the Roman people to commit the blunder of an immediate assault on the imperial city. He crossed the Appenines toward the Adriatic hoping for the dissolution of the Roman federation and the enlisting of the local communities in his cause. In this hope he was doomed to disappointment.

Thoroughly aroused and alarmed the Romans now appointed to the post of Dictator, Quintus Fabius Maximus, an old and conservative aristocrat, who became famous principally on account of the policy of delay which he pursued. Fabius had four new legions and with these he set out to follow Hannibal. He was determined, however, not to invite the fate of Flaminius by risking a battle and in spite of Hannibal's shrewdest efforts, Fabius refused to be tricked into a conflict. Weary of this inactivity, Hannibal led his troops into Campania where he inaugurated a season of plundering, burning, looting and laying waste the country as far as Capua which he hoped would join him. That city remained loyal for the time being, and Hannibal started back for Apulia. Fabius, who had been following with his impatient army along the crests of the mountains, seized a pass and attempted to hinder the retreat of Hannibal.

It was on this occasion that Hannibal employed a trick which has made his name familiar to even those uninterested in the details of the histories of nations. He waited for the darkness and had a detachment of his light armed troops tie burning faggots to the horns of oxen and drive the animals up a pass weakly guarded by the Romans. Thinking that Hannibal was about to escape, the enemy hastened after the torches and Hannibal marched his army through the pass which the Romans had deserted.

Dissatisfaction with the policy of Fabius led the Romans to declare Marcus Minucius, master of the horse, co-director. He bravely engaged Hannibal's army and his force would have been annihilated had it not been for the timely assistance of Fabius.

In the following year, 216 B. C., Hannibal won his greatest victory. His army now numbered about 40,000 infantry and 10,000 cavalry. With this force he seized Cannæ, a Roman magazine, on the river Aufidus. Here he was confronted by a Roman army of 80,000 infantry and 6,000 cavalry under Paulus and Varro, the newly elected consuls. The conditions were excellent for Hannibal. His cavalry which comprised a fifth parth of his army, outnumbered that of the Romans and the wide plain on which the foes had met served to give this arm of his forces its greatest efficiency. Paulus saw the advantage which the position afforded to Hannibal and concluded to avoid battle. He stationed his forces so as to prevent foraging and hoped to starve the Carthaginians out of their favorable situation. With this object in view he pitched two camps a mile apart on either bank of the stream, but Varro was impatient of these tactics and determined to strike as quickly as possible. On the day on which the command, according to Roman custom, alternated to him, he led the bulk of the Roman army across the river and took up a position opposite Cannæ. He placed his infantry in the center with the cavalry on either wing.

Hannibal crossed the river and drew up his infantry in a semicircle in the center with the wings composed of the Gallic and Numidian horse. The Roman legions forced their way through Hannibal's center but the Libyans in the wings swung around by the movement, menaced their flanks. The onslaught of Hannibal's cavalry was irresistible, and Hasdrubal, his brother, who commanded the left, pushed in the Roman right and then swept across the rear and attacked Varro's cavalry on the Roman left. Then he reformed the legions from behind. The Roman army was hemmed in with no chance of escape. Livy puts its total loss at 71,100, Polybius at 92,500. Mommsen says 70,000 covered the field. Among the slain were Paulus, Servilius and eighty men of senatorial rank. Varro was saved only by the speed of his horse. Ten thousand Romans left as a garrison at Paulus' camp were nearly all made prisoners of war and included in the Roman losses. The total Carthaginian loss did not exceed six thousand.

In spite of this the victory was a disappointment to Hannibal. Among the cities which fell into his hands was the important one of Capua, but even this failed to satisfy him as only a few of the tribes which he had expected to gain as allies consented to join him.

While these events were taking place in Italy, Gnaeus and Publius Scipio were meeting with considerable success against the Carthaginians in Spain and it was impossible for Hannibal to receive any re-inforcements from that quarter. Later, the Carthaginians recovered their foothold and drove out the Romans, both the Scipios being

slain.   Another Scipio, afterward named Africanus for
his victory over Hannibal in Africa, led an army back to
Spain and re-conquered that country.   After Hannibal's
great victory at Cannæ, his fortune began to decline.   It
is true that he afterward won a number of victories, captured many cities and ravaged the country even up to the
walls of Rome, once pitching his camp within three miles
of the city.   But the Romans had learned caution from
defeat and industry from failure.   They placed six armies
in the field and even forced slaves into the service.   It
became a question of the relative resources of Rome and
Carthage and against Carthage the odds were too great.

In the year 212 B. C. Hannibal took the City of Tarentum.   He also received from Carthage re-enforcements
of elephants and cavalry.   Two Roman armies besieged
Capua so persistently that Hannibal himself was forced
to go there to raise the siege.   It was only a temporary
relief, for two years later the Romans were again before
Capua with three armies.   Hannibal attempted to draw
them away by a feint against Rome but in this instance
his strategy failed and Capua was forced to surrender.
During the same year, Hannibal defeated Fulvius at Her-
donea in Apulia, but the next year he lost Tarentum.   In
the following year, however, the consuls Crispenus and
Marcellus, the latter probably the ablest Roman General
of the second Punic war with the exception of Scipio Africanus, were killed by the Numidian cavalry and a Roman
army was destroyed near Locri.

In 207 B. C. was fought the battle of Metaurus in
which Hannibal took no part, but which practically decided
the war.   Claudius Nero and Marcus Livius were the
Roman consuls for that year.   In the autumn of the year
208 B. C. word reached Rome that Hannibal's brother,
Hasdrubal, was leading an army from Spain to the assist-

ance of Hannibal.   Livius was to oppose Hasdrubal in
Cisalpine Gaul, while Nero remained to watch Hannibal
in Apulia, but Livius retreated before the invader and when
Hasdrubal reached the Metaurus he sent dispatches to
Hannibal arranging for the juncture of the two armies
at Narnia sixty miles from Rome.   The dispatches fell
into Nero's hands and the consul made forced marches
for two hundred miles with part of his army to join his
colleague and crush Hasdrubal.

The stroke succeeded.   The Carthaginians were completely defeated and Hasdrubal was slain.   Nero hastened
back to Apulia, and Hannibal received his first information
of the catastrophe which had overtaken his brother when
the bloody head of Hasdrubal was tossed into his camp
by the directions of Nero.   This ended the last hope of
the cause of Carthage in Italy.   Hannibal retreated to
Bruttium in the far southern part of Italy and there for
four years bravely and successfully defended himself
against army after army sent out to crush him.

Scipio had long desired to "carry the war into Africa,"
and at last his wish was gratified.   He landed near the
city of Utica which he unsuccessfully besieged.   But
though Utica held out, Carthage, which was also threatened, began negotiations for peace.   Hannibal was
recalled.   The return of the leader inspired the Carthaginians with new hope and courage and they broke off
the peace negotiations.   Hannibal was supplied with fresh
mercenaries and he advanced against Scipio at Zama.
Although he commanded his indifferent army with his
old skill and valor he was nearly annihilated in the conflict.   Carthage was conquered and Hannibal himself
advised the State to abandon the war.   Carthage agreed
to surrender all prisoners and deserters, relinquish her
claims on Spain and on the islands between Africa and

Italy, deliver up all her ships of war, except twenty, pay 250 talents to Rome annually for fifty years and bound herself not to wage war anywhere without the consent of Rome. Carthage was, in fact, completely subjugated and humiliated.

The second Punic war ended in 201 B. C. Then Hannibal, the warrior, now but 46 years old, became a statesman. He had waged one of the greatest wars of history during which he had demonstrated his ability as a commander. His personal courage and daring and his skill as a tactician have never been surpassed for brilliancy of conception and execution, and although he failed in the ultimate achievement of his original purpose, his name must forever remain emblazoned on history's page as one of the greatest among the world's great warriors.

As chief magistrate of Carthage he brought order into Carthaginian financial affairs so that the war tribute could be paid without extra taxation. Carthage prospered under his rule until the Romans again became alarmed and demanded, seven years after the battle of Zama, the surrender of Hannibal. To save his country the choice between the shame of giving him up to his enemies and suffering punishment for refusing to do so, he left his native land and became an exile and an unhappy wanderer, a condition which continued until his tragic death. His wanderings took him to Tyre and then to Ephesus, where the King of Syria, Antiochus, was preparing for war with Rome. Hannibal was received with joy. He advised the King against engaging in war with Rome but Antiochus, conceited and arrogant, pointed to his army assembled at Ephesus, and asked the old warrior if he did not think those forces would be enough for the Romans. "Yes," replied Hannibal, "enough for the Romans, however greedy they may be."

Antiochus' army was easily defeated by the Romans who now demanded Hannibal's surrender from him. The wretched warrior fled to Crete and thence to Bithynia, whose King, Prusias, weakly agreed to give him up to his enemies. Hannibal then fled to Libyssa on the eastern shore of the Sea of Marmora, where, broken in spirit and unwilling to bring further misfortune on his friends he took poison, which, according to narrators of that time, he had long carried about him in a ring. Some doubt exists as to the exact year of his death but it is generally believed to have been in 183 B. C.

Out of the long struggles between Carthage and Rome for the mastery of the Mediterranean and the world, there arose no grander figure than this half black descendant of old Tyre, whose savage patriotism and thirst for vengeance so nearly led to the imposing of Carthaginian instead of Roman-Greek civilization upon the world.

JULIUS CÆSAR
B. C. 100-44

"THE FOREMOST MAN OF ALL THE WORLD"

Caius Julius Cæsar, whom Shakespeare called "the
foremost man of all the world," was born in the year 100
B. C., on the twelfth day of the month Sextilis, the month
afterward named in honor of his birthday, July. By
Mommsen and one or two other historians, it is claimed
that the year of his birth was 102 B. C., but this claim is
now generally conceded to be erroneous. Roman history
contains no other name as honored as that of Cæsar. He
was an orator, a statesman, a man of letters, and a warrior. In all of these capacities he was great, and in the
last mentioned his genius excelled to an extraordinary
degree. From his youth he remained steadfastly the
friend and champion of the people. He began life during
one of the most turbulent of the many critical periods
experienced by the Roman Nation. He was, in his youth,
persecuted owing to his political connections, to the extent
that his property was confiscated and his life endangered.
His aspirations and steadfastness of purpose, however,
carried him to the highest honors that could be bestowed
upon a Roman, and yet the conspirators who slew him
in the Senate chamber and ran with reeking daggers
through the streets boasting of their deed, were so powerful and so much feared by the partisans of Cæsar, that
his body lay where he fell, at the base of the Pompeiian
statue, for many hours before anyone dared to bear it to
his home. Had he been a traitor as was proclaimed, the

custom would have been followed of dragging his body through the streets and casting it into the Tiber. His murderers favored such action, but the people were now aroused and his funeral services witnessed such a demonstration of popular grief and devotion as history does not record in any other instance. As leader of the Roman armies, his prompt and unfailing courage, his supreme confidence of victory in every venture, his keen insight and ready resource in every desperate undertaking, and the boldness with which he entered upon and executed his military plans and achievements, attained for him the just renown and greatness which all the world has conceded, and gave added brilliance to a career which has few parallels either in tradition or recorded history.

Cæsar came of pure patrician blood. His ancestors for many generations, the Julii, prior to the adoption of the name Cæsar, had ranked high in Rome as statesmen and warriors, and had held some of the highest offices obtainable in the Nation. This Cæsar knew, and he aspired, though not until manhood had been reached, to rival the honorable careers which they had lived. Before entering further upon the life and deeds of the "real founder of Imperial Rome," it will be necessary to briefly recite a few facts in Roman history which bear directly upon the time and conditions which surrounded Cæsar's advent as a factor in that nation's history. The destruction of Corinth and Carthage left Rome without a rival in the civilized world. For the emolument of the Roman nobility, Asia Minor, Macedonia, Greece and its dependencies, with the exception of Crete, northern Italy, the south of Gaul and the northern coast of Africa, had been divided into satrapies. The practice of relieving the city of congestion by sending out colonies composed of every class of Roman citizens, had ceased. The bulk of the lands in the provinces which had long before joined Hannibal in his war against the Romans, had passed into the hands of the great families and was used chiefly for pastures, or was tilled by slaves. Money had decreased in value as a result of the influx of precious metals, in consequence of conquests, the freeholds had passed into the hands of the great proprietors, and the petty freeholders who were the strength and stability of ancient Rome, were ruined. The capital was overcrowded with this class and with the yeomanry, willing to work, but unable to secure it, owing to the preference for slave labor. Of manufacturing and commerce Rome had none. This vast population was therefore left without healthy activity, and gradually became uneasy, discontented, vicious, and ripe for revolution. Tiberius Gracchus was the first to attempt to apply a remedy to this dangerous condition. Part of his plan was to enforce the Licinian laws, which provided that no single person could rent more than 500 acres of land. He proposed to take the land away from the illegal holders and divide it among the needy. Naturally he met with resistance from the oligarchical faction. His term as Tribune was drawing to a close, and before he could put his plans into execution, it was necessary that he should be re-elected. The popular party supported him, and his re-election was assured, but on election day Tiberius and 300 of his adherents were attacked and murdered by the opposition. The conditions existing may readily be seen from the fact that although the blood of a Tribune had been illegally shed, the murderers remained unpunished. Ten years later Caius Gracchus, in spite of the fate that had befallen his brother, set about carrying out the same plans, and he would possibly have succeeded had not the bitterness he entertained as a result of his brother's murder, led him to excesses. Every needy citizen was supplied

with corn from the public granaries, and this soon converted a great body into clamorous paupers.   For two
years he carried out his plans with a high hand, but by the
decree of the Senate at the beginning of the third year,
he and his followers were condemned and slain to the
number of 3,000. Affairs again returned to the previous
condition.   No champion of democracy now appeared
until the year 111 B. C., when the Jugurthine War enabled
the democracy once more to rally and elect Caius
Marius first to the consulship and later to the greatest
height of power. During his sixth consulship he repaid
his obligations to his party by reviving the Gracchian
laws, but placed their execution in unworthy hands, those
of the Prætor Glaucias and the Tribune Saturninus, who
were condemned by the Senate and treacherously slain by
the oligarchists.

In the meantime, the freedom of the city had risen in
value, and the Italian allies had become eager to partici-
pate in this privilege.   In the year 95 B. C., a law was
passed against allowing them to enjoy the franchise. This
fomented the disaffection which was already prevalent.
Four years later the social war burst out. It lasted three
years, and is said to have resulted fatally to 300,000 sons of
Italy, fighting one another. The leading Roman Generals
who were employed in conducting this war were Caius Marius and his ancient rival, the aristocratic Cornelius Sulla.
The latter had carried off the greater share of the glories of
the war, and near its close he was elected consul, and at
its termination was commissioned to avenge the wrongs
which the Romans in Asia had suffered at the hands of
King Mithridates. Marius, who was now in his 70th year,
grudged this opportunity for greatness afforded his political antagonist and personal enemy. The Tribune Sul-

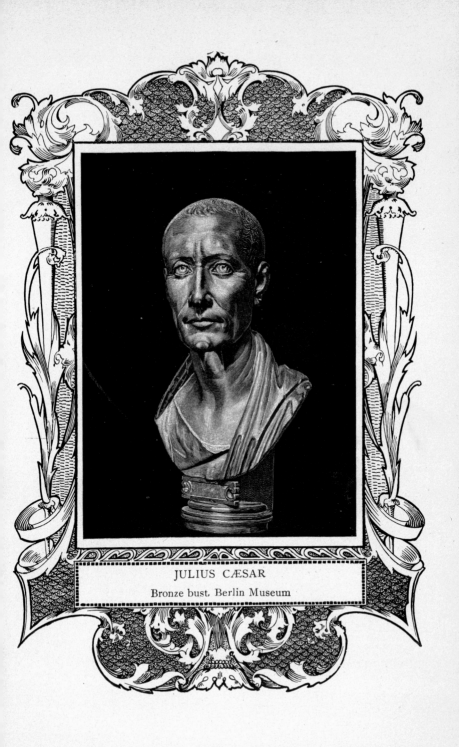

JULIUS CÆSAR
Bronze bust. Berlin Museum

picius had in the meantime placed himself at the head of the popular party and proposed a law whereby the allies should have representation in the Senate. Sulla, still consul, protested, but with his colleagues was compelled to flee before an armed force brought forward by Sulpicius. The old Senate, threatened with death, then passed the law, the council of the allies at once revoked the commission of Sulla and authorized Marius to lead the armies against Mithridates. Sulla's first step after having escaped was to visit the army, then in the vicinity of Nola. He called upon them to march with him to Rome to deliver the city from the lawless party in power. Soon was presented the spectacle of Rome's own consul marching against Rome with an army at his back. Rome was taken by storm, the Marians put to flight, Sulpicius slain and Marius himself, his son and nine leading senators of their party, proscribed and rewards offered for their murders. The Sulpician laws were repealed and Sulla's friends were given supreme power. As soon as the army was removed from Rome, however, the Consul, Cornelius Cinna, though bound by oaths to Sulla, proclaimed himself leader of the popular party. He was opposed by his colleague, Octavius. The two factions fought in the streets of Rome, and 10,000 lives were sacrificed. Cinna was defeated and fled from the city to appeal to the Italian allies and various bodies of troops. He gathered a considerable force and was joined by Marius, then marched upon Rome and starved the Senate into submission. In violation of the terms of capitulation, as soon as the gates were thrown open, an indiscriminate slaughter of all the Roman and Latin opponents who could be reached, took place. Marius entered upon his seventh consulship, but died soon after of an acute fever. For three years peace reigned in Rome, ruled despotically by Cinna after the death of Marius. Then Sulla returned with his victorious armies and once more assumed power.

These were the conditions in the midst of which Julius Cæsar spent his early years. Marius was the uncle of Julius, and under Cinna's rule, his father, holding Prætorian rank, coincided with the opinions of the democratic party. He was therefore surrounded with those influences and embued with them. As Cæsar was born the twelfth of July, 100 B. C., and as Marius lived until the thirteenth of January, 86 B. C., the nephew had ample opportunity of imbibing the sentiments of his uncle from personal intercourse. He had also already had opportunity to witness actual scenes connected with war during the social war and the subsequent civil strifes of those years. Sulla, having once more established himself in power, did not fail to inaugurate persecutions against those who had opposed him, as well as against their families. One of the steps which he took in pursuance of this plan was to detach young men of the opposite party by ordering them to divorce wives married from among Marian partisans. Young Cæsar had married Cornelia, the daughter of Cinna, and naturally Sulla did not fail to seek to bring the young man who naturally belonged to the highest rank of the patricians, away from the connections he had thus formed with the democracy. Like others, Cæsar was ordered to divorce his wife. But the dictator was not obeyed in his mandate to this youth, who was destined to become a greater ruler than Sulla himself. Suetonius intimates that repeated efforts were made to compel him to comply with the dictatorial demand, as may be seen from the following expression: "He married Cornelia, the daughter of Cinna, fourth time Consul, who soon after gave birth to a daughter Julia, nor could he by any means be compelled by the dictator to divorce her."

Sulla therefore pronounced him a Marian at heart, and deprived him of rank and fortune, as well as his wife's dowry. Cæsar had been appointed a priest of Jupiter, and of this honor he was also shorn. Moreover, Cæsar had reason to believe that his life was in danger, not so much from Sulla himself as from some of his vengeful adherents. He disguised himself and fled to the Sabine Mountains, where he lived a wandering life, and, being as yet unaccustomed to hardships, was stricken with a severe fever. But the future ruler of Rome was not destined to die thus obscurely. He recovered, and, through the intervention of influential friends, who pressed Sulla to pardon so young and highborn an offender and restore to him his title and property, was enabled to return to Rome. Sulla consented reluctantly to the pleadings of the fugitive's noble relatives, but, according to an ancient historian, quoted by Williams, uttered these prophetic words: "Have then your way and take him with you, but be assured that this young man, whom you are so anxious to preserve in all his rights, will, at a future period, be the destruction of the aristocratic party which you have assisted me to defend. For in Cæsar there are many Marii." Having rescued him from the possible wrath of Sulla, these relatives became in a measure personally responsible for his good conduct, and he was therefore sent according to the law to give his term of service in the camp. The youth of the nobility during this service were usually attached to the staff of some General, and, while not commissioned, were often employed in important work. Cæsar was sent to the camp of one of Sulla's lieutenant's, Minutius Thermus, who was engaged in the invasion of Chios for the purpose of inflicting punishment on the Mitylenians as a result of their conduct during the war against Mithridates. Through this plan it was thought Cæsar could be kept away from contact with the Marians. During this campaign, Cæsar distinguished himself at the storming of Mitylene and received from Thermus a civic crown for saving a Roman life. This was in the year 79 B. C. When these operations ceased his services were transferred to the camp of Servilius, also a partisan of Sulla. Suetonius writes that Cæsar did not serve long under Servilius, but that on learning of the death of Sulla he hurried to Italy. This was in the year 78 B. C. He did not long remain in Rome, but proceeded to Rhodes for the purpose of perfecting himself in oratory. During the period of his stay at Rhodes, he appears to have diversified his studies by spending some of his time at military camps and visits to Asia. He returned again to Rome in the year 74 B. C., and was active in the plans of the democratic party, but it was not until the year 69 B. C. that he entered the arena of public life. He was then elected to the office of quæstor, although in the struggle for preference he was surrounded by antagonists of high standing and great ability and influence. Although the grandest days of the Roman Nation were even then past, the true conditions were concealed by surface facts and affairs. The Nation was in a condition favorable to quick transitions. Four factions were waging a bitter fight for supremacy, the oligarchical faction, consisting of families of chiefs, who directed the Senate, was represented by Cicero at home and by Cn. Pompey, the successful General, abroad. This party practically governed the republic. Marcus Crassus, formerly Pompey's colleague but now his personal rival, led the aristocratic faction, composed of a mass of Senators who were anxious to obtain the power usurped by their colleagues. Cataline headed the military faction. His one object, like that of dissolute adherents was to incite some revolution, and thereby replenish purses grown lean since the time of Sulla. Cæsar was identified with the Marian faction, and naturally became its chief. By far the leading figure in the ruling aristocratic faction, and probably in the republic, at this time, was Pompey. He had been a lieutenant under Sulla, and in that capacity his career had been distinguished. He had won fresh laurels by his forceful management of two campaigns, in which important Roman interests were at stake. The first achievement was the suppression of a revolution under the formidable leadership of Sertorius (77-72 B. C.), the other was the crushing out of a revolt brought about by Sparticus, the leader of a band of gladiators. This small body of men, supported by a force of discontented citizens, had kept Italy in a state of alarm for three years (73-71 B. C.). Made a popular favorite by these exploits, Pompey was rewarded in the year 70 B. C. with a position as Consul together with Crassus, the rich Senator. At the expiration of the year Pompey retired. It was not long afterward, however, before he became weary of the life of repose which he was leading, and again left Rome, in the spring of 67 B. C. In the meantime Cæsar returned from a trip to Spain, where he had begun the acquaintance with the provinces of the West, which he was later to renew under different circumstances and on a more expansive scale. Pompey went forth and cleared the seas of piracy. The following year he superceded Lucullus in command of the war against Mithridates. He did not return to Rome until 61 B. C. He had completely rid the seas of pirates, annihilated the forces of Mithridates, received the submission of Tigranes of Armenia, and added to the

Empire the greater portions of the possessions of both monarchs. Pompey was the man of the hour. Had he been as great a statesman as he was a successful general, his power in Rome might have been extended without limit. But during his long absence plotting and intrigue had been prevalent. Cæsar had completed his term of office as Quæstor and had readily been made Ædile. As such, he had charge of the amusements and decorations of the city. In each department he made startling innovations. He began and continued his administration with a recklessly profuse display. He restored to their former places the trophies and statues of Marius and thereby caused many of the old democratic soldiers to come forth from their retreats and weep for joy at what they believed to be the dawning of a new Marian era. His expenditures were not less bold than his political moves. His prodigality resulted in fabulous outlays, in order to present to the public entertainments never before witnessed in Rome, 300 pairs of gladiators, equipped in silver armor were sent into the arena to combat for the amusement of the people. Rome forgot the dismal calamities of the past and remembered Cæsar. His term as Ædile over, Cæsar set about to obtain the office of Pontifix Maximus. Although opposed by men of great eminence, he so adroitly manipulated his friends and enemies alike that he was triumphantly elected.

In the year 61 B. C., as Prætor, he became Governor of Spain and was in the west at the time of Pompey's return to Rome. His labors in the provinces placed him on the way to the fulfillment of his cherished ambition to achieve military power. Then, for the first time, the real genius of the man began to make itself apparent. He incidentally made use of his position to pay off the enormous debts which he had contracted while holding the position

of Ædile. He ate the common food on which his soldiers
subsisted, he swam icy streams with them, withstood the
rigors of camp life and made progress with the passing of
each day. He was at this time pale, slender, shaken by
excesses, prematurely bald as a result of the dissipated life
he had led in Rome, according to Chamberlin, and was a
victim of epilepsy. In spite of these physical impediments
to personal success, he at this time started on a career as a
General, Statesman, Orator, Historian and Lawgiver,
which was to continue for seventeen years and leave its
impress on the civilization of twenty centuries. For the
purposes of his ambition it was necessary for Cæsar to
obtain command of an army for a number of years. In
order to secure such a command he decided to return to
Rome and have himself made Consul. With characteristic promptness he carried out his plan, not even taking time
to indulge in a triumph upon the occasion of his entrance
into the Eternal City. In order that he might the more
easily obtain the desired consulship, he brought about a
reconciliation between Pompey and Crassus. His only
daughter was given in marriage to Pompey, and the friendship was begun between the two great men which was to
change to rivalry and ultimately to personal hatred. Pompey had influence. Crassus possessed wealth, as Cæsar
had occasion to know, having had the rich senator as his
security for the great debts he owed prior to receiving the
Governorship of Spain, which enabled him to clear himself of debt. By making promises to the two men Cæsar
induced them to join their fortunes with his and thus the
first Triumvirate was formed. Cæsar was to have the
consulship and be Governor afterward. Pompey was to
see his plan for the distribution of lands to his veterans
carried out and the capitalists were to be favored as an
equivalent for the support lent by Crassus. Cæsar was

elected without difficulty as Consul together with a non-
entity purposely chosen so that the youngest Triumvirate
should have supreme power in the consulate.   It was not
long afterward that laws were passed authorizing Cæsar
to take charge of the three legions stationed in Cisalpine
Gaul.   His command was to extend over five years.   His
jurisdiction was to reach south as far as the Rubicon and
was to include Lucca and Ravenna.   Before departing to
assume the government of his province, Cæsar took care
to leave his interests in Rome in friendly and competent
hands.   Publius Clodius Pulcher was chosen the Procon-
sul's representative.   Clodius was of Patrician birth and
upon the advice of Cæsar, he secured his adoption into a
Plebeian family, so that he might be elected to the Tribu-
nate.   Clodius became active immediately after he assumed
the duties of Tribune and proposed four new measures
which were adopted.   The first law provided for free distribution of corn; the second placed a ban upon the practice of
censors in impeding legislation on the pretext of augury;
the third revived the old time associations which formerly
had exercised considerable political influence throughout
the State, and the fourth stripped the censors of a part of
their powers.   Not satisfied with these radical steps Clodius introduced resolutions which were intended to deprive
the Senate of its leaders.   By their provisions the resolutions forced Cicero into exile and compelled Cato to take
the Governorship of Cypress, which effectually removed
Cicero's friend from the seat of Roman affairs.   Cicero
pleaded in vain against the order.   He besought the intercession of Pompey but the sentence was carried out and the
great orator went into exile.

Lucius Calpuanius Piso, Cæsar's father-in-law, had
been elected Consul and thus he felt safe in leaving Rome
to take up his five year term as Governor of the two Gauls

and Illyricum. Pompey was assigned to the Governorship of Italy and the East was given into the charge of Crassus.

Upon reaching Cisalpine Gaul with eight legions of soldiers Cæsar was informed that the Helvetians were preparing to leave their pent-up territories between the Jura and the Rhine and settle in a more fertile region. In the commentaries which the General himself wrote, he claims to have come to the conclusion that the proposed emigration was not compatible with the good of the province. Accordingly he reached the Rhone by forced marches and constructed a line of fortifications from Lake Lemanus to the Jura. In this way he hoped to prevent the passage of the Helvetians. The tribe made an attempt to secure egress by another route but Cæsar overtook them at Bilrax and dealt them such a blow that the nation was practically annihilated. The remaining members of the tride were forced to return to their original territory.

This problem had scarcely been solved when the Roman legions were called upon to combat 120,000 Suevi, who had crossed the Rhine and entered Gaul under the leadership of Ariovistus. The latter declared he had come thither to settle differences between Gaulish tribes. He and his forces were driven back across the Rhine and Cæsar found himself in the country of the Belgæ. This race, which had become accustomed to warfare through continual battle with the Germans, was subdued by the Romans during the year 57 B. C. Cæsar completed the conquest of all Gaul within a year, by overthrowing the Veneti on land and sea and subduing the Morini and Menopii. Cæsar's naval victory over the Veneti was the first great engagement on the Atlantic Ocean and it served to illustrate the versatility of the Roman. Cæsar was now prepared for a German war and in the year 55 B. C. he devoted

his attention to this campaign.   Several Teutonic tribes
had crossed the Rhine and it was Cæsar's purpose to beat
them back to their former possessions.   He engaged in
an important battle and then built a bridge across the river,
a formidable undertaking, and then made his way into
Germany.   The result of his invasion proved a great success and Cæsar led his thus far invincible legions to the
seacoast.   He made a voyage to Britain but soon afterward transported his army back to the mainland and withdrew to winter quarters in Gaul.   In the succeeding summer he returned to the British Isle and defeated the armies
who opposed his progress under the leadership of Cassi-
vellaunus.   Britain speedily acknowledged dependence
and gave the aggressive Roman tribute and hostages.

While Cæsar was winning these splendid victories,
Rome was celebrating what they believed to be the return
of the Republic's former power.   All praised the Procon-
sul who was making additions of territory to the Nation
with as great rapidity and display of genius as was exhibited by Alexander the Great in the interests of Greece.

Reverses seemed imminent, however, during the winter
of 54-53.   The Roman army was dispersed to several quarters in order to make a supply of provisions possible and
the Gallic tribes seized upon the opportunity to start a general revolt.   The Aduatici attacked and drove into confused retreat what remained of one portion of the army.
Sixty thousand Nervii and soldiers of other native tribes
surrounded the camp of Quintus Cicero.   When it seemed
that the legions were about to be annihilated Cæsar suddenly fell upon the swarming tribes and punished their
boldness by causing fearful loss of life in their ranks.   He
also compelled them to give up great treasure. In order to
break the power of a combination which had again formed
between the Gallic tribes and the Germans, Cæsar under-

took a second campaign in Germany.   He took this step
in the latter part of the year 54 B. C. and early in the next
year brought his scheme to a successful outcome by punishing the Eburones, the leading spirits in the coalition and
revolt.   In 52 B. C. he was obliged to meet a general insurrection in all parts of ulterior Gaul.   With characteristic
promptness Cæsar made his way back over the mountains,
fell upon the city of Genobum, which the natives had recaptured.   Cæsar burned the city and was laying plans for
immediate action before the enemy had recovered from its
surprise at his sudden return.   Vercingetorix, the leader
of the strong Averni and for that reason generally regarded as the proper leader of the tribes, adopted a plan
of wasting the country and thus preventing Cæsar from
obtaining adequate supplies.   The Roman got the better of
his antagonist by taking Avaricum and possessing himself
of all the supplies stored there.   Disaster attended the next
movements of the army. Siege was laid to Gergovia, capital of the Avernian territory, but Cæsar was set upon and
so signally defeated that he was forced to retreat in order
to escape destruction.   It was the first real defeat suffered
by the aggressive Romans and the news traveled over
Gaul like wildfire.   Hope was once more fired in the savage breasts and all the barbarian tribes with but one exception, re-entered the lists against the Roman host.   They
poured down upon the small army of invaders like an ava-
lanche.   In the face of grave danger Cæsar's genius only
shone the brighter. He called for reinforcements from the
province of Cisalpina. His forces were concentrated and
the barbarian hordes thus had but one army to fight.   His
ten legions swept aside the defenders of Alesia.   In spite
of the almost countless hosts at the back of the leader Vercingetorix, that intrepid leader and dangerous enemy was
captured.   His life was spared in order that he might be

used in the triumph which Cæsar felt certain would follow
his campaigns.   Other Gauls were reduced to slavery.
Thousands of them laid aside their spears and shields and
submitted to become servants of the Roman soldiers.   The
army of savages was completely overthrown.   The tribes
sought terms of peace.   It was the successful outcome of
a long campaign, the realization of hopes cherished by
Cæsar while that conqueror was a young man studying
the business of government and arranging his chessmen
so that he might reach the goal of his ambition.   Gaul was
conquered but Cæsar's labors were not completed.   He
spent the following winter in settling the terms of peace.
He organized the vast territory into the provinces, Gallia
and Belgica.   The General's task done, the duties of the
statesman and the diplomat opened.   Cæsar met all emer-
gencies with promptness and judgment.   There was no
further persecution of the Gauls.   Their leaders were
treated with magnanimity.   They were honored and made
to appreciate the fact that they were dealing with kindly
victors.   Some of them were honored with Roman citizen-
ship and others were admitted to the Roman Senate.   Being
Roman provinces, a successful effort was made to intro-
duce the Latin tongue into the conquered territories and
the usual system of Romanizing the peoples was introduced along substantial and enduring lines.

Cæsar in the campaigns thus concluded had arrested
the emigration of the Helvetians and expelled the Germans under Ariovistus in 58 B. C.   He subdued the Belgæ
in 57 B. C. and in 56 B. C. he overcame the Aquitani.   He
had made successful invasions of Britain twice in 55 and
54 B. C.   From 53 to 51 B. C. he had penetrated Germany,
had overthrown the Gauls after their repeated revolts, had
conquered and taken Vercingetorix and completely subdued the country.   In this way he had improved the oppor-

tunity afforded his genius during the five years granted
him to be "Governor" of the two Gauls and Illyricum.

While he had been winning battles in the provinces
Cæsar's enemies at home had been making new plots. They
were silenced for the time by the Triumvir's victorious
career in Gaul. In celebration of the continued successes
the Senate granted fifteen days "supplicatio" to the gods.
From the Senators and Politicians who went to Ravenna
to confer with Cæsar he learned that one of the support-
ers of the motion to award him this unprecedented honor
was Cicero. The Orator had returned from exile upon permission of the Senate, granted only after the bitterest sort
of opposition by Clodius. Cicero realized that his residence
in Rome might be terminated any time at the pleasure
of leaders who had got start of the world and were bearing
the palm alone. It behooved him, therefore, to secure the
confidence of Cæsar, Pompey and Crassus. In the meantime he secretly looked and longed for a breach between the
members of the powerful Triumvirate which might enable
himself and his sympathizers to obtain a foothold in the
government. But Cicero was sorely disappointed.
Before the beginning of his third campaign in 56 B. C.
Cæsar made his way to the Roman colony at Lucca and
called a rendezvous. He had had intimations that Pompey and Crassus had again become jealous of one another.
Pompey was attempting to heal the breach between himself and the senatorial party. Cæsar was not through
with the services of his two fellow members of the Triumvirate, and the conference at Lucca was intended to mend
the broken machinery of their administration. As usual,
he broke down opposition and succeeded completely. Two
hundred Senators who attended the conference were practically ignored while Cæsar, Pompey and Crassus made
plans looking toward the maintenance of their power. By

the agreement reached Pompey and Crassus were to hold the joint consulship during the following year, and after the year's time had expired, they were to have the proconsular governments of Spain and Syria. Before Cæsar's five years' governorship of Gaul expired, Pompey and Crassus were to secure for him a reappointment to another five years. In the year 55 B. C. laws were passed making the terms of Pompey and Crassus five years in Spain and Syria. By this renewed demonstration of the power of the triumvirate Cicero saw the downfall of his hopes for immediate preference and Cato saw the passing of republican institutions.

In 54 B. C. Crassus set out with seven legions, with the purpose to vanquish the Parthians. The millionaire-Senator-General was led into the desert by an Arab traitor. The Roman army was suddenly surrounded by Parthian horsemen. The legions fled over the burning sands, but could not escape disastrous defeat. Crassus, a few days afterward (June 9, 53 B. C.) was called to a conference with the Parthian commander and treacherously assassinated. The next year Pompey lent Cæsar a legion, but despite this ostensible co-operation he was beginning to feel that natural antagonism against Cæsar which had formerly existed. In the meantime Pompey's wife died, and as she was the only daughter of Cæsar, another strong tie between the members of the duumvir was broken.

While T. Annius Milo and Clodius, one the candidate for the consulship, and the other working to secure the prætorship, were turning the streets of Rome into a gladiatorial arena, Pompey was quietly resting in his beautiful villa, fondly hoping that dictatorial power would be invested in him. Instead he was named sole Consul February 4, 52 B. C., and in five months he had his new father-in-law Metellus as his colleague. It was the

notion of Cato that giving Pompey the legal position of
Consul would deter him from taking active steps toward
securing a larger and less constitutional administrative
office. He was allowed to maintain control over Spain
and all Africa, his annual charge out of the public treasury
being a thousand talents. Pompey was beginning to fully
realize the influence of Cæsar. All that either of the two
men needed to become the greatest man in Rome was the
overthrow of the other. They had long since secretly
resolved upon this very thing. Pompey had undoubtedly
harbored such an idea from the commencement of his
career, but Cæsar had looked upon his son-in-law as a
leader to be despised and shorn of power at will. Pompey
had been spoken of as a fit man to become dictator, and he
had been secretly striving to obtain that position. He had
not the temerity to seize it with the aid of his legions.
Affairs were in this condition when Marcellus was named
consul for the year 51 B. C. The crisis advanced a step
nearer upon the request of Cæsar for the consulship and
the continuance of his provinces. Marcellus openly defied
Cæsar and heaped insults upon him. After the term of
Marcellus had expired Cæsar became active in establishing himself in the favor of the leaders in Rome. From
the wealth taken in Gaul he paid the debts of Curio, the
tribune; gave Paulus, the Consul, 1,500 talents wherewith
to build the Court of Justice adjoining the Forum. At
these preparations Pompey organized his friends and immediately demanded of Cæsar the legion which he had
lent him several years before. Cæsar returned the soldiers,
giving each one a gift of 250 drachmæ. In order to settle
the now open dispute Cæsar proposed that both he and
Pompey should lay down their arms and retire to private
life. Curio and Anthony, the latter being tribune, made
this proposal to the people, and the scheme met with popu-

lar approval. Cæsar wrote letters to be read publicly in which he offered to relinquish all except Gaul within the Alps, Illyricum and two legions. His reason for expressing this wish was that he did not think it expedient to go to Rome as a private citizen seeking the consulate. Cicero now offered his services toward effecting an amicable settlement of the differences. He interceded with Pompey, who was willing to accept Cæsar's proposition with the exception that he did not want the conqueror of Gaul to retain his soldiers. Finally Cicero prevailed upon Pompey and his friends to consent to Cæsar's keeping the provinces and a small army of 6,000 men. But Lentulus, the Consul, appeared in the Senate and opposed the plan with fiery energy. He heaped insult and abuse upon Antony and Curio, and those two men left the Senate. They were compelled to flee Rome disguised as slaves. At this time Cæsar was at Ravenna, and his available forces consisted of but 300 horse and 5,000 foot. The rest of his army was across the Alps, but his plans, made up after the flight of his friends from Rome, did not require a large force. He decided upon a sudden and bold step. Rome was to remain no longer in ignorance of the extent of his power and ambition. The Senate had passed a resolution to the effect that if he did not lay down his arms he should be considered a public enemy, and Cæsar had no idea of laying down his arms.

Sending the most of his troops ahead of him, he made a night march south from Ravenna in the direction of Ariminum. In his path lay the River Rubicon, a stream formed by the union of three mountain currents and marking the frontier of Italy. To cross it meant that Cæsar had directed himself against his own government. It was in the month of November, 49 B. C., and the river had grown into a torrent. Authorities differ as to the hesita-

tion of Cæsar before he took this final step. He has been
pictured as standing on the northern bank of the stream
pondering for hours over the advisability of his course.
Few of them allege that this hesitation was due to fear,
however. It has been written that Cæsar addressed himself in an impassioned speech to his soldiers shouting at
last "The die is cast" and leaped into the river. However this may be, Cæsar does not enlighten us in his commentaries and, in fact, he does not mention the commission of this irrevocable act in his own account. Merrivale
is of opinion that instead of thinking upon the effects of
the move upon posterity his mind was probably absorbed
in plans for the marching of his legions and the approaching combat at Ariminum. Cæsar crossed the Rubicon and
paused at the latter city. There messages went to and fro
between Cæsar and Pompey, all of them seeking a reconciliation. Each demanded that the other abandon his
position. The correspondence was finally terminated by
a demand upon Cæsar to retire from Ariminum and disperse his army. Seeing that further negotiations were
useless, Cæsar sent a portion of his small army further
into Roman territory. Arezzo was occupied by Mark
Antony with five cohorts, and Cæsar took possession of
three other cities, using one cohort for each. From the
fact that Pompey did not attack and drive back the
intrepid invader Trollope draws the conclusion that
although Pompey had the command of a great army his
soldiers could not be depended upon to make war against
the popular Cæsar. Although the conqueror's power had
been shorn by the forced withdrawal of two of his legions
he was still strong enough to frighten Pompey, the Consuls
and a host of Senators out of Rome and southwards to
Brundusium, whence they expected to leave Italy. Cæsar
also made for the south, and the first battle in this historic

civil war was fought at Corfinium. Cæsar took possession of this town after coming out of a small engagement, victor. As the future founder of a line of despots traveled through his native country many soldiers who had followed him over mountains and across plains in Gaul, but who had been taken from him and placed under the command of Pompey, once more joined his army and prepared to fight under his standards. Cæsar passed the capital and advanced rapidly toward Brundusium. Here were gathered with Pompey the Consuls, Senators, remnants of the nobility and all prominent adherents of that party which depended for its success and indeed for its very existence upon the genius and ability of Pompey. The fleeing host continued to retreat and Cæsar advanced by the forced marches he knew so well how to conduct. Cæsar laid siege to Brundusium, and Pompey, who had made the boast that he had but to stamp on Italian soil and legions of soldiers would arise to obey his behests, took flight from his native shores with his Consuls and Senators never more to see the sunny slopes of Italy or the Eternal City.

Pompey's fleet sailed to Dyrrachium in Illyria. After making an effort to intercept him and his fleet, and failing, Cæsar proceeded to Rome, he could not follow Pompey because he had no transportation facilities. He therefore decided to arrange the Government of Italy during a short stay in Rome and then set out for Spain, whose valuable resources and government were in the hands of Pompey's lieutenants. In accordance with these plans he called together such of the Senators who had dared to remain in and around Rome and obtained their sanction to his various acts. He did not himself enter the city, thus showing a scrupulous regard for legal forms, which might scarcely have been expected of him. The appropriation of the sacred treasure heaped up in the vaults of the temple of Saturn was authorized upon his recommendation. This wealth had been reserved for generations and was to have been used for no purpose except the repelling of Gallic invasion, which danger had been threatening the Romans for many years. Cæsar insisted that because he had put an end to that fear he was entitled to the treasure. Cæsar obtained these funds and laid the foundations of government in the month of April, 49 B. C.

Pompey's design was evidently to gather a great army in the East and then return and overthrow the "usurper." Cæsar resolved to secure the submission of all the West before he followed Pompey into Greece. Each sought the mastery in Rome and each left that city, going in opposite directions, in their preliminary preparations for the final conflict. Cæsar now had legions and he possessed the advantage of having his headquarters in Italy. Before departing for Spain he sent Claudius Fabius with three legions from Southern Gaul to take possession and maintain control of principal Spanish roads and the passes of the Pyrenees. Fabius fulfilled his mission with commendable zeal and energy. When Cæsar arrived in the West his representative was confronting the Pompeian forces at Ilerda on the river Sicoris, this place having been chosen for the scene of battle. Afranius and Petreius, the Generals in command of the armies of Pompey in Spain, had five legions of hardy and seasoned veterans and were supported by a considerable number of native allies. Cæsar's army was of about the same proportions. The Pompeian forces arrived first on the spot, however, and had all the advantage of position. The river had been spanned by a substantial stone bridge and their ranks were being supplied with provisions supplied by the entire surrounding country. Cæsar was compelled to build temporary

bridges. A storm and subsequent flood swept these struc-
tures away, and left the invading army under still more
disheartening circumstances. In spite of natural impediments Cæsar succeeded in driving the enemy from their
superior position. Upon their retreat he intercepted them
and without any general engagement, forced them to surrender unconditionally.

This campaign, which had occupied but forty days and
which gave to Cæsar final supremacy in all Spain, was one
of the most brilliant of the General's achievements. It
was won by mere force of strategy and military skill and
energy. After his decisive victory Cæsar turned his
attention to the Greek city of Massilia. This place was
supposed to be independent and an ally of Rome. All
about Massilia the Gallic tribes had been subdued.
Despite these conditions the city had refused to open its
gates for Cæsar when the latter set out upon his advance
against Spain.

Not willing to overlook this unfriendly act, Cæsar left
three legions before the city and went on his way with his
materially diminished army. He ordered a fleet to be
built for coöperation with the land forces in the seige
which followed. The army was under command of Tre-
bonius, and Decimus Brutus was given charge of the naval
force. When Cæsar returned from Spain he found the
beleaguered city had undertaken extensive engineering
operations against the Roman army, but was now ready to
surrender. Cæsar incurred the anger of his soldiers by
refusing to destroy and sack the city. His veterans had
expected rich booty, and their disappointment led to a
dangerous mutiny soon afterward, at Placentia. In the
meantime Curio had led an expedition into Africa, whose
provinces were also governed by lieutenants of Pompey.
Curio was slain at the battle of Bragadas. The disasters

attending this campaign were more than offset by subsequent seizure of the granaries of Sicily, which were
used to supply Cæsar's army.   In 48 B. C. Cæsar was
elected Consul.   He thus legalized the establishment of
his authority in Italy, Gaul and Spain.   He now prepared
to cross the Adriatic sea and force issues with Pompey.
He arrived at Brundusium in January and prepared to
take ship.   He had few vessels at his command and was
able to transport only 15,500 men.   With this army he
landed at Palæste on the coast of Epirus.   He had difficulty in making his way through the fleets of his enemy,
which far outnumbered his own, and the second detachment of his army was prevented by Pompey's vigilant
cruisers from joining him until the winter had nearly
passed.   Many of the ships which had been sent back to
Italy to bring over the remainder of Cæsar's army had
been destroyed.   But before the arrival of Mark Antony,
Cæsar had boldly made his way into Macedonia, taking
towns in his path and reducing fortresses.   Cæsar was
anxious to confront Pompey, whose army now numbered
nearly 100,000 men, gathered in Macedonia during the
months Cæsar had been busy in the West.   With his small
army Cæsar pressed for a battle, but was unable to precipitate an engagement.   Antony joined him, and the reinforced army pushed after the enemy.

Pompey withdrew his hosts into a strongly fortified
camp at Petra and defied Cæsar to force him out.   Pompey's enemy, however, was in no hurry to dislodge him
and undertook to wall the immense camp on the seacoast
on the land side by ramparts and towers reaching across
the country seventeen miles.   Cæsar found his forces
insufficient for the undertaking and was placed in great
peril by a sudden flank movement by Pompey.   His plans
were disconcerted, and he suffered serious loss.   While

Cæsar was recovering from this blow, Pompey and his adherents celebrated their victory. Cæsar withdrew into the interior of the country to intercept reinforcements then on the way to join Pompey. As he had expected, Pompey followed him. This gave Cæsar the opportunity he had sought of arraying his trained legions against the motley hosts of the enemy in an open country. On the plain of Pharsalia, in Thessaly, on August 9, 48 B. C., the decisive battle was fought. In spite of the fact that his foot soldiers were outnumbered two to one and that he had but few horsemen to meet the cavalry of Pompey, composed largely of young Roman nobles, Cæsar broke the ranks of the enemy and speedily turned the defeat into a rout.

Pompey, utterly crushed, fled to Alexandria with a few attendants. When he landed in the harbor of Pelusium and set foot in Egypt, he was assassinated by a man sent to commit the bloody deed in the hope that the Court of Alexandria would thereby win the favor of Cæsar. Other leaders of the Senatorial party escaped. Brutus and a few companions submitted to Cæsar. When Cæsar carried his pursuit of Pompey to Alexandria and was shown the gory head of his late opponent, former colleague and friend, he turned sadly away and refused fellowship with the murderers of his daughter's husband. Upon his order Pompey's ashes were buried with every mark of honor. Cæsar then undertook to settle a civil broil between the forces of Cleopatra and those of her brother, Ptolemy. An attempt had been made to expel "The Sorceress of the Nile." Both factions appealed to Cæsar and he threw his fortunes into the balance with those of the beautiful Princess. It has been claimed that Cæsar's decision in this matter was influenced by the personal charms of Cleopatra, and his attachment to the woman who was in later years to win the heart of another Cæsar. During the conflict, extending over nine months, the forces of Ptolemy were defeated and dispersed and Cleopatra was able to maintain possession of half of the Kingdom left to her by the will of her father.

While Cæsar was engaged in this civil strife in foreign land, rumors were circulated in Rome to the effect that his army had mutinied and that Pompey's victor had lost his ability to win further battles. Moved by such reports as these, Pharnaces, son of Mithridates, resolved to regain the Kingdom of his father. He had proven traitor to his father, and for this treachery Pompey had rewarded him with the small Kingdom of Bosporus in the Crimea. Pharnaces now sought to obtain possession of Pontus, Cappadocia and Lesser Armenia. Domitus Calvinus, Cæsar's lieutenant in Asia Minor, attacked Pharnaces at Nicopolis in 48 B. C., with a small force, but was defeated. Although he was needed in Rome, Cæsar determined to restore Roman dominion in Asia Minor before returning to the Imperial City. At the battle of Zela he struck the forces of Pharnaces a blow which shattered the throne and the hopes of the young King. It was after this battle that the laconic words, "Veni, Vidi, Vici," were penned as a message to Italy. Cæsar set out for Italy and arrived at Tarentum before any one was aware that he was coming. At a point between Tarentum and Brundusium Cæsar met Cicero, who had been awaiting his return for a year. The General embraced his old friend and one-time enemy. The two men walked side by side for some distance, and during the conversation it is supposed that Cicero was influenced to retire to private life. The orator separated himself from public affairs and spent the remaining years of Cæsar's lifetime in literary labors.

Cæsar's progress toward Rome had a salutary effect

upon the seditious tendencies of the people. Rome became quiet. The government was in Cæsar's hands. He had been made Dictator and administered affairs much like an absolute Monarch. For three months be busied himself raising money, passing bills, recruiting the Senate and appointing Magistrates and provincial Governors.

He proved himself enough of a skilled leader and keen judge of human nature to quell a serious mutiny in the army and made preparations to wrest Africa from his enemies. The Senatorial party had made headquarters in the city of Utica. Juba, the Numidian King, was their active ally. They had gathered a formidable army during Cæsar's absence. Near the end of the year 47 B. C. Cæsar assembled his forces at Lilybæum and sailed with a detachment for Africa. Troops which were to follow were delayed by storms, and he was placed in a perilous position before their arrival. Upon arrival of the reinforcements he forced a battle at Thapsus, a coast town in possession of the senatorial party. The first charge of the Roman legions won the battle. Cæsar lost but fifty men, while the enemy had 10,000 killed. The battle was fought April 6, 46 B. C. Scipio, the commander of the Senatorial forces, attempted to flee to Spain, but was intercepted and took his own life. Cato also committed suicide and the Numidian King followed his example. Numidia became a Roman province, and almost the last vestage of Pompey's former strength was swept away. There was one more battle which Cæsar had to win before he could return to Rome and enjoy the fruits of his many campaigns. Cnæus Pompey, son of the former Triumvir, had brought together in Spain a new army of disaffected officers and soldiers. Cæsar sped over the Alps and the Pyrenees, and after a number of minor engagements, met and defeated Pompey in the decisive battle of

Munda, on March 17, B. C. 45.   It was a desperate conflict, but at its close 30,000 dead lay on the field and only Sextus Pompeius remained of the leaders of Cæsar's enemies.

In Rome, Cæsar was now regarded as a demigod and his praises were sounded from one end of Italy to the other.   A statue inscribed "To the Invincible God" was raised to him in the Empire of Quirinus.   The Conqueror returned to Rome in September, 45 B. C., entering without a triumph.   That celebration was reserved until the following month.

Cæsar was now supreme, and many citizens of Rome believed he would wreak summary vengeance on his enemies at home.   He surprised these persons by restoring the statues of Sulla and Pompey.   He pardoned Cassius, who had sought to assassinate him.   The same magnanimous clemency was extended to Marcellus, who had stirred up war against him and to Quintus Sigarius, who had betrayed him in Africa.   He maintained the existing institutions, only centering public action in himself by combining all the republican offices in his own hands.

In other days it had been the custom for a General to lay aside, after his triumph, his title of Imperator, but Cæsar received sanction from the Senate for a departure from this course.   Cæsar retained for life absolute control over the army, the judicial department and the administrative power.   The right was also accorded him to draw freely from the public treasury.   Members of the majestracy were sworn to do nothing contrary to the acts of the Dictator, such acts being laws.

Cæsar's seat in the tribunal, at the circus or at the theater was a throne of gold.   His robe was of the royal purple and his image was stamped upon the coins of the realm.   The Senate became a mere committee to consult upon the propositions of the Dictator, if so be the Dictator took the trouble to ask their advice. This was the power vested in one man. He is said to have desired a crown and the title of Monarch. The question of a kingship caused vague alarms in Rome, and the Optimates were well pleased at the uneasiness. The members of the broken-down party had sworn to protect the life of Cæsar. Taking them at their word, the Dictator went daily to the Senate unarmed and apparently unafraid. Cæsar was at the mercy of the men whom he had pardoned, and who hated him because he was able to show such clemency. A conspiracy, involving sixty Senators, was formed with the assassination of the Imperator as its chief purpose. The co-öperation of Marcus Brutus was secured. This was a valuable acquisition to the ranks of the conspirators, because Brutus was the only member of the Senatorial party whom Cæsar really trusted. Cato was his uncle, and Brutus had expressed deep gratitude to Cæsar for sparing him his life and liberty after all that had transpired.

Notwithstanding these facts Brutus became with Cassius the leader of the conspiracy. The date upon which Cæsar's life was to be taken was set for the Ides of March. Cæsar was to set out in a few days for Parthia. The party for whch Pompey died would be separated by appointments to distant offices within a few weeks. There was to be an important meeting of the Senate on March 15. It was whispered that the question of making Cæsar King was to come up for consideration by the Pontifices. The night of the fourteenth, a meeting of the conspirators was held in Cassius' house. The Senate hour was chosen for the time of the murder. Cæsar would attend unarmed. The Senators were to carry poniards in their paper boxes. A gang of gladiators was engaged to

lie in readiness in an adjoining building in case some
unforseen circumstance should disconcert the plans.
Anthony was to be detained in conversation at the door so
that there would be no friendly hand to stay the poniards.
The date arrived, but when the Senate convened Cæsar's
chair was vacant. His friend Decimus Brutus was sent
to his house to bring him, as delay was considered dangerous. Cæsar was uneasy and depressed. He shook off
this feeling and started up to accompany Brutus to the
Senate. As he crossed the hall his statue fell and was
shivered to fragments on the floor. On the way to the
Senate a man thrust a manuscript into Cæsar's hand, with
the request that he read it immediately. Cæsar placed
the roll, which contained an expose of the entire plot,
among his other papers and walked on. Upon taking his
place he was surrounded by Senators. Under some pretext, one after another joined the group of conspirators.
Tullius Cimber came forward with a request, and caught
the Imperator's gown as if in entreaty. The folds of
Cæsar's robe were pulled tightly about his arms. Cassius,
from behind, stabbed him in the throat. Cæsar started
up, and seized Cassius' arm, but at that instant another
poniard entered his breast, inflicting a mortal wound. He
looked about him, and seeing poniards flashing in scores of
hands, he gathered his robes over his head and about his
form and fell. The Senate rose in confusion, and ran into
the forum. The news of the assassination caused intense
excitement and fear in the city. Antony fled for his life.
The murderers ran through the streets announcing the
fact that the tyrant was dead and Rome was free.

The far-reaching effect of the life-work of Julius
Cæsar was probably not appreciated or anticipated by the
Dictator himself, nor by his contemporaries. In carving
out the ideal of his own ambition the man of genius had

brought civilization to hundreds of thousands of savages in the North.

He undoubtedly enabled the tribes in Gaul to advance farther in the line of progress in government and civilization than they would otherwise have done for centuries. He opened the country where Christianity took root in later years and left the impress of his genius upon all with which he came in contact.

He died before he could carry out gigantic schemes for the advancement of commerce, science and letters, but left the world a reformed calendar, which has been in use more than 2,000 years.

What he might have done for the state if his career had not been terminated so soon after the close of his series of military campaigns, has been the subject of much conjecture. Recent writers have inclined to the belief that too much glamour has been written into his history, but the weight of authority still tends toward accepting the statement that he was the greatest man of his Century, and one of the greatest of all Centuries.

CHARLEMAGNE
A.D. 742-814

CHAMPION OF CHRISTIANITY AND CIVILIZATION

Charlemagne, or Karl the Great, King of the Franks and, during the final fourteen years of his life and reign, Emperor of the Romans, was born in the year 742. He was the elder son of King Pepin, known in history as Pepin the Short. That worthy ruler died in the year 768, leaving as heritage to his sons, Charles and Carloman, not only a kingdom which extended from the Rhine to the Pyrenees and from the Alps to the ocean, but an unfinished double task as well—the Christianizing of the Teutonic races and the uniting of all Germanic tribes in one Empire. By the death of his brother Carloman three years later, Charlemagne became sole ruler of the kingdom, and upon him devolved the fulfillment of the mission which his father had begun. He became, as had been his father, the champion of Christianity and the protector of the Popes, and in this capacity, during thirty-three years of his eventful reign, conducted a fierce and unrelenting warfare against barbarians and heathens, in which the bloodshed on both sides, if we are to believe such records as have come down from that period, is almost without a parallel in history, In addition to the cause for which he fought battles and added to the extent of his kingdom, Charlemagne is also entitled to the gratitude of posterity for his efforts in behalf of the noble aim of advancing civilization and reviving education, which, during the two previous Centuries, had been at its lowest ebb as a result of perpetual wars.　Himself an ardent seeker for knowledge and a diligent student, he surrounded himself with men of learning, and throughout his vast Empire established schools, which were open to all.　Charlemagne was physically and mentally a giant of his age, a man of immense energy, of great administrative ability, firm alike in adversity or prosperity, magnanimous to his enemies, imperious but not tyrannical.　In every respect he proved equal to the task imposed upon him, and successfully accomplished the mission of his life.　He reigned 46 years and died at the age of 72 years.　Prior to his death, he designated his son Ludwig as his successor and crowned him as Emperor, but shortly after the passing of this indomitable spirit, the great Empire which he had created was broken to pieces.　Each fragment, however, retained the impress of his genius.　The civilization and Christianity he had conferred upon barbarians was not obliterated and the influence he wielded on future generations was lasting and wholesome.

The Franks were originally composed of tribes of fierce warriors.　Their earliest settlements were located between the rivers Scheld and the Rhine.　They were Teutons and spoke the Low German tongue.　Their dress was fashioned from skins of the bear, wolf and boar, they were light complexioned and wore their fair hair long and streaming.　In battle they were formidable, and even their appearance was enough to strike terror to the more civilized nations against whom they waged savage and continuous war.　The first traces of them on record dates to the Third Century, when they came in contact with the Roman Empire.　During this and the following Century they also carried on hostilities against the peaceful inhabitants of Gaul, crossing the Rhine on rafts, raiding the cities and slaughtering the inhabitants.　Considerable of the territory and some of the cities thus laid waste by them became permanent Frankish possessions. The first Frankish King identified in history was Chlodion. Under his rule they extended their southern boundary into the Roman territory as far south as the river Somme. Later on, under the rule of King Merwing, they became allies of the Romans and aided them against the invasion of Attila and his terrible Huns. The Franks were divided into two great divisions, the Saliens and the Ripuarians. To the Saliens belongs the credit of founding the Frankish Kingdom under the royal line of the Merwings, although the Ripuarians were more numerous and powerful. Until King Chlodwig became King of the Saliens in the year 481, the two tribes maintained separate governments, but during his reign he was chosen by the Ripuarians to become their King also. This formed the first great Teutonic confederation. Even at this time, although they were savage and cruel in their warfare, it is noted that they were more amenable to government and given to more settled habits than other barbarian tribes of the period. They worshiped the heathen gods Thor and Wodin (Odin). Gradually they enlarged their kingdom by conquest, and gradually, also, they built up and strengthened their original possessions on the banks of the Rhine. Under Chlodwig's reign they made the most notable additions to their kingdom. The victory over Syagrius at Soissons in the year 486 gave the Franks possession of all Gaul as far as the River Loire. This territory was at once flooded by Teuton settlers. In the battle of Zulpich, ten years later, Chlodwig defeated the Alemanni League, who dwelt on the upper Rhine, and were contending with the Franks for German supremacy. They were compelled to join the Frankish confederation, thus extending his dominion as far as the River Inn and to the Alps. It was at this time that the Franks embraced Christianity. Chlodwig, during the desperate battle with the Alemanni, invoked the aid of the God of the Christians and after the victory all the Frankish warriors were baptised and adopted into the church by Remigius, the Bishop of Rheims. This was the beginning of Frankish Christianity, and the new converts became zealous champions in the cause of the church. In the year 507 the Franks defeated the Visigoths, who then inhabited Spain and Gaul as far as the River Loire and to the Burgundian borders. The Visigoths were compelled to relinquish their Gothic possessions, but retained Spain for 200 years longer, when the Moors invaded the country and vanquished the Visigoths, whose name then disappeared from history. Chlodwig's avowed purpose in making war on the Visigoths was to gain this territory for Catholicism. The Franks now became the rising power in Europe, and the Burgundians were easily brought into subjection. After Chlodwig's death his kingdom was divided among his four sons. Clothair, the youngest, survived his brothers and became, eventually, ruler of the whole kingdom, but at his death it was again divided. Later it was again united under Clothair II and his son Dagobert, the latter reigning until 638. Following several divisions at different dates the whole kingdom was finally divided into two great parts, Austrasia, occupied by the eastern Franks, and Neustria, inhabited by the western Franks. Both thrones were occupied by the descendants of Merwing, who had deteriorated into such weak and worthless rulers that their power was exercised by the chief officer of state, the Mayor of the palace, instead of by the Kings. In Austrasia, the office of Mayor had become hereditary in the family of Pepin of Landi, whose valor and ability in the field and in the councils of the nation had long been

CHARLEMAGNE

(Ideal)

established.   To all intents and purposes these Mayors
ruled, the King being but nominally in power.   Dissen-
tions between the two divisions of the Franks had led to
war on several occasions, until finally, under the Mayor-
ship of Pepin of Heerstall, the rupture assumed serious
proportions.   The Teutonic blood had almost disappeared
in Neustria from the intermingling with the Romano-
Gallic element, and even of the Teutonic tongue but a
remnant remained.   Under Pepin, the Austrasians were
victorious over the Neustrians and Pepin assumed government over them as their Mayor as well as over the
Austrasians, and once more the Frankish dominions were
united.   The Pepin line of Mayors continued until in 752
when Pepin the Short held the office, he applied to the
Pope for a decision whether the title and throne should
not pass to him, inasmuch as he exercised the power and
Childeric, who occupied the throne, was a mere figurehead.
Pepin was supported by the nobility, and, as the reply of
the Pope was favorable, Pepin was duly declared King and
crowned, while Childeric was deprived of the long hair
which was a distinguishing mark of royalty, and sent to
the cloister at Monte Cassino.   King Pepin ruled as such
for sixteen years, during which time, as has been stated,
he labored diligently in the interest of the Church of Rome
and the power which had crowned him, until his death
caused his mission naturally to fall to his son Charlemagne.

Immediately following the death of Pepin a revolt was
instituted in Aquitania.   It was led by Hunald, who
claimed to be a descendant of the ancient dynasty. Owing
to a disagreement between the two King brothers, in
which Carloman withdrew his forces, Charlemagne was
compelled to carry on the war against the rebels alone.
At the first encounter he won a decisive victory.   Hunald

fled to Gascony for refuge. Lupus, the ruler of Gascony, at the demand of Charlemagne, surrendered the refugee, and here Charlemagne gave the first example of his magnanimity, by sparing the life of the revolutionist and simply compelling him to retire to a cloister. The Aquitanians submitted and Charlemagne built a fortress on the banks of the Dordogne and left a strong garrison to secure against further revolts in the province. At this time the throne of Lombardy in Italy was occupied by Dedier, who had a son, Adelgis. Bertrada, Queen-mother of the Franks, was anxious to bring about an alliance between the Frankish kingdom and Lombardy, and in furtherance of this plan, offered her daughter Gisela to become the wife of Adelgis, heir to the Lombard throne, and at the same time sought Desiderata for one of her sons, although they had both already taken brides in their own nation. Pope Stephen III, who naturally hated the Lombards because of their aggressions against the Roman Empire, denounced the plan, but Bertrada persisted, and Charlemagne repudiated his wife Himiltrude and married Desiderata. The marriage of Adelgis and Gisela did not take place. Desiderata was of a sickly constitution, and a few months later Charlemagne divorced her, and the alliance which had been brought about with Lombardy was broken off. In 771 Carloman died, and, owing to the unfriendly relations which had existed between the brothers, his wife fled with her two infants to the court of Lombardy.

In 772 the wars against the Saxons was begun, or rather renewed, for war had existed for generations between the Saxons and Franks. The Saxons still retained their rude barbarism and their idolatrous religion, and made frequent incursions into Frankish territory, just as the Franks, Centuries before had ravaged and invaded the Roman Empire. Eginhard, the secretary of Charle-

magne, who was educated under the King's direction and
was his almost constant companion, and who has given
us the most authentic history of the ruler's life, says of
the Saxons and the Saxon wars: "No war undertaken
by the Franks was so protracted or so fierce, or so full
of toil and hardship, since the Saxons, like most of the
nations inhabiting Germany, were naturally brave, and,
being addicted to heathenism, were hostile to our religion,
and thought it no disgrace to dishonor divine laws or vio-
late human ones. Causes, too, daily arose which contributed to disturb the peace. The boundaries of their
country and ours were in the open, almost everywhere
contiguous. It was only in a few places that large forests,
or ranges of mountains, coming between, formed a well-
defined and natural boundary line to both countries. On
the borders, therefore, plundering, burning, and bloodshed never ceased. The Franks were so enraged at this
that they judged it now to be no longer a matter of
making reprisals, but so important that it warranted them
in undertaking an avowed war against them. War therefore was declared, and was carried on continuously during thirty-three years with much bitterness on both sides,
but with greater loss to the Saxons than to the Franks.
It was the bad faith of the Saxons which prevented a more
speedy termination. It is hard to say how often they
were beaten, and humbly surrendered to the King, promising to obey his orders, giving up at once the hostages
he asked, and acknowledging the Ambassadors sent to
them; how sometimes they were so tame and compliant
as even to promise to give up their idolatry, declaring they
wished to embrace Christianity. But ready as they were
at times to undertake all these things, they were always
far readier to renounce them."

During the first year's campaign against these

marauders along the Eastern borders of the Frank dominions, Charlemagne crossed the Rhine, and marched rapidly into the very heart of the Saxon territory. He took
the fortress of Eresburg after a desperate assault, and
proceeded to the religious center of Saxony, where stood
the Irminsul, that dread pillar before which stood an altar
where half the captives taken in war were with barbaric
ceremonies sacrificed to the god Wodin. The idol was
destroyed and the rich treasure which had been offered
to the god was taken as booty and shared by the troops.
On the banks of the Weser he was met by Saxon emis-
saries, who sued for peace. It was granted on the simple
condition that Christian missionaries were to be allowed
to work unmolested among the Saxons. On returning
to his own country, Charlemagne received information
which caused him to undertake a winter campaign into
Italy. The King of Lombardy had demanded of Pope
Adrian I that he consecrate the infant sons of Carloman
as Frankish Kings. When the Pope refused, the King
seized several towns of the exarchate and then marched
on Rome. The Romans appealed to Charlemagne for
protection, and the champion of Christianity, without hesitation, divided his troops, and, by two separate routes,
crossed the Alps into Italy. The Lombards were caught
between the two sections, and, not daring to risk a battle,
retreated, each contingent seeking its own territory. The
Lombard King retired to Pavia and prepared to withstand
a siege. The siege lasted many months, at the end of
which time the citizens revolted against their King and
opened the gates to Charlemagne. The royal family of
Lombardy was sent into France, and Charlemagne
assumed the crown and title of King of Lombardy. This
was in 774. In the meantime the Saxons had taken
advantage of his absence and harried his borders as on

previous occasions. Charlemagne again took the field
against the barbarians, and proved easily victorious in
every engagement. He ravaged their country as far as
the sources of the Lippe, and was, as usual, met by deputies, who implored peace and pardon. His army was
accompanied by priests and monks, and these baptized
thousands of men and women and children in the river,
while the victorious army looked on. The following
spring the King called the Champ de Mai, which was the
primitive assemblies held annually by the Franks in the
open air, hence, the May-field, to meet at Paderborn, and
the Saxons were admitted to it on the same terms as other
constituent states of the monarchy. Some of the fiercest
of the Saxon chiefs, however, were not present, and one
of them, Witikind, was even then among the Scandina-
vians of the North, inflaming them against the Franks.
In 778 Witikind returned from the North, having reinforced his band of fugitive Saxons with hordes of Norman warriors, and many of the subdued Saxons joined
his ranks. He inaugurated a campaign of revenge, invading the Frankish territory and destroying life and property without regard to age, sex or condition. The nearest
Frankish troops were sent against him, and before Witikind reached the shelter of the trackless forests most
of his adherents had been slain. He mustered another
force during the winter, and when Charlemagne personally led his army against the barbarian in the spring, Witikind again suffered ignominious defeat and fled beyond
the Danish borders. Three years later he once more
returned and operated in the country between the Ems
and the Elbe, massacring Christians and burning the
churches and monasteries. When Charlemagne appeared
with a great force, the rebel retired again to the North.
The anger of the King was thoroughly aroused. He sum-

moned the Saxon administrators at Verden, accused them
of complicity with Witikind in not having prevented his
cruel work, and demanded the surrender of all who had
participated in the outrage. Fugitives were hunted down
to the number of 4,500, and they were all condemned to
death and beheaded. Instead of having the desired effect
of terrorizing the Saxons, this act inspired them to
revenge, and they rallied in greater numbers than ever to
the standard of Witikind. He had secured Norman allies
and at the same time the Frisians arose in insurrection
and made common cause with the Saxons. Charlemagne
was preparing to move against these combined forces in
the spring of 783, when his Queen, Hildegarde, died at
Thionville. Having attended her burial, he pushed rapidly across the Rhine with an advance guard, ordering
the main body of his troops to follow. For the first time
the Saxons awaited an attack of the Franks. They held
the heights of Osneggberge and fought with desperation,
but were forced to retreat. This was followed by another
battle at the River Hase, in which Witikind sustained a
crushing defeat. Charlemagne laid to waste the country
as far as the Elbe, and returned the following spring to
inflict further punishment. He also made a winter campaign against the Saxons and in the spring, with an irresistible force at his back, issued an edict which made
refusal to accept baptism punishable with death. He also
opened negotiations with Witikind. That unfortunate
warrior consented to accept Christianity and be baptised.
The King himself stood as godfather to the ceremony, and
in that period this relationship bound the principals in
the most sacred ties. This accomplished, the conquest and
Christianizing of Saxony proper, and within less than
twenty years thereafter, there had grown up around each
of eight sees, established by the Church, as many pow-

erful cities, which continued to be centers of population, wealth and education through many Centuries, viz., Minden, Halberstadt, Verden, Bremen, Munster, Hildesheim, Osnabruck, and Paderborn.

But there still remained outside the Frankish monarchy tribes of unsubdued Saxons between the mouth of the Elbe and the Baltic, warlike Normans in the Danish and Scandinavian peninsulas, and races of Slavs and Tartars were scattered beyond the northern and eastern borders. Having received the submission of Witikind and broken, at least for the time being, the opposition of Saxony, Charlemagne went to Italy to organize his affairs there. He crossed the Alps in the autumn of 786, celebrated the Christmas festival at Florence, and visited Rome. Then he proceeded, accompanied by a strong army, without opposition through the duchy of Beneventum and was soon before Capua. The Duke was powerless to offer resistance against the forces of Charlemagne and sent ambassadors, among them his son Romuald, to treat for peace. Charlemagne demanded that he should be recognized as sovereign, that an annual tribute should be paid, and that the Duke restore to Rome the estates whose revenues he had seized. The conditions were accepted and the victor returned to Rome and there spent the Easter festival of 787. Returning then to his native land, he determined to put an end to the troubles which had for some time stirred Bavaria, which was a dependency of the Franks and presided over by Tassilo, who had long been planning to throw off the yoke. Charlemagne summoned the intriguer to appear at the Champ de Mai at Worms of 787. He did not appear, and this resolved the King to incorporate Bavaria in the Frank kingdom. Armies invaded the doubtful duchy from every side. Troops from Italy poured across its southern border, from the north, Thuringians and Saxons entered the rebel territory and the King himself advanced upon Augsburg with a mixed army of Burgundians, Aquitanians, Neustrians and Allemanni. Tassilo had in the meantime entered into an agreement with the Huns and Slavs, but they repudiated the compact, and he surrendered to Charlemagne. The rebel Duke was tried at the Champ de Mai of 788 and condemned for high treason, but again the King's magnanimity intervened and the Duke and his family were committed to the cloister. During this same year, one of Charlemagne's armies overcame the Greeks in Liburnia and added it to the Frankish kingdom.

For the purpose of setting forth connectedly Charlemagne's campaigns against the Saxons, we have thus far refrained from recording Charlemagne's first expedition into Spain, although it occurred ten years prior to the invasion of Bavaria, and just at that time, when the Saxon Witikind returned from his first flight into the North to renew with the aid of Norman allies the struggle against the Franks. Charlemagne's tremendous activity was such that if the narrative were to follow in strictly chronological order, his marvelous rushes from one side of Europe to the other and from the northern boundaries of his kingdom to the southern extremities of Italy, the consecutiveness of the chronicle as concerning the campaigns against especial localities and the results thereby attained would to a considerable extent be sacrificed.

It was while attending the great Champ de Mai of 777 at Paderborn, that Charlemagne was visited by a number of Moorish envoys, who sought his aid. The Emirs of Northern Spain were anxious to escape from the rule of the Caliph at Cordova. Charlemagne, with a well-appointed army, hastily crossed the Pyrenees, but met with no opposition in his onward march. He had divided his army into two divisions, in the same manner as when he invaded Italy, and the principal cities opened their gates to him and acknowledged submission without even a show of resistance. Pampeluna, Barcelona, and Girone, together with many lesser cities, surrendered. The two armies effected a junction at Saragossa. It had been the hope of those who applied to the King for aid that he would proceed against the Caliph of Cordova, but when they discovered that he was merely taking advantage of the opportunity to extend the borders of his own kingdom and providing an additional safeguard for it, they repented of their request. The accounts of this campaign are meager, but on the return journey, probably because of the bad faith shown by the Emirs, Charlemagne dismantled the city of Pampeluna. The district was mountainous, subsistence scarce, and transportation extremely difficult. For this reason a speedy retreat was necessary. The retiring armies marched out by way of the old Roman road through the gorge of Roncevaux. The main body was well in advance, while a strong rear guard followed with the baggage. Of the disaster which here befell the troops of the rear guard, Eginhard says: "The Gascons had placed themselves in ambush on the crest of the mountain, which, by the extent and density of the woods, concealed their ambuscades. They threw themselves upon the rear of the column, hurled it back into the depths of the valley, slew all the men to the very last, pillaged the baggage, and, favored by the shadows of night, which already darkened, scattered on all sides with amazing rapidity, and without a possibility of following up their traces. The assailants had in this engagement lighter arms and the advantage of position. The weight of their equipment and the difficulty of the ground, on the other hand, put the Franks entirely at a disadvantage."

Twenty years later the conquest of Spain was completed. The Christian inhabitants of Gallicia and Asturias, under the leadership of Alphonso, aided Charlemagne in this conquest, and the enemy was driven back defeated. As a result of this final campaign in Spain the boundary of Charlemagne's kingdom was extended to the banks of the Ebro.

The Huns and Slavs, who had been excited by Tassilo, the Duke of Bavaria, to begin hostilities against the Franks, although they failed to come to the aid of Tassilo, began a series of incursions into Bavaria and Lombardy. They were repeatedly defeated and great numbers slaughtered, but the barbarian hordes continued to pour in from Pannonia, then occupied by them, together with the districts farther east. Charlemagne himself made one expedition into Pannonia, but these campaigns were mostly conducted by his lieutenants. This conflict continued, according to Eginhard, for eight years, from 789 to 796 inclusive. The Franks were in every way superior to the Huns or Avars as warriors, and that their losses were slight as compared with the practical extermination of the barbarians, may be gathered from the following account quoted from Eginhard: "How many battles were fought, and how much blood was shed, is fully attested by the complete depopulation of Pannonia; even the situation of the royal palace of the Kegan (king or chieftain) is so obliterated that no trace remains of a human habitation. In this war the whole nobility of the Avars perished, and the glory of their nation was destroyed. All their riches and treasures, which they had long been accumulating, were carried away, nor can memory recall any war of the Franks in which they have gained greater booty or by which they have been more enriched. Indeed, we may confess that up to this time the Franks appeared to

be a poor nation; but so much gold and silver was found
in the palace, and such a quantity of valuable spoil was
taken in the battles, as can scarcely be believed.   The
Franks justly spoiled the Huns of this booty, for the Huns
themselves had no right to it, it being the plunder they
had carried off from other nations.   Only two of the
chief nobility of the Franks fell in this war—Eric, Duke
of Friuli, killed in Liburnia, near Tharsatica, a maritime
state, having been cut off by an ambush of the inhabitants;
and Gerold, Prefect of the Bavarians, who was killed in
Pannonia while drawing up his line of battle, just before
engaging the Huns.   By whom he was killed is uncertain, since he was slain, with two others who accompanied
him, while riding up and down the ranks and encouraging each man individually.   With these exceptions the war
was almost a bloodless one for the Franks, and although
it lasted longer than its magnitude seemed to warrant, its
result was most successful."

Another account, given by Edward L. Cutts, holds
that the losses were extremely heavy, though sickness contracted in the marshy plains is given as the cause.   This
account also asserts that the Franks were unable to gain
entrance to the center of the "ring," the stronghold of the
Huns, a circular enclosure forty to fifty miles in extent, and
surrounded by nine circles of barriers, composed of earth,
stones and trees, between each of which were located villages, the rude palace of the chief occupying the inner
enclosure.   Of all the accounts of the life of Charlemagne,
it is scarcely possible that any can be more reliable than
that of Eginhard, who was the King's secretary, and had
easy access to all information, and besides accompanied
the King in all of his campaigns.   In the spring of 792,
Count Theodore and a large number of troops marching
against the Huns were treacherously murdered by Saxons.

The Saxons were to have joined in the expedition again.t the Huns, but on meeting the command of Count Theodore on the banks of the Weser, they surrounded his troops and massacred them. At this time, also, a second revolution took place in Beneventum, the Duke having married into the Imperial family of Byzantine and intrigued to assert his independence. The allies he expected apparently failed to come to his aid, although there is no definite record of this affair except that the impending revolt was suppressed by an army under Louis, the son of Charlemagne.   In the year 794 Charlemagne found leisure to punish the treacherous Saxons who had slain Count Theodore and his command. With two armies he entered Saxony, but the rebellious subjects surrendered without striking a blow. He sent thousands of the Saxons into other states of his empire as a safeguard against further insurrections, and also established strong military colonies in various of the most troublesome sections of Saxony. The following two years he occupied in subjecting the whole country to a vigorous military discipline. The defeat of the Huns had added Pannonia to the kingdom and the close of the war against the Saxons practically ended the campaigns of this remarkable conqueror. Eginhard relates that after this there were two short campaigns against the Bohemians and Linonians, but in these the King did not personally engage. The final war during the reign of Charlemagne was undertaken against the Northmen in 810, when as pirates they began ravaging the coasts of Gaul and Germany. King Geofrey, the leader of these incursions, was assassinated by one of his own servants, and this ended the piratical expeditions against the Franks. On Christmas Eve, in the year 800, Charlemagne was crowned by Pope Leo as Emperor of the Romans.

The last years of his life Charlemagne devoted to spreading education and civilization throughout his vast Empire, organized by his wonderful genius and unflagging energy. There are few acts of cruelty to be found in the annals of Charlemagne's reign. He was merciful and forbearing on many occasions where such a course would not be expected. His favorite punishment seemed to be to send offenders to a cloister. He died on the 28th day of January, 814, at Aix-la-Chapelle, after a brief illness with fever. He was buried in the great church which he had himself built. His remains were placed in the crypt beneath the dome, seated as in life in a great marble chair, ornamented with gold, clad in his royal garb, with his crown upon his head and scepter in hand, and his famous sword, "Joyeuse," girded to his side; the pilgrim's pouch which he had worn in life in his pilgrimages to Rome hanging to his girdle, and on his knees a copy of the gospels. On the stone beneath the dome which closed the entrance to the tomb was carved the following epitaph: "Beneath this tomb lies the body of Charles the Great, an orthodox Emperor, who gloriously extended the kingdom of the Franks, and ruled it fortunately for forty-seven years. He died in the seventy-third year of his age, in the year of our Lord 814, the seventh year of the Indiction, the fifth of the Kalends of February."

WILLIAM THE CONQUEROR
1027-1087

CREATOR OF AN ERA

Chroniclers of the life of William the Conqueror do not agree in regard to the date of his birth. The generally reported and most common acceptation is that this interesting event took place in the year 1027, though the addition is usually made that it may have been 1028. Thomas Roscoe, who in 1846 published a life of William the Conqueror, after immense research and being the first to have taken advantage of the then recently discovered Haddon manuscript, asserts definitely that "William I., surnamed the Conqueror, King of England, and Duke of Normandy, was born on the 14th day of October, in the year 1024." Jacob Abbott, in his history of the Conqueror, gives an elaborate chronological table of the Norman line from the time of the banishment from Norway of Rollo, who became the first of the Dukes of Normandy; until after the birth of William. In this table the death of Richard II is placed at 1026, and the assertion is made that William had been born two years before this time. However, while it is interesting, in the life of so strong and gigantic a character to know the exact date of birth, it is not essentially important as compared with the events of his youth, manhood and mature years; combining as they do a career of illustrious achievements. Ambition, supported by a daring and indomitable spirit and by wisdom which seems little short of marvelous, places him at once as the foremost figure of that stirring age. As a mighty warrior, a

wise legislator and an educator, his genius shines forth
with equal brilliancy. He was the creator of an era, the
influence of which stamped itself indelibly upon all future
generations of England and to a large extent upon all
Europe. He overcame obstacles of the most formidable
character and by his own exertions reached an eminence
so lofty that the characteristics of his Kingdom have
remained through centuries the pathway followed by his
successors in the great dynasty founded by him. He was
stern and strong, great power made him to a degree tyrannical and sometimes cruel, but he was also magnanimous
and progressive, so progressive that the Dukedom of Normandy even after by conquest he had greatly extended its
boundaries, was too small to contain the full measure of
his genius. For this he required a great nation and the
Anglo-Saxons became the instrument of his ambition.
William the Conqueror was the son of Robert, sixth Duke
of Normandy. His mother was Arlette, the daughter of
a tanner at Falaise. She was, according to the modern
expression, a common law wife, a circumstance which
at that period was not regarded in the same spirit which
it is to-day. Of the boyhood of William, historians pre-
tend to know but little, although it is recorded in the Nouvelle Histoire de Normandie that at the early age of five
he engaged in mimic war as commander of a troop of
infantile warriors. When the boy was nine years of age
his father, being about to set out on a pilgrimage, called
together the nobles of his dukedom and formally designated his son, who had no legitimate claim to the succession, as his heir. He named King Henry of France as
the guardian of the child and when he set out took the lad
to Paris and placed him with King Henry's court during
his absence. There are no details of William's life at
the French court, but it is presumed that the education
which his father had begun was carefully proceeded with

and the chroniclers announce that he was assiduously
eager in the acquisition of knowledge. In the year 1035
while William was still at the French court, his father
died. In the meantime his uncles and other relatives in
Normandy had intrigued to usurp the ducal crown and
the death of Duke Robert became the signal for a great
movement toward arming among the Barons of the duchy,
who were as jealous of each other as they were of the
new and youthful Duke. Among these aspirants were
many who had sworn to protect and cherish him at the
time he was named successor by his father. But the
young Duke was not without friends, though they were
few. The brave De Gace became at once the protector
and first tutor in war of the young Duke. Under the
leadership of this faithful warrior and through the efforts
of the Ducal Council sufficient order was restored to formally install William as Duke of Normandy at Falaise.
Scarcely had this been accomplished when the Earl of
Arques, brother of the late Duke Robert, laid claim to
the crown. He succeeded in bringing to his side the vacillating King Henry and their armies took the field against
William. Here the future conqueror displayed for the
first time his ability to cope with great difficulties. He
personally led an army against the strongest castle of the
Earl, left a force to besiege it and gave orders to the pre-
tender to appear at Rouen to do homage, while he marched
with a body of select troops to meet the army of King
Henry which was approaching to join that of the Earl.
William resorted to one of those stratagems for which he
afterward became noted. King Henry led a brave array
of knights, nobles and German allies directly into the trap
that had been prepared for him, a valley with rocky sides
where were posted the Norman bowmen. When the
French army entered the valley, it received from both
sides a storm of deadly arrows and in the confusion which

followed, the Norman men-at-arms and a body of horse fell upon the luckless French and wrought terrific carnage. The King retreated as he had come with his shattered forces, leaving many prisoners of rank in the hands of the victor. The young Duke magnanimously set the prisoners free and continued the siege of Arques. Soon after he learned that the King of France was again advancing with an army. Then, according to Abbe Prevost, "he first began to know himself, and to devote his mind to war in earnest as one covetous only of honor." Here, too, it was for the first time that he uttered the great oath which became memorable amidst the perils of his future eventful career. Surrounded by his knights and vassals, with uncovered head, he swore: "By the splendor of God, I swear never to depart from this spot until the strong place of Arques shall be in my power." The oath was responded to by all and soon after the fortress capitulated without striking a blow upon the approach of the determined-appearing array. William allowed his traitorous uncle to escape but confiscated his estate. The result of this victory was that the King of France made peace with William. Revolts continued with frequency in various parts of Normandy and William continued his campaigns wherever necessity required, always successful and always magnanimous. In the meantime he administered the civil and ecclesiastical power in a most judicious manner. He published a general amnesty after five years of this strife and offered clemency to the still turbulent factions. "Be it known," was one of the clauses of this amnesty, according to the Nouvelle Histoire de Normandie, "that barons, knights, vassals and all other Normans, shall lay down their arms and not make use of them till necessary to defend their own hearths and homes." He encouraged arts and industries in the cities, and, says Walsingham, "promoted commerce, public buildings and free ports." Instead of indulging his genius for war he advocated peace and sought to maintain it with neighboring States. He even made overtures along these lines to King Henry, but at the same time made himself friendly with those Princes who were jealous of the monarch. In the midst of these peaceful pursuits a conspiracy was hatched against him by Guy of Burgundy, his relative and the companion of his boyhood, whom he had enriched and favored in many ways. Guy's castles became the rendezvous for William's enemies and they conspired to overthrow the young ruler and establish Guy in his place. Grenoult du Plessis, lord of the powerful district of Cotentin, was one of those who joined this league. It happened that William entered this district on a hunting trip and when it became known, the conspirators determined to assassinate him at the town of Valognes, where he was stopping. A jester attached to William's court discovered the plot and informed his master, who fled in the night, pursued by the conspirators and it was only after a most perilous journey that he safely reached Falaise. The incident is believed to have occurred in 1044 and Roscoe asserts that it is well authenticated. Knowing that their plot had been discovered, the conspirators had to choose between war and flight, and decided on the former. They raised an army of 20,000, composed of mercenaries and adventures, and marched against William, who was illy prepared after the campaigns of the recent years. In this extremity he appealed to the King of France with such strong arguments that the former foemen furnished troops and William signally defeated his enemies. He mercifully forgave most of them and the most severe punishment inflicted was banishment. This practically ended the wars of the Barons and attempts at usurpation in Normandy, and from this time on William was only engaged in wars with foreign Princes and potentates. In 1046 William is again found in peaceful pursuits, enacting laws and promoting commerce and attempting to form a naval power. Once more he was interrupted by the outbreak of war in which he was called upon to aid his ally and suzerain, the King of France. Geoffrey Martel, Earl of Anjou, laid claim to an integral portion of the French monarchy. He prepared to besiege the King in his capital. Not daunted by the much-heralded skill and strength of Geoffrey's arms, William threw himself into the breach, stood between the army of the Earl and the city of Paris and completely out-generaled his adversary by capturing the castle of Moulines, and penetrated into the very heart of the Earl's dominions. In this campaign he personally directed every operation in the field and was ever in the thickest of the conflict. But such was the ingratitude of King Henry that when he made peace with the Earl, William was not made a party to the compact. This treaty, which was made in 1048, placed William in a position of the greatest peril, finding himself in an enemy's country and deserted by his ally. His only expedient was to retreat, and this was accomplished with consummate skill. Geoffrey with his army was in pursuit and carried the fortress of Alencon by assault and also captured the fortress of Dumfront. William retreated to Falaise, which he fortified and having reinforced his army, at once set out to meet the enemy in the open field. He appeared before Dumfront and demanded its surrender. At the same time the foe was marching upon him with a greatly superior force. William now received aid from an unexpected source, the result of his clemency on a previous occasion. The able military leader, Niel, one of the conspirators who had been pardoned, came to pay a debt of gratitude and brought with him 5,000 warriors. With this aid the fortress was compelled to capitulate and Geoffrey made no further effort upon Normandy. He started for his own capital with Niel in pursuit and William and his army following. This campaign resulted in wresting the city and territory of Mayenne from the Earl of Anjou, thus extending the power and frontier of Normandy. He then marched upon Alencon, which was still in the hands of the enemy. The Normans besieged it and the besieged amused themselves by shouting taunts and jests at the troops of William, reflecting on his birth and coarsely alluding to his mother by shaking hides and leather aprons over the walls and calling upon the Norman tanners to come forward. This so enraged William, that having made an assault and captured some prisoners, he had their hands and feet cut off and had them thrown over the walls. This had a terrifying effect upon the defenders of the place and they surrendered. Geoffrey was now glad to make peace at any cost, but William did not take advantage of the opportunity to dishonor his adversary. On returning to Normandy in 1051 with his victorious army, he called a council of the nobles, had them renew their pledge of fealty and distributed honors and rewards among those who had been faithful and had served him well. He announced on this occasion that he intended to pay a visit to his relative and ally, King Edward of the English court. The claim is made by some historians that King Edward had promised Duke Robert of Normandy that he would name William as his heir in the event that he died without issue. But whatever the motive that took William to England he was magnificently received and entertained, King Edward having during his exile found comfort and protection at the court of Normandy. The King was still childless and aged and the question of succession in England was becoming critical. When William returned to Normandy, he decided to enter into a matrimonial alliance. He had selected Matilda of Flanders, daughter of Baldwin V., Earl of Brittany, and descended on the maternal side from the great King Alfred. She was highly accomplished and beautiful, but she herself and her relatives opposed the alliance. Historians relate that William pursued his suit for seven years before he finally succeeded in winning her consent. There was also another difficulty. They were first cousins and the bulls of the papal court forbade marriages of relatives within certain prescribed limits. The marriage took place, it is stated, at Augi, and after a tour with his bride of his dominions, he opened his court at Rouen. William's uncle, the Archbishop Mauger, soon afterward excommunicated the couple on alleged grounds of close consanguinity, though the claims of William were that his uncle was prompted by malice. In vain he sought to appease the prelate and finally appealed directly to Pope Victor, through the afterward celebrated Lanfranc, with the result that he was finally absolved. But again the clouds of war were gathering. The close connection of William with the court of England, his conquest of a part of Anjou, and finally the alliance with Flanders brought about by the marriage, gave umbrage to the King of France, who began to suspect and fear the growing power of his vassal. In this attitude the King was sustained by his nobles, who had not yet forgotten the defeat at Arques and were eager for revenge. The King was advised to strike a decisive blow and annex Normandy to the crown of France. The vain monarch needed but little urging. He collected his army and started for Normandy after having invited the powers with whom he was allied to take part in the conquest. His real intentions were kept secret and his apparent

object was to restore to Geoffrey the tracts which William
had taken by conquest.   The Earl naturally joined the
King against William.   But the alert and able ruler of
Normandy was not to be taken by surprise, as his enemies intended.   Hastily he marshalled two powerful
armies, composed of his veterans, vassals and free bands
who had been drawn to his banners by the fame he had
acquired in previous campaigns.   William, with his own
force, marched to oppose the King and sent the other
army, under Count d'Eu, to occupy the district of Caux
before the arrival there of Earl Eude, King Henry's
brother, who was advancing at the head of a powerful
army.   Eude proved to be not an able general, for at
Evreux, Guiffard, one of William's distinguished leaders,
fell upon the French army and won a complete and bloody
victory.   The entire baggage of this section of the French
army was captured and ten thousand dead are said to
have been left upon the field.   The announcement of this
defeat filled King Henry with terror and he began a
retreat, while the troops of William harried him on every
side.   The victor made reprisals upon the dominions of
his enemy, captured Tilliers, which he had long coveted
for a border, and there built the fortress of Breteuil.
Fearful of further encroachments by the victorious William, the French King sued for peace and this was concluded and ratified in 1059.   About this period the Count
de Maine died and, having named William his heir, that
vast and rich territory was added to Normandy.   In 1060,
another desperate effort was made to wrest from William the fruits of his many victories.   The young Count
of Anjou, nephew of the famous Geoffrey Martel, at the
head of a numerous host aspired to bring about the downfall of William.   Preparations were going forward to
have the fickle King Henry join the movement, but the

death of that monarch prevented the proposed juncture. William, in the campaigns against his new enemy, trusted not so much to force of numbers as to the quickness of his movements and the skill in guerilla warfare of which he had become master.   Combats were frequent but none of a decisive nature until the young Martel and his confederates had advanced to the Dive, threatening Rouen itself.   Then, at Varaville, came the opportunity for which William had waited, and here, after a forced march, he fell upon the enemy and the havoc wrought by the Norman spear and sword and the deadly Norman arrows, was, according to Duchesne and others, so terrific that this battle, with the exception of Hastings, must rank as the most sanguinary of the conflicts engaged in by the Conqueror.   This victory made William undisputed master and enabled him once more to turn his attention to bringing prosperity and progress to his dominions.   How successful he was is still evidenced by the remnants still to be seen of the once beautiful edifices scattered throughout Normandy.   His court, which was conducted with much magnificence and splendor, became the rendezvous for men of learning and high character.   But the time was now fast approaching when William was destined to enter upon the greatest of his achievements—the conquest of England.   It was in 1064, according to all of the narrators of those times, that Harold, the son of Earl Godwin, of England, paid a visit to Normandy and a brief glance must be taken at the object and the result of this visit.   King Edward of England was growing old.   He had no son nor any direct successor and as has already been shown, William of Normandy would probably be designated by him as his successor.   Harold was an aspirant to the throne, and but one thing stood in the way of open efforts on his part in this direction.   King

Edward and Earl Godwin, Harold's father, had been at war, and when they agreed to terms of peace, Godwin had given hostages to Edward as a pledge of fealty. The hostages were Woolnoth (or Ulnoth), Harold's younger brother, and Hacon (Haakon), his nephew. When Godwin died, Harold applied to King Edward for the release of the hostages. But the wary King had sent them to Normandy and placed them in charge of William. This placed a power in William's hands which would aid him in his effort to succeed Edward as King, and Harold determined to visit William and secure the release of his brother and nephew, which would leave him free to pursue and forward his own aspirations. Harold set out with a splendid retinue, intended to impress William with his wealth and power, but all pomp disappeared when his galley was shipwrecked on the coast of Ponthieu. He was received with every mark of honor and friendship by William, whose acute mind at once grasped the favorable opportunity which had presented itself to him. He announced to Harold in due time his aspirations to the throne of England, and asserted that such was the desire of King Edward. He further requested of Harold his goodwill and coöperation in the fulfillment of these prospects and promised in return to make Harold and his family among the greatest in the Nation. Harold, being practically a prisoner in William's hands, acquiesced to this proposition. But William was suspicious, and to make the compact more binding he arranged a pledge-troth between his daughter, Princess Adeliza, and Harold, and the ceremony between the affianced parties was celebrated with great show before the assembled nobles and dignitaries of the Church. Adeliza was at this time a mere child and the troth to which Harold swore was that he would marry her when she became of suitable age.

Still William was not satisfied that he had sufficiently bound Harold and finally required him to solemnly swear in the midst of a great assemblage, with his hand upon a chapter of the evangelists, to support William's claims to the throne. The missal upon which he swore was laid upon a cloth of gold and when the oath had been taken, William had the cloth removed and revealed to Harold that he had also sworn upon a casket containing the sacred relics of the Church, which made the oath doubly binding. All was now in readiness for the departure of Harold for his own country, and while William consented that one of the hostages should return with him, the brother of Harold was required to remain in Normandy as a further guarantee that Harold would remain faithful to his promises. In this instance as in most other cases in history, of compulsory compacts, they were made but to break. Shortly after Harold's return to England, King Edward died. His death took place January 5th, 1066. The only legitimate heir to the throne was Edgar Atheling, son of the King's nephew, Edward. Although in the lineage, he was a foreigner, too young to make any pretensions in his own behalf and had none to take his part. According to the Haddon manuscript, Edgar was present on the day following the death of the King; when Harold, with the assistance of Aldred, Archbishop of York, crowned himself King, with the full approval of the nobility. Before leaving St. Paul's, where the ceremony took place, Harold knighted young Edgar and made him Earl of Oxford. It was evident from the first that the reign of Harold was not destined to be one of peace. The Danes were already preparing for another invasion and Harold's brother, Tostig, was, soon after his brother's accession, busily engaged in foreign courts urging strife against his own brother. These reports coming to

Harold did not disturb him, for he was more of a warrior
than a statesman.   Normandy had by this time, under a
strong, able and enlightened government, completely
recovered from the ravages wrought by foreign foe and
domestic struggles, and William had to all appearances
been busily making preparations for the great move which
he was now about to undertake, for he had given much
attention to shipping, the construction of good harbors and
the improvement of ports.   Tostig was the first to bring
to William the intelligence of Edward's death and Harold's accession.   He called a council of his lords and prelates and with their sanction sent an embassy to England
to remind Harold of his sacred promise and calling upon
him to renounce the crown.   The reply, that Harold held
himself in no manner responsible to the Duke of Normandy, was anticipated by William.   He laid the matter
before an assembly which represented every interest in his
dominions and received their unanimous pledge of swords
and fortunes.   After several months of the most strenuous toil William had assembled a fleet of three thousand
vessels of all sizes and a well-equipped army of 60,000
men, under the leadership of some of the most distinguished warriors of the day.   He had been joined by volunteers from every nation, had received the sanction of
the papal court and exacted aid even from his inimical
vassals of Anjou and Brittany.   France had absolutely
declined to enter into the enterprise.

After a discouraging delay caused by adverse winds,
William's fleet finally got under way and on September
28, 1066, arrived in the Bay of Pevensey on the Sussex
coast.   William was the first to land, and as he sprang
from the boat, he, like Cæsar when he landed in Africa,
slipped and fell.   Like Cæsar, too, he turned the accident
into a good omen with the exclamation, "By the splendor

of the earth, I have seized England with both my hands."
He sent out scouting parties in various directions and
finding no trace of the enemy, pitched camp, had his ships
taken into deep water and scuttled, and set about constructing a wooden fortress upon which to fall back in
case of need.   Four days after his arrival he learned that
the Danes, who had preceded him with an invasion of
the country, had been defeated by Harold at Stamford
bridge.   William made no movement to leave the place
where he had first encamped but calmly waited the arrival
of Harold, meanwhile occupying his army with evolutions
and particularly in the stratagem of feigned retreat, which
he afterward employed to good advantage.   He still had
some hope of attaining the English crown without bloodshed and sent a monk to once more remind Harold of his
vows.   He received in reply announcement that vows
made while a captive could not be counted upon, and ad-
vising him to retire at once to Normandy.   William's
position between Pevensey and Hastings was well adapted
for a battleground and especially for the movements of the
Norman horse.   In this arm as well as in archers the English army was deficient, relying mainly on the solid masses
of infantry armed with the sword and battleaxe.   When
Harold finally approached the Norman invaders, he established a strongly intrenched camp seven miles from the
encampment of William. Some further negotiations were
attempted by William.   Among other propositions made
by him was one to fight Harold in single combat.   Finding these efforts useless he decided to give battle.   On
Saturday, October 14th, William's birthday, was fought,
according to "Lives of the Queens of England," the battle
of Hastings, as it is known, but the encounter took place
at a spot called Heathfield, seven miles from Hastings,
where the town of Battle now stands.   At dawn the Nor-

man army was drawn up in battle array. William
addressed those within sound of his voice from a small
eminence, inspiring them with valor and confidence.
Beside him was the consecrated banner that had been presented to him by the Pope.   Then mounting his famous
horse, Bayard, William placed himself at the head of the
corps of Normans and cavalry.   He had divided his army
into three corps.   The first was in command of Roger de
Montgomery, and the second of the young Geoffrey Martel.   The point of each corps was occupied by archers.
The whole army advanced into attack led by Taillefer,
the minstrel-warrior, singing the song of Roland, in which
the whole army joined.   He challenged anyone in the
English army to single combat.   He killed his first adversary and his second, but was himself slain by the third.
The Normans now began the attack.   Harold's army was
in two divisions, one to defend the intrenched position,
the second forming the rear and reserve.   In point of
strength the armies were about equal.   Following a storm
of arrows from the bowmen, the Normans made a terrific
onslaught upon the English and none but veterans would
have withstood the shock.   William led the attack with
his right wing but made little impression upon the enemy,
which was here composed of the stanchest warriors of
the army, headed by the famous Kentish men.   A cavalry
charge was tried against them but the charge was received
without faltering, upon the point of the English lance, and
William then called upon his veteran infantry to charge.
The carnage which now began was terrible.   Spears and
lances were soon cast aside and in their place the sword
and battleaxe were employed.   Both sides fought with
the greatest valor.   The English feared more the arrows
of the archers than the hand-to-hand conflict with the Normans.   Harold displayed the greatest bravery, appearing

everywhere in the thickest of the fighting. The stubborn combat continued for hours. During this time William had three horses killed under him and served as an inspiring example for his troops. Harold also engaged in the battle with the greatest recklessness and although he had been wounded by an arrow continued to mingle with his men and keep them from getting into disorder and confusion. At noon neither side could have been said to have gained any advantage, although the slaughter had been enormous. It was stratagem that won the day for William. Finding that his repeated attacks upon the positions of the English availed nothing, he ordered a general attack with the understanding that in the midst of the melée a feigned retreat was to be inaugurated. The English fell completely into the snare and the Normans suddenly fell in compact forces upon the confused pursuit of the English, pierced their squares on all sides and inaugurated a butchery that was appalling. Still they fought with desperation until almost nightfall. The intrenchments were carried and the English cut down by thousands. Harold, fighting to the very last, was struck by an arrow which pierced his eye and killed him. Still the English stood their ground. There was no rout or retreat according to the chronicles of the time. Nor were any prisoners taken. The army of Harold was practically exterminated, including his brother and all the leaders. The number of slain among the Normans is variously placed at from six to twelve thousand, while the registry rolls deposited in Westminster at the time, show the English loss to have amounted to the tremendous figure of sixty thousand, the army being exterminated almost to a man. The following day William rested at Hastings to refresh his soldiers, dispatched messengers to carry the news of his victory to Normandy and his allies, and marched on London.

There were none to oppose him. The Nation seemed unable to rally after the blow it had received. With the conqueror's entry into London, a new epoch in his remarkable career began. His march to London left behind him a vast trail of devastation, and panic seized upon the inhabitants wherever he approached. He left a strong garrison at Dover and also garrisoned and fortified other points of importance along his triumphal march.

Terror reigned in the councils of the nobles and prelates. One effort was made to raise Edgar Atheling to the throne before the arrival of the Conqueror, but the effort was quickly abandoned on his approach. A weak attempt was also made to oppose the approach of William by the Earls Edwin and Morcar, but their armies were routed by a charge of five hundred Norman horsemen, which demonstrates the extent of the terror which had been inspired into the breasts of soldiers and civilians alike. On nearing London he was met by a delegation of nobles, who invited him to ascend the throne. Two months after entering London, William was crowned King of England. For a brief time he remained, or feigned to remain, the same affable, magnanimous ruler which he had shown himself to be in Normandy, but he soon became arrogant, harsh, unjust and cruel. He established a system of secret police and threw off the mask as soon as these and his troops had made him feel secure, and began a system of almost pauperizing the nobility of the Nation. He also permitted his army to carry out the most violent excesses and neither sex, age, beauty nor virtue were regarded by the ruffianly soldiers in their enormities. William indiscriminately dismissed Englishmen from positions of trust or honor and installed Normans, and in addition to depriving the English of their rank and positions he also seized their estates, erected barracks in positions to overawe the chief towns, and ruled with a rod of iron. In March, 1067, William set out for a visit to Normandy and carried with him a vast quantity of spoil, together with such of the English nobles whom he feared might organize a revolt against him. In spite of his precautions he was compelled to hastily return to England December 6, arriving at Winchelsea the following day, and while his appearance at London served to overawe those who were there plotting against him, the English in several sections of the country were preparing in deadly earnest for revolt. Early in the following year these revolts began to take on a serious aspect.

At Exeter, the people rose at the instigation of Githa, the mother of Harold, seized the fortress and called upon the neighboring inhabitants to join in the revolt. William soon appeared upon the scene with an army, and after a siege of eighteen days compelled the rebels to surrender and sue for mercy. Githa escaped with her life and treasure into Flanders. The Conqueror next marched into Cornwall and suppressed the symptoms of revolt there, returning to Winchester to celebrate the Easter festival with Queen Matilde, his consort, who had arrived from Normandy. Their joint coronation was celebrated on a magnificent scale in the abbey of Westminster on Whit-Sunday, 1068. In this year a fourth son was born to William. He was named Henry and afterward ascended the throne of England. William, during this time, spent several months in tranquillity with his family, devoting himself largely to the making and changing of laws. In 1069 insurrections again called the attention of the monarch and he sent his family back to Normandy. The persistent system of confiscations and unjust violence perpetrated against vassals and lords under the name of law, had rekindled the torch of rebellion. Both clergy and

laity, deprived of office and robbed of their lands and
estates, eagerly rallied under the banners of Earls Edwin
and Morcar in the North.   They were aided by Malcolm,
King of Scotland.   William was not taken unawares.
With a powerful army which he had already equipped
for this very purpose, he proceeded north by forced
marches and before the confederates had fully prepared
and while still waiting some of their reinforcements, he
fell upon them and won an easy victory.   The city of York
surrendered and its citizens were compelled to build a
mighty fortress in which William installed a strong Norman garrison.   Returning in triumph, he now began to
carry out his confiscatory system against the English
nobility to the fullest extent.   The estates of rebel lords
were transferred and ecclesiastical offices of trust turned
over from the English to Norman hands.   The noblest
families, according to Ingulphus, were imprisoned, banished or reduced to penury.   He struck boldly, fiercely and
relentlessly at the base of the English power, civic, military and ecclesiastical.   But he had not yet blotted out
all his enemies.   The sons of Harold, with the aid of Der-
mot, King of Ireland, made a sudden descent upon the
Devonshire coast with sixty-six vessels.   They were
defeated and driven back to their ships.   Next to join
in the insurrection were Cornwall, Somerset, Dorset,
Salop, and the Isle of Ely.   In the North, the Governor
of Durham, with seven hundred of his followers, had been
set upon and massacred.   This, according to Robert Cum-
min, took place the 29th of January, 1069.   There was an
uprising of the people of York and they slew the Governor,
Fitz Richard, and laid siege to the castle.   Soon afterward a Danish fleet appeared upon the Humber with an
army under Earl Osborne, and this was followed by
another under Hacon.   These were induced to withdraw

from the contest by the payment of large sums of money.
In the meantime King Malcolm, at the head of a strong
force composed in part of English exiles, invaded Cumberland and Northumberland, ravaged the country as far
as Durham, destroyed Holderness, and perpetrated acts
of great cruelty and sacrilege.   Edgar Atheling and Earls
Waltheof and Werleswain marched to the support of the
York insurgents.   On September 19th the Normans made
a sally from their castle and set fire to the town, destroying a part of it.   Then the infuriated inhabitants carried
the castle by assault and put the entire garrison of three
thousand to the sword.   The movement to throw off the
Norman yoke spread rapidly and the revolt became more
formidable each day.   Walsingham and others record
that William became so enraged that he swore not to
leave a single soul alive in Northumberland.   With an
imposing army he hurried to the support of his generals
and his advent seemed to paralize the efforts of the rebels.
The inhabitants were made to suffer the devastation of
both armies.   The rebels scattered and William pursued
the army of Malcolm and came up with him in Lothian,
where peace was effected and William pardoned many of
the exiles.   He spent Christmas at York after having
reëstablished his power.   It was the third insurrection
and by no means the last.   For a brief period a deceitful
calm ensued, but in the following year on the outbreak
of fresh disturbances, William again resumed arms and
went into the North.   From the Humber to the Scottish
borders fire and famine marked his path.   The country
was completely devastated and Hoveden asserts that
almost the entire population was swept away.   It became
a desert, maintains that chronicler, without dwellings and
without people and so remained for ten years.   From this
period forward William left no means unemployed to keep

the people in abject subjection. The vice of avarice was also growing upon him. He learned that some of the English had concealed their riches in the monasteries and at once ordered a thorough search for the treasure. Everything that his agents and spies could find was confiscated to the crown. Having crushed another insurrection, William tried a conciliatory measure by making Waltheof, with whom he had come to terms, Earl of Northumberland. The Earl married Judith, the niece of William; and later on he entered into another rebellious conspiracy, repented and informed his wife, who betrayed him to William with the result that on April 29, 1075, the unhappy Earl was executed near Winchester, being almost the last survivor of the Anglo-Saxon nobles. After an expedition against the Scotch and one against the Welsh, William once more found himself master of the situation. By a gradual deprivation and confiscation every interest had been merged in the crown. The clergy had shared the same fate as the nobles. They no longer divided penalties and forfeitures with the King. He had totally deprived them of their temporal power and confined them strictly to the limits of the Church. The privileges of cities, towns corporate, and other chartered bodies were inquired into and in order to maintain their previous standing they were compelled to pay over great sums of money. Vast wealth was thus transferred into the public exchecquer. As a final resort to deprive the people of the means of rebellion, he compelled them to give up all arms. Punishments of the most severe character were inaugurated for the slightest infractions and especially was this so in regard to any violation of the forest regulations. Having thus thoroughly cut off all resources for outbreaks among the crushed and disheartened people of England, he turned his attention to Normandy, where a serious revolt, headed by Fulk, Earl of Anjou, had just broken out.   As he had conquered the English with Normans, so he now defeated his rebellious Normans with English troops which he carried into Normandy.   From this time, he began to appreciate the military capacity of the English and this caused him to somewhat abate the discrimination he had shown against that nationality.   During William's absence in Normandy another conspiracy was inaugurated in England, this time by some of the Norman Barons who called to their aid the Danes and English.   After a brief struggle the malcontents either fled the country or were captured and imprisoned.   The following year was tranquil, but in 1076, being called to Normandy by the hostilities carried on by the Earl of Norfolk, he pursued the enemy into Brittany and besieged him at the city of Dol. The Duke of Brittany and the King of France, however, came to the assistance of the Earl and William was compelled to abandon his project, losing at the same time his entire baggage.   At this time discord in William's domestic life began to assume such formidable proportions that it resulted at last in a revolution carried on against the monarch by his own son Robert.   The son demanded the fulfillment of his father's promise to give him possession of Maine when he became of age.   To these demands William paid no heed.   Robert openly revolted, gathered about him an army of the adventurous youth who espoused his cause, and aided by allies who were anxious to widen the breach between father and son, he took the field against his father.   William drove the rebels before him to the castle of Gerberoy, to which he laid siege.   To add to his chagrin at this time William discovered that his wife was supplying the renegade son with funds to carry on the rebellion.   Having received reinforcements Robert finally confronted his father's army in the open field and

during the battle wounded his father.   This led to a reconciliation.   Robert was placed at the head of an army in
England to operate against the incursions of the Scotch
and this served to keep him out of further mischief.   In
1081 William commenced the great national census which
resulted in the famous Doomsday book.   The survey conducted by his commissioners gave the most minute particulars in regard to every city, town and hamlet in the
Kingdom and by this system he contrived to add to his
annual revenues a sum equal to five million dollars in our
money.   In 1083 William was called to Normandy to
attend the deathbed of his consort, to whom, according
to the best authorities, he had been faithfully attached
through all of his trials and successes.   There are stories
attributing to him great cruelty to her, but their sources
are of a questionable character.   One of these was to the
effect that he beat her to death with a bridle.   At this
time King Canute IV of Denmark was preparing to invade
England, but during the following year, on learning of
the preparations made to resist him, abandoned the project.
King Philip of France and his allies had not yet
given up their designs on Normandy, however, and in
1086 William took the field against the confederates.
The French armies had already crossed into Normandy
and were ravaging the country when the Conqueror
advanced against the enemy.   The French retreated and
William entered the city of Beauvais in triumph.   Here
he fell sick and in this condition agreed to the peace proposed by Philip.   By slow marches he returned to Rouen
and was placed under a course of treatment by physicians,
one of the objects to be attained being to reduce his
extreme corpulence.   King Philip at this time on a public
occasion inquired in a scoffing tone, whether "the good
old woman of England was yet in the straw."   This

remark was reported to William and in great rage he announced his intention to punish Philip for the insolence. Immediately on his recovery he led an army into France and laid waste everything in his path. The town of Mantes, among others, was attacked and burned. Here he received the injury which resulted in his death. He had entered the town in triumph at the head of his army when the animal he was riding stepped among some hot embers and plunged, throwing the Conqueror forward on the pummel of his saddle, and severely injuring him. He was at once conveyed to Rouen where, notwithstanding the efforts of the best physicians, he grew gradually worse. Finding that he must die, the monarch had himself removed to the monastery of St. Gervas in order that he might die on holy ground. He was struck with keen remorse for the many great wrongs committed by him during the closing years of his life and did what he could to atone for his sins by liberal donations to the Church and charities. He also ordered that the English nobles and other prisoners be set at liberty. He bequeathed to his son Robert the Duchy of Normandy and Maine and to his second son, William, the crown of England. His death took place September 9, 1087, at the age of sixty-three. He had reigned over England nearly twenty-one years and held the ducal power of Normandy fifty-three years. It is narrated in the ancient chronicles that after death the Conqueror's body was left in charge of some inferior officers, his sons having hastened to possess themselves of the bequests left to them. The officers plundered the personal belongings of the monarch, stripped the body and left it on the floor where it remained until the Archbishop of Rouen ordered that it be taken to Caen and buried in the Church of St. Stephen. None, however, cared to undertake the charge until a poor knight, Herl-

wein, took it upon himself to convey the body to Caen.
There he was met by the abbot and monks and while carrying the remains to the Church, a fire broke out and the
body was once more abandoned.   Finally it was brought
to the abbey Church and the ceremonies begun.   At the
end of a discourse by the Bishop of Evreux, a young man
named Anselm Fitz Arthur sprang up and protested
against the burial of the body on that spot, which he
claimed had been forcibly seized from his father by the
Conqueror and afterward given to the Church.   He
produced witnesses and was subsequently remunerated for
his lost inheritance.   It is asserted that when Chatillon
occupied Caen in 1562, the tomb was plundered by soldiers, who, finding nothing of value, scattered the bones
about the street.

RICHARD THE LION-HEARTED

1157-1199

HERO OF THE THIRD CRUSADE

Richard I, King of England, called "the Lion" or
"Cœur de Lion," was the third of the five sons of Henry
II and Eleanor of Aquitaine. As a doughty warrior-
King, principal figure in the Third Crusade, and personal
director of extended campaigns against the French, Richard won in his forty-two years of life credit for being a
typical representative of the brave and generous, but often
barbarously cruel, chivalry of his time. Eleanor, Richard's mother, had been the wife of Louis VII of France.
Like other women of rank of her time she had become
imbued with the spirit of the age and prevailed upon Louis
to allow her and others of her court to accompany him
upon the crusade against the Saracens.* The rigorous life
which followed for the Queen was indirectly the cause
of an estrangement between herself and Louis, and on
March 18, 1152, they were divorced. Six weeks later,
according to Lamb, Eleanor bestowed her hand upon
Henry, Duke of Normandy, who afterward became Henry
II of England. Richard was born of this union September
8, 1157, probably, Lamb reasons, in the King's palace
of Beau Monte at Oxford. The King and Queen went
to Normandy in 1167 to be present at the marriage of
their daughter, Matilda. After the ceremony, King
Henry and his eldest son returned to England, while
Queen Eleanor remained abroad with Princess Marguer-
ite and the two sons, Geoffrey and Richard. The latter

had already been invested with certain territories and some chroniclers state that as the young Prince grew in understanding, the mother sought to impress him with the idea that he should become a ruler independent of his father in these territories. At any rate it was not long before revolts against parental control took place. Aided by the French King, Henry, Geoffrey and Richard entered into a conspiracy in 1173 with William of Scotland and several disaffected English nobles to attack their father's possessions, English and Continental. Henry longed for the territory as well as the title of King of England. Richard was eager to possess himself of the territory of Poitou, and Geoffrey claimed right to the Duchy of Bretagne. For this treacherous conduct they were afterward pardoned by their father, but in 1189, after the death of Geoffrey and his brother Henry, Richard renewed his opposition to his father and was joined in this unfilial conduct by his younger brother, John. An alliance was formed with Philip, who had ascended the French throne, and the allies invaded Maine and Touraine and wrested these possessions from Henry, who retired to Normandy, hunted by his own sons, and there died, at the castle of Chinon, July 6, 1189. Richard now became King of England and was crowned at Westminster, September 3, 1189, with a great display of pomp and magnificence. The formalities adopted on that occasion have been quite faithfully followed in all subsequent English coronations. Richard had, during the years of his youth, shown that spirit of adventure and personal bravery which was later so fully developed in his campaigns for the recovery of Jerusalem. He had taken the cross in 1187 and immediately upon becoming King, he began extensive preparations for a crusade. His first act, however, was to order the liberation of his mother, Queen Eleanor, who had been under restraint for sixteen years as a punishment for having incited her sons to rebellion.   Upon his only surviving brother, John, he conferred the earldoms of Cornwall, Dorset, Somerset, Nottingham, Derby and Leicester.   He entrusted the government of the nation to Longchamp, Bishop of Ely, and Chancellor of England; and Hugh, Bishop of Durham.   He then gave his attention to raising funds for the crusade.   He levied taxes, disposed of crown lands, sold ecclesiastical and temporal offices to the highest bidders and for a certain large sum, released the King of Scotland from the vassalage to which he had been subjected by Henry II.   By these and other means he raised a vast sum, equipped himself and his followers for the undertaking which he proposed to carry out, and crossed to Calais on December 12, 1189.   Having entered into a treaty with Philip of France to join him in the crusade, the two Kings met with their armies on the plains of Vezelai, in Burgundy, June 27, 1190.   Here the two monarchs bound themselves with elaborate pledges and marks of affection to make the recovery of Jerusalem from the Saracens a common cause.   A code of laws for the armies was drafted and the French and English forces marched together as far as Lyons.   Philip here set out for Sicily, taking the route to Genoa, while Richard took another route, going by way of Marseilles and a temporary separation of the forces was brought about.   Richard arrived at Messina September 23d and was there joined by the French army.   Here the fleets which were to carry them had been assembled.

Several years previously Richard had met and fallen in love with Berengaria, daughter of Sancho the Wise, of Spain.   He now commissioned Eleanor, his mother, to go to Navarre and urge his cause.   As a result of this mission Berengaria promised to meet her royal suitor in Messina.   In the meantime a conflict arose between the two young monarchs which for a time threatened to put an end to the joint crusade. Philip had established himself in the palace of Tancred, who had seized the throne of Sicily, shortly before, on the death of William II, who was the husband of Richard's sister, Joanna. Richard peremptorily ordered the banners of Philip taken down from the palace walls and his own placed there. A conflict as a result of this arbitrary act seemed imminent, but a clash was avoided. The incident, however, served to sever the ties of friendship and affection to which they had pledged themselves and jealousy and hatred of each other dated from this rupture. Philip with his army left Sicily for the Holy Land, without waiting for Richard, who remained to await the arrival of Berengaria. When his fiancée, accompanied by his mother, arrived, he fitted out a ship for their services and then with his army embarked for his original destination. Near the Port of Cyprus, some of the ships were wrecked and on the shipwrecked soldiers reaching shore a conflict between them and the Cypriotes was precipitated. Richard and three thousand of his men drove the enemy back into Limoussa, their capital, and captured the city. The whole island yielded to his army and in May, 1191, the marriage between Richard and Berengaria was celebrated and the pair were crowned King and Queen of Cyprus.

Well satisfied with the ultimate outcome of the shipwreck, Richard now proceeded toward Acre, arriving there June 8th and finding Philip and his army already on the ground, having arrived two months previously. Acre had been undergoing a siege since 1189, the attacking force being under command of Guy of Lusignan, who laid claim to the throne of Jerusalem. With the forces of the crusaders added to the besieging army, the city readily surrendered. It was occupied by the Christians on July 12, 1191. Saladin, the leader of the Moslems, agreed in the terms of surrender to pay the Christians,

within forty days, 200,000 pieces of gold and to restore
to them the wood of the true cross which had been taken
in battle.   There was still a dispute over the claim of
sovereignty over Palestine, Guy of Lusignan's rival being
Conrad of Montferrat.   Richard favored the claim of
Lusignan and Philip supported that of Conrad.   It was
finally agreed that Guy should have the title of King of
Jerusalem and that Conrad, in the event that he survived
his rival, should be entitled to the throne and that his heirs
were to have the sovereignty perpetually.   Lusignan was
given the crown of Cyprus.   Shortly after this adjust-
ment Conrad was murdered and the crime was by some
laid at Richard's door.   A few days later, Philip pleaded
ill-health and the necessity of his presence in France, and
announced that he had decided to return to his own country.   Richard prevailed upon the French monarch to leave
ten thousand foot soldiers and five hundred knights with
the crusaders, under the command of the Duke of Burgundy.   Philip pledged himself to make no hostile move
against the possessions of Richard during his absence,
and with the bulk of his army set out for France.   Upon
his arrival there he at once violated the pledge he had
made and set about an attempt to capture some of the
English strongholds.   Failing in this he entered into
negotiations with John, the younger brother of Richard,
to join forces across the channel.   The threats of the English council deterred John from his treacherous purpose.

In the meantime, Richard was waiting at Acre for
Saladin to fulfill the terms of surrender.   Finally the time
limit expired without the promises having been kept and
Richard cruelly ordered the massacre of three thousand
Moslem captives within sight of the camp of the Saracens.
Richard fortified Acre and started out along the seacoast
in the direction of Ascalon.   During this journey a ter-

rific battle was fought with the Saracens between Cesarea
and Jaffa.   The enemy fell suddenly upon the Christians
with savage fury, but were beaten back after a bloody
struggle in which Richard's famous sword-arm played an
important part.   The Moslem loss, while no definite figures are given, is reported to have been enormous.   That
of the crusaders was also large, but not in comparison.
While Richard and his forces proceeded to Jaffa, the Mussulmans took occasion to recruit their shattered army.
He caused the rebuilding of Jaffa, which had been partially destroyed, and then began the march upon Jerusalem.   The crusaders arrived within sight of the goal of
their long pilgrimage, but owing to the reluctance of the
allies to join in an attack, Richard was prevented from
capturing the Holy City.   With his army he now withdrew to the coast.   Ascalon was found to have been
stripped of its ramparts and citadel.   The stronghold was
rebuilt by the hands that were better accustomed to the
wielding of swords.   The winter of 1191-1192 was given
up in fortifying the maritime towns, and in June, 1192,
Richard once more set out in the direction of Jerusalem.
He had in the meantime received disquieting news from
England, but was anxious to accomplish the conquest upon
which he had come, hoping with one more effort to capture the Holy City.   The army encamped in the valley of
Hebron and thence proceeded to Bethlehem.   Here, again
in sight of the towers of the city which he had vowed to
subdue, Richard found himself unable to carry out his
designs owing to the objections of his councillors.   The
army of crusaders now retired to Jaffa and Acre.
The strength thus being divided, Saladin fell upon the division at Jaffa and succeeded in capturing that city.   Richard
on learning of the result of the conflict, hastened from Acre
by sea and made a sudden onslaught on the Moslem

hosts. The Mussulmans were under the impression that he had sailed for England and his appearance with his army and assault upon them was so sudden that they were compelled to retreat into the interior and once more the cross was raised over Jaffa. This was on August 1, 1192, but a few days later the Turks returned with augmented forces and, although many times outnumbered, the crusaders, after listening to a vow by Richard that he would decapitate any one of his knights who shirked duty, attacked the enemy and after a bloody encounter completely routed the Moslems. In this battle Richard displayed such bravery in personal encounters that his acts were regarded as miracles. After the battle a truce was arranged for three years, three months, three days and three hours. The Christians were under this arrangement to retain possession of the seacoast from Jaffa to Tyre and Christian pilgrims were to be allowed to enter Jerusalem free of tribute. In the winter of 1193 Richard started upon the home voyage. The ship which bore him away from the Holy Land was wrecked at Aquileia and he was cast ashore. Realizing the dangers of attempting to pass through France and thus placing himself in the power of Philip, he determined to go on foot through Germany and with a few followers, disguised as pilgrims, reached Erdburg. His plan to escape recognition did not succeed. He was discovered by Count Meinhard, a near relation of Conrad, of whose murder Richard had been accused. He was seized and made a prisoner and loaded with irons and turned over to the Emperor of Germany. It was in March, 1193, that he became the prisoner of Emperor Henry VI of Germany, and after being imprisoned for some time at Trifels was transferred to Worms. Here the warrior lay in the castle dungeon for fifteen months; his only amusement was wrestling with his

guards and composing poetry.   In early life he had won
some fame as a minstrel and now devoted his talents to
writing pleas in rhyme for aid from his friends in England.   Efforts to discover the location of Richard's prison
were for some time futile and his continued detention
created much concern in England.   Prince John, in the
meantime was looking with envy upon the territories of
his brother, and only the intercession of Queen Eleanor
prevented him from usurping the throne.   Philip of
France also saw an opportunity for revenging himself
upon his former sworn friend.   He offered to aid John in
an attempt on the throne and proposed a marriage between
the English Prince and Alice, the sister of Philip. John did
homage to the French King and was furnished with an
army of mercenaries with which he proceeded to England
and captured the castles of Windsor and Wallingford.
He then proceeded toward London, proclaiming that
King Richard was dead.   It was, however, discovered
that Richard was still alive and messengers from England discovered his whereabouts.   At Worms a diet was
held in which Richard was charged with recognition of
Tancred, who had usurped the throne of Sicily.   He was
also accused of the murder of Conrad and the conquest
of Cyprus, as well as the betrayal of the Holy Land to
Saladin.   The royal prisoner defended himself with fiery
eloquence against these accusations and was fully vindicated.   When the information reached France and the
expectation was that Richard would be released, King
Philip wrote to Prince John, "Beware, for the devil is let
loose."   King Henry of Germany set a price of 150,000
marks upon Richard's liberty and efforts were at once
instituted in England to raise this sum.   In the meantime Philip and John offered a like amount to the German monarch to withdraw his offer and keep his captive.

Such severe criticism of the acceptance of this proposal by King Henry ensued, however, that he once more demanded the original amount, and Queen Eleanor brought the sum which secured the release of the captive.

Richard arrived in England March 13, 1194, after an absence of four years. It was not until the following month that Queen Berengaria was able to rejoin her husband. The reunion of the royal couple was marked with acclamations of joy throughout England. A second coronation which took place at Winchester, April 17, 1194, was attended with magnificent ceremony. Prince John now sought his brother's pardon and Richard granted it with the remark, "I forgive you, John, and I wish I could as easily forget your treachery as you will my pardon." Richard, learning that King Philip was besieging an English stronghold in the Continental possessions, organized an expedition and started for France. Philip fled from the advance of Richard's army to Verneuil. Shortly after this a truce was entered into between the two Kings— the first of a long series of short-lived treaties. For five years there were encounters, sieges and fresh reconciliations, though neither of the armies were formidable enough to decisively crush the other. In January, 1199, a treaty of peace to cover a period of five years was solemnly entered into. It was not long after this that Richard was apprised that Vidomar, Lord of Chaluz, had found an iron chest in one of his fields, filled with golden statues and vases full of diamonds. The historian Green relates that Richard desired a share of this treasure and advanced upon the castle of Lord Vidomar to secure it. Vidomar resisted and siege was laid to the castle. While Richard was demanding surrender, an arrow from the crossbow of Bertrand de Gourdon pierced the King's shoulder, inflicting a severe wound. It is a question whether the arrow wound was mortal or whether the bungling work of the surgeon in withdrawing the shaft was responsible for the result which followed. When Richard found that he had but a brief space left of life, he had de Gourdon brought before him and generously extended pardon to his slayer. He died of the wound April 6, 1199. His body was buried at Fontevraud. His closing hours were filled with remorse on account of his undutiful treatment of his father and his last request was that he be buried as near the grave of Henry II as possible. He was succeeded on the throne by his brother John. The history of Richard the Lion-Hearted is interwoven with romantic incident, such as abounds in the lore of the knights of old. Of this vague evidence there is sufficient of an authentic nature to prove that he was a great warrior, personally brave and naturally magnanimous, though imbued with the greed for power which was one of the prevalent diseases of the age. No excuse can be found for the wanton massacre of Moslem captives of which he was guilty, though in this he displayed only the ferocity which at that period was entertained by Christians generally toward their enemies. His record fails to show that he accomplished any great result either for his own country or any other. His sole ambition lay in the direction of war and while he was not successful in attaining the objects for which the greatest of his campaigns were undertaken, his courage and skill as a leader of armies, coupled with his personal bravery and prowess, deservedly won for him the proud title of "Cœur de Lion."

ROBERT THE BRUCE

1274-1329

SCOTLAND'S WARRIOR-KING

Robert I, King of Scotland, or, as he is more commonly known, Robert the Bruce, was born on the eleventh day of July, 1274. His father was the seventh Lord of Annandale and Earl of Carrick, and Robert, on the death of his father, succeeded to the title and a number of great estates which had come down from the first Robert de Bruce, who received them as a reward for his services while a follower of William the Conqueror. Of the early life and boyhood of the Bruce who became, after a series of most remarkable exploits as a warrior, the King of Scotland, neither contemporaneous nor subsequent histories throw any light. His grandfather was a claimant to the throne of Scotland, but this had been decided in favor of Baliol. Our first glimpse of the future King is when, in 1293, on the 3d day of August, he presents the resignation of his father as Earl of Carrick in his favor, to Baliol and swears fealty to Edward I of England. In this same year arose the disputes between King Edward and Baliol which resulted in the latter losing his crown. In October, 1295, the father, having done homage to King Edward, was made Governor of Carlisle. Baliol in revenge deprived de Bruce of Annandale and conferred it upon the Earl of Buchan, John Comyn. Soon after this we find the younger Bruce arrayed, in spite of his oath of fealty to Edward, with the rebels of the patriotic Wallace, who had come forward in Baliol's name to fight for Scottish inde-

pendence.   On July 7, 1297, came the capitulation of
Irvine, when Bruce with other insurgents sued the King's
peace and was restored to his former standing. Even after
this he again took sides with his countrymen, for two years
later he was elected one of the three guardians of Scotland
in the name of Baliol, and led an attack against King Edward's garrison in Lochmaben castle.   In 1304, however,
when Edward renewed his campaign against Scotland and
reduced Sterling, Bruce is shown to have been on the
King's side. The King seems to have had a strong appreciation of the value of the young Earle's coöperation to so
readily restore him in favor after flagrant rebellion.   This
vacillating conduct on Bruce's part cannot be explained,
and it serves as one of the shadows which tends to somewhat dim his otherwise glorious career.   His life was divided into three epochs: The one which has been related
was the first.   The second was that romance-surrounded
period through which he struggled through despair and
defeat for the freedom of Scotland and the third his triumphal succession of victories over the foes of his nation.

In October, 1302, Bruce attended King Edward's Parliament.   It is considered probable that he was at that
time looking after his own interests.   The old Lord of
Annandale, his father, was rapidly approaching his end,
and the son's care was necessary to keep the family estates
on English soil from falling into other hands.   In 1303,
Bruce was ordered to lead forces from Galloway to attend
muster at Roxburgh.   Bain is authority for the statement
that Bruce took with him to this muster all the men at
arms he could gather, including 1,000 foot soldiers from
Carrick and Galloway.   He seems at this time to have
fully decided to cast his fortunes with the English.   He
received advanced pay for his services, being Edward's
sheriff at Lanark and Governor at Ayr castle.   The Scots
lost all their strongholds upon the advance of the English

forces with the exception of Sterling. The Scots under Comyn and his friends surrendered at Strathord, February 9, 1304. A few of them were sentenced to various terms of exile, but the periods of punishment were shortened on condition that the offenders would devote themselves toward effecting the capture of the patriot, Wallace. The King of England thus showed leniency to those who had repeatedly broken their promises of allegiance and made them his assistants in an effort to arrest Wallace, who had never sworn fealty to him. About that time King Edward wrote a letter to Robert, Earl of Carrick, and the contents of that communication brings to us the information that Bruce was one of the most diligent among those in pursuit of the fugitive patriot. The father of Bruce died in 1304 and Robert went to London to look after his properties. In the meantime he maintained a correspondence with King Edward, who had decided to begin a formidable siege of Sterling, and Bruce assisted in this enterprise by furnishing a number of engines of war. So determined was the King to reduce this last stronghold, that he ordered the Prince of Wales to strip lead from all the churches in the vicinity of Perth to use as missiles. Sterling castle withstood the fierce onslaught but a brief time, and then Sir William D. Oliphant and his men surrendered and were taken to England as prisoners of war. This gave the last of the fortresses of Scotland into the hands of the English. Wallace, however, was still at large, and the search for him was prosecuted with greater energy. He was finally captured in Glasgow in the summer of 1305. The prisoner was conveyed to London, arriving there August 22. The following day he was brought before the judges and mockingly crowned with laurel. Wallace protested that he was not guilty of treason to the King, never having sworn fealty to him. The argument availed him nothing, and he was convicted of treason, sacrilege, homicide, robbery, and arson. On the charges of robbery and homicide he was hanged that same day. As an outlaw his head was cut off. For burning churches and relics his entrails were taken out and burned. As a traitor his head was fixed on London bridge and his quarters were suspended on gibbets at Newcastle-on-Tyne, Berwick, Sterling, and Perth. Some authorities assert that Robert Bruce was a witness of the execution of William Wallace.

This concludes the record of Bruce's career up to the time he was 31 years of age. Scotch writers have called it a humiliating chronicle, but they have annexed to the statement that his subsequent achievements in behalf of Scotland were of sufficient glory to efface the transgressions of his early history. At the time of Wallace's untimely death Bruce was a stalwart warrior, of engaging manners, and always able to find followers in any cause he was willing to undertake. What led him finally to sever his affiliations with King Edward and once for all take up the cause of Scotland has been a matter of dispute. Fascinating romance has been interwoven into the record of his deeds to such an extent that it has become difficult to separate the embellishments from the authentic historical facts. He had fought valiantly against his own countrymen, and, although strongly impressed by the courageous warfare maintained by Wallace, his sympathies for Scotland do not seem to have been stirred until after the execution of the patriot, when King Edward felt secure in the belief that the long extended rebellion of the Scots was forever at an end. He entertained the hope of conciliating the nobles by a policy of clemency and rewards and thus securing undisputed authority over Scotland. The King called a parliament in London during the month following Wallace's execution, which was attended by Scotch representatives, Bruce among them, and a plan of government for Scotland was arranged. From the fact that an agreement was here made that Bruce's estates at Kildrummy were to be placed in charge of a person answerable to the King, it is evident that Edward had already some suspicion that Bruce harbored hostile motives.

At any rate Bruce hastened to Scotland and suddenly decided to revive his claims to the throne of Scotland. After the abdication of King John, his most formidable competitor for this honor was John Comyn, called John the Red. According to Fordun, Bruce offered Comyn all the Carrick estates if he would renounce his claims to the throne and support Bruce for King. Also that he made the alternative proposition to support Comyn's claims if the latter would give over his estates to Bruce. Fordun's version is to the effect that the two entered into a sworn agreement by which Comyn was to aid Bruce to secure the crown, but that immediately afterward he treacherously revealed the plot to King Edward and urged the monarch to put Bruce to death. Bruce, the narration continues, learned of this, and whatever the true account may be, it is certain that on February the tenth, 1306, Bruce and Comyn met before the altar in the Church of the Minorite friars at Dumfries, and that Bruce there slew Comyn. Bruce hastened to his castle at Lochmaben, gathered some of his friends and proceeded to Glasgow and made the preparations which resulted in his coronation as King of Scotland, at Scone, March 29, 1306. The ceremony was conducted by the Bishops of St. Andrews and Glasgow and Bruce's four brothers and a gathering of friendly Scotch earls and others of the nobility. As a result of the fact that it was the recognized and hereditary right of the family of Macduff, Earls of Fife, to place the crown on the King's head, this feature was carried out by Isabella, Countess of Buchan, notwithstanding the fact that her husband was of the family of the man Bruce had slain. The new King now set out to secure a kingdom.

When the tidings of this sudden turn in events reached King Edward in England, he at once ordered preparations for a campaign against his new enemy. All the estates of Bruce were declared forfeited. King Robert thus found himself poor and minus even the title of Earl of Carrick. Aymer de Valence, King Edward's lieutenant in the north, was directed in a series of fiery letters, written almost daily by the King, to capture all the lords and bishops who had aided Bruce, yet he also directed that the life of Bruce should be spared in the event of his capture.

On June 5, 1306, the greater excommunication was passed upon Bruce in St. Paul's Cathedral. There soon followed a blow to the cause of the insurgent Scots which seemed to be final, so completely were Bruce's forces confused and scattered. Edward was unable to go north, but Aymer de Valence succeeded in taking King Robert by surprise near Methven. On Sunday, June 26, de Valence, with a force outnumbering that of Bruce by 1,500 men, fell upon the Scots. It became a hand-to-hand conflict. Bruce led his men into the fray with the personal bravery for which he long since had become distinguished. In the charge he was unhorsed and was with difficulty rescued from his perilous position. The battle went against him most decisively, and Bruce, with a few of his knights, fled from the field, after his army had been completely routed.

Bruce and his constant friend, James of Douglas, wandered about in the Highland hills for some time after the battle of Methven, and then proceeded to Aberdeen. Robert there met his wife and was joined by his daughter Marjory and his two sisters. The party went westward, and at a place called Dalry, near the borders of Lorn, Bruce

and his handful of men met in battle a much larger number
under John of Lorn. The Scots under Bruce were again
badly defeated, and it was with great difficulty that Robert escaped from the field with his life. Among the many
incidents told of his personal valor it is related that
while riding away from the scene of this combat he was
waylaid by three brothers. One of the men attempted to
seize the bridle of Bruce's horse, but his arm was cut off
with one sweep of the warrior's battle-axe. Another
brother clutched the stirrup, but Bruce crushed his hand
beneath his foot and finally killed his attempted captor, and
the third was dispatched as he attempted to leap upon the
horse behind Bruce. In spite of the danger King Robert
proceeded to give the ladies of the party safe escort to
Kildrummy castle. He here separated from the Queen at
this time, and it was many years before he was able to rejoin her.

King Robert's wife and his sisters were soon afterward
taken by the English, the castle of Kildrummy having
fallen before the onslaught of the Prince of Wales. The
Queen and Princess, and Marie de Brus, were confined in
cages in the castles of Roxburgh, Berwick, and in the tower
of London. Partisans of Bruce were captured and executed or imprisoned in great numbers. The prospect
which King Robert saw before him at that time was an
extremely dismal one. He started westward again after
the fight at Dalry. Sir James Douglas and 200 followers
were all he had upon which he might depend to make good
his claim to be master of Scotland. He was on foot and
anxious to escape to some island. He arrived at Loch
Lomond, but there was no boat on the shore with which
to transport his men. An old sunken hull was found,
however, and this was pressed into service. It required a
day and a night to carry the little army across, and Bruce

is said to have read aloud from romances in order to make the tedious hours pass more quickly. The days that followed were dark ones for the King of the Scots. Cooped up in the hills, in dangerous proximity to Lorn and Mentieth, he and his men would have added starvation to their other sufferings had not Malcolm, Earl of Lennox, come to their relief. Having procured some more worthy vessels, the band left their unsafe resting place and embarked on the Clyde near Dunbarton and sailed for Cantyre. With his force augmented to 300 men Bruce set sail from Cantyre for Rachrin, an island off the Irish coast. The winter of 1306-1307 was spent here, according to Bartour, and Bruce then left the bleak and barren island for the island of Arran. In the midst of the rugged hills and vales, densely wooded, Bruce might have avoided any enemies for an indefinite period, but he did not wish to remain on the defensive. The outlawed King was within twenty-five miles of his own earldom of Carrick, and could almost see the smoke rising from his own buildings nearer Arran.

He was anxious as to the fate of his wife and child. He sent a spy called Cuthbert into Scotland to find what the feeling was regarding himself. Cuthbert was to build a fire on a great hill near the coast if in his opinion the conditions were favorable to the return of Bruce to the land where he was King in name. Cuthbert found matters very unfavorable so far as an immediate return of Bruce was concerned, and built no fire. A fire was built by peasants, however, and Bruce thinking this was the signal for him, set sail in his galleys for the coast. He landed only to find Cuthbert on the shore, frantic with fear lest the innocent beacon light on the hill had drawn his chief into a position of peril. Bruce determined to stay in Scotland, notwithstanding the fact that he had gone there under a misapprehension. His first move was to place himself at the head of his 300 men and make an attack on his own castle of Turnberry, which was then under the control of Henry de Percy, who was stationed there with a garrison of 300 men. Bruce led his men stealthily in the night to the cottages surrounding the castle, and raising the Highland war cry, fell upon the English soldiers occupying them, killing many. Henry de Percy feared to come to the rescue from his position within the castle, as he knew not the strength of the attacking party. Bruce secured arms, provisions, and clothing, and then withdrew into the hills again.

It was not long after this first success of the King of Scots that his two brothers, Thomas and Alexander, landed south of Turnberry and were attacked and routed. The brothers were taken to Carlisle and instantly hanged. After King Robert had sought safety in the Galloway Hills, following his hasty visit to his own estate, Sir James de Douglas, Bruce's right-hand man, set off for his home in Lanarkshire, with only two companions. Douglas disguised himself and went among his old friends and organized a band to retake his own castles from the English. His confederates attacked the garrison on Palm Sunday in St. Bride's castle of Douglas. The English were put to the sword or taken prisoners. There was no resistance offered when Douglas and his men entered the halls of the castle. The great pile of masonry was totally destroyed, and the Douglas band joined Bruce in the Galloway Hills, where the King was in desperate straits. His enemies were closing in on him from every side, and treacherous Scots who had been employed to assassinate him, increased his danger. De Valence was advancing at the head of a formidable force of English to crush the little band of Scots and affairs were daily assuming a more serious aspect. Bruce divided his force into three bands and began a retreat. Bloodhounds were used by Lorn to trace the retreating King, and when this was discovered Bruce ordered his men to scatter, retaining with himself only his foster brother. On one occasion five men of Lorn's command came up with them. In the combat which followed all five were slain. By following the channel of a stream the bloodhounds were thrown off the scent. While continuing their flight through a wood, Bruce's companion was slain by peasants, and the King narrowly escaped sharing the same fate. After many stirring incidents Bruce at last reached Craigencallie, where he was joined by the faithful Douglas and Edward, the only surviving brother of Bruce. Here he gathered under his banner 150 loyal friends. Soon after this he was attacked by a force under De Valence, who was repulsed with great loss.

The English recovered, however, and Bruce found himself hemmed in on all sides by disciplined troops, but he managed to make his escape from the mountain passes and suddenly appeared in Ayrshire. De Valence, foiled again, retired to Bothwell on the Clyde. Bruce now had with him 600 fighting men and a battle was fought between the two armies on the face of Loudon Hill. De Valence found himself unable to take the position assumed by Bruce, and before night the English army was in full retreat; put to flight, Barber writes, in spite of the fact that they had 3,000 men to the Scot's 600. This was the first time Bruce had met the English in the open fields, and it served to help his cause materially. Minor battles were fought in the following months, and King Edward, greatly exercised over the failure of his lieutenants to crush Bruce, himself set out to take charge of the campaign. He died on June 7, 1307, after just coming in sight of the land of the Scots. It now devolved upon Edward II to take issue with King Robert. The son had little of the resolute spirit of the father, and the effect of the change of English monarchs made itself apparent in Scotland. The new king allowed the most critical period of the war to pass without striking a blow, giving himself up to the pleasures and diversions of his court while his leaders were meeting failure after failure. He finally headed an army and marched to Cumnock, but failing to meet the enemy he returned with his army without having struck a blow. On returning south he celebrated his marriage with Isabella of France, and the conduct of the war was again left to the generals who had already proven themselves too feeble for the task.

These opportunities were not allowed to pass by Bruce, who took advantage of the neglect and indolence with which the English were carrying on the war to inaugurate a series of rapid and brilliant campaigns and meeting in nearly every instance with great success. Bruce placed his brother Edward in charge of affairs in Galloway, and suddenly made his own appearance in Aberdeenshire. During the closing months of 1307 and the early part of the year 1308, he invaded Buchan, defeating the Earl of Buchan at Inverary and thus disposing of one of the most persistent and troublesome of the Scottish leaders who opposed him. By quick and stratgetic marches he next made his appearance in Argyll, where he surprised Lord Lorn in the Pass of Brander, defeated him in a fierce engagement and took Dunstaffnage.

His cause was now gaining rapidly and support came to him from every hand. During 1309 a truce was arranged by the Pope and Philip of France, but it cannot be said to have been observed. During the following year the clergy of Scotland formally recognized Bruce as King. This was of the greatest importance to him, as it gained for him the support of many sections which were previously doubtful. The three succeeding years were marked by a series of small but none the less important victories. Linlithgow was won at the end of 1310, in October of the following year Dumbarton was added to the list of victories, and in January of 1312 Bruce himself took Perth. He even made a raid into the north of England, and on re-entering Scotland reduced Butel, in Galloway, Dumfries, and a number of other places of minor importance.

The memorable year of 1313 closed with the capture of the Roxburgh castle by Sir James Douglas. This feat was followed by the capture of Edinburgh castle by Thomas Randolph, another of Bruce's strong allies. Edward de Brus attempted to take Sterling castle in 1313, but had agreed to suspend hostilities until Midsummer Day (June 24), 1314. De Brus was to receive the surrender of Sir Philip de Moubray, in command of the garrison, if the latter did not receive reinforcements by the date stipulated. This arrangement eventually brought about the battle of Bannockburn, which effectually settled the opposition to King Robert. The King of England made immense preparations to supply de Moubray with reinforcements. The muster of 21,540 foot soldiers was ordered at Wark, for July 11. Auxiliaries in Wales and Ireland were summoned to gather under the English banner against The Bruce. Maxwell is inclined to the belief that the number of troops brought together for the expedition in relief of Stirling castle was 50,000. Others have placed it much higher. The same authority places the strength of the Scots at 20,000, with the probability that this is too generous an estimate. Bruce chose to meet the enemy near the Bannockburn near Parkmill. When the English hosts appeared the King of Scots was riding up and down his lines, swinging his battle-axe and waiting calmly for the beginning of the conflict which might lose to him all he had gained.   Sir Henry de Bohun advanced from the English lines and offered to meet any knight among the Scots.   Bruce accepted the challenge.   De Bohun rode at him with poised spear.   Bruce nimbly took himself out of the way and brought his axe down upon the head of the English knight with such force that de Bohun's helmet was cloven from crown to chin.

The real combat soon began and Bruce, Randolph, Douglas, and Edward de Brus led the fight for the Scots. The English took flight after a bloody conflict, some going to Stirling castle and some back the way they came. Fighting was renewed the following day and King Edward watched the progress of the engagement from the elevation of Charters Hall.   He was very nearly captured, and as he realized that all was lost, fled from the scene of bloodshed.   By strategy, brawn, and endurance the Scots had pounded the English columns until even the superior forces of Edward could not withstand the strain.   Knights and common soldiers went down under the axes of the Scots on all sides, and hosts of prisoners were taken.   It is estimated that 30,000 Englishmen perished in the battle and during the flight.   King Edward escaped to Berwick. The loss sustained by the Scots in this memorable battle was insignificant.

This was the decisive turning point in the career of Bruce. The whole Nation was wildly enthusiastic over his victory.   At the Parliament of Ayr, held April 25, 1315, it was unanimously settled that the succession to the throne of Scotland rested in him.   The result of the war in Scotland decided the whole Celtic race to rise against England, and at the persistent invitation of the natives, Edward Bruce in 1315 crossed to Ireland.   This decided the Welsh in the following year to become his allies.   In the autumn of 1315, King Robert joined his brother in Ireland. During the campaigns in Ireland no fewer than nineteen victories were won. In May, 1316, Robert returned to his own country while Edward continued the campaigns in Ireland. With his army he was finally, after meeting with reverses, compelled to retreat to Dundalk, where a battle was fought in which Edward was slain and his army defeated. This ended the efforts of the Scots in behalf of the Irish race.

In the meantime King Robert, having returned to Scotland, took up the siege of Berwick. At this time ambassadors from the Pope arrived in England to effect a truce, threatening in the event of the refusal of the Scottish King to comply, to renew the excommunication against him. Bruce firmly refused to treat with the messengers sent to him and the siege of Berwick continued. In March, 1318, the town and castle of Berwick capitulated and the Scots ravaged the English territory as far as Ripon. The following December a great Scottish Parliament was held at Scone. It was here decided that inasmuch as the brother and daughter of Bruce having died, and there being no heir to the throne, that the succession go in favor of Randolph, and in the event of his death to Douglas, both of whom had been the most trustworthy generals of Bruce during the wars. Bruce showed his wisdom by arranging extensively for the defense of the country and regulating a system of justice for the Nation, which showed no partiality between rich and poor.

The great champion of Scottish liberty, having achieved the ambition of his life, left the conduct of further wars to his generals, Randolph and Douglas, and spent the few remaining years of his life at Cardross Castle on the Clyde, where he engaged himself with shipbuilding and the civil affairs of the Nation. As his years advanced he became of a pious turn. He had already been excommunicated, but one of his chief provisions was for masses for his soul. On the seventh day of June, 1329, he died as the result of leprosy, contracted during the hardships of his campaigns. He was buried at Dunfernline. He was succeeded by his only son, David, born to him by his second wife, Elizabeth de Burgh.

WALLENSTEIN
1583-1634

WAS HE HERO OR KNAVE?

Schiller, who made Wallenstein the central figure in three of his dramas, and in his history of the Thirty Years' War devotes much attention to the important part taken in it by Wallenstein, says: "His character has been so obscured by the hatred and applause of factions, as still to float unfixed and stationless in history." For two centuries the biographers of Wallenstein paid due homage to his greatness as a warrior and the remarkable part he played in the sanguinary struggle which marks one of Europe's most important periods. But no effort was made to shed light upon the dark and mysterious chapters which closed his career. The question whether he was a man of honor and integrity or a great and ambitious criminal, whose treachery merited the cold-blooded tragedy which ended his life, was left unsettled. All were guided by the official account of the court of Vienna, published immediately after the authorized assassination at Eger. Doctor Forster, in 1828, was the first to attempt the defense of the famous Duke of Friedland. Others have followed him and have endeavored to prove that Wallenstein was the victim of his enemies, and thus remove the stain of infamy from the name of this powerful actor in the great events which so materially affected the destinies of Europe. Wallenstein's high standing as a military genius is nowhere disputed. He organized armies out of the most unpromising material and conducted a series of cam-

ALBRECHT VON WALLENSTEIN

Painting by Van Dyck, Pinakothek, Munich

paigns which reflect the greatest luster upon his ability, intrepidity and skill. From the humble beginning of a common soldier he rose through his own indomitable energy and resistless perseverance to a height so commanding as to place almost within his reach the crown of Bohemia.

Albrecht Eusebius Wenzeslaus von Waldstein, known in history as Wallenstein, Duke of Friedland, Sagan, and Mecklenburg, was born September 15, 1583, the third and youngest son of John Waldstein of Hermanic, Bohemia. His parents being Protestants, the lad received his first religious instruction in that faith. His boyhood was anything but promising. Before he reached the age of twelve years, both of his parents died and he was taken under the protection of an uncle—Lord Slavata, of Chulm. A little later he was transferred to another uncle—Lord Kavka, of Ricam. This man was a zealous Jesuit and sent the boy to the College of Nobles at Olmütz. Here he was converted to the Catholic faith. At the age of 16, according to some of his biographers, he was sent to Altorf University near Nuremburg, where the records, still preserved, show that he was punished for misconduct. Forster, however, asserts that Wallenstein never attended at Altorf, and left Olmütz only when, through the exertions of Father Pachta, an arrangement was made for him to accompany Lord Liek, a wealthy young nobleman, on an extensive tour of Europe. France, Spain, Germany, Holland, and England were visited, and the youth had ample opportunity to acquire a store of knowledge and experience during these travels. While in Italy he became interested in the study of astrology and remained for some time at Padua, receiving instruction in that branch from Professor Argoli. It is said that the teacher, by the aid of his art, predicted for his pupil great martial fame and a brilliant destiny. Whether or not this prophecy induced

him to take the next step of his life is not known, but
on leaving Padua, he joined the imperial army, then struggling against the Turks in Hungary. At the siege of
Gran, after having served through several campaigns, the
young soldier was promoted to command a company of
infantry. As money, in those days, formed the only
means, practically, of promotion in rank, and as Wallenstein at this period was poor, it is concluded that he must
have shown an extraordinary degree of merit. In 1606,
after peace had been concluded, Wallenstein returned to
Bohemia and received his share of the estate left by his
father. As he had two brothers and three sisters, his
part most probably was not large. At this time, Wallenstein's brother-in-law, Count Zerotin, whose letters are
still preserved, wrote, in an effort to secure for Wallenstein a position as chamberlain to the Archduke Mathias:
"He is extremely reserved and entertains the most ardent
predilection for the profession of arms." Following the
advice of friends, soon after his return to Bohemia, he
sought the Lady Lucretia Nikkessin, of Landeck, in marriage. She was possessed of great wealth, but accepted
the poor youth for a husband. Little is recorded in connection with the domestic affairs of Wallenstein nor of
his own actions during this period. In 1617, however,
having inherited the wealth of the Lady Lucretia, who
died in 1614, Wallenstein at his own expense equipped
200 horsemen and set out to aid Archduke Ferdinand of
Gratz in his war against Venice. In this campaign, Wallenstein first demonstrated his superiority as a military
genius by getting supplies into the fortress of Granitza,
which had for a considerable time been blockaded by the
enemy. He accomplished the feat without striking a blow,
and his exploit attracted the attention of the surrounding
states.   His troops, it is recorded, were magnificently
equipped, well paid, and lavishly fed out of his private

purse, and such liberality did not fail to attract the attention of the Emperor, who conferred on him the rank of Count and placed him in command of the Moravian militia, a post of considerable importance. At this period, Wallenstein married Isabella Catherine, Countess of Harrach, daughter of the imperial minister, Count Harrach. She brought Wallenstein a great fortune and an influence which he might not otherwise have obtained. Soon after this marriage he went to Olmütz, where he had been placed in command of the provincial militia.

The year 1618 was now well advanced, and the first acts of violence which led to the Thirty Years' War transpired, and the slumbering volcano of religious dissension burst into eruption. In the charter which Emperor Rudolph had granted to the people of Bohemia and which both Emperor Mathias and Ferdinand had sworn to maintain, there was a specific stipulation that the Protestants should have full right to build schools and churches in cities and in the country. The Protestant citizens of Prague, under this stipulation, had built two churches and the evangelical congregations of Brunau and Klostergraben were about to dedicate their new edifices, when the Catholic clergy, claiming to be acting under direct instructions from the Emperor, seized the churches and destroyed one, while they closed up the other. The two congregations joined in a complaint to the Lords of the Council, the representatives of the Emperor at Prague. Instead of granting redress, the dignitaries caused the deputies of the complainants to be imprisoned. The Protestant members of the states then assembled and sent a strong remonstrance to the Emperor. From the fact that the Catholics were in full control at Vienna, where the Emperor was held completely under their influence and also on the advice of Ferdinand of Bohemia, whose hatred of "heresy" had previously been demonstrated, the

Emperor returned the remonstrance with a harsh reply.
It was on May 22, 1618, that the deputies of the Protestant states appeared before the Council of Prague to listen
to the decision of the Emperor in regard to their appeal.
The reply set forth that "His Imperial Majesty had, for
good and sufficient reasons, deemed it right to command
that the church of Brunau should be closed and the one of
Klostergraben demolished. His Imperial Majesty further
thought that the states had abused the charter, and that
the deputies had rendered themselves liable to be punished
as rebels and traitors."

The decision caused no surprise, as it had already been
given publicity, and the Protestant clergymen had vigorously denounced this encroachment on their religious lib-
erties and had taken every means in their power to arouse
the indignation of the people. The deputation therefore
had but to follow out a prearranged programme. They
requested a copy of the Imperial letter and asked permission to again appear before the Council the following day
to make their explanations. On the following morning
the Protestant noblemen who had been chosen proceeded
to the castle in full armor, followed by a great crowd of
armed Protestants. After some argument, the crowd
seized the Lords of the Council and threw them out of a
window and fired several shots at them. None of them
were injured, but the leaders of the Protestants realized
that their act would be likely to be followed by the vengeance of the Emperor, and at once sent a contrite appeal
for clemency. There was, however, little hope that such
a request would be granted and precautionary measures
were promptly taken. Many of the Catholic clergy were
banished, Count Thurn, one of the Protestant leaders,
was placed at the head of an army, alliances were entered
into with the neighboring countries of Lusatia and Silesia,

and appeals for aid were sent to the Protestants of all German states.

Wallenstein was asked to take sides with the insurgents, but declined, preferring to cast his lot with the imperial armies. Two Austrian armies were sent against the Bohemians to disarm them, but the imperial troops were repulsed. Wallenstein tried in vain to hold the Moravians in allegiance to the Emperor, and in return the deputies of the States passed a decree relieving him of his command. His imperial commission availed him nothing, and he was compelled to evacuate Olmütz, against which, Count Thurn was then marching with an army. Wallenstein was provided by the Emperor with a regiment of cuirassiers, and in the following June he was present with his command at the battle of Teyne, and defeated the insurgents under Count Mansfield. This battle and victory, small as it might appear when compared with Wallenstein's subsequent exploits, was really of the greatest importance, coming as it did at a most critical period. By the death of Emperor Mathias just previously, Ferdinand of Gratz, King of Hungary and Bohemia, had succeeded to the imperial throne and his position in Vienna was daily becoming more insecure, inasmuch as the town was destitute of troops, while the Protestant armies were advancing upon it from every direction. Count Thurn, at the head of the Bohemian army, was already at the Danube bridge, and the sound of his guns could be heard at the palace. Gabor, Prince of Transylvania, was advancing with 50,000 men, and the Protestants of both upper and lower Austria were arming and coming to the aid of the Bohemians. All seemed lost to Emperor Ferdinand, when suddenly came the announcement of the insignificant defeat of Mansfield at Teyne, coupled with the information that Wallenstein and the Austrians under Bocquoi were marching on Prague. The effect was instantaneous. The Bohemians gave up their project against Vienna, broke camp and hastened toward Prague to defend it. Thus the Austrian capital was saved and Ferdinand found time to secure himself against his adversaries. His first step was to proceed to Frankfort, where, in spite of Protestant opposition, he was formally elected to the imperial throne in August. Almost simultaneously with this event the Bohemians renounced their allegiance to Austria and selected Frederick V, Elector of the Palatinate, as their sovereign. In the meantime the army of Transylvanians met and defeated General Bocquoi, and would have entered Vienna but for the resistance of the troops of Wallenstein. Finding that their allies, the Bohemians, had departed, the Transylvanians also retired. Maximilian of Bavaria, one of the ablest and most powerful of the Catholic Princes, by an agreement with Ferdinand, marched into Bohemia and was joined by the troops of Wallenstein and Bocquoi. These armies met with no resistance until November 8, 1620, when the Bohemians and their allies made a stand at the White Mountain, near Prague. These defenders of Bohemia were illy disciplined and mutinous as a result of internal dissensions, and while they numbered 25,000 men and could have made a tremendous defense against the 30,000 which composed the invading army, they were completely routed. King Frederick V, on learning of the result, fled with all speed to Holland, forfeiting his crown, and Prague surrendered the next day. This restored to Ferdinand his dominions. Practically the war was at an end, and peace would perhaps have been made lasting, had not Ferdinand in revenge for the revolt of his subjects given over the unhappy Kingdom to the remorseless vengeance of inquisitors and

executioners. According to Habernfeld and Erhard, the
most barbarous cruelty was practiced upon those found
to have been connected with the insurrection. Three
months were allowed to elapse before this bloody work was
begun, and many who had fled the Kingdom were lulled
into security and returned, only to fall victims to the
executioner. Members of the nobility were beheaded, the
plebeians were hanged. With his own hand Ferdinand
destroyed the Bohemian Magna Charta, and thus relieved
of its obligations, banished the Protestant clergy and subjected their congregations to oppression of every sort. In
less than two years the estates of 622 Protestant nobles
were confiscated for the benefit of the crown. Wallenstein took no part in the battle at Prague, having been sent
with an expedition into Moravia. He met with no resistance, and on entering Olmütz, repossessed himself of his
own estates and bought up numerous confiscated estates
at extremely low prices, as a result of his services to the
Emperor. After the fall of Prague, the Transylvanians
again invaded Austria. The imperial generals failed to
arrest the progress of Gabor's army, and it remained for
Wallenstein to add to his renown by administering a
crushing defeat upon the forces of Prince Gabor at Sha-
nutz, October 18, 1621. In 1623, however, Gabor
renewed the war in pursuance of his claims upon the crown
of Hungary. In this campaign he succeeded in surrounding the imperial army sent against him, and surrender
must have resulted but for the timely arrival of Wallenstein with an army of relief. Toward the end of this year,
as a reward for his services, Wallenstein was created
Count Palatine and Duke of Friedland, with the right of
striking coin and granting patents of nobility. The
domain forming the duchy was composed of confiscated
lands which had been purchased by him. Some historians

hold that Wallenstein was also created a Prince, in translation of the German word "Furst," but there is some doubt on this point. His own letters during the period spent by him in actively ruling his dukedom throw considerable light on his character. They show that he lived in the most sumptuous style, ordered liveries at one time for fifty servants, commands the citizens of Leipa to send their children to a school which he had founded, and offers a reward of 5,000 crowns for the capture of an intruder who organized a revolt in the dukedom. These letters also show that he patronized agriculture to a large extent, built roads and bridges, issued a constitution for his subjects, and invited artisans and instructors to his court from foreign countries. There is an abundance of evidence that he strove to educate and benefit his vassals in every way. While Wallenstein was thus peacefully employed, the armies of the Emperor, under Tilly, had invaded the Palatinate, the hereditary dominions of the fugitive King Frederick V, and accomplishing its conquest after meeting with no resistance except that of an army led by Count Ernest of Mansfield, an adventurer, who, though courageous and resourceful, could not long maintain himself against the combined armies of the Emperor and the League. The movements of the imperial army became such as to evoke protests from the States, and when Tilly's forces gathered on the frontiers of lower Saxony, the States began arming. Aided by English subsidies, the Duke of Brunswick and Mansfield again appeared on the scene and an alliance was entered into with the King of Denmark, Christian IV. An army of 60,000 was soon organized and its avowed object was for self-protection and to maintain peace. At Vienna it was construed to mean that an effort would be made to reconquer the Palatinate, and the Emperor, after ordering the

forces disbanded, and meeting with refusal, sent his
armies into the Circle. King Christian, who was Commander-in-Chief of the Protestant forces, was an able General, and Tilly made little progress. He demanded reinforcements, but the Emperor had none to send. Tilly's
forces were composed almost entirely of the troops of
Maximilian and the Catholic League. The imperial troops
were engaged in watching Gabor and preserving peace in
the newly acquired territories. The Emperor was badly
in need of troops, but his resources were almost exhausted.
At this juncture Wallenstein came forward and offered
to raise and equip at his own expense an army of 50,000
men. While the Emperor hesitated to put so much power
into his hands he finally consented to the proposition, and
Wallenstein was promised a salary of 6,000 florins per
month and empowered to reward himself and his men
from out of the fruits of their conquests. Wallenstein's
fame for liberality caused soldiers to flock to his standard from all of the surrounding nations. At the end of a
month he had an army of 20,000, and, leaving Eger on
September 3, 1625, he soon appeared on the borders of
Lower Saxony with an army of 30,000. Wallenstein
placed himself in communication with Tilly with a view
to coöperating, but differences arose and the armies continued to act separately. On entering Lower Saxony, Wallenstein followed the Elbe River, and in order to command
its passage, secured the bridge of Dessau. He fortified it
by building strong redoubts on the right bank. On the
first of April, 1626, Count Mansfield made a gallant
attack on Wallenstein's position, but was repulsed. A
second attack was made April 11th, which was equally
unsuccessful. On April 15th the persistent Mansfield was
again advancing to the attack, when Wallenstein crossed
the river, attacked Mansfield's army, and won a victory.

The number of slain in Mansfield's ranks is given as
9,000. Mansfield fled, but reappeared in the field in
June at the head of 20,000 men. A letter from Wallenstein to the Emperor at this time relates that "6,000 British soldiers for Mansfield's army were reported landed
at Hamburgh," but this is discredited by historians. With
his new army Mansfield marched through Silesia for the
purpose of joining Prince Gabor in Hungary. Wallenstein pursued him into Hungary, sustaining severe losses
during the marches through the Carpathian Mountains,
owing to lack of supplies. Mansfield could not come to
terms with Gabor and his Transylvanians and Turks, and
after turning over his command to Prince Ernest of Weimar, set out for Venice, but died on the way. Gabor, finding Wallenstein's army in his vicinity, effected another
truce with the Emperor. Wallenstein placed his fatigued
army into winter quarters on the Danube, made a visit to
Vienna, secured reinforcements and supplies, and, in the
spring of 1627, had a well-equipped army of 40,000. During his absence in Hungary Tilly had defeated the army
of the King of Denmark, and several of the German States,
terrified at the possible results, renounced the alliance with
Denmark. Wallenstein's first move in the campaign of
1627 was to occupy Silesia, where he met with no resistance from the small forces of Danish troops. He next
occupied Mecklenburg and Pomerania, in spite of remonstrances and assurances of neutrality. Wallenstein's
reply, according to Forster, to these remonstrances was
that the time had come to dispense with electors and unite
the country under one absolute sovereign, the same as
France and Spain. He marched toward the frontiers of
Holstein, following the retreating Danes, and in a series
of engagements near Heilighausen, defeated and scattered them, and ravaged the entire peninsula of Jutland.

The sea arrested the further progress of the victorious army. Those States of Lower Germany who had renounced the alliance with Denmark, were soon made to suffer the consequences of their policy of refusing to supply the army of their defenders. Wallenstein had increased his force to 100,000 men and overran the country, levying contributions and following out the theory of making the war pay for the war. Tremendous sums were extorted from the provinces, and complaints to the Emperor, who had through Wallenstein's prowess been made absolute ruler from the Baltic to the Adriatic, availed nothing. Wallenstein did not fail to improve this opportunity to add to his already enormous wealth. With the end of the campaign, he repaired to Prague, where the Emperor was then established, and solicited the transfer to him of the Duchy of Mecklenburg, as a reward for his services. Incidentally he presented an account for three millions of florins for war expenses. It was an easy way for the Emperor to settle the account, and on February 1, 1628, letters patent were granted, declaring that the Dukes of Mecklenburg had forfeited their domains because they had made an alliance with the King of Denmark, and transferring the duchy to Wallenstein to hold as pledge for the payment of certain war expenses. The months that Wallenstein remained at Prague during this visit, he was laying plans for the conquest of Denmark and also for an alliance with Sweden to conquer Norway. He ordered all seaport towns invested, fortresses built along the coasts of Mecklenburg and Pomerania and collected vessels which he intended to use in his invasion of Denmark. Arnheim, second in command to Wallenstein, in pursuance of these orders, attempted to occupy Stralsund, strongly located on the Baltic. The citizens refused to comply with these demands, claiming the privileges of a Hanseatic free town.

Arnheim besieged the town, and on May 16, 1628, attempted to carry it by assault, but was repulsed. Failing to receive aid from the Duke of Pomerania, the people of Stralsund placed themselves under the protection of the King of Sweden, Gustavus Adolphus, who, fully aware of the importance of the place, sent 600 men under David Leslie and later 1,000 more under Count Brahe to aid in its defense. Wallenstein joined his army before Stralsund, June 27th. He led a general assault in which heavy losses were inflicted on both sides, and while his troops even penetrated to the inner lines, they were unable to withstand the desperate resistance offered. The bombardment of the town continued, and deputies came to Wallenstein to make terms. An armistice of a few days was agreed upon, while terms could be discussed. Before this was accomplished, a Danish fleet appeared off the harbor and the besieged refused to carry the negotiations further, asserting that they would not submit. The attack was renewed, but continued rains filled the trenches with water, the camp became inundated, and sickness spread rapidly among the troops, and a force of Danes landed at Jasmund. Wallenstein was therefore compelled to abandon the siege, and marched with his troops to oppose the Danes at Jasmund. They had, however, reëmbarked, and later landed at Wolgast, where they were surprised by Wallenstein and signally defeated. He next proceeded to Holstein, where he captured Krempe, but failed to reduce Gluckstadt, which continually received reinforcements from the ships of the Danes. Realizing the impossibility of accomplishing his purpose without the aid of a fleet, Wallenstein was ready to make peace with the Danes. Consequently a treaty was entered into at Lübeck in January, 1629, by which Denmark recovered all her former possessions, but pledging herself not to further interfere in the affairs of the Empire. All of Germany now hoped the peace they had longed for would come. The country had suffered to a great extent from the ravages of the imperial armies, and protests and petitions poured in upon the Emperor from every side. Instead of peace, however, Ferdinand signed the "Edict of Restitution," calling upon all Protestants to restore to the Catholic Church all church property that had been sequestered since the pacification of 1555. The edict fell like the knell of doom upon Protestant Germany. It meant that numberless convents and clerical domains which had been confiscated must now be returned. Commissioners were appointed to see that the mandate was carried into effect. Summary proceedings were instituted, the estates of all persons who had served with any of the armies arrayed against Ferdinand, were confiscated. Raumer writes that the largest sum paid to any of those who were deprived of their estates was twenty florins. It became the part of Wallenstein to carry the edict into effect in all sections occupied by his troops, and history records that he proceeded with the work with merciless rigor. In 1630 a great Diet was convoked to meet at Ratisbon to settle all remaining differences. At this Diet complaints of every description and nature were made to the Emperor of the cruelty and savage barbarity practiced by the imperial troops in their campaigns. These reports reflected severely upon Wallenstein, and plainly demonstrated that his enemies were legion. At different times it was reported that his life had been attempted, but there is no authentic record of any effort in this direction being made prior to the assassination which ended his life. The greatest among his enemies were members of the nobility, both Catholic and Protestant, and at the head of this hostile party was Maximilian of Bavaria, second Prince of the Empire. The Diet

made a report and Ferdinand was advised from all sides
to dismiss Wallenstein. The Emperor yielded finally and
dispatched two Counts to communicate the order of dismissal to Wallenstein, who was then encamped at Mem-
mingen with an army of 100,000 men, and who would
have obeyed any order he might choose to give. It was
expected that he would refuse to be dismissed. On the
contrary, he failed even to utter a protest, but showed by
an astrological calculation that the Emperor was not to
blame, inasmuch as the spirit of Maximilian predominated
over the spirit of Ferdinand. Not long before his dismissal King Gustavus Adolphus of Sweden landed in Pomerania with less than 20,000 men and for more than a year
continued to defeat the imperial army in every engagement
and quickly made himself master of great sections of
Ferdinand's territory. Meanwhile, his allies, the Saxons,
invaded and occupied Bohemia and every effort to drive
them out proved futile. At the battle of Breitenfeld, Tilly
was badly defeated by the Swedes, and at the battle of the
Lech the imperial army was again beaten and Tilly
received a mortal wound from which he died the following day. Gustavus Adolphus then advanced on Munich,
which dared not resist him, and continued his triumphal
march until he was master from the Baltic to the Rhine.
During all this time Wallenstein was living in splendor
and luxury in his magnificent castle and apparently paying no heed to the victorious progress of the Swedish
army. In his extremity the Emperor, after seeing the
troops of the Empire shattered and defeated, applied to
Wallenstein to resume his former position. At first he
positively refused to comply with the demands of the
Emperor, but on being further pressed he agreed to take
the command for three months, during which time he
undertook to raise an army of 40,000 or 50,000 men. The

Emperor was practically destitute of troops, and lacking in means to procure them. As soon as it was announced that Wallenstein was to take up a campaign against the invaders, soldiers flocked to his standard by the thousands. Those who had served under him before were the first to come forward. They well knew the severity of his discipline and the rigorous penalties inflicted by him, but they also remembered his lavish generosity in rewards. Before the expiration of the three months an army of 40,000 stood ready, fully equipped and officered by experienced soldiers from every nation, ready to follow him against the enemies of the Empire. Wallenstein was given absolute and unrestricted power, not even the Emperor reserving the right to control his movements or dispose of rewards. General Arnheim at this time occupied Bohemia with an army of Saxons, but had permitted the organization of this army without making a move to stop it. On May 4th Wallenstein suddenly stood with his army before Prague. Arnheim and the Saxons retreated after a small garrison had been left to defend the town. As soon as the guns of the attacking army opened, the Capucian friars, whose convent walls formed part of the town wall, began to break it down. Two breaches were soon made and an assault undertaken. The first attempt failed, but the second was successful and the imperial troops entered the city and plundered it, notwithstanding that it was a part of the domain they had been organized to defend. Wallenstein rewarded every soldier who had been wounded during the attack. The towns of Egra and Leumeritz capitulated without resistance and Bohemia was more quickly recovered than it had been taken by the Saxons. At Egra Wallenstein was joined by Maximilian with Bavarian troops, after humbling his former enemy by having it stipulated that Maximilian was to be under the orders of Wallenstein. The imperial and Bavarian forces numbered 60,000. By rapid marches he reached the Upper Palatinate determined to attack Gustavus at the first opportunity. The Swedish army at this time did not exceed 20,000, and retreated before Wallenstein to Nuremburg, situated in the midst of the country it had conquered.

Before Wallenstein with his army arrived in front of Nuremburg, Gustavus had strongly fortified and entrenched the town, and so well was the work done that Wallenstein considered the position unassailable and determined to conquer the enemy by the aid of famine. He selected a commanding position about five miles to the southwest of Nuremburg on a range of wooded hills, where his camp formed an irregular parallelogram about four miles in length and one to two in breadth. The camp was strengthened with redoubts at the most important points and all approaches were guarded and fortified. From this secure post, detachments of Croats and light troops were sent to cut off supplies for the Swedish army and harass their foragers. This led to a continual series of skirmishes between detached parties of the two armies. The most important of these was the surprise of Frienstadt. Here the principal magazine of the imperial army was located and a large convoy from Austria and Bavaria assembled there on its way to Wallenstein's camp. The town was attacked by the Swedes in the night and the convoy captured. This caused want in the camp of Wallenstein. In the meantime the King of Sweden had called upon the allied and Swedish troops acting in various parts of the Empire to come to his aid, and on August 16th these troops, having assembled at Kinzingen, entered the camp of Gustavus and added to his forces 36,000 men. Wallenstein made no effort to prevent the entry of these reinforcements into Nuremburg. He rather regarded their arrival as aiding his plan of starving the Swedes into submission, and indeed it was not long before hunger became common and was soon supplemented by disease and crime. August 22d the Swedes cannonaded the camp of Wallenstein all day, but without result. Two days later Gustavus with his whole army assailed his position. After repeated efforts, renewed time and again, with all the bravery for which these troops of Gustavus were noted, the attempt was finally abandoned. Wallenstein's troops, though but newly organized, made the most valiant resistance, and the wisdom of the manner in which he had fortified his camp was amply demonstrated by the failure of the enemy to make any considerable impression at any point along the imperial lines. Wallenstein, as in all of his previous battles, displayed the most undaunted courage by appearing wherever the battle raged most fiercely, and urging and encouraging his troops. At one point he discovered some of his troops deserting their post under the terrific fire being poured upon them. Personally he drove the fugitives back to their places, and while thus engaged his horse was shot from under him. After the Swedes had withdrawn, and it was assured that the repulse had been a success, Wallenstein, as at the capture of Prague, distributed money to every wounded soldier and lavishly rewarded the troops having displayed the greatest bravery. In a letter to the Emperor, giving an account of the engagement, he acknowledges having lost 400 men and a number of officers, and estimates the loss to the Swedes at 2,000. For a time the two armies remained opposite each other, neither making a move to attack the other. Gustavus, unable to lure Wallenstein from his strong position, determined to break up his camp. He placed 5,000 men in Nuremburg as a garrison and on September 8th,

with flags flying and drums beating, marched slowly in
review before the imperial entrenchments and marched
away to Neustadt. In spite of this taunting defiance and
challenge on the part of the Swedish King, Wallenstein
firmly refused to hazard a battle without, as he explains
in a letter, the presence of Pappenheim and his cavalry,
at this time absent from the camp. Schiller calls this same
Pappenheim, "the Telamon of the army and the most
formidable warrior of the House of Austria and of the
church," so that Wallenstein's decision was evidently
based on wise principles. From Neustadt, the King of
Sweden dispatched Bernhard, Duke of Weimar, to Wurts-
burg for the defense of the Maine, and with the rest of
his army proceeded into Bavaria to complete the conquest
of that country. Five days later Wallenstein broke up his
camp, and, after separating from Maximilian, who with
his troops hastened to the defense of his own country,
directed his march on Bamburg with the object of separating the Saxons from the Swedes. After vainly attempting to reduce the castle of Cobourg, defended by a Swedish
garrison, Wallenstein rapidly advanced into the very heart
of Saxony and captured Leipsic on October 23d. Schiller
and other historians, who have presented Wallenstein
from but one- view, assert that he here gave orders that
the country be plundered and laid waste. This is conclu-
sively disproved by the letters written at this time by Wallenstein to Holk and Gallas, two of his generals, and published by Dr. Förster along with many other letters, still
preserved in the archives of the War Department. In one
of these letters, Wallenstein says: "Let nothing be
destroyed or taken from the peasantry, for we must live
during the winter on the supplies we can find here." Also,
"The Croats must not, under pain of death, presume to
take a single thing from the people." No directions to

refrain from acts of violence could be more positive. Wallenstein had at this time ordered Pappenheim, who with his corps was on the Lower Rhine, to join him at Leipsic. In the meantime the King of Sweden had almost reduced Ingolstadt, brilliant prospects were opening for him toward the south, and the road to Vienna was almost clear, when the news of Wallenstein's successes in Saxony reached him, and he hastened to the aid of his allies there. He left a sufficient force to protect the territory conquered in Bavaria, and by forced marches reached Erfurth. There he was joined by the Duke of Weimar, and the army rapidly advanced upon Naumburg and seized it before Wallenstein had time to reinforce the garrison which he had placed there. At this time Wallenstein was on his way to Torgau, where he hoped to destroy the Saxon army. Learning, however, of the arrival of the Swedes at Naumburg, he determined to countermarch and fall with his whole army upon the King's forces. He advanced to Weisenfels and found, on reconnoitering, that the Swedes had as strongly entrenched themselves at Naumburg, as they previously had at Nurenberg. To attack such a position would be unsuccessful and perhaps fatal, and he called a consultation of his generals to form a plan of procedure. Although Wallenstein's army was composed of 40,000 men, and the Swedes had but 22,000, an attack was regarded as out of the question. The generals came to the conclusion also that Gustavus had decided to make a long stay at Naumburg, and the plan of the council therefore was that Pappenheim should hasten with a detachment of Croats to the relief of Cologne while the rest of the imperial army went into winter quarters. Wallenstein himself was not present at these deliberations but when they were laid before him agreed to the plans. Pappenheim was therefore dispatched toward Cologne and in order that he might while on his way dislodge a Swedish garrison at Halle, his original force was increased by six regiments of infantry and six of cavalry. To cover the expedition, Wallenstein, after placing most of his troops in cantonments, took post at Lützen. Before daybreak on the morning of November 5th, the Swedes suddenly broke camp and marched in the direction of Pagau, evidently with the intention of joining the Saxons at Dresden. At ten o'clock in the forenoon, Gustavus discovered through some intercepted letters and from prisoners, what had transpired in the imperial army. With Pappenheim at a distance, the army scattered in cantonments, and Wallenstein surrounded with but 12,000 troops, the opportunity was not to be lost and instantly the necessary orders were given which started the Swedish army at a rapid rate towards the famous field of Lützen. Wallenstein's position was precarious and a less resolute spirit would doubtless have faltered. But he determined, being apprised of the advance of the Swedes, to make a stand with the troops at hand until he could gather his scattered army. Orders were sent to all corps to march with speed to Lützen and couriers were dispatched to bring Pappenheim back. That fortune favors the brave proved true upon this occasion. The Swedes in their march toward Lützen were hampered by miry roads and delayed in crossing the Ripach, a small stream with high clayey banks. Detachments of Croats and cuirassiers had been hastily sent forward to dispute the passage of the stream and while the Swedes routed them with heavy loss, the fighting meant delay and every hour was of importance and the time thus gained was made good use of. The plain of Lützen is a great level stretch without even a bush. But the roads were separated from the fields by ditches, and these ditches were turned to good advantage. They were deepened and as the various corps arrived during the night, they were posted behind the road leading from Weisenfels to Leipsic with the village of Lützen on the right, and the left without cover of any kind. Two hundred yards behind the road the main body of the army was formed. The garden walls around Lützen were loopholed and lined with troops armed with muskets. The number of troops gathered here during the night is uncertain, but from the plan drawn by Wallenstein the number is estimated by Förster and others at 26,000 or 28,000. Pappenheim and his troops had joined Wallenstein before daybreak, and when morning dawned the troops were in battle array and waiting the arrival of the enemy. The morning of September saw the plain of Lützen deeply enveloped in a mist so dense that the Swedish army advanced to within a thousand yards of the occupied road before either army could perceive the other. Here a halt was made and while waiting for the fog to clear, the King employed his time by riding along his lines and addressing words of encouragement to his troops. It was half past eleven o'clock before the sun broke through the mist. Lützen was seen to be in flames and firing here and there told that the contending armies were at some points already beginning the battle. Gustavus now ordered the advance, and although the forward rush is met by a terrific fire from the trenches, both of musketry and artillery, the charge sweeps forward over the trenches and in an instant the two armies come together with a crash. Wallenstein's right and center give way before the terrific onslaught, but the left succeeds in checking the division under the Duke of Weimar, from behind the loopholed garden walls. While Gustavus hastened with aid in this direction, Wallenstein rallied his shattered corps and fiercely fell upon the Swedish center. They were forced back across the road and Wallenstein recaptured his lost battery. But again the progress of the imperialists was arrested, and they were swept back before the resistless mass of Swedes. Gustavus at this period looked upon the battle as already won and rode forward with a few attendants to determine how best to follow up his advantage. Here the King received a musket shot in the arm, and growing faint, was being led out of the battle when another shot struck him in the back. He fell from his horse, and as the enemy pushed forward his attendants fled with the exception of Lubeling, a page, who attempted to help the King to remount. A party of imperialists surrounded them, and as the Swedes were now advancing, the imperialists dispatched Gustavus and mortally wounded the faithful page. The battle continued unabated. Backward and forward across the road again, the imperialist batteries were alternately employed in dealing death to which army held possession. Pappenheim fell at the head of his cavalry, the imperialists forces became more and more scattered and thinned and Wallenstein was at last forced to withdraw from the disputed field. When darkness came he retreated to Leipsic with the remnant of his troops. What the losses were is nowhere definitely recorded, but 9,000 are said to have been slain in both armies, and three times that number wounded. Wallenstein had no alternative but to retreat, and led his shattered troops into Bohemia, and placed them in winter quarters, while the Swedes proceeded to Weissenfels and accepted the Duke of Weimar as their leader. Despite the fact that the imperialist army had been almost annihilated and had been compelled to seek safety in flight, the battle was regarded by Ferdinand as a victory owing to the death of the King of Sweden and a *Te Deum* was sung in all Catholic countries. Having settled his army in winter quarters, Wallenstein set about rewarding the deserving and punishing those who had failed to do their duty. He had twelve of his officers beheaded at Prague on February 4, 1633. These punishments took place three months after the battle of Lützen and there were those who asserted that Wallenstein here attempted to wash out the disgrace of his defeat with the blood of innocent men, though Förster and Mitchell—the latter, himself an army officer and a follower of Förster in the defense of Wallenstein—maintain that the punishments were justly deserved. During the winter months "the creator of mighty armies" recruited and reorganized another powerful army so that on May 5, 1633, he left Prague with 40,000 men to begin what proved to be his last campaign. He proceeded to Silesia, which had been conquered by the Saxons during the Lützen campaign. Among the many other charges against him is one that he here attempted to make peace with the Saxons in order to advance a design which he was reported to have on the throne of Bohemia. He certainly displayed at this period a suspicious inactivity and while it is certain that he entered into negotiations looking toward peace not only with the Saxons but also with Brandenburg, Sweden, and France, his true object is not made clear. France having heard the report that Wallenstein was intriguing against the House of Austria, made overtures to place him upon the throne of Bohemia and pay him a subsidy, providing he would turn against Ferdinand. The well-known jealousy which existed against Wallenstein at Vienna tended to confirm those with whom he was negotiating in the belief that he was sincere, although it had already been asserted that the negotiations amounted to nothing more than a ruse. Whatever the true object may have been, the summer and much of the fall passed in armistices and Wallenstein seems to have accomplished nothing by it. It was not until October that operations of a hostile nature were made. He then surrounded a Swedish column of 5,000 men under Count Thurn at Sreinau on the Oder, and compelled them to capitulate. This victory was rapidly followed up by the reduction of Glogow, Leignitz, Goldberg, and Crossen. Having cleared Silesia of the enemy, Wallenstein, at the solicitation of Maximilian, started for Bavaria in order to save it from the Duke of Weimar, who on October 24th had reduced the last of its strongholds by capturing Ratisbon. During this march he had an interview at the town of Pilsen with Count Trautmansdorff, the imperial minister, who happened to be in the vicinity. During this interview, according to the report made by the Count to Ferdinand, Wallenstein was considerably excited, owing to information received in letters from Vienna that high functionaries of state there spoke of him in the most injurious terms, and attributed to him the most sinister purposes. He also complained that orders had come to some of his generals from Vienna without his knowledge, and finally spoke strongly in favor of concluding peace. In the Emperor's reply to this report, he denies having any knowledge of evil discourses against Wallenstein and desires the names of the authors in order to call them to account. This was but two months before the tragedy at Eger. In December Wallenstein learned that the Emperor had determined to deprive him of his command. He determined to resign before this intention was put into execution and called his officers together and informed them of his purpose. The officers pressed him to reconsider and to remain at their head. In return, he demanded from them a promise that they would pledge themselves to adhere to him. As a consequence, soon afterward a banquet was given by Count Illo at which forty-two officers signed a paper pledging themselves to "adhere to Wallenstein to the last drop of blood, so long as he should continue to command the army, in the service, and for the good of the Emperor." The following day he called them together and informed them that nothing was intended against the Emperor or the Catholic religion by the compact which they had formed. In the meantime his enemies were rapidly spinning the web of treachery against him. The Emperor was continually receiving reports of alleged intrigues and on January 24th an order was issued by Ferdinand depriving him of his command. The same document granted amnesty to those who had signed the compact at Pilsen and concluded by declaring Wallenstein an outlaw and ordering him to be taken dead or alive. The command of the army was divided between Gallas and Arlinger, but the whole matter was kept secret for the time being. On February 13th Gallas made the order known to a number of the officers under him and furnished at the same time a list of "heretics" among the officers, whose property was to be confiscated. On that very day the Emperor was still dissembling with Wallenstein, for he wrote him a letter commending Bohemia to his care and protection. It is clear that murder was intended and only the opportunity wanting. On February 20th Wallenstein once more called his officers together and this time signed with them a pledge of entire devotion to the Emperor and readiness to shed every drop of blood in his service. Two days later, having become convinced of the Emperor's intentions, Wallenstein, accompanied by a few trusty officers—Illo, Terzky, Kinsky, Butler, and Neumann—and seven companies of infantry and 200 dragoons fled from Pilsen. He was suffering from the gout and was carried in a sedan chair between two horses.   On the evening of the day following they arrived at Eger, the last Bohemian fortress on the road leading onto the Palatinate.   Colonel Gordon was in charge of the post. Butler showed to Gordon and Major Leslie the Emperor's proclamation, of which, up to that time, they knew nothing.   It is evident that Butler had direct instructions to murder and authority to reward those who should aid him in the crime.   In no other way can the prompt readiness of those whom he called upon to assist him be accounted for.   He took first Gordon and Leslie into the conspiracy, and after they had sworn to stand by him, seven other officers were brought into the ring.   They were Geraldine, Devereux, Brown, Macdonald, Birch, Pestaluzi, and Lerda.   The two last named were Spaniards; Gordon, Leslie, and Butler were Scotch, and the others were Irish.   It was decided first to kill the four trusty friends of Wallenstein, Illo, Terzky, Kinsky, and Neumann, and to this end they were invited to sup with Gordon in the citadel on the following evening.   At the conclusion of the meal, upon a given signal, the conspirators fell upon the unsuspecting victims and brutally murdered them.   Wallenstein had taken up quarters at the house of the Mayor in the town.   At midnight (February 25, 1634) Devereux, who had been chosen to commit the murder, proceeded with half a dozen troopers to his chief's quarters.   Wallenstein was in the act of retiring when the assassins burst into his apartment.   "Thou must die," exclaimed Devereux and immediately plunged his blade into his breast.   "Thus fell," says Gualdo, "one of the greatest commanders, most generous princes and most enlightened ministers of his own or of any preceding time."   Wallenstein's body was rolled in a carpet and carried to the citadel and placed with the other victims. By the Emperor's orders the body was afterward given over to friends, who deposited the remains in the vault of a Carthusian convent which Wallenstein had himself built near Gitchen. When the Swedes penetrated to that section in 1639 General Banner had the coffin opened and removed the skull and right arm, which he sent to Stockholm. The slayer of Wallenstein was rewarded with a gold chain and several confiscated domains. The Emperor shook hands with Butler and caused the Archbishop of Vienna to place a golden chain about his neck. He was also made a Count and presented with the estate of Terzky in Bohemia. All the others were also handsomely rewarded, even to the common soldiers who had aided in the assassination. Wallenstein, it seems, remained a firm believer in astrology to the very last, for it is related that only a few minutes before he was slain, he had consulted an Italian astrologer named Seni, who declared that the stars still boded impending danger.

OLIVER CROMWELL
1599-1658

DEFENDER OF CIVIL FREEDOM

Many able and far-sighted historians, such as Lingard,
Bossuet, Hume, and Voltaire, in painting the portrait of
Oliver Cromwell, saw in him nothing of a laudable character, though they were forced to recognize his magnificent military genius.   By these and others Cromwell has
been stamped as an ambitious, crafty usurper, a ferocious
tyrant, a hypocritical and cunning traitor.   Robert
Southey charges Cromwell with a consciousness of guilt
and wrongdoing throughout the whole struggle which
finally attained for him sovereign power, and holds him
little less guilty than Macbeth.   Guizot accuses him of
selfishness and holds that his sole object was self-aggran-
disement and that his life effort was directed toward
founding a dynasty and clutching the sovereignty.   "Sup-
pose," said Eliot Warburton, "all the letters of the crafty
Cromwell had been discovered, what a revelation we
should then have had."   Finally, as a result of the patience
and effort of Thomas Carlyle the correspondence of Cromwell was discovered, and gleaned from public and private
archives, and there was a revelation, but not such a revelation as Warburton expected.   Carlyle presents in the
domestic, political, and military life of Cromwell, based
on these letters, the true Cromwell, a man of singular
intellect, of consistent integrity, of honest purpose, fear-
less, without personal ambition, the champion of the Puri-
tanical faith, the defender of civil freedom, displaying

throughout his career the zeal of a fanatic for what he honestly believed to be the right, a great and daring political leader and a soldier, who, though he knew nothing of the military art or the conduct of war until a man of mature years, attained an eminence as a warrior, rivaled by but few names in all history. He was sincere in his religion, possessed of an indomitable will, personal bravery, and singleness of resolve. He was stern and terrible to his enemies. His whole life was dominated by religious conviction, with which he allowed neither mercy nor reason to interfere. Every important act in the life of this human enigma must be charged to this religious fanaticism, regarding himself as he did an instrument in the hands of the Lord to carry out the Divine will, whether by fire and sword or in the councils of the nation. Lamartine shows how great fanatics generally spring from sad and sterile countries. Mohammed sprang from the scorching valleys of Arabia, Luther from the frozen mountains of Lower Germany, Calvin from the somber plains of Picardy, Cromwell from the dismal fens and stagnant marshes of the Ouse.

Cromwell came from an ancient and noble English family. His great uncle was Thomas Cromwell, created Earl of Essex by Henry VIII and after that monarch had established Protestantism in England, was one of the most zealous despoilers of Romish churches and persecutors of Catholic adherents. When this Cromwell became the minister of Henry VIII, he delegated to Richard, one of his nephews, the task of wreaking vengeance upon Catholics and of demolishing their convents and monasteries. Richard was the great-grandfather of Oliver, the Protector. His grandfather, Henry, was known as "The Golden Knight," owing to his great riches, and lived in Lincolnshire on the domain of Hinchinbrook. His

manor house had formerly been a convent from which
the nuns had been expelled.   Robert, the youngest son of
Henry, married Elizabeth Steward (or Stuart), connected with the royal line of Scotland.   In some manner
the wealth of the family had become reduced.   Robert
settled upon a small estate in Huntingdonshire, called Ely,
where Oliver was born.   Amidst the lonely fens where
the quiet, winding Ouse pursued its way, his boyhood
was spent.   His first impressions of the world were,
therefore, influenced by the mean nature of the country,
with its stunted poplars and willows, its marshy fields,
unbroken horizon and poor, scattered cottages.   The
character of this scene was well calculated to sadden the
disposition of the child.   Oliver Cromwell was born
April 25, 1599, and it is related that when he was four
years of age King James I, then on his way to take possession of the English crown, paid a visit to the dwelling
of the Cromwells, owing to his relationship with Elizabeth Steward.   Thus it was possible for Cromwell to
remember in after years having seen at his father's table
the father of the monarch he dethroned and beheaded.
Oliver attended first the Huntingdon grammar school
and later the University of Cambridge, not far distant
from his home.   Upon the death of his father in 1617
he left college to aid in the support of his mother and
became a second parent to his sisters.   At the age of 21
he married Elizabeth Bourchier, the young and beautiful
daughter of Sir James Bourchier, of Felsted, in Essex.
For ten years subsequent to his marriage he pursued the
ordinary life of a country gentleman upon the estate of
his father.   Like others at this period he was devoutly
attached to the comparatively new cause of Puritanic
Protestantism.   He trembled for his eternal salvation and
was impressed with the idea of an early death.   Religious
melancholy settled upon him and made him its victim.

One of his contemporaries, Warwick, relates that on a particular occasion, while laboring under the weight of this depression, he sent frequently during the night for his physician, from the neighboring village, in order to relieve himself of the terrors which hung over him. He studied the Bible assiduously, sought solitude and meditated upon the sacred words until his piety developed into fanaticism. In the meantime, he was an industrious and frugal farmer, cultivated his fields and attended his flocks. He disposed of a part of his estate and with the proceeds purchased one with more pasture land near the town of St. Ives, a few miles from Huntingdon. His family already consisted of two sons and four daughters. He was at this time thirty-six years of age and his correspondence showed affection for his family, interest in domestic details and more than all else solicitude for the welfare of his soul. He aided by voluntary contributions the work of the Puritan missionaries and in every way encouraged them. His exemplary life and intelligent attention to the interests of the county in which he lived gave him popularity and respect among the people. He gave no evidences of ambition and when the electors of Huntingdon and St. Ives offered him their suffrage, he accepted only from a conscientious feeling that in this manner he could promote the interests of the faith which had laid such a strong hold upon him. It was on March 17, 1627, that he was elected a member of Parliament from his county. Here his public career commences, soon to develop with those political storms which caused a nation to take up arms and consigned a King to the scaffold.

To appreciate the conduct of Cromwell in this position in which destiny had placed him, a passing glimpse at the recently prior events of England and its state at the time when Cromwell so inauspiciously entered upon the scene will be necessary. In the time of Cromwell's great-grandfather, King Henry VIII, in a fit of anger against the Church of Rome, changed the religion of his Kingdom. The Roman Catholic faith became a crime and its adherents were the legitimate prey of the King's favorites. A medium between the Catholic Church and the Church of Luther was selected and the Church of England came into being. The change was followed by the right of liberty of conscience and different sects sprung up from this condition of religious anarchy. The people refused to submit to the Church organized by the King, with debauchery and blood for its basis, without a murmur, and the organization of new sects eased the conscience of the Nation. One of the most widely extended of the new sects was Puritanism, and its devotees struggled against the Anglican Church and also against what remained of the proscribed Church of Rome. Through three succeeding reigns religious dissensions formed the chief cause for disturbance. Mary, the Catholic daughter of Henry VIII, favored the return of her subjects to their original faith, Elizabeth, the Protestant daughter of the same king by another wife, persecuted the Catholics, sacrificed Mary Stuart and compelled obedience to the Reformed Church. James the First, son of Mary Stuart, who had received his education in the Protestant faith from Scotch Puritans, was an indulgent monarch, who desired to tolerate both faiths and tried to make the rival sects live in peace together. Then came Charles I, who succeeded to the throne in his twenty-sixth year. He retained in his service the prime minister of his father, the Duke of Buckingham, a man who sought only to satisfy his own aims. The diffidence of Charles gave Buckingham rein to agitate England and embroil the State according to the dictates of his own interest. Thus

OLIVER CROMWELL

Painting by Sir Peter Lely, Ufizzi Gallery, Florence

he caused the King to lessen or increase that relationship between the Crown and Parliament which right or tradition attributed to these two powers and thus a spirit of resistance and encroachment on the part of Parliament was created.   Buckingham was at last assassinated and the young King attempted to struggle on alone.   In a few years the struggles between the Crown and Parliament, augmented by religious more than political factions, reached a crisis.   Such was the condition of affairs when Cromwell became a member of Parliament.   The only traces of his presence in Parliament for ten years are a few brief addresses made by him at long intervals in defense or in favor of the Puritanic missionaries or against the aspirations of the Anglican Church and of the Roman Catholics.   Cromwell sat in three of Charles' Parliaments from Huntingdon, but in the fourth, which met in April, 1640, he was returned from Cambridge. In three weeks it was dissolved and another was called November 3 in which he also sat for Cambridge.   Sir Philip Warwick furnishes an interesting picture of Cromwell at this time.   "It was in November, 1640," he writes, "that I, who was also a member, and vain enough to think myself a model of elegance and nobility, for we young courtiers pride ourselves on our attire, beheld on entering the House a person speaking.   I knew him not; he was dressed in the most ordinary manner, in a plain cloth suit which appeared to have been cut by some village tailor.   His linen, too, was coarse and soiled.   His hat was without a hatband; his stature was of a good size; his sword stuck close to his side, his countenance swollen and reddish; his voice sharp and untunable; and his eloquence full of fervor, for the subject matter would not bear much of reason, it being in behalf of a libeler in the hands of the executioner.   I must avow that the attention bestowed by the Assembly on the discourse of this gentleman has much diminished my respect for the House of Commons." It seems that the man in whose favor Cromwell was pleading was guilty of having dispersed libels against the Queen for dancing "and such like innocent and courtly sports." In the meantime, Cromwell had attracted attention in another manner. King Charles had attempted to replenish his exchequer by laying claim to 95,000 acres of drained land in Huntingdon, a part of the work which was then in progress, and known as Bedford level. Cromwell led the opposition against the claims of the King and for this was long known as "Lord of the Fens." The unpopularity of King Charles was rapidly growing. He was charged with illegal seizure of ship-money, and taxes were weighing heavily upon the people. The so-called "Long Parliament" greatly hastened the inevitable rupture between the King and his discontented subjects. January 19, 1641, a bill was proposed which prescribed the calling a Parliament every three years at most. If the King did not convoke one, twelve peers, assembled at Westminster, might do so without his coöperation; in default of this, the sheriff and municipal officers were to proceed with the elections. The King protested against delegating the royal prerogative to sheriffs and municipal officers and this made it all the more certain that the bill would pass. The crisis now approached rapidly. The popular party in Parliament drew the lines closer and closer around the Royal power and eventually came the "Grand Remonstrance" which carried in the House after a stormy debate, by a majority, according to Hood, of but nine, and which was concurred in by the upper House. The "remonstrance" was a catalogue of the sins and shortcomings of the King. In royalist eyes such a document had the appearance not only of disloyalty but of treachery. In this light the bishops looked upon it and made a solemn "Protestation" to the upper House. It only served to precipitate matters and ten of the bishops were sent to the Tower for their presumption. The King entered a declaration against the "remonstrance" also, and went to the House with some soldiers to demand the arrest on a charge of treason of some of the most violent agitators—Hampden, Pym, Vane, and others. The House defied him and he was compelled to retire in humiliation. The members whom he had intended to arrest had fled temporarily, but quickly returned in triumph. Already, in anticipation of armed resistance to the King, companies and regiments were being formed and armed throughout the Kingdom. The King heard the shouts of the populace, "Long live the Parliament," and from his windows in Whitehall could see the people of London arming and forming themselves into military organizations. Thus menaced and trembling for the safety of his Queen and children, the King, on January 12, 1642, left Whitehall and saw it not again until he found himself there a prisoner, and finally left it for the scaffold. King Charles retired to Hampton Court, a solitary, but imposing and strongly fortified country palace some distance from London. If anything was needed to further inflame the people and embolden the Parliament it was this retreat. The Parliament took possession of fortresses and conferred military authority on the ground of protecting the people, and when the King in a proclamation, pronounced against this proceeding, the proclamation was summarily declared void in law. The King, forseeing what was about to transpire, sent Queen Henrietta to the Continent and with the few retainers who had accompanied him to Hampton court, proceeded to the loyal city of York, taking his children with him. Here the royal army was rallied and the Parliament, representing this act as one of public danger, authorized the raising of an army to oppose that of the King, which consisted of the nobility, to a great extent. The King established his first camp at Nottingham in August, 1642, and began preparations for putting down, what he termed the insurrection.

Meantime, as already stated, the Parliament was also preparing. The Earl of Essex, an experienced, but as developed later, a temporising general, was placed at the head of the Parliamentary forces, which were growing rapidly. These forces had others, also, who made some pretensions to being leaders; least of all among them, at that time, perhaps, was Cromwell, who at the outset was made a captain of horse, as he himself says in one of his letters, "and I did labor to discharge my trust." Thus in the fall of 1642, Oliver Cromwell, a man forty-three years of age, knowing little or nothing about military science or the conduct of war, buckled on his armor and during four succeeding years amazed the world as the greatest figure of this terrible and dramatic civil contest. From among his friends and neighbors in and around Huntingdon, he organized a regiment of men, inspired, like himself, with religious enthusiasm, the terrible and invincible "Ironsides." Other leaders of the Parliamentary army failed, were beaten, slain. Cromwell alone among them all, never sustained a defeat. On many a tottering field his immortal troop turned the tide and snatched victory out of defeat. Cromwell struck the first as well as the final blows in that fearful struggle. As soon as he had been commissioned Captain he began his victorious career. He seized the magazine at Cambridge, spent his own money in supplying arms and confiscated the Royal University plate. He stopped those who were about to throw their fortunes with the King and disarmed Crown partisans in his vicinity. Before spring came, he had become Colonel of the famous "Ironsides" which he had raised and drilled himself. "I raised such men as had the fear of God before them," he says in a letter, "and made some conscience of what they did, and from that day forward, I must say to you, they were never beaten, and wherever they engaged against the enemy, they beat continually." Förster asserts that had Cromwell's history ceased with the creation of this body of troops, "it would have left a sufficient warrant of his greatness to posterity." This intense piety is shown in every act of his career. Inspired as he was with the conviction that he was doing the service of the Lord as well as of Parliament, he marched fearlessly from victory to victory. After the capture of Worcester and Bristol, he wrote: "This is a fresh favor conferred on us by Heaven. I again repeat, the Lord be praised for this, for it is His work." His dispatches and military notes are filled with this spirit. In narrating the account of the battle of Worcester, he says anyone "must see that there has been no other hand in it but God." After the victory at Preston he writes, "This is a glorious day. God grant that England may prove worthy of, and grateful for His mercies." That this sentiment was not confined to the commander but also to his soldiers, is shown by the following: "While we were digging the mine under the castle Mr. Stapleton preached, and the soldiers showed their compunctions by tears and groans." Carlyle, who gathered the correspondence of Cromwell, gives scores of similar examples. Such was the man and such were the soldiers under him, who began, in the spring of 1843, a series of remarkable achievements scarcely equaled in all the annals of warfare. Hood furnishes a sarcastic allusion to Cromwell and his men, published in a newspaper of the period, by the then celebrated Marchmont Needham, as follows: "As for Noll Cromwell, he is gone forth in the might of his spirit, with all the train of his disciples; everyone of whom is as David, a man of war and a prophet, gifted men all, that resolve to do their work better than the sons of Levi."

The first notable exploit of Cromwell was the capture of the town of Lowestoft, a Royalist stronghold, where he captured a great quantity of valuable war stores. In July, after doing good service in Lincolnshire, he saved the town of Gainsborough from falling into the hands of the Royalist army under the Marquis of Newcastle, who was marching upon it and would have had little difficulty in taking it from the small Parliamentary force under Lord Willoughby.   Cromwell took up a position between the town and the advancing army, and after a desperate charge up the sides of a precipitous hill, fell upon the vanguard of the Royalist army under General Cavandish, and although outnumbered three to one, completely routed the enemy, whose loss included their general.   While Cromwell had been thus successful, the Parliamentary armies, or Roundheads, as they were called, under other leaders, had suffered reverses in almost every section.   In the early autumn the outlook for the Roundheads was extremely dark.   At this time the Earl of Manchester was given command of the Eastern Association, in which Cromwell was Colonel.   In October, Cromwell joined the division of the Parliamentary army commanded by Lord Fairfax, and on the 11th of that month was fought the sanguinary battle of Winceby.   The Royalists were led by Sir John Henderson, and though they made a brave resistance, they could not withstand the terrible charges of the Ironsides and finally broke and fled, while the vic-

OLIVER CROMWELL   199

tors pursued them for miles and indiscriminately slaughtered those who were overtaken.   There is no record of
any further fighting done by Cromwell during the balance
of this year, and in fact it was not until the middle of
the following year that the next great battle of the war
was fought.   This was the battle of Marston Moor.
Whitelocke holds that Cromwell's greatness as a military
leader was first shown in the battle which saved the town
of Gainsborough from falling into the hands of the Royalists, but Hood maintains that his military genius first
shone conspicuously on the field of Marston.   It was one
of the first great critical periods of the struggle.   York
was in the possession of the Royalists, while all around
were scattered the camps of the besieging Puritans under
Fairfax, whose forces had but recently been augmented
by the arrival of the Scotch Covenented army under Les-
ley, a body of 21,000 men.   Cromwell had been raised to
second in command.   York had but a weak garrison
and must soon have fallen, but King Charles had written
to Prince Rupert, "If York be lost, I shall esteem my
crown to be little less," and Rupert, a dashing and daring
leader, responded by hastening from the Lancashire hills
with 20,000 warriors at his back to save York.   On his
approach the Parliamentary army was withdrawn to Marston Moor.   Had Rupert been satisfied with thus liberat-
ing York, the whole history of the war might have
changed, but reckless and fiery, he sought battle and was
confident of success.   He lay with his army outside of
York and not far distant lay the Roundheads—the Scotch
and Cromwell and his praying, psalm-singing Ironsides.
Throughout the beautiful, calm summer day of July 2,
1644, but a few scattering shots had been fired between
the outposts of the two armies, and on each side it was
expected that no considerable conflict would come until

the following day. As the evening advanced, clouds began to gather and soon a storm broke upon the scene. It is related by Hood that some of Rupert's men had captured a prisoner belonging to the opposing army and that the Prince had particularly inquired whether Cromwell was there. The prisoner was released, and returning to his own ranks informed Cromwell what had been said by the Prince, among other things having promised that they should have fighting enough. "And," said Cromwell solemnly, "if it please God, so they shall." In the meantime the firing had gradually increased and forward movements began in both armies. Cromwell, who occupied the left of the Scots and the troops under Fairfax, brought his cavalry to the front and became the target for a body of musketeers sent forward by Prince Rupert. At the same time the Royalists suddenly attacked the center of the Parliamentary army and put the Scots to rout. An incessant cannonading was kept up from the Royalist batteries advantageously planted on a height to the rear. The troops of Fairfax began to flee, and that general himself put spurs to his horse, left the field with all possible haste, and reaching Cawood castle, calmly went to bed. Goring, with the Royalist cavalry, was remorselessly cutting down the fugitive soldiers of Fairfax and two-thirds of the field had already been won by the Royalists. But in the midst of it was Cromwell. He saw how fast the enemy was gaining ground and then turned his cavalry toward the terrible batteries. "Charge in the name of the Most High," was his command, and following their intrepid leader the Ironsides poured through the Royalist ranks, cut down the gunners, captured the guns and turned their fire upon the hosts of Prince Rupert, who at that moment still believed himself victor of the field. Then

as the Royalists rallied to regain this lost portion of the
field, Cromwell charged again, broke and shattered the
cavalry of Goring and mercilessly fell upon the cavalry
under the immediate command of Rupert himself.   The
terrible and irresistible work of the Puritans continued
until the Royalist army was completely scattered and dispersed.   The field was strewn with dead and wounded,
1,500 of Rupert's soldiers were taken prisoners, all of his
artillery, tents, and baggage fell into the hands of the victorious Cromwell, together with the standard of Prince
Rupert and a hundred others.   With what remained of
his former magnificent army Rupert retired into York
and from there proceeded southward, leaving Newcastle,
who had command of the forces which defended York, to
shift for himself.   But Newcastle, who had advised
against engaging the enemy, now deserted his post and
went to the seaside and thence to the Continent, leaving
York to fall easy prey to the Parliamentary forces.   Thus
the battle of Marston Moor irretrievably ruined the hopes
of success for the King so far as the North was concerned.
Just after the battle, on July 5, Cromwell, as soldier and
saint combined, wrote one of those letters which gives
such clear insight into his character.   It was addressed to
his brother-in-law, Colonel Valentine Walton, husband of
Cromwell's youngest sister, Margaret, and bluntly but
feelingly informs them of the death of their son during
the battle and recalls that his own son, Oliver, had been
but recently slain in battle.   In this letter, too, it is seen,
that Cromwell takes upon himself not a particle of the
credit for the great victory, nor does he in the slightest
degree criticise the conduct of his superior officers, who
had failed to do their share in the contest.   The letter
reads in part as follows: "Truly England and the Church
of God hath had a great favor from the Lord, in this

great victory given unto us, such as the like never was since this war began. It had all the evidence of an absolute victory, obtained, by the Lord's blessing, upon the Godless party principally. We never charged but we routed the enemy. The left wing, which I commanded, being our own horse, saving a few Scots in our rear, beat all the Prince's horse. God made them as stubble to our swords. We charged their regiments of foot with our horse and routed all we charged. The particulars I cannot relate now; but I believe, of 20,000 the Prince hath not 4,000 left. Give glory, all the glory, to God. Sir, God hath taken away your eldest son by a cannon shot. It broke his leg. We were necessitated to have it cut off, whereof he died. Sir, you know my own trials in this way; but the Lord supported me in this—that the Lord took him into the happiness we all pant for, and live for."

Nearly half of the Kingdom was now in the hands of the Parliamentary party, but here arose an obstacle which for a time prevented and delayed further successes. Many of the nobility, notwithstanding that they had supported and acquiesced in the earlier measures in opposition to the King, began to realize that they had in the headlong rush placed the common people, under the guidance of the House of Commons, upon a footing so nearly equal with that held by themselves that the mastership of the nobility was threatened. They began to show a disposition to coalesce with the Scotch and looked toward a peace with the King, which should fully secure themselves, while not allowing the sovereign as he had previously held and which he had employed as a means of oppression. In the Parliamentary army this nobility was represented by the Earls of Essex and Manchester. They had shown little vigor in their engagements with the

troops of the King, and the campaigns of Essex were such
absolute failures that he finally disbanded the remnant
of his army and fled to London to make his explanations
to Parliament.   The Earl of Manchester, under whom
Cromwell was now serving, showed an equal spirit of
indolence.   Manchester and Cromwell had been ordered
into the West and on October 27 engaged the King's forces
at Newbury.   The forces of the King were beaten and
Cromwell saw that more aggressive measures would have
completely crushed the Royalist forces.   During the night
the King's forces began a retreat and Cromwell implored
Manchester to allow him to make a forward movement
with his horse and completely overthrow the Royalists.
But Manchester persistently refused to grant permission.
Again and again Cromwell entreated his superior to pursue the retreating army, but to no avail.   In the meantime, the King had removed all his heavy guns and stores
into the Castle of Donnington and quietly fell back on
Oxford.   Twelve days later, having been reinforced by
the command of Prince Rupert, the King returned
assumed the offensive against Manchester, removed his
stores and cannon from the castle and with his army and
entire equipment made his way to Oxford while the Parliamentary army looked on without attempting to molest
the enemy, in spite of Cromwell's repeated appeals to Manchester to attack.   Cromwell is reported to have remarked
as a result of this stand by Manchester, "There will never
be a good time in England till we have done with the
Lords."   Manchester and Cromwell quarreled and
thenceforth opposed each other.   Carlyle says, "Manchester was reported to have said, if they lost this army
pursuing the King, they had no other.   The King might
hang them.   To Cromwell and the thorough-going party
it had become very clear that high Essexes and Manches-

ters, of limited notions and large estates and anxieties, who, besides their fear of being beaten utterly, and forfeited and 'hanged,' were afraid of beating the King too well—would never end this cause in a good way." Thus the Parliamentary cause was failing in the midst of successes. Added to the obstacles thrown in the way of success by the nobility were the Scots, who had marched into England to aid the Parliament for the purpose of elevating Presbyterianism, while the great party which Cromwell represented was rather given to tolerance in regard to religious matter. Cromwell saw, and advocated a change in the tactics. He was confident that he could bring affairs quickly to an issue. He had grown powerful enough to excite jealousy and both the Presbyterians and the nobility leaders in the army feared him. The result was a conspiracy entered into between the Scots Commissioners and the Lords connected with the army. Whitelocke gives the particulars of this plot, having himself been present when the effort was made to arrange it, and while it does not appear that the intention was to kill Cromwell, still the expression used by the spokesman of the occasion, the Lord Chancellor of Scotland, at the meeting which was held at the house of Lord-General Essex, was sufficiently broad to include even murder. He simply stated that "Lieutenant-General Cromwell is no friend of ours," referred to him as an "obstacle," and stated that it had been thought requisite that he "may be removed out of the way." Cromwell was defended at the meeting of the conspirators and nothing further was undertaken in the matter. At the same moment Cromwell went before the House of Commons and impeached Manchester with backwardness in attacking the enemy and neglect of the Parliamentary interests. In his turn Manchester charged Cromwell with having

stated that it would never be well with England until
he, the Earl, was plain Mr. Montague, and that the Scots
had crossed the Tweed with no other purpose than to
establish Presbyterianism, for which reason, he, Cromwell would as soon draw his sword against them as against
the King. This resulted in the passage of the Self-denying Ordinance, which provided that members of Parliament could not serve in the army. This was passed April
3, 1645, the discussions having continued all through the
winter. Sir Thomas Fairfax, not being a member of
Parliament was elected to have supreme command of the
army, but the need of having Cromwell in the field to
look after the interests of Parliament is shown by the fact
that but twenty days later he was specially exempted from
the Self-denying Ordinance and dispatched to join Fairfax at Windsor. Fairfax had been engaged in remodel-
ing the army and had as yet not commenced engagements
against the Royalists. Cromwell, on joining Fairfax,
was not invested with any military title, yet he was immediately given command of a body of horse with orders to
proceed to the road between Oxford and Worcester and
prevent communication between Prince Rupert and the
King. He set out on his mission the same evening, April
23, and the following day at Islip Bridge, encountered
and defeated 2,000 Royalists. Two days later he
engaged the enemy again at Witney and won a victory, and
the next day, April 27, defeated another detachment of
the Royalists at Bampton Bush. He had on the same
day at the battle of Islip Bridge also captured Bletching-
ton. On May 7, the King left Oxford and joined the
forces under Prince Rupert. Together they marched
northward. On May 10 Cromwell was ordered to continue his services with the army for another forty days.
On the last day of May the forces of the King captured

Leicester, and this left the Eastern counties at the mercy of the Royalists. Fairfax and his chief officers now appealed to Parliament to establish Cromwell in his former position in the army, as he was indispensable as commander of the cavalry. On June 13, Cromwell, with 6,000 cavalry, including the illustrious Ironsides, joined the army of Fairfax near Northampton, while the Royalists were drawing together near Leicester. Within a few hours after his arrival, Cromwell with his squadron was already engaged in harassing the rear of the King's army. The following morning, June 14, 1645, the two armies met in deadly conflict on the field of Naseby, a wide open tract between slight elevations, not of sufficient height to be designated as hills, and close to the town of Naseby in Leicestershire. As at Marston field, Cromwell and his Ironsides saved the day and turned defeat into a glorious victory. The Parliamentary army had taken up a strong position. The center was held by Fairfax. On the left Ireton commanded and on the right stood Cromwell with his irresistible cavalry. Prince Rupert made the opening attack at 10 o'clock in the morning of that bright summer day, and fell upon Ireton's division with such fury that he routed it. Fairfax struggled desperately to maintain himself against the onslaught on the center. The charge against Cromwell was directed by Sir Marmaduke Langdale. But here the Royalists recoiled and were so fiercely attacked that they fled in every direction. Cromwell sent three of his squadrons to pursue and keep them from rallying and with his remaining four squadrons went to the aid of Fairfax in the center. Here King Charles commanded in person and tried in vain to rally his men from the charges of the Ironsides. The Royalists could not withstand the shocks, and at last with thousands cut down and the formation completely shat-

tered, they fled, leaving in the possession of the victors
all the artillery, 8,000 stand of arms, and of prisoners,
5,000 foot and 3,000 cavalry.   The King's cabinet of letters and the entire baggage of the camp were also taken.
From this time on Cromwell conducted a long series of
attacks on the towns held by the Royalist forces.   With
remarkable rapidity he rushed from one victory to another.
Everywhere he proved invincible.   One town after
another fell before him.   Leicester was the first, then
Bridgewater, Shaftesbury, Bristol, and Devizes.   Berke-
ley followed, and then he suddenly advanced upon Winchester, which capitulated.   Basing Castle was regarded
as impregnable, but he beat it to pieces.   This was in the
early part of October.   During the succeeding few months
he reduced Salisbury, fought Lord Wentworth at Exeter
and captured 500 prisoners, and then poured along Cornwall, driving before him and scattering the last remnants
of the Royalist forces.   April 22, 1646, he returned to
London and was greeted with extraordinary honors by
Parliament.   Cromwell now had two years of repose from
fighting, but during this time he was active with the affairs
of Parliament.   Negotiations were carried on with the
King, who was held a prisoner at Hampton Court.   These
negotiations were not completely broken off until January,
1648.   The King had during the previous November
made his escape from Hampton Court and managed to
reach the Isle of Wight, where he took refuge in a castle
commanded by an officer whom he believed friendly to
him.   The King believed that he could here negotiate for
his restoration to better advantage.   But he found himself as much a prisoner as before and the negotiations
which he continued to carry on were of little account,
owing to the fact that prior to his escape from Hampton
Court a message which he had written to his wife, had

been intercepted by Cromwell, and had practically sealed the doom of the unhappy King. In this message he stated that while each faction was eager to have him join them, he thought he ought to conclude with the Scotch. His trial was decided upon, and he was conducted from the Isle of Wight to London and lodged in Whitehall. A High Court of Justice had been convened and the King was placed on trial for his life. He refused to defend himself and was found guilty and executed three days later. Cromwell has been condemned for surrendering the King to the scaffold. Lamartine shows that Cromwell's correspondence at this time reveals that he only desired to protect the Nation from monarchial enterprises until religious liberty was too solidly founded to ever again be interfered with by the Romish or Anglican Church.

In March of the year 1648, the Duke of Hamilton had organized a Royalist army in Scotland, and this intelligence stirred the remnants of the cause in England into life, so that uprisings took place in various parts of the Kingdom. One of the most serious revolts took place in Wales, and while Cromwell himself hastened there, Lambert was sent to check the progress of Hamilton. Cromwell suppressed the revolt in Wales in a little over two months and then with his army joined Lambert in Yorkshire. Sir Langdale with 4,000 Yorkshiremen had joined Hamilton's army of 17,000 Scots, and it was not until August 17 that Cromwell came up with the enemy at Preston. He had but 8,000 men, but attacked without hesitation, routed the enemy and for three days pursued the fleeing army, killing 2,000 and taking 10,000 prisoners. He then continued his march across the border and straight to Edinburgh, where he arrived October 4 and was received with every evidence of delight. He was feasted and shown every attention, and after a stay of two days he retraced his steps and reached London early in December. Having disposed of King Charles as already shown, Cromwell was confronted with a new danger. A faction known as the Levelers had sprung up in the army and in some instances had mutinied. Several executions and other decisive measures soon put an end to the Levelers. Early in the year 1649 Parliament turned its attention to rebellious Ireland. In 1640 the Catholics of Ireland had taken advantage of the feebleness of Royal authority and began the perpetration of a series of massacres upon the English colonists and Protestants, which for wanton cruelty and revengeful fury stand without a parallel in the annals of any Nation. More than 100,000 are said to have been murdered during this terrible period. In 1649 Dublin and Londonderry were the only places that stood favorable to Parliament. The Marquis of Ormond had aroused the whole country into rebellion and had entered into a union with the Royalists. Parliament decided that the rebels must be suppressed and named Cromwell Lord-Governor of Ireland, with absolute civil and military power. On July 10 Cromwell left London amidst much pomp and ceremony, proceeded to Bristol and thence to Wales, sailing from Milford with an army of 12,000 men. He arrived in Dublin August 18. He at once advanced against Drogheda or Tredagh. "Cromwell," says Lamartine, "converted his victories into massacres and pacified Ireland through a deluge of blood." Hood recites the cruelties committed by the Irish against the Protestants and says, "Let these facts always be borne in mind when we look on Cromwell in Ireland." When Tredagh fell the entire garrison of 3,000 were massacred. After this he met with but feeble resistance. Having captured the fighting Bishop of Ross, who used to say that there was no way of curing the English, but by hanging them, Cromwell had him hanged before the walls of Clonmel in sight of the garrison, which at once capitulated. In the brief space of nine months Ireland was completely reduced to submission. He left Ireton to maintain order and returned to England, arriving in London May 31, 1650. He was received with the wildest demonstrations ever accorded a conqueror and Parliament again expressed its thanks and appreciation. Affairs had at this time grown threatening in Scotland. The Prince of Wales, Charles II, eldest son of the King who had been beheaded, had taken refuge first in Holland and later in the Isle of Jersey to wait for a favorable opportunity to enter England by way of Scotland. The Scotch Parliament offered him the throne of Scotland, demanding of him but one thing, that he should sign the Covenant and adhere to the Presbyterian faith. Their position was this, that if with their aid he could finally be placed on the throne of England, their object of bringing Presbyterianism upon England would through him be brought about. Under these circumstances armies were raised in Scotland to oppose the Commonwealth. The English Parliament had offered to Fairfax the command of the expedition against Scotland, but he declined on the ground that his wife was a Presbyterian and he would not fight against them unless they should invade England. Cromwell was then named Lord-General of the Parliamentary armies. This was June 26 and three days later he marched from London at the head of his army. July 23 he crossed the border and five days later encamped at Musselburgh. The Scotch army numbered 27,000 men, that of Cromwell 11,000 horse and foot. Two days after his arrival Cromwell was attacked by the Scotch but easily repulsed them. He waited a month and attempted in every way to bring about an engagement but to no avail, and finally decided to fall back upon Dunbar. The Scotch army managed to head him off and reached the heights above Dunbar in advance. Encamped here, Cromwell writes to Sir Arthur Hazlerig, Governor of Newcastle: "We are here upon an engagement very difficult. The enemy doth block up our way at the Pass at Copperspath through which we cannot go without a miracle." But Cromwell had no doubt but that the miracle would be forthcoming at the proper moment. His faith had not in the least been dimmed, for further along in the letter he says, "All shall work for good. Our spirits are comfortable, praised be the Lord, though our present condition be as it is." During the wild, wet night of September 2, Cromwell's soldiers held prayer meetings and "kept their powder dry." At the first grey of the morning was fought the terrible battle of Dunbar. Cromwell and his inspired host fell upon the Scots like a storm and before the sun had scarce come above the horizon, the Scotch army had been cut to pieces, was scattered and flying in all directions. Cromwell called a halt in the carnage and his army sang the 117th Psalm. Out of that army of 27,000, the soldiers of Cromwell had slain outright 3,000 had taken 10,000 prisoners, captured 200 colors, 15,000 stands of arms, and the entire artillery. The loss to Cromwell's ranks was but twenty men. Cromwell spent the winter at Edinburgh and during the following spring fell ill as a result of the exposures through which he had passed. By June, 1651, he was well enough to again take the field, and dividing his army into several bodies under command of chosen generals, sent them upon various expeditions against the enemy. In the meantime an army of Scots under young Charles II had invaded England and had found no trouble in taking Worcester, which threw open its gates and received him with all deference. It was first intended to at once march upon

London, but the Scotch army determined to remain at Worcester to recuperate and in the interim Cromwell was not idle. He rapidly marched upon Worcester and as he advanced he was constantly joined by bodies of militia so that when he appeared before Worcester he had an army of 30,000 men. The enemy was well intrenched, however, Cromwell himself wrote of the battle, "as stiff a contest, for many hours, on both sides of the river as I have ever seen." The battle was fought on the walls of the town and through the streets on September 3, 1651. The streets were filled with bodies of horses and men, great ruin had been wrought in every part of the city, all of the leading generals were slain or captured and the young King, with a few followers, fled, and, after many romantic adventures, escaped to the Continent. The battle of Worcester was the last of Cromwell's career as a warrior. He had left the conclusion of the war in Scotland to General Monk and the country was thoroughly subjugated, and eventually was united to the Commonwealth by Act of Paliament. The great spirits of the Parliament were not at this time a part of the Government. Pym and Hampden and other strong leaders were dead. The famous "Rump" Parliament was fast exhausting the patience of the people. Months were wasted in debate over technicalities, and finally the members concocted a plan to continue themselves continually in office. They had come to the conclusion that Cromwell was too much their master and some of the Republican leaders had practically decided to bring about his fall. Sir Henry Vane, according to Lamartine, was the leader of this contingent and shortly before the blow fell, which put an end to their schemes, he delivered a speech in the House, disputing the intervention of military authority. The applause which followed it was significant. On April 20, 1653, Crom-

well was notified that the measure to continue themselves
in office was being hurried through the House. Cromwell had been warned before to stop the proceedings, but he
had hesitated to act. Now he hesitated no longer. He
proceeded to his own place in the House and sat down to
listen. The bill was about to be put to the question when
Cromwell arose and walked to the desk of the President
and began to speak. First he addressed a few quiet words
about the services of Parliament in the cause of liberty,
then suddenly breaking forth in a fury of wrath, he
denounced the body as corrupt and unfit to serve. An
attempt to check him was made under the rules of the
House. At this his fury increased. He put his hat on,
advanced to the middle of the floor, stamped loudly in his
rage and, in a voice of thunder, shouted, "You are no
longer a Parliament. Make room for better men." On
his way to the House, Cromwell had given hasty instructions to General Harrison and that soldier now appeared
at the head of thirty veterans of the wars. They surrounded Cromwell with their naked weapons, and at his
orders drove or dragged the members from their seats and
ejected them. Cromwell himself locked the doors of
Westminster Hall and put the keys in his pocket. He was
now absolute and sole ruler of England. Later Cromwell
selected 140 men to act as a Parliament. They sat for the
first time July 4th. Entering too eagerly into the work of
reform, they aroused from many quarters a storm of protest, and December 12th the body resigned, having first,
however, invested Cromwell with the title of Lord Protector of the English Commonwealth. December 16th
he was under that title installed at Westminster Hall. He
was recognized by the principal courts of Europe. He
proceeded at once to establish new ordinances and instituted many worthy reforms calculated to avoid factional

strife both in Church and State affairs. In July, 1654, a plot to assassinate him was discovered and the conspirators were promptly apprehended and executed. Don Pantaleon Sa, brother of the Ambassador from Portugal, was on the same day beheaded for the murder of an Englishman. Cromwell concluded peace treaties with several of the Nations of Europe and called a Parliament which sat September 3, 1654. This Parliament could not agree whether to confirm the reforms which Cromwell had instituted and was soon dissolved. In the summer of 1655, the attention of Cromwell was attracted to the sufferings of the Protestants in the Piedmont valleys in France. He was about to sign a treaty with France, but refused to do so until assured by that Government that the persecutions should cease. Cromwell had also turned his attention to increasing the naval power of England and to protect her commerce. The able Blake had, under the direction of the Protector, cleared the Mediterranean of the barbarian pirates which infested the region. Nearly all of the Barbary States had been compelled to make reparation for misdeeds against English ships and subjects. In 1656 Cromwell made another experiment with a Parliament. It sat September 17th. This Parliament proposed to make Cromwell King. April 13, 1657, in replying to this proposition and refusing it, he says, "I am ready to serve, not as King, but as Constable." June 26, 1657, he was again invested with the Protectorate. The following year he called another Parliament, which met January 20th. February 4th the body was dissolved because the House of Commons was dissatisfied with the House of Peers. But Cromwell's life was rapidly drawing to a close. In August of this year he was seized with a slow intermittent fever. He knew that death was upon him.

That confidence in the power and mercy of God which had caused him to sing Psalms on the field of battle remained with him now as firmly as ever. He spent his last days in agonized prayer. On August 30th he declared in favor of his eldest son, Richard, as his successor. He breathed his last on September 3, 1658, the anniversary of the battle of Dunbar. He died in Whitehall and when his spirit had departed, he was mourned and prayed for and accorded a magnificent funeral. It is a matter of doubt where the remains of Cromwell were laid to eternal repose. It was announced that he had been buried in the old Abbey and when Charles Stuart came upon the throne, he had what was supposed to be the remains of Cromwell taken up and the head exposed over Westminster Hall. But there is an old story which asserts that the remains were secretly removed after the funeral and consigned to the Thames, in order that no indignity might be offered to the body by his enemies. The illustrious essayist Macaulay, years before the correspondence of Cromwell came to light and Carlyle had prepared his magnificent vindication of the Protector, wrote of Cromwell: "The ambition of Oliver was of no vulgar kind. He never seems to have coveted despotic power. He, at first, fought sincerely and manfully for the Parliament, and never deserted it till it had deserted its duty. But even thus placed by violence at the head of affairs, he did not assume unlimited power. He gave the country a constitution far more perfect than any which had, at that time, been known to the world. For himself, he demanded indeed the first place in the Commonwealth, but with powers scarcely so great as those of a Dutch stadtholder or an American President. He gave to Parliament a voice in the appointment of ministers and left it to the whole legislative authority, not even reserving to himself a veto on its enactments; and he did not require that the chief magistracy should be hereditary in his family. Thus far, if the circumstances of the time and the opportunities which he had for aggrandising himself be fairly considered, he will not lose by comparison with Washington and Boliver."

FREDERICK THE GREAT

After a drawing by Adolph Menzel

FREDERICK THE GREAT

1712-1786

Frederick II, King of Prussia, and universally styled, Frederick the Great, concluded his last will and testament with the following words: "My most fervent aspirations, when breathing my last, shall be for the prosperity of my Kingdom. May its government be ever conducted with justice, wisdom, and decision. May the mildness of its laws render it the happiest, and the due administration of its finances the most prosperous of States. May its army, mindful of nought but honor and renown, render it the most valiently defended of Kingdoms. Oh, may it continue in the enjoyment of the most perfect prosperity to the end of time." Such were the sentiments for which Frederick had labored and fought during his long and eventful reign and such an ideal condition, indeed, he had in a great measure succeeded in establishing. This giant figure in modern history ascended a throne that was none too secure and through his valiant conduct in war and wise administration in peace, virtually founded the present monarchy of Prussia and brought the Nation to a higher place than it had ever occupied before; for while flattering distinction must be accorded him as one of the foremost of warriors, so amply demonstrated in the campaigns against Silesia and the more remarkable ones of the Seven Years' War; he is also entitled to merit as a statesman of distinguished ability, and a scholar of extensive attainments. In the cabinet and upon the field of battle he was alike a genius of surpassing brilliancy; his heroism and sagacity made an impress on Germany which time cannot obliterate, his faithful and successful service in the interests of his Kingdom and its people, caused his name to be cherished and honored in life and his memory to be revered and blessed after death.

When Frederick II was born in the royal palace at Berlin on the 21st day of January, 1712, his grandfather, Frederick I, occupied the Prussian throne. Frederick William I, father of the infant Prince, was the only son of the aged ruler and as he had already lost two sons, the birth of a direct heir was hailed with joy. The mother of Frederick was Sophia Dorothea, daughter of the then King of Hanover, who later became King George I, of England. On the 28th day of February, in the year following the birth of Frederick II, the grandfather died after having the infant brought to his bedside and solemnly blessing him. Frederick William I now became King and the infant Frederick, Prince Royal. His education was entrusted, first to Madame de Kamecke and Madame de Rocouilles, and after his seventh year, to Count Finkemstein and Count Kalkstein. Later Duhan, a French refugee, became the leading educator of the Prince. The orders of the King were that chief above all else, religion should be inculcated into the boyish mind and Latin was strictly forbidden as a study. The King was a hard, stern and practical man, who shunned frivolity in all its forms and was practically a fanatic in religious matters, yet he was intensely interested and solicitous about the army and military affairs. As his son grew into boyhood, the King treated him more as a subject than as a son and the childhood, boyhood, and early youth of Frederick became, under the harsh and cruel treatment of his father, a bitter experience and the saddest period of his life. Frederick possessed a fiery spirit which did not take kindly to the system of control mapped out for him. He was compelled at a very early age to don an uncomfortable military uniform and be tonsured. Gradually the ties between father and son widened. This breach grew rapidly when the Queen suggested a double marriage between Frederick and an English Princess, and between her daughter, Wilhelmina, and the Prince Royal of England. To this the father of Frederick was violently opposed. The Prince in his studies made rapid progress. His military instruction was not neglected. At fourteen he was made a Captain, at sixteen a Major, and at seventeen a Lieutenant-Colonel, and he was compelled to discharge the duties of his various posts.

He grew more and more dissatisfied with the conditions imposed upon him and only the pleas of his sister Wilhelmina, who sympathized with him, prevented him from open rebellion. He finally, however, determined to escape and communicated with his uncle, King George, of England, who agreed to receive him, the more so as a strong feeling of dislike existed between Frederick's father and the King of England. The fact of this correspondence reached the ears of the Prussian King, and his conduct toward his son increased in bitterness. Frederick and Wilhelmina were practically banished from the presence of their father and mother, and strife between husband and wife made the situation worse. Frederick was fully determined to fly, despite his sister's importuning. He laid the ignominy of his situation before her in the following words, according to her memoirs: "They are daily preaching patience to me, but none knows how much I have to bear. I am daily beaten, treated as a slave, and debarred every amusement. Even the enjoyments of reading and music are denied me. . . . But that which completely overpowers me is my father's recent treatment of me at Potsdam. The King summoned me,

and on my entering, he seized me by the hair, flung me to
the ground, and, having beaten me with his fists, dragged
me toward the window, and there coiling the string of the
curtain around my throat, pulled both ends with his
utmost might. I had, fortunately, time to get upon my
feet and seize his arms, but as he tugged with both his
hands I felt I was being strangled and cried for aid. A
chamberlain rushed to my assistance and rescued me by
force out of the hands of the King." Frederick made
arrangements with his two closest friends, Lieutenants
Katte and Keith, to aid him to escape and to fly with him.
He expected the opportunity might come during a journey
on which he was to accompany his father, for he was continually closely watched. His plans were discovered
through a misdirected letter, and although he made the
effort to escape, he was prevented, and at the King's orders
was taken aboard a vessel that was to convey the royal
party down the River Maine. When he received the absolute evidence in the shape of the strayed letter he became
so enraged that he attacked his son and beat him unmerci-
fully with his cane, so that the blood streamed down
Frederick's face. The unhappy youth managed to warn
his two friends of their danger. Keith escaped to England, but Katte delayed too long, and was arrested. He
was tried and sentenced to death. In the meantime Frederick was imprisoned, for a time in the palace, and then
transferred to Custrin, where he was confined in a barren
room. The King had determined that he should die for
desertion under the military law, and only the most strenuous intervention saved him from this fate. The cruelty of
this father, however, was shown in another manner. The
condemned Katte was taken to a position under the windows of the imprisoned Prince, and while the latter was
compelled to look on, his friend was decapitated. On
approaching the place of execution, Katte looked up and

saw the Prince. "Forgive me, my dear Katte," called Frederick, in heartbroken tones. "Death for a Prince so beloved is sweet," returned the undaunted victim, and went calmly to his death. Months afterward, Frederick, on declaring submission to his father and taking an oath to implicitly obey him in everything, was released from his prison. He took care not to further offend his father, and in 1732, on the petition of sympathizers in the nobility he was made Colonel of a regiment, and the following year, in accordance with the wishes of his father, married Princess Elizabeth Christine, daughter of the Duke of Brunswick-Bevern. He was provided with a palace at Rheinsberg, near Ruppin, where his regiment was stationed, and there he resided with his bride until the death of his father and his own ascension of the throne.

In June, 1735, the King promoted Frederick to the rank of Major-General. He now returned to his castle at Rheinsberg, and there surrounded himself with some of the most illustrious men of the time. The Princess entered fully into the life which so delighted her husband, and Rheinsberg soon assumed the tone of an intellectual center. Among the men whose associations Frederick availed himself of during this period were Wolff, the philosopher; Jordan, a former clergyman, noted for his remarkable conversational powers; Baron Beilfiel; Pesne, the famous court painter; Graun, a musician of great ability; Beausobre, the learned divine, and many others. But personal contact with distinguished officers, scholars, artists, and musicians was not enough to satisfy the thirst for knowledge which Frederick possessed and which, as has been shown, he had hitherto been prevented from obtaining. He entered into correspondence with Voltaire, for whom he had long entertained the greatest admiration; with Grumbkow, the diplomat, and with the Prince of

Anhalt-Dessau and other warriors of distinction.   He was
systematically preparing himself for the high post he was
to fill.   Through French translations, he became thoroughly familiar with the histories of the Nations. He read
and conversed and corresponded.   He possessed the facul-
ty of "extracting their learning from the learned," thus
adding to the culture of his mind with all the diligence
of an enthusiastic student.   During this period, also, he
produced two works of considerable merit : "Considera-
tions of the Present State of the Political Relations of
Europe," and the well known "Anti-Machiavelli."   In
the first he discusses the coalition of France and Austria
and the dangerous results to Europe unless some new
power is developed to even the balance.   His second
treatise relates to the attainment and maintenance of sovereignty—a reply to the arguments of the Florentine historian, Niccolo Machiavelli.   Another step in the direction of attaining knowledge taken by the Prince at this
time was his entrance into the order of Freemasonry.   On
the 31st day of May, 1740, after a most affecting parting
from his son, the King breathed his last.

While Frederick sincerely mourned the death of his
father, he immediately began to exercise that vigorous
policy which made him famous in peace as well as war.
He retained nearly all of his father's advisors at their
posts.   Almost his first step was to care for those who
through him had suffered at the hands of his father.   The
fugitive Keith was recalled and restored to the army with
a higher rank than he previously held.   Toward his
mother and brothers and sisters he showed the most loyal
spirit.   It is related that when his mother at the funeral
addressed her son as "Your Majesty," he quickly checked
her with, "Call me your son, I am prouder of this title
than that of King."   Toward his wife he showed the same

devotion which he had always entertained for her, and
on presenting her to the assembled court, embraced and
kissed her tenderly. One of Frederick's first acts was in
behalf of the poorer classes of his Kingdom. The winter
had been a hard one and there was much suffering. In
consequence of this condition, on the second day after
accession, he ordered the granaries opened and cereals sold
to the masses at reduced rates. Taxes were for a time
remitted, and money was distributed among the most destitute. His next task was one of military reform. That
expensive and practically useless body, the guard of giants,
which had been his father's personal command, was disbanded and the 10,000 members divided among other regiments. Frederick at once invaded those branches of the
national life which had been most neglected by his father.
Freedom of speech was granted. Greater liberty was
accorded the press. An Academy of Sciences was founded
and men of eminence invited to come to Berlin and Prussia. The order of Freemasons, against which much preju-
dice had existed, received public recognition. Religious
toleration and freedom was enforced. In the administration of law and justice he found much room for reform,
but the first ordinance given in this department was the
abolition of the torture, except in extreme cases. Frederick's activity was so boundless that he found time to
examine into and observe everything himself. He even
personally attended to affairs brought forward by foreign
ambassadors. In the midst of it all he wrote poetry,
studied diligently, and devoted himself much to music.
In July Frederick proceeded to Königsberg, and on the
20th day of that month was formally crowned King of
Prussia.

The fall of the year 1840 was well advanced, when
suddenly a courier arrived with the information that

Charles VI, Emperor of Austria, had died on the 20th day of October. This quickly decided the young King to action in a matter which he had long meditated upon. "Now is the time," he wrote to Voltaire, "in which the old political system may be made to undergo a change. The stone is loosed which shall fall on Nebuchadnezzar's statue of many metals and crush them all." A glance at the Empire, which he likened to the statue, fashioned of metals, but with feet of iron and clay—making it incapable of withstanding a shock—must here be taken. Austria had suffered much in the war with the Turks. Her resources were not what they once had been. Prince Eugene, in whom the military ability of the Empire was rooted, had gone to his final accounting. The Emperor had given more attention to securing from the rulers of Europe their consent to the succession of his daughter, Maria Theresa, and had in consequence greatly neglected the affairs of state. His dealings with Prussia had been unjust, but in this he had only followed the example of previous rulers of Austria. Several provinces in Silesia, which rightfully belonged to Prussia, having come to the ancestors of Frederick by inheritance, were stubbornly withheld by Austria. During the reign of the Great Elector, Austria needed his aid against the Turks, and at that time acknowledged the claims of Prussia to the principalities of Jägerndorf, Liegnitz, Brieg, and Wohlau in Silesia, but proposed instead, to cede to Prussia the Schwiebusian district. By underhand methods, the Austrians then extracted a promise from the son of the Great Elector that he would restore the district to Austria when he came to occupy the throne. When as King Frederick I he succeeded to his father's place and informed his ministers of the promise he had made, the duplicity of the Austrians was exposed, but the promise was faithfully kept, though with a protest and the expressed desire that his successors would prosecute their claims to the Silesian principalities above named. Frederick had already formulated the intention to carry out this act of justice on behalf of his Kingdom, and now the opportunity presented itself. Prussia was in splendid condition to carry out this bold design. The army, which had been the hobby of Frederick's father, was perfectly equipped and disciplined, there was prosperity in the provinces, Prussia had no national debt, but, on the contrary, the royal exchequer contained nine millions of thalers. Frederick has been severely criticised for his campaigns against Silesia, by some historians, but in his memoirs has made out a case which would appear to justify his actions, showing that the territory invaded by him was his by lawful inheritance. His intentions against Silesia he kept as secret as possible. Everyone knew, as a consequence of the unusual activity in the army, that some movement was on foot, but only a few of his closest friends knew the facts in regard to his project. He personally looked after the forwarding of troops, the disposition of artillery, and the construction of magazines. December 15 everything was in readiness for the opening of the campaign, and Frederick joined his troops at Crossen, on the Silesian boundary. Two days later he set foot for the first time on the soil of the territory he had set out to conquer. Reinforcements from Austria had not yet arrived in the disputed territory, and the soldiers which garrisoned the towns were not numerous enough to come forth and dispute the progress of the invader. The first fortified town which made any show of resistance was Glogau. Frederick left a large detachment here to besiege it, and with the main army pushed forward toward Breslau, the seat of government. On January 7, 1741, he made his formal entry into Breslau. Ohlau and Namslau were taken without a blow. Brieg, a fortress, was invested and Ottmachau, in upper Silesia, was easily taken. The only important point which was not now in the hands of the Prussians was Neisse, the most formidable fortress in Silesia, and here the strength of Frederick's army was concentrated. Neisse withstood the bombardment, and as the season was such as to preclude a regular siege, the effort was abandoned. The Austrian troops, which had arrived too late to defend Silesia, retired to Moravia, and the Prussian troops went into winter quarters. The number of Prussian troops engaged in this, the first Silesian campaign, was 30,000. King Frederick had returned to Berlin by the end of January. His bold move had created amazement in every corner of Europe. That Prussia should thus array herself against the mighty Austria was almost beyond belief. Sometimes Frederick was charitably spoken of as imprudent, but there was no lack of those who declared that he must be insane. Toward the end of February Frederick returned to his troops, and about the same time the Austrians under Field-Marshal Count Neïpperg advanced on Silesia. On the 9th of March the fortress of Glogau was assaulted by the Prussians and captured, the garrison being made prisoners of war. Frederick proceeded to the camp of General Schwerin, his most experienced General, in Upper Silesia. On learning that the Austrians were proceeding to the relief of Neisse, an effort was made to effect a junction with the Lower Silesian detachment of the army, at the River Neisse. The Austrians arrived there first and prevented the junction, making Frederick's position at this time extremely critical. He was cut off from his main army and could not even communicate with his own States. There was but one thing to do, and Frederick resolutely

faced the situation and decided to bring about an engagement with the enemy as quickly as possible. The center
of the Austrian army lay at the village of Mollwitz, not
far from Brieg. At this point on the 10th day of April,
1741, was fought the battle of Mollwitz. At one period
in the conflict, all seemed lost to the Prussians, but the
steady resolution of the infantry saved the day, and the
Austrians retreated with a heavy loss. Subsequently, in
writing his memoirs, Frederick unsparingly criticised
himself for blunders committed in this his first serious
military operation. The Prussians now proceeded with
the siege of Brieg, which, after a brief resistance, capitulated. Frederick was now master over Lower Silesia.
The army then moved on Neisse, which was still in the
hands of the Austrians, who, however, soon retired. The
Austrian court now offered to cede Lower Silesia and
Neisse to Frederick on condition that he withdraw his
troops. He reluctantly accepted this offer, as the French
were making serious inroads in Germany, and it was not
a part of Frederick's plan that Austria should be enfeebled
in order to aggrandize France. After receiving the homage of the Princes and estates of Lower Silesia at Breslau
on November 7, Frederick returned to Berlin. Suddenly
there came a change in the situation. The Hungarians
rallied to the aid of Maria Theresa, and began a savage
warfare against the Franco-Bavarian army. The Hungarians marked a path of blood and devastation through
Bavaria, and entered Munich February 12, 1742. Under
an agrement with France and Bavaria, made during the
previous campaign to support the claim of Charles Alfred
of Bavaria to the Austrian throne, Frederick was obliged
to take part in this warfare. He induced Saxony to furnish an army, and, joining this with an army of his own
Prussians, burst into Upper Austria and swept every-

thing before him.   On April 17, the Prince of Dessau with
a Prussian corps joined Frederick in Bohemia.   Then an
Austrian army advanced upon Prague, and Frederick
divided his force, sending the Prince of Dessau toward the
town of Czaslau, with orders to invest it.   The King, with
his section of the army, awaited the advance of the Austrians.   But the enemy had already entered Czaslau, and
the Prussian army was reunited at Chotusitz, near Czaslau.   The junction had barely been effected on May 17,
1742, when the Austrians attacked.   Frederick in person
led an attack upon the left wing of the Austrians, driving
it back upon the right wing, and charging irresistibly into
the ranks of both, routed the whole Austrian army.
Negotiations with Austria were renewed, and Maria
Theresa readily agreed to the terms stipulated.   On June
11, 1742, the treaty was entered into whereby the whole
of Silesia, the province of Glatz, and a district of Moravia
was ceded to Frederick.   Peace was now declared throughout his dominions.   It lasted for two years, during which
time Frederick applied himself with ardor to the develop-
ment of their resources, strengthened his fortresses, both
in Prussia and in his new territories, and further improving his army.   During the first months of the year 1744, it
became more and more apparent that Austria was planning to dislodge his rule from Silesia, and therefore, on
July 5 of that year, he entered into a secret agreement
with France to maintain the imperial rights of Charles
VII, who was established at Frankfort, and to protect his
Bavarian possessions; France agreed to advance with two
corps upon the Lower and Upper Rhine, while Frederick
was to attack Bohemia and retain out of his conquests
Austrian Silesia and sections of Bohemia adjoining
Silesia.   Thus began Frederick's second war against
Silesia in 1744.   While the French king, Louis XV, in

person led an army into the Austrian Netherlands, the
Prussian king advanced according to agreement into
Bohemia. The Prussians reached the Bohemian frontier
August 15, 1744. The advancing columns met with no
resistance, and on September 2 was concentrated around
Prague. The siege of the Bohemian capital was taken up
at once and prosecuted with great vigor. The assault began September 11, and although the town was garrisoned
by 12,000 troops, it capitulated five days later.

On the 20th of January, 1745, Charles VII died. This
dissolved the treaty into which France and Prussia had
entered, and being no longer able to count on French coöperation the position of Frederick became perilous. He
joined his army in Silesia and waited for the Austrians,
who were already advancing, having been joined by the
Saxons. The king retired with his troops to Schweidnitz
and took up a favorable position. He caused the report to
be spread that he was retiring to Breslau and then prepared
an ambush for the enemy. Near Striegau he collected his
troops in the night and waited for daybreak and the enemy.
At daylight, the Saxons, who had been ordered to seize
Striegau, were descending from the heights when the
Prussian right wing fell upon and almost annihilated them.
The Austrians then advanced and desperately attacked
the Prussians, but not a corps wavered, and when the
bloody day was ended the Austrians had lost 4,000 slain
and 7,000 prisoners. In this battle Frederick gave undisputed evidence of his personal bravery and prowess as
a warrior. He advanced with the utter contempt of death
with three battalions in the face of the Austrian guns,
which mowed down men on every side of him and reached
the heights with but 360 men, whom he then headed in a
bayonet charge against a battery. The battle of Soor was
the next great victory of the Prussians. Frederick had

pursued the flying Austrians into Bohemia and had taken up a position in the hills between Lower Silesia and the province of Glatz. It was his object to strip this section of its provisions, so as to protect Silesia during the approaching winter from hostile incursion. Various corps were detached to guard the passes through the hills, and his collective force did not exceed 18,000. The Austrian forces who were watching his movements and waiting to crush him amounted to 40,000. As he was advancing from his camp in the village of Staudenz he was suddenly attacked by the Austrians. The Austrians were completely cut to pieces and routed, retreating in great disorder. The pursuit continued as far as the village of Soor, from which the battle derives its name. After ravaging the country and returning into Silesia, Frederick learned in November of the intended junction in Lusatia of Saxon and Austrian armies to attack Silesia from the Bohemian side. By rapid marches he came upon the Saxon regiments at Hennersdorff on September 23 and attacked and so badly defeated them that the Austrians, seeing the fate of their allies, retreated from place to place, so that within a brief space the whole of Lusatia was in the King's hands. The Prussians now invaded Saxony and successes followed each other fast, until Frederick was notified that Austria was ready to conclude peace. The treaty was entered into on December 25, 1745. It was similar to the treaty of two years previous, and in addition Saxony was compelled to pay to Prussia one million thalers indemnity. Three days later, the King entered Berlin and received such a welcome and ovation as has been accorded to but few men. He was now but 33 years of age, and yet the famous ruler of his time.

During the eleven years of peace which now followed, Frederick devoted his time to the best interests of civil pursuits of the Nation.   He built canals, reclaimed marsh lands, encouraged manufacturing, and in every way exerted himself for the internal welfare of his people. The population and revenues of Prussia soon increased to a considerable extent.   The administration of justice received his particular attention.   The defects of the Prussian code were amended and a judicious reform was instituted throughout the whole monarchy.   Frederick did not fail to give a large share of his time and attention to the army.   Camps were formed each year, and the various branches of the military brought up to the highest standard in manœuvers and in excellence of equipment.   He summoned distinguished cavalry officers from Hungary to instruct his officers in this arm of the service.   He provided every facility for the diffusion of education, and aside from all of these numerous affairs, managed to give himself time to engage in literary pursuits and music, and found his greatest enjoyment in the seclusion of Sans Souci, a beautiful mansion which he had erected on a hillside near Potsdam, in the midst of one of the most beautiful stretches of scenery to be found in that section of the Kingdom.   Here he passed all of his leisure hours, and here, after his life work had been completed, he found repose in his declining years until the time of his death. But fate had not destined that his life should pass without another demonstration of the ability and genius which he had displayed in the second Silesian War.   Maria never forgot Silesia, and Francis Kugler in his history relates that she could not look upon a Silesian for years after this gem of her possessions had been torn from her, without bursting into tears.   Her hatred of Prussia and Frederick was shared to a considerable extent by other Nations, though in the form of jealousy.   Prussia was a rapidly growing power, and its constant claims to superiority over

other Nations led to fear lest its power should extend
beyond its own borders, to the humiliation of its enemies.
Next to Austria, the bitterest foe of Prussia was Saxony.
In Russia, Empress Catherine was hostile to Frederick,
and even France declared against him. Maria Theresa
was not slow to take advantage of this condition, and did
all in her power by intrigue and by the use of gold to
revenge herself upon him who had humbled her haughty
spirit. Treaties were entered into among these rulers,
and each of them was directed against Prussia. Of all
of the plots and plans against him, however, Frederick
was totally informed through a treacherous official of
Saxony, who supplied the King with copies of all docu-
ments and correspondence on the subject. England alone
evinced a friendly spirit, resulting probably from Prussia's
refusal to join France in an enterprise of plunder against
Hanover. This friendship resulted in 1756 in a recip-
rocal treaty between the two powers. But it was plainly
to be seen that Austria, through machinations, was bringing affairs to a crisis. An alliance was formed between
France and Austria May 9, 1756, and following this
extraordinary levies of troops were made in Bohemia, and
Frederick also learned that there was a movement to raise
a large army in Saxony by the allies. Matters began to
assume so serious an aspect in the neighborhood of Prussia that on July 12, 1756, he demanded from the Empress
of Austria a declaration as to the purpose of these equipments. He received an unsatisfactory and vague reply.
Two other similar demands, one of which directly asked
whether Prussia was to be attacked, brought no better
results, and Frederick immediately took steps to prevent
his enemies from taking him at a disadvantage. He acted
quickly and decisively. He decided to direct his main
forces against Saxony and Bohemia, and to strongly

intrench himself in Saxony, so as to cover any hostile approach upon Brandenburg. His disposition of troops were made with the utmost secrecy, and his first great step came as a complete surprise, when on August 29 he suddenly moved upon Saxony with a force of 60,000 Prussian troops.

It had been generally expected that war would break out, yet no one was prepared for this sudden move on the part of King Frederick. In Saxony, the approach of the Prussians caused the greatest consternation. Saxon troops to the number of 17,000 were gathered in a great camp at Pirna, and thither fled King Augustus and his minister, Bruhl. But there was none to hinder the advance of the Prussian army. Wittenberg, Torgau, Leipsic, and last, on September 9, Dresden was occupied. The contents of the arsenals at Dresden, Weissenfels, and Zeitz were seized by Frederick and transferred to Magdeburg. The funds in the royal exchequer were appropriated, but the rights of citizens were scrupulously respected. The camp of the Saxons was surrounded and blockaded in the hope that famine would compel them to surrender. This occupied so great a part of Frederick's troops that he was prevented from acting promptly against the Austrian troops in Bohemia. These were advancing in two columns upon Saxony and Silesia. The Austrian corps under Browne was concentrated at Budin, and he prepared to cross the Eger. Frederick posted an inconsiderable body of troops in the narrow passes connecting Bohemia and Saxony to watch the movements of the enemy. In order to prevent or at least delay the junction of the Austrians with the Saxons, he determined to attack Browne's corps with the force occupying the passes, and himself took command of the enterprise. The two armies came together during a heavy fog on the morning of October 1, close to the village of Lowositz on the Elbe. After a battle of six hours the Austrians were completely routed. The besieged Saxons were in the meantime being starved into submission, and in the middle of October, after vainly waiting for aid, they laid down their arms and surrendered as prisoners of war. This ended operations for the year 1756, and was but a small beginning to the great struggle which was to follow. France and Poland declared against Prussia, and in January, 1757, Russia made a new pact with Austria. In the spring of 1757 Frederick pushed into Bohemia, and after some minor conflicts with the Austrians, advanced on Prague, where the main army was located. On May 6 the Prussians reached a position below Prague, on the Elbe. The Austrians occupied a strong position on rising ground, and protected by a marsh. Through this marsh the Prussian battalions under Gen. Schwerin struggled, in order to fall upon the left wing of the enemy. On reaching dry land, each battalion rushed at the Austrians, but the fire was so murderous that it could not be withstood. Schwerin rallied his men after the first repulse, and again attacked, when he was shot from his horse. Five grape shot had entered his body, and this shows the ferocity of the enemy's fire. The battle was at its height in all quarters when King Frederick, at the head of three battalions, charged through a storm of cannonading into a breach in the Austrians' center. This started the rout, which soon became general, and the Austrians sought safety inside the gates of the city of Prague. The losses on both sides were tremendous. Prussia, according to Kugler's history of these battles, lost 12,000 men, and the losses of the Austrians were even greater. Frederick now drew a cordon around Prague and besieged it for five weeks, until the arrival of Marshal Daun, with an army of Austrians far superior to the Prussian army, who took up a position on the heights near Panian. In the battle which here took place June 18, Frederick sustained his first considerable defeat. His troops, after hard marching, were permitted to rest but three hours, when they were ordered to the attack. Had the plan of battle as first decided upon been carried out, the result would perhaps have been different, but for some unexplained reason, Frederick suddenly altered his plans. The result was most disastrous. While the Prussians gallantly charged the enemy, the nature of the ground was such that their advance was slow and fatiguing, and the fire of the Austrians mowed them down by regiments. Then the Saxon cavalry fell upon them and a slaughter ensued. The whole Prussian center was annihilated, the left wing had suffered severely, and the right wing alone had escaped until Frederick ordered a retreat, when it became the duty of the right to protect the retreat of the shattered left. This caused the right wing also to become engaged, and another fierce struggle was carried on, in which the Prussians were again at a disadvantage and lost heavily. In spite of the continued and terrible disasters of the day, the Prussians were not subjected to the rout, such as they often inflicted upon their enemies. The Prussians lost in this day's carnage nearly 14,000 men, while the Austrian losses did not exceed 8,000. Historians have found no manner of excuse for this defeat, and that it resulted from Frederick's change of plans after the battle had begun, is conceded.

This calamity was followed by the capture of Zittau by the Austrians and the destruction of the town and the Prussian stores which had been collected there. The prospects of the Prussians had also become dark in other directions. Frederick, with 12,000 men, hastened to the defense of Saxony, which was threatened by the imperial

armies and French forces which had been sent to aid the
Austrians. The great part of the Prussian army had been
left to protect Lusatia and Silesia. During an attack by
the Austrians on an isolated Prussian position, Winter-
feldt, Frederick's favorite General after Schwerin, was
killed, and this information, when it reached the King,
during his march into Saxony, served to depress him
exceedingly. On the lower Rhine a great French army
had entered Westphalia, opposed only by an allied army
of Hanoverians, Hessians, and Brunswickers, under the
Duke of Cumberland. After one battle the allied army
retreated and the Duke concluded an ignominious treaty
by which he agreed to disperse his troops. The French
poured into the Prussian provinces of the Elbe. An army
of Russians had at the same time entered Prussia. They
advanced to the River Pregel, and there defeated the Prussians under Lewald. An army of Swedes landed at Stralsund, ravaged Pomerania and Uppermark, and, in pursuance of a treaty with Austria, took possession of Erfurt.
Every part of the Prussian Kingdom was thus assailed,
but what affected Frederick more than all else at this time
was the death of his mother. Under these conditions and
circumstances it was not strange that the King should
be seized with melancholy and that his closest friends
feared that he might at any moment resort to the use of
poison, which he always carried with him, and which he
had resolved to employ rather than survive the downfall
of his Kingdom. In this desperate situation Frederick
found relief from despair in poetry. Thus in the darkest
moments of this period he dedicated to his brother, Prince
Henry, an ode in which he sets up the conduct of the
Romans, who reached the glorious heights of supremacy
only after surmounting countless adversities; as an example for the Prussian Nation, and expresses confidence in

the future greatness and brilliant achievements of Prussia. From this time on, success seemed to crown his every effort.

He advanced upon Erfurt, fighting his way, and the enemy retired, were soon after driven out of Gotha, and pursued as far as Eisenach. A concerted movement of French and imperial troops upon Saxony, caused Frederick to hastily concentrate troops to cover Leipsic, in which vicinity the enemy had already arrived. They were driven back across the River Saale, and although in the retreat they burned the bridges, Frederick with his army soon after crossed the river by means of pontoons and encamped on the same side of the river as the enemy. On the 5th day of November the enemy moved against Frederick's camp. The wonderful rapidity with which the Prussians broke camp and started on a rapid retreat toward Rossbach astonished the French, who pushed forward with all speed, fearing that the Prussians would escape. But suddenly the scene changed. By rapid movements the Prussian cannon were planted on surrounding heights and the cavalry, under Seidlitz, by a quick detour, outflanked the French columns, which had thus been caught in a most unfavorable position. The battle lasted two hours. The Prussian army, numbering 22,000, lost 165 slain, 376 wounded. The losses of the enemy out of its army of 64,000 was over 600 killed and more than 2,000 wounded. Upward of 5,000 prisoners were taken and the greater part of the baggage captured. In England the greatest joy was manifested and more substantial aid was accorded Frederick than had been the case up to this time, by protecting the Prussian frontier with Hanoverian armies against the French and relieving him from further danger in that direction. In the meantime the Austrians had defeated the Prussians under the Duke of Bevern in front of Breslau, and that city fell into the hands of the enemy. It was the key to Silesia. Frederick hurried forward with his army to Breslau, and after being joined by the remnant of the Duke of Bevern's forces, captured, on December 4, Neumarkt, a Prussian outpost. On the following day, the Austrians, having left their intrenchments and come forward to meet the Prussians, were completely defeated, although the Austrian army numbered over 80,000 and the Prussian forces were but 32,000. The Austrians lost during the awful four hours of battle 27,000 men in killed, wounded, and prisoners, while the Prussian losses were about 6,000. On December 21, the town of Breslau, with its garrison of 18,000 men, was compelled to surrender to Frederick, and great quantities of military stores fell into his hands. A few days later Liegnitz also surrendered. Thus ended the eventful year of 1757, with the whole of Silesia again in Frederick's grasp with the single exception of Schweidnitz. During the winter overtures of peace were made to the Austrian Empress and refused. The alliance between Austria, France, and Russia was more closely drawn, and Russia, whose troops had withdrawn after the first incursion, again invaded Prussia and seized Königsberg. Frederick's first move in the spring of 1758 was to compel the Austrians to evacuate Schweidnitz. This was accomplished April 18. Early in May Frederick furnished another of his surprises by suddenly appearing with his army in Moravia and besieging Olmütz. The arrival of a large Austrian army under Field-Marshal Daun and the destruction of a convoy of ordnance and ammunition for Frederick from Silesia, forced him to abandon the siege. Frederick now received information that the Russians under Fermor, having advanced through Poland had crossed the Neumarkt frontier and were threatening the heart of Prussia. Count

Dohna, who had been holding the Swedes locked in at Stralsund, advanced to the Oder and strengthened the fortress at Custrin upon which the Russians were advancing. As the invaders approached they left a scene of desolation behind them. The country was plundered, villages destroyed and the most wanton and uncivilized warfare carried on. On August 15 the town of Custrin was bombarded and totally destroyed, but the fortress held out and refused to surrender. On August 21, King Frederick joined Count Dohna with 14,000 picked men, having made a series of remarkable marches from Silesia. Two days later he crossed the Oder, and making a wide circuit, deployed in such a manner as to hem in the enemy between an arm of the Oder and some extensive marshes. The Russians numbered 52,000, the Prussians 32,750. The Russian right flank was separated from the main army by a marsh, and on this, at 9 o'clock on the morning of August 25, the attack opened with a terrific cannonade which inflicted great damage. This was followed by a furious charge by the Prussian infantry, which overthrew the ranks of the enemy, but were soon compelled to fall back, and were being pursued and annihilated by the Russians when Seidlitz with his cavalry came to the rescue, and a scene ensued which has few parallels in the history of warfare. The lines of Russians were cut down one after another, but they refused to yield, and were sabered by thousands by their adversaries. Their ammunition was finally spent, and still they continued to resist, so that the massacre was continued for hours. Meanwhile confusion spread throughout other divisions of the Russian ranks. The soldiers plundered their own baggage and seized the brandy casks, from which they drank until crazed. Russian officers who attempted to interfere were murdered. Until noon the combat was confined to this right flank

of the Russians, but at that time the signal for a general
attack was given by Frederick. The Prussian left wing
soon began to give way before the wild charges of the Russian cavalry, and Count Dohna's troops were seized with
a panic and fled. Seidlitz with his valiant followers again
saved the day. He drove back the Russian cavalry as
Frederick brought up the veteran battalions of infantry,
and together they forced the enemy into one compressed
mass. King Frederick was in the midst of the attack and
soon the battle became a hand to hand conflict, in which
Prussians and Russians, infantry and cavalry, formed one
vast, struggling mass, which continued until dark. From
the fact that the village of Zorndorf lay between the two
armies, the battle has become known by that name. The
Prussian losses amounted to 11,000 men and those of the
Russians nearly double that number. Frederick left
16,000 troops to watch the Russians, and with the balance
of the army marched toward Saxony. On September 10
he arrived in the vicinity of Dresden and faced the army
of Daun, and then followed a series of manœuvers for a
month, at the end of which time Frederick was encamped
in the village of Hochkirchen, and Daun occupied the
heights above the village. On the night of October 13,
the Austrians made an attack on the Prussian camp, and
in the battle that continued all night each side lost about
9,000 men, though the Prussians also suffered the loss
of 100 cannon and many of Frederick's best leaders were
slain. Winter was now approaching and Frederick went
into camp and spent the winter months in preparing his
army for the campaigns of the following year. Hostilities
were not opened by the Prussians in 1759 until the summer
was well advanced. Late in July a Russian army under
General Soltikoff, having beaten the Prussians under
Wedell at Züllichau, inflicting a loss of 8,000 men, pushed

on to Frankfort where a junction was effected with a corps
of Austrians under Loudon.   This movement involved
the greatest danger to Frederick and he determined to
march in person upon the Russians and their Austrian
auxiliaries.   With an army of 43,000 he crossed the river
between Frankfort and Custrin, and on August 11 took
up a position facing the Russians, who were camped on
a ridge of hills running toward the east of Frankfort and
to the rear of the village of Cunnersdorf (now Kuners-
dorf).   The camp was well intrenched and the declivities
strengthened the batteries.   The attack opened with a
violent cannonade, to which the hostile batteries replied
with alacrity.   The Prussian infantry then assailed the
heights, and in the face of the most desperate resistance
stormed the barricades and captured the battery.   The
main body of the Russian left wing retreated across a
ravine and rallied, but the assaults of the Prussians again
proved victorious.   This occupied several hours, and the
right wing of the Russians, occupying a commanding position on adjoining heights, had not yet been attacked.
Although his troops were exhausted and against the
remonstrances of his Generals, Frederick resolved to move
against the Russian right.   The assault was begun with
the greatest bravery and continued for an hour, while the
Russian cannon played havoc with the Prussians.   Thus
far but one regiment of Austrians had taken part in the
engagement, and now Loudon suddenly burst across a valley with his cavalry and fell upon the Prussian flank.   Still
Frederick refused to yield.   His horse was shot from
under him and several balls passed through his uniform.
He had scarcely mounted a fresh horse when the animal
was shot in the breast, and when he had received a third
horse a bullet struck the King's hip, but was turned aside
by a golden case which he carried.   The Prussians began

to fly from certain destruction and finally the King was left alone with but a single page, when a company of his own Hussars, fleeing before the Cossack cavalry, compelled him to seek safety with them in flight. He found shelter in a peasant's hut on the Oder, and his page and one servant remained with him while he sent the Hussars to collect his shattered and scattered army. Frederick firmly believed that all hope of escape was past, and, determined not to survive the humiliation of capture, he made his final depositions. He named Prince Henry to command the army and his nephew Frederick William as his successor to the crown. To Count Finkenstein, the Minister of State, he wrote as follows: "I am now wholly bereft of all aid, and, to speak the truth, I believe that all is lost. I will not outlive the downfall of my native land. Farewell forever."

The following morning the remnants of Frederick's army gathered together and formed a body of 18,000 men. The losses sustained by the Russians in their victory was 16,000 men, and Soltikoff paid his adversary a compliment when he wrote to the Empress as follows: "The King of Prussia generally sells his defeats dear, and should I have to communicate intelligence of a second victory of this kind, I shall be obliged to take a staff in my hand and bring the tidings myself." The victorious armies made no move upon Berlin, as Frederick fully expected they would, having, with his army, taken up a position in Fursttenwalde, on the Spree, in order to cover the road to Berlin.

During the winter and spring Frederick managed to organize an army of 90,000 men. His adversaries in the field numbered 200,000. The first great enterprise of the year 1760 was Frederick's effort to reduce Dresden. From July 14 to the 29th he kept up the siege, but the fall of Glatz and the approach of large forces of the enemy caused him to abandon the enterprise. The Russians were moving on Silesia and he set out to prevent their junction with the Austrians. Daun and his army hung close after Frederick but did not seem disposed to risk an engagement. Loudon with 50,000 Austrians attempted to invest Breslau, but was prevented by the timely arrival of Prince Henry's troops. Daun and Loudon joined forces on the Katzbach near Liegnitz. The Austrians after this junction numbered 95,000 men, while the force that Frederick was leading into Silesia composed but 30,000. On August 14 Frederick saw from the movements of his adversaries that he was about to be attacked and rightly guessed that another night attack would be attempted. He, therefore, after dark changed his position somewhat and when the combined forces of the Austrians advanced upon him several hours before daybreak on the following morning, it was they and not Frederick who received the surprise. It was a hard fought battle, but the Prussians were completely victorious and lost but 3,500 men, while the Austrians lost 10,000 men and eighty-two guns. Frederick now pushed forward and joined Prince Henry at Breslau. Daun retired to the Bohemian frontier and the Russians who had entered Silesia, hastily retreated to the borders of Poland. Soon thereafter, the information came that the Russians were marching on Berlin. On October 6, Frederick with his army set out to save the Capital. Nine days later, on reaching the frontier of Mark Brandenburg, he learned that the Russians and Austrians had already occupied Berlin. But the occupation was of brief duration. On learning of the approach of the King, the forces withdrew. The enemy had secured 2,000,000 thalers and destroyed or carried away great stores of ammunition. Worse even than this disaster was the fact that nearly all of Saxony had again fallen into the hands of the enemy. In driving them out, success attended the Prussian arms from the outset. Wittenberg and Leipsic were recaptured and Daun with his army of 64,000 went into camp near Torgau. His position was in many respects the same as that of the Russians at Cunnersdorf. The army of King Frederick numbered but 44,000, but he decided to attack, and did so on the third day of November. The battle lasted through the afternoon and far into the night. During the battle Frederick was unhorsed by being struck in the breast by a bullet. The wound was, however, slight, as he had been protected by a heavy fur coat which he wore. When darkness came it was doubtful which army had gained the victory, but the matter was definitely settled after darkness had set in by the arrival of General Zieten upon the rear of the Austrians. Daun was wounded and the Austrians retreated across the Elbe. The losses on both sides had been tremendous. Those of the Prussians were 12,000, and those of the Austrians 16,000. Frederick advanced into Silesia in May, 1761, to prevent the junction of Loudon, with 75,000 men, and the Russians, numbering 60,000. After maneuvering for three months the two armies affected a junction in spite of Frederick's efforts. He realized the folly of attempting an attack on this force and went into camp near Bungelwitz. The army labored day and night to make it unconquerable. Intrenchments were thrown up, pits and trenches were dug and the ground was undermined. The hostile forces formed a crescent about the camp and several weeks passed in watching and waiting. Finally, the Russians, lacking in provisions, grew discontented and departed, with the exception of 12,000 men, who were left with the Austrians. A little later Loudon moved his camp to the hills, some distance from the Prussians. On the night of Sep-

tember 30 Loudon attacked and captured the town of
Schweidnitz.   Frederick now removed his camp to Streh-
len.   Here, during the following month, he was visited
by deputies from the Tartar, Kerim Geray, the enemy of
Russia, who offered to furnish troops for a consideration.
A treaty was made, but changes transpired in the political situation the following year which prevented its execution.   Winter came on and still the hostile armies maintained their positions.   On January 5, 1762, Empress
Elizabeth, of Russia, died and was succeeded by Peter
III, her nephew, a stanch friend and admirer of King
Frederick.   On May 5 a treaty of peace was made between
them and Russia restored to Frederick the possessions
previously taken by the Russians.   Corps of Russian
troops who had been allies of the Austrians were recalled
or transferred to become the allies of Frederick.   With this
unexpected and welcome aid, Frederick concentrated his
forces in Silesia.   Before he could use the allies of Russia against his enemies to any great advantage, Peter III
of Russia, who had made himself intensely unpopular,
was dethroned and soon after died.   Empress Catherine,
who succeeded him, revoked the treaty with Prussia and
recalled the troops.   On July 21, therefore, Frederick,
without the aid of the Russians, attacked the posts established by Daun and the Austrians were completely routed
and cut off from Schweidnitz.   The siege of Schweidnitz
occupied two months and was ended on October 9, 1762,
by a Prussian grenade which struck the powder magazine
of the Austrians and blew up the fort and many of the
garrison.   The last battle of the Seven Years' War was
fought October 29 near Freiberg, when the Prussians
won a brilliant victory.   After this battle both sides went
into winter quarters.   In England George II had died
and was succeeded by George III.   His minister, Lord

Bute, desired peace and early in November Frederick
received overtures for a cessation of hostilities from Austria. The necessary preliminaries were soon arranged,
and representatives of Prussia, Austria, and Saxony met
at Hubertsburg December 31 and began negotiations.
On February 15, 1763, the treaty was concluded. One
provision was that all possessions acquired by conquest
should be restored. Seven years of misery, toil, and bloodshed had resulted from the hatred and jealousy of one
sovereign for another. Yet the war had taught the world
a lesson in heroism and the possibilities of human attainment and had placed Prussia high among the Nations of
the earth. King Frederick returned to Berlin late in the
night on May 30 and was received with joyous acclamations by the populace. From this day to the close of his
life Frederick devoted himself to restoring and further
upbuilding the Nation and mending the injuries that had
been brought about by the war. Trade which had become
inactive was made once more to flourish, and lands which
had been neglected were made fruitful. The widows and
orphans of fallen heroes were provided for, and those
States which had suffered most were remunerated, and
every encouragement afforded them to fully recover from
the burdens they had been compelled to bear. The military department was also reorganized. The army was
brought up to its full strength, the fortresses repaired and
better equipped and the magazines replenished. In 1764
Frederick concluded an alliance with Russia. In 1769
Emperor Joseph II, of Austria, gratified a long desired
ambition in personally meeting Frederick and expressing his admiration, as he expressed it, for the "first of
Kings and greatest of warriors." The visit lasted several days and a treaty was entered into which bound the
two royal houses, long separated by strife, in a close bond

of friendship. Eight years later this bond was broken.
Maxamilian Joseph, Prince elector of Bavaria, died
December 30, 1777, and with him the royal family of
Pfalz-Bavaria became extinct. The succession would
naturally revert to Charles Theodore, Prince elector of
Pfalz, to whom, having no issue, Charles, Duke of Pfalz-
Zweibrucken, stood next in succession. Austria had long
coveted the possession of Bavaria and now interfered with
some unfounded pretensions, and sent an armed force
into Lower Bavaria and Upper Pfalz, demanded and
secured a compromise from Charles Theodore of one half
of his inheritance. The next in succession had not been
consulted at all. King Frederick decided that an act so
arbitrary could not be allowed to pass unchallenged.
Negotiations with the Emperor of Austria proved fruitless. Under these circumstances Frederick quickly concluded to take decisive action. He was now in his 67th
year, but promptly called his army together and himself
set out to take command of one division of the army. He
met the Austrian van at the borders of Bohemia. In the
meantime Prince Henry, with the Prussians under him,
had penetrated Bohemia and seized several magazines
belonging to Austria. Troops of the two Nations to the
number of 400,000 now faced each other and every indication pointed to a fierce and bloody war, but no great
battle took place during the disturbance, which continued
until 1779. Frederick's name carried fear and respect
with it and the Austrians never ventured further than to
make a few weak skirmishes against the Prussians.
Frederick contented himself with holding the enemy in
check and holding himself in readiness to take advantage
of any opportunity that might afford should the Austrians leave their intrenchments. France and Russia
finally interfered, and Austria, seeing the determination

of Frederick to continue the course he had taken, deemed
it prudent to yield and peace was signed on May 13, 1779,
Austria annulling the compromise made with Charles
Theodore.

Frederick spent the closing years of his life at his
beloved Sans Souci with his greyhounds and his literary
pursuits, yet attending with the greatest fidelity to the
affairs of the Kingdom. His solicitude for the welfare
of his people never abated while the breath of life remained
in him. His subjects, in turn, loved and revered him
as they would a father. From 1780 and thereafter he
was frequently attacked with illness and suffered considerably with the gout, but in spite of this and his age he
kept up the daily routine unremittingly. He even continued the tours through the provinces as late as 1785.
In August of that year he sat for five hours on horseback,
during a review in Silesia, through a drenching storm.
This perhaps hastened the end, although at the time it
seemed to affect him only to the extent of a slight indis-
position. Late in the fall symptoms of dropsy were
noticeable, and though tortured with this malady his activity did not abate. As the dropsy increased his sufferings
became acute, but no murmur of complaint escaped him.
At 4 and 5 o'clock in the morning he summoned his coun-
cilors and gave his orders and transacted all affairs relating to the State. By the middle of August his condition
became critical. On the morning of the 15th instant, he
continued to sleep until 11 o'clock. That day his voice
was extremely feeble, but his faculties were as active as
ever. The next day he was worse and for the first time
be failed to summon his cabinet. At 11 o'clock that
night, after inquiring the time, he announced that he
would rise at four the next morning. A few hours later,
on the morning of August 17, 1786, he died in the arms

of an attendant. Two other attendants and his physician were the only persons present. The next day, as the remains lay extended on a camp bedstead, clad in the uniform of the first battalion of the Guards, and the officers of the garrison came to pay their tribute, there were few among them who could restrain the flow of tears.

JOHN PAUL JONES
1747-1792

AMERICA'S FIRST GREAT SEA FIGHTER

Born among the peasantry of Scotland, John Paul,
the son of an humble gardener, without encouragement
and lacking in the advantage of even a meager education,
but possessed of an indomitable spirit and a constant and
passionate desire for fame, advanced, entirely through his
own exertions, to an eminence among the naval heroes of
the world which will forever keep his memory glorious
among Americans; while the greatness of his achievements compels the admiration and respect of every Nation.
To his imperturbable bravery, surpassing skill and unquestioned daring was added a singularly acute and conceptive
mind, which possessed the power to frame great projects
and forcefully convey the inspiration to others.   His was
a calm enthusiasm.   The apparent recklessness which
marked the execution of even his most hazardous exploits
had no part in the workings of his creative mind during
the time he evolved these desperate plans.   With cool
deliberations he estimated every chance for success or
failure and having once concluded to act he entered upon
the undertaking with a dash and persistence which death
alone could have dismayed.

The life of this brilliant man naturally had its blemishes.   Much of his earlier nautical experience had been
gained as a smuggler and in the slave trade.   He deserted
from service in the British navy, into which he had been
impressed, and to which his spirit of independence could

not submit. All of this was during his early youth and came about as a natural sequence of the influences which had up to that time surrounded him and practically made this restless soul a willing victim to circumstances. It was his advent in America at the time when the colonies were struggling to throw off the yoke of despotism that opened a new sphere for his ambitions and transformed him from a purposeless adventurer into a determined warrior in the cause of freedom against oppression. He entered upon this new career with earnestness and ardor and his devoted and illustrious services in behalf of his adopted country and the cause he espoused, stands out in untarnished splendor which totally obscures the misguided passions and erring judgment of his early life. Among the heroes of the world and among the great benefactors of the American Nation his name must continue to stand for all time in undiminished glory.

John Paul was born July 6, 1747, on the estate of Arbigland in the parish of Kirkbean and Stewartry of Kirkcudbright, Scotland. His father was employed as gardener on this estate, which occupies a jutting promontory on the sea shore. Both the mansion of Arbigland and the cottage in which John Paul was born, stand to this day and are pointed out by the passing mariner. Between the only two conditions which presented themselves to the lad, the sea with its enchanting view and the great ships passing by, and the irksome monotony of the peasant's life, it was but natural that his inclination should lean toward the former. His desires in this direction strengthened as he grew until, at the age of twelve, after persistent importunity, his father took him across the Firth to Whitehaven, where he was apprenticed to a merchant in the American trade. His first voyage was on the Friendship. He had already formed studious habits and applied himself zealously to everything that regarded

navigation.   While in the American port he remained
under the roof of an elder brother, William, who had
come to America some years previously and settled at
Fredericksburg, Virginia.   After several voyages his
skill became such that he was offered the place of third
mate on the King George, slaver of Whitehaven.

In 1766, though but 19 years of age, young Paul, who
had already sustained a considerable reputation as a navigator, became chief mate of a Jamaica slaver, a berth
which in those days required not only a sailor of no mean
ability, but a man of firm and decided character.   Two
years later he gave up his position in connection with this
nefarious business, having become disgusted with it, and
sailed as a passenger from Jamaica for Scotland on the
brigantine John, of Kirkcudbright.   During the voyage
both the master and the mate died of fever and Paul
assumed command and brought the vessel safely home.
The owners rewarded his skill by making him master
and supercargo, and as such he made two voyages to the
West Indies.   During the second voyage he caused a
sailor named Mungo Maxwell to be flogged for a breach
of discipline.   Shortly afterward, the sailor, having
embarked on another vessel, died of fever.   Claims were
made, but later substantially refuted, that Maxwell died
as a result of the punishment inflicted upon him by John
Paul.   The young navigator was extremely sensitive in
regard to this accusation and went to considerable trouble
and expense to disprove it.   This attitude tends to demonstrate that even then he was zealous to maintain a good
reputation as a commander and there is no instance during his whole career in which he is shown to have exercised cruelty either to his own men or his enemies.   Subsequent to this, according to general report, he engaged
extensively in smuggling, his base of operations being the
Isle of Man and later on Dover.   After a varied experi-

ence in this line he entered into the West India trade and while thus engaged was impressed into the Royal navy, a condition which was of short duration, for at the first opportunity he deserted, knowing that his position would never be anything but subordinate. He went to France, fitted out a ship of his own in the India trade, which also involved smuggling, and brought him into frequent clashes with the authorities. During this time he was, rightfully or wrongfully, accused of piracy.

In 1773 he sailed to America and settled in Virginia on the estate of his brother, who had died. He remained there long enough to make a failure of agriculture as a pursuit, and at the first outbreak of the colonies against the mother country he offered his services to America. During his residence in Virginia he had assumed the name of Jones. There are two versions of his reason for adopting this name. One is that he was sent on a secret mission to Great Britain in the interest of America, another that gratitude to a General Jones of Virginia, who had befriended him, induced him to take the name. At any rate the first authentic record of his entering the service of the colonies is on December 22, 1775, when Congress passed a resolution providing for equipping thirteen frigates and, among a number of other officers, appointed John Paul Jones as a first Lieutenant. The ship Alfred was made flagship of the squadron fitted out and to her Lieutenant Jones was assigned. E. Hopkins had been appointed Commander-in-Chief of the fleet and when he boarded the Alfred, Lieutenant Jones hoisted and displayed for the first time an American flag. It was not, however, the stars and stripes, that national standard not being adopted until two years later. The first flag as flown in this instance is believed to have represented a pine tree with a rattlesnake at its root in a position to strike. Jones was at this time 29 years of age, a per-

fect specimen of physical manhood, and every inch a sailor
and commander, as was subsequently demonstrated in the
most ample manner.

The squadron had been intended to operate against
Lord Dunsmore, who was at this time terrorizing the Virginia coast, but the Delaware river, in which the fleet
was fitted out, froze up so that the sea was not reached
until February of the following year. The British island
of New Providence in the Bahamas was then made the
objective goal and here, as a result of the Commander-
in-Chief's distrust of the pilots, Jones distinguished himself by guiding the ships safely into the harbor. Nearly
one hundred cannon and valuable munitions of war were
captured and on the return trip several prizes were taken.
Soon after this Jones was given command of the sloop
Providence of twelve guns and a crew of seventy men.
For some time he was engaged in convoying along the
coast from Boston to the Delaware and showed great
skill in avoiding and outwitting the enemy's cruisers.
Twice he engaged in running fights with the British frigate, Cerberus, and each time managed to escape and safely
deliver his convoys. For this service he was on August
8, 1776, presented by Congress with a commission as Captain and ordered on a six weeks' cruise against the enemy's
commerce. This was an adventurous cruise, during which
he encountered at different times two of the enemy's large
frigates and caused them to waste great quantities of
ammunition in vain efforts to capture him. He destroyed
the shipping and fisheries at the harbor of Canso and at
the island of Madam by swift, daring, and irresistible
moves, and at the expiration of forty-seven days returned
to Newport with sixteen prizes. These successful enterprises inspired the naval authorities with still greater confidence in his ability and valor, and an expedition was

planned for him which was well calculated to test his
intrepid soul.   He was directed to proceed to Isle Royale,
where over one hundred American prisoners were reported
to be incarcerated in the coal mines, and liberate them;
also to capture the coal fleet and destroy the fisheries.

November 2, 1776, Jones set out in the Alfred accompanied by the Providence.   Off Lauisburg he captured
three prizes, the most important being the Mellish, which
carried 10,000 uniforms and stores for Burgoyne's army.
These uniforms and stores were soon turned over to Washington's army, and that at a time when the Continental
troops were in an almost destitute condition.   The following day the Providence deserted and left the Alfred
to proceed alone on its mission.   Jones, nothing daunted,
continued on his way with his prizes, stopped at Canso
to destroy a transport and burn an oil warehouse and
buildings connected with the whale and cod fisheries.
Once more setting out for his destination, Jones during
a fog, captured and destroyed three coal vessels, notwithstanding the fact that they were under convoy, and two
days later a Liverpool privateer of sixteen guns fell into
his hands.   Arriving off Isle Royale he found the harbor
frozen up.   He was short of water and provisions, had
150 prisoners on his hands aside from the flotilla of prizes
and concluded to abandon the original enterprise.   During his return voyage he encountered, on St. George's
bank, the British frigate Milford, which gave chase.   He
was no match for the frigate and was in danger of losing
all his prizes.   But here again his quick judgment and
seamanship saved him.   As darkness approached and the
chase continued he directed his crews on the prizes to sail
for the nearest port, placed the Alfred between them and
the pursuing frigate and after raising the lights on the
Alfred, suddenly changed his course.   The frigate fol-

lowed and the next day came up with and engaged the
Alfred. Jones continued to maneuver and fight until a
favorable opportunity offered when he made his escape,
and on December 1 entered the harbor of Boston in triumph with his prizes. Instead of being rewarded for
this enterprise, Jones was superseded in the command of
the Alfred and by the appointment of a fresh batch of
captains, most of whom had seen no service, but were
commissioned as the result of wealth, social standing or
influence, Jones found himself eighteenth on the list
instead of sixth. He strove in every way possible to
have this injustice corrected but without avail. Still
eager for action he proposed to Congress an expedition
to the West Indies and was ordered by the marine committee to proceed with his plans and five vessels were put
at his disposal, but before his scheme could be carried into
action the jealousy of superior officers served to have the
order countermanded. He was, however, given the new
ship Ranger, of 18 guns, and ordered to France, carrying instructions to the American commissioners there to
supply him with a frigate. In the Ranger he sailed from
Portsmouth the first day of November, 1777, and arrived
safely at Nantes thirty-one days later, having captured
two prizes on his passage across. On presenting himself
at Paris he was disappointed and chagrined to discover
that the powerful frigate he had expected could not be
provided for him. Nevertheless he proceeded on the
Ranger to Quiberon bay, where a French fleet under command of Admiral la Motte Piquet was preparing to convoy some vessels to America with stores. Here, after
communicating with the Admiral, an exchange of salutes
was arranged and it was the first time that the flag of
America was recognized and saluted by a foreign power.

But inactivity was not to the liking of Paul Jones.

He left the coast of France April 10, having in contemplation a series of daring dashes along the British coast. April 14 he captured a brigantine bound for Ireland with flaxseed. Not desiring to divide his crew, he burned the ship and cargo. Three days later a second prize, convoying a cargo of great value fell into his hands, and this he sent into Brest. Next evening, when the Ranger was off the Isle of Man, he determined to destroy the shipping of Whitehaven, the port from which he first sailed as a boy. The project was an exceedingly daring one, and while the first attempt was delayed by untoward weather, a second effort was made, Jones himself leading a small party, which scaled the cliffs, captured a small fort and spiked forty cannon. The men detailed to fire the shipping failed in their duty and the only ship burned was one fired by Jones himself after the dawn had come and while, pistol in hand, he stood off the dismayed residents who had gathered to learn what was transpiring. Following this desperate, but not particularly valuable exploit, Jones decided to capture the Earl of Selkirk, with the idea of exchanging him for some desirable American prisoner. The Earl happened to be away from home and Jones' men allayed their disappointment by carrying away the family plate. This was afterward bought up by Jones and returned to Lady Selkirk with a letter of regret, for which Jones received the warm thanks of the Earl. On the morning of April 24 Jones was off Carrickfergus and discovered the Drake, a ship of twenty guns, coming out of the harbor. The commander of the Drake had been informed of what had happened at Whitehaven and was setting out to seek the Ranger. The Drake had, in addition to her own men, taken aboard a number of volunteers, so that her crew numbered 160 men. Jones disguised his ship as much as possible and kept her stern to

the Drake, which sent out a boat to reconnoiter the
stranger. The boat was captured and its crew made prisoners, whereupon the Drake bore down upon the Ranger
and a desperate battle at close range began and continued
for one hour and four minutes, at the end of which time,
the Drake having suffered greatly and her captain having
received a mortal wound, her crew called for quarter. The
losses in killed and wounded on the Drake were forty-two,
while on the Ranger but two were killed and six wounded.
After making repairs Jones, with the Drake and other
prizes, and over 200 prisoners, entered Brest, May 7, 1778.
The narrative of this gallant victory reached King Louis
XVI, who ordered Jones to Versailles to receive a better
command. Many honors were shown the intrepid sea-
fighter, but delay followed delay and not until Jones had
determined to return to the Ranger was an ill-fitted
squadron got ready for him in order that he might
under the American flag, fight against England both on
behalf of America and France. This squadron was made
up of the Alliance, an American frigate of thirty guns, in
which Lafayette had just returned from America; an old
French frigate which Jones named Bonhomme Richard,
hastily armed with a miscellaneous collection of forty guns,
mostly twelve pounders, but including six indifferent
eighteen pounders; the Pallas of thirty-two guns; the
Cerf of eighteen guns, and the Vengeance of twelve guns.
The crews comprised sailors of all nations and
tongues, men undisciplined, inexperienced and accepted
only owing to the desire of Jones to get to sea
after the months lost waiting for French promises to be
fulfilled. Finally, August 14, 1779, the redoubtable
squadron sailed from L'Orient. Within a few days disaffection and jealousies grew into mutinies and desertions.
Captain Landais, of the Alliance, was especially insolent,

NOTICE.

HOW TO OPEN A BOOK.

From "Modern Bookbinding."

Hold the book with its back on a smooth covered table; let the front board down, then the other, holding the leaves in one hand while you open a few leaves at the back, then a few at the front, and so on, alternately opening back and front, gently pressing open the sections till you reach the center of the volume. Do this two or three times and you will obtain the best results. Open the volume violently or carelessly in any one place and you will likely break the back and cause a start in the leaves. Never force the back of the book.

"A connoisseur many years ago, an excellent customer of mine, who thought he knew perfectly how to handle books, came into my office when I had an expensive binding just brought from the bindery ready to be sent home; he, before my eyes, took hold of the volume and tightly holding the leaves in each hand, instead of allowing them free play, violently opened in the center and exclaimed: 'How beautiful your bindings open!' I almost fainted. He had broken the back of the volume and it had to be rebound."

and by disobeying orders lost two valuable prizes. Many prizes were, however, safely taken into French ports. Finally on September 23 the Baltic fleet, of which Jones had been in quest, was sighted off Flamborough Head, in which vicinity he had been cruising after an unsuccessful effort, due to a gale, to attack Leith. The Baltic fleet was under the convoy of the powerful English frigate Serapis, and the Countess of Scarborough of twenty-two guns. They were within two leagues of the coast and in sight of Scarborough castle. Jones' squadron, owing to the lack of harmony and discipline which existed, was widely scattered. He signaled his three companion ships to form in line of battle, and the captain of the Alliance as usual disregarded the order, following it up during the desperate conflict, which shortly ensued, by deliberately firing upon the Bonhomme Richard and exhibiting the most treasonable conduct. The battle between the Serapis and the Bonhomme Richard was unquestionably one of the most terrific encounters in the history of naval warfare, and this victory of John Paul Jones over an enemy greatly his superior from every standpoint places him, when the battle is calmly viewed in its various stages, preëminently as the highest type of the heroic, undaunted warrior ready to die in glorious combat, but proudly unyielding and unwavering. It may here be of interest to peruse the brief and modest official account of the battle written by Jones himself aboard the Serapis off the Texel, several days after the encounter.

"I have only time, my dear friends," he writes, "to inform you, that I have this day anchored here, having taken this ship in the night of the 23d ult., on the coast of England, after a battle of three hours and a half; two hours and a half of that time the Good Man Richard and this ship being fast along side of one another, both ships being in flames, and the Good Man Richard making water faster than all the pumps could deliver it.   This ship mounts forty-four guns, and has two entire batteries, one of them eighteen pounders, so that my situation was severe enough, to have to deal with such an enemy in such a dreadful situation.   Judge then, what it must have been when the Alliance came up, toward the close of the action, and, instead of assisting me, directed her whole fire against the Good Man Richard, not once or twice, but repeatedly, after being spoke to, and showing a private signal of recognizance.

"The Alliance killed eleven men, and mortally wounded an officer on the Good Man Richard's forecastle at one volley.   I have lost, in killed and wounded, the best part of my men.   The Good Man Richard went to the bottom on the morning of the 25th ult. in spite of every effort to bring her into port.   No action before was ever, in all respects, so bloody, so severe, and so lasting.   I beg of you to communicate this, with my best respects, to the gentlemen of your port.

"The fire was not quite extinguished on board of the Good Man Richard till eight hours after the enemy had struck; and at last it had reached within a few feet of the magazine.   We lost all the stores and all our private effects; but no lives were lost from the conflagration. The Pallas took at the same time an armed ship of twenty six pounders.   The prizes taken and ransomed by the Good Man Richard during her cruise of about three months' amount to at least one million livres."

It was 7 o'clock in the evening with beautiful serene weather and a light southwesterly breeze when the action really began.   For several hours previously the vessels had been slowly maneuvering and gradually approaching each other.   The Scarborough had drawn close to the

Serapis, and the English cruisers were confident of victory. The decks had long been cleared for action and there had been ample time for reflection as the rival craft silently drew near each other. Coming within pistol shot, Captain Pearson, from the bridge of the formidable appearing Serapis, hailed the Richard with, "What ship is that?" "I cannot hear what you say," was the sarcastic retort from the Richard. The hail was repeated with a threat to fire unless immediate answer was made. The answer was a shot from the Richard. Immediately there was an exchange of broadsides. This was the beginning of that memorable conflict which continued unabated through the twilight of that September evening, grew fiercer as the dusk deepened and waged with relentless fury far into the darkness of the night. At the very first fire of the Richard two of the miserable eighteen pounders burst, spreading death and ruin on every hand. Jones ordered the lower deck ports closed and made no further effort to use that battery during the engagement.

After many terrific exchanges of broadsides, during which the rotten sides of the Richard suffered so that she began to leak, the constant maneuvering for position, in which the Serapis, owing to her superior qualities, usually fared best, although her crew were suffering terribly from the musketry and grenades in the Richard's tops, Jones determined to get at closer quarters and succeeded in bringing his ship alongside the Serapis. With his own hands he assisted in lashing them together. The guns of each ship touched the sides or protruded into the decks of the other; there were frequent hand to hand skirmishes. Fires were frequent on both vessels and every part of the decks presented a scene of carnage. An hour after the battle began and just after the ships had grappled and an attempt at boarding by Jones had been repelled, Cap-

tain Pearson hailed him with, "Has your ship struck?"
Jones proudly retorted, "I have not yet begun to fight."
Later on when most of the guns on the Richard were disabled and her decks strewn with dead and wounded a
report spread that Jones and his only Lieutenant were
dead.   One of the crew ran to the quarter deck to strike
the flag and there found Jones undismayed and calm,
helping to work his three remaining guns.

"If you do not strike," shouted Pearson, "I will sink
you at the next broadside."   "Sink me if you can," was
Jones' reply.   "If I must go to the devil, I would rather
strike to him than to you."

In the midst of this the Alliance, which had attempted
to take no part in the engagement, came up on the larboard side of the Richard and deliberately fired into her
several times, despite the fact that signals of recognition
were flashed and voices shouted out in protest to Captain
Landais.   This fire killed and wounded several of the
Richard's men.

Finally, with the best part of the men on both ships
killed or wounded, with the Richard in a sinking condition and men at the pumps, with the yards and spars of
the Serapis destroyed and her upper decks rendered untenable by the effective work of the men in the Richard's tops,
and with both ships on fire, the commander of the Serapis
surrendered to his indomitable adversary.   The Richard
was kept afloat two days, when she went to the bottom,
Jones having transferred his wounded and prisoners
to the Serapis.   The victory was solely due to the immov-
able courage, self composure, and brilliant skill of Jones.
Throughout the engagement he displayed the noblest
heroism, taking an active part from time to time in every
phase of the fighting, from firing cannon to repelling in
hand-to-hand conflicts boarders from the Serapis.   On

October 7 Jones reached Amsterdam, where he was lionized and where his presence did much to inspire friendly feeling for his adopted country and the cause of the colonies. Another "glorious accomplishment," as Dr. Franklin expressed it, resulting from the services of Jones was the liberation of American captives who had long languished in English prisons. Including the prisoners captured by the Pallas, which gave a good account of herself while Jones was fighting the Serapis by defeating the Scarborough, he had in his custody over 500 Englishmen, and these were eventually exchanged for Americans. Of this accomplishment Jones was as proud as of his victories, showing that he possessed the virtue of sympathetic humanity as well as bravery.

While his squadron lay anchored at the Texel, Holland, undergoing repairs with a score of British cruisers waiting outside for him to make his appearance, Jones remained for a season in Paris, was feted and applauded and presented with a sword by Louis XVI. He soon grew weary of court surroundings and boarded the Alliance, from which Captain Landais had been dismissed in disgrace, and during a favorable gale at night slipped out of the harbor and away from the British cruisers so anxiously watching for him. His resulting cruise in the Alliance was disheartening, and owing to the constant clamor of his crew for the prize money due them, Jones conveyed his ship to L'Orient arriving there February 10, 1780. In October of that year, being furnished with the Ariel, a King's ship of twenty guns, by the French minister of marine, Jones sailed for America. During the passage he engaged the English privateer, Triumph, whose captain after brief resistance struck his colors but made all sail and escaped before a prize crew could board her. Jones arrived in Philadelphia February 18, 1781. Here the highest honors awaited him. In April Congress passed a vote of thanks for the "zeal, prudence, and intrepidity with which he had sustained the honor of the American flag; for his bold and successful enterprise, with a view to redeem from captivity the citizens of America, who had fallen into the hands of the English; and for the eminent services by which he had added luster to his own character and his associates."

He was also presented by Congress with a gold medal as a token of the high estimation in which he was held by the government of the Republic.

For these honors bestowed upon him Jones was deeply grateful, but he had not forgotten the injustice done him when he was relieved of the command of the Alfred, and again besought Congress to give him proper recognition. The committee to which the memorial was referred recommended that Jones be promoted to the rank of Rear Admiral, but again the jealousies of others whom he would supersede interfered and the matter was referred back to the committee and never again brought forward. At this time there was on the stocks at Plymouth the first American ship of the line, America, and on June 23 Congress authorized her speedy launching and equipping. Three days later Congress balloted for a commander of the America and Jones was unanimously chosen. This was entirely satisfactory to him. It appears that during all of his time of service Jones had received no funds from Congress in the line of pay and there was due him something like $13,000. He had out of his own resources paid the crews of the Alfred and Ranger, and we find him on the 28 of June petitioning the President of Congress for $1,000 with which to pay his debts in Philadelphia that he might go to Portsmouth to superintend the equipping of the America. On reaching Portsmouth late in August he was chagrined to find that the ship was only half completed and there was even a lack of material with which to proceed with the work. It was not until toward the close of 1782 that the completion of the America, which Jones had so enthusiastically awaited, was perfected. It was the largest ship of seventy-four guns in the world, measuring 182 feet 6 inches on the upper-gun decks and 50 feet 6 inches in extreme breadth. Jones eagerly looked forward to the moment when he should be given the opportunity with this ship to add further glory to his country and himself. Again he was doomed to disappointment. About this time a squadron of French line of battleships entered Boston harbor when one of them, the Magnifique, was stranded and lost. Congress considered it a duty to make good this loss and decided to present the America to France to replace the Magnifique. This was done. Jones had remained inactive for nearly two years and finally received consent from Congress to serve on the French frigate Triumphant as a volunteer. Not long after joining this ship, and before any further opportunities had presented themselves for him to reap more glory, peace was declared and hostilities ceased.

Jones returned to Philadelphia, and having recovered from a fever which, however, left his constitution greatly shattered, he repaired for a time to the country. America had as yet received none of the prize money due for ships captured in European waters, and Jones was delegated, on recovering his health, to proceed to Paris and collect the same. After more than a year of persistence he succeeded. In December, 1787, while in Paris it was reported to him that the Russian ambassador at Versailles had intimated that he would be a valuable acquisition to the navy of Empress Catherine in the war then being waged by Russia against the Turks. This awakened anew his enthusiasm. Soon after this Jones was offered the position of Captain Commandant in the Russian navy. He did not think the honor was high enough and he was made a Rear Admiral and given a squadron in the Black sea. He rendered distinguished service in the engagements in which he participated, but at the expiration of eight months as a result of jealousies and rivalry he was recalled and kept in idleness for a time and finally given two years' leave of absence. This virtually amounted to a dismissal and Jones repaired to Paris, from whence he kept up a fruitless correspondence with Russia in an effort to be restored to favor and active service.

His constitution had gradually broken down, dropsy manifested itself and he became a helpless invalid. He declined rapidly and on July 18, 1792, after making his will as "a citizen of the United States," the unconquered hero of the seas gave up the ghost. Two days later his remains were followed to the grave by many distinguished men of the day, including twelve members of the National assembly.

NELSON
1758-1805

THE HERO OF TRAFALGAR

From his earliest years Horatio Nelson was endowed with that daring spirit and love of adventure, which, put to the test in the service of his King and country, established his memory for all time as one of the most illustrious among the men who have filled the front rank in National contests.

Courageous to the degree of rashness, of sound judgment, self possessed, confident, full of resources, he combined to an extraordinary degree all of the qualifications which made his career glorious, startled the world and changed the history of Europe.

His history contains one dark chapter. The responsibility for this is due to the one ruling weakness in this strong man's nature—susceptibility to the influence of a wicked, intriguing woman, who caused him to place a blot upon his own name and brought the blush of shame to the cheeks of his countrymen.

He was born at Burnham-Thorpe, Norfolk, England, September 29, 1758. His father was Edmund Nelson, a rector, and Horatio was the younger son in a family of eleven children. His mother died shortly after his birth and the shaping of his young mind was left entirely to the father, who acted both as parent and schoolmaster. Young Nelson's connection with the British navy began when he was twelve years old. At this time, through the aid of Captain Maurice Suckling, his uncle, who commanded the Raisonable, permission was reluctantly given, and the lad was taken aboard. After completing two cruises with his uncle he embarked on a merchant vessel for a protracted voyage and after his return to England, enlisted with a North polar expedition which occupied a year of his life.

These enterprises, fraught as they were with all the rude experiences, the hardships and rigors of a sailor's life, served the double purpose of bestowing upon the youth a thorough knowledge of seamanship, strengthened his constitution, which had been feeble from infancy, and thus fortified him mentally and physically to meet the exigencies which the future demanded of him.

Returning again to England from this severe schooling in the arctic regions he once more found service in the navy, being placed by his uncle on board a corvette bound for a voyage in the Indian ocean. He was there affected by the unhealthy latitude and at one period during this time, according to his own accounts, was so overcome with melancholy that he felt prompted to abandon his profession and even contemplated suicide. But at this critical moment in his life the heroic impulses of his boyhood triumphed and he declared that if perish he must it should be in the service of his native land. He was permitted to return to England to recover his health and after a course of study, at the conclusion of which he passed a brilliant examination, he was appointed a Lieutenant in the Royal navy and ordered to American seas for service against the colonies then struggling for independence.

Soon afterward he participated in expeditions fitted out against French and Spanish colonies and in this service he was repeatedly marked for distinction owing to the many hazardous tasks in which he was involved, and which he persistently sought. His services were recognized and appreciated to the extent that although but twenty-one years of age he was given command of a sloop of twenty-six guns. His first winter as Post Captain was passed in a cruise of the North sea and in the spring he was ordered to return to the American coast where he further distinguished himself by a number of exploits and captures which secured for him high compliments from the King and enabled him to triumph over the naval authorities in a controversy involving prize money.

Following this came practically the only period of peace in Nelson's life. He was on March 11, 1787, married to Mrs. Nisbet, a young widow of nineteen. With his bride he returned to the home of his father and his childhood. Here he gave himself up to absolute repose and to all appearances had banished entirely from his mind all thoughts of the ocean and occupied himself wholly with the interests which surrounded him in his rural abode. His retirement from the navy was deplored not only by his companions in arms but the Nation at large as he had already been singled out as a hero and it is of record in the journal of one of his fellow officers, written at the time, that Nelson's retirement was a most serious loss to the navy as "he would have been the greatest naval commander this country has ever produced."

But Nelson had not lost the indomitable spirit which had thus far controlled him, for when the occasion arose he was as ready and eager as ever to respond to the call of his country. The interruption to his peaceful domestic life came in 1792 when war broke out with France. Nelson was then, at the recommendation of Lord Hood, appointed to the command of the Agamemnon, a ship of the line. He was ordered to the Mediterranean to protect the coast and harbor of Naples. While thus engaged he took part in land engagements, among them being the

siege of Bastia and the investment of Cadiz.   In the latter engagement he suffered the loss of one of his eyes.

It was during Nelson's early operations in the Mediterranean that the most baneful event in his career was
brought about.   Always susceptible to the attentions of
women he here permitted himself to take a step which
ruined his domestic relations and would doubtless, but for
the splendor of his achievements in the service of his
country, have blighted his future.   This circumstance in
his life began with an attachment for Lady Hamilton,
wife of the English ambassador at Naples.   Nelson was
received by Sir Hamilton with great pomp and ceremony.
Sir Hamilton's announcement to Lady Hamilton of the
coming of Nelson was prophetic.   "I am going to in-
troduce to you," he said, "an officer who has not much
pretension to personal beauty, but who is one day destined
to astonish the world by his great achievements."

Thus prepared by her husband, Lady Hamilton, a
beautiful and talented adventuress of obscure birth, at
once planned to exercise her blandishments upon Nelson
to enslave him in order that she might further her own
interests in the intrigues of the court of Naples against
France.   Nelson willingly abandoned himself to the influences of this wily woman and to such an extent that it
eventually led to separation from his wife, incurred dis-
pleasure of his Sovereign, and ultimately resulted in his
acquiescence to a cruel crime which forms a dark blot
upon the glory of his career.   His infatuation for Lady
Hamilton was such that on several occasions he even dis-
obeyed the orders of his Government in order that he
might remain near Naples and Lady Hamilton.

Grave, however, as were his errors during this period
he still continued to retain the confidence of his superiors
and following his successful operations during the winter
of 1795 and 1796 in cutting off the supplies for the French

army on the Italian coast, he was made Commodore. In
1796, when Spain formed an alliance with France and
declared war, Nelson succeeded in another of those
remarkable enterprises of reckless courage and audacious
bravery which caused the world to marvel. During the
battle off Cape St. Vincent on February 13, 1797, while
the Spanish Admiral was endeavoring to re-form his
broken line of battle and was on the point of succeeding,
Nelson, disregarding the explicit orders of his superiors,
boldly attacked a detached section of the Spanish squadron
with his single ship and so vigorously and skillfully did
he engage the greatly superior number of the enemy that
the Spanish Admiral was compelled to withdraw in defeat.
For his promptitude and valor on this occasion, even
though he acted in disregard of the rules of the service,
Nelson was made an Admiral and decorated with the
order of the Bath. It was shortly after this while
engaged in an attack on Santa Cruz that he lost an arm.

We now come to a period in Nelson's career where his
recognized genius and superiority as a sea fighter received
an additional and signal impetus by the conferring upon
him of an independent command. Bonaparte had
embarked at Toulon a force on the most formidable fleet
that had navigated the Mediterranean since the Crusades.
This move, secretly and hastily accomplished, left the
British ministry in doubt regarding the real object of the
expedition. Lord St. Vincent, then in command of the
English naval forces, did not dare to abandon the blockade of Cadiz and the French ports. He selected Nelson
to pursue and if possibly destroy the armament of the
French. With sixteen ships of the line, including his
flagship, the Vanguard, Nelson set out blindly to seek
the enemy, having no information of a definite nature
concerning their course. His task was one of extreme
difficulty. He visited Corsica and vainly searched the

Spanish Main, finally returning to Naples January 16,
1798, discouraged and sadly lacking in stores and
ammunition. Added to the unenviable condition in
which he found himself he here received the disheartening information that the French had reduced Malta and
had again departed upon some unknown course. Nelson
concluded that the French were destined for Egypt, but
before reëntering the pursuit it was necessary that his
ships should receive fresh equipments. Through Lady
Hamilton's influence at the Neapolitan court he was
enabled to supply his wants notwithstanding the openly
avowed neutrality of Naples, and within a few days he
was once more scouring the seas in quest of the French
fleet.

After traversing the Mediterranean and the Egyptian
sea and receiving from time to time bitter reports
from his native land of accusations of incapacity and
dilatoriousness which were being made against him
there, his persistence was finally rewarded at dawn on
August 1st when he discovered the French fleet at
anchor in the Bay of Aboukir, six leagues from Alexandria and close to the mouth of the Nile. With the
quickness and precision which always characterized his
judgment on occasions of great moment, Nelson's plan
of attack was hastily formed and promptly put into execution. The French squadron was located in an
apparently secure position. Admiral Brueys had
moored his fleet, which consisted of seventeen men-of-
war and a number of smaller vessels, in the Bay of
Aboukir. Six of the most powerful of his vessels he
had arranged in a concave crescent following the sweep
of the shore, supported on one side by the Island of
Aboukir well fortified with cannon; the other side had
the protection of an advanced arm of the bay.

ADMIRAL NELSON

Painting by John Abbott, National Portrait Gallery,
London

An attack from the rear was deemed impossible, owing to the presence of treacherous shoals which were counted upon to prevent the advance of an enemy's ships from that quarter. Brueys' first act on sighting the English fleet was to send out two light brigs with instructions to reconnoiter the enemy and then to seek refuge in the bay by crossing the shoals, thus attempting to decoy the British into following the same course in the hope that their ships would run aground. Nelson, however, was cognizant of the danger, and paid no attention to the brigs. Instead he advanced directly upon the head of the French line, suddenly altered his course and passed between the Island of Aboukir and the French fleet with half of his squadron and, gaining the desired position in the rear of the French, after being compelled to leave one of his vessels—the Culloden—stranded on the sandbanks. The other half of Nelson's squadron remained in front of the French line. Until the maneuver had been fully carried out, Nelson did not fire a shot, but immediately upon obtaining his point of vantage, the anchored French fleet was simultaneously attacked upon both flanks. The fate of the French ships became at once apparent. There could be but one result. Although the French fought with desperation and displayed the greatest bravery, they were completely at the mercy of the foe. One by one the warships of France were disabled and wrecked, while their decks presented scenes of indescribable carnage and destruction. With the exception of two ships which escaped by taking to flight, the French fleet was utterly destroyed. The battle had raged far into the night, and the final and most spectacular incident in the catastrophe occurred an hour before midnight, when Admiral Brueys' flagship, the Orient, blew up with a

terrific detonation. When the morning sun rose over
the Bay of Aboukir all that remained of the proud
French fleet was but the remnants of stranded hulls and
burning vessels tossed about by the action of the waves.

The victory of Nelson was conceded by contemporary historians to be the most complete since the inven-
tion of gunpowder. Nelson's fleet had not escaped
injury in the battle. Eighteen days were required to
repair his squadron sufficiently to enable him to put to
sea. As a consequence of the annihilation of so great a
share of the French navy Nelson was directly responsible
for the capitulation of the French army in Egypt which,
without the aid and support of the navy, was practically
imprisoned in the land it had conquered. Toward the
conclusion of the battle of the Nile Nelson received a
wound in the forehead which he believed to be mortal.
Confident that complete victory had been gained, he
called his chaplain and calmly imparted to him the last
remembrances to his family and country. It was soon
determined, however, that his injury was superficial, and
this knowledge among the crews caused as great rejoic-
ing as did the outcome of the engagement.

Nelson's victory in the Bay of Aboukir furnished
conclusive and corroborative proof of the supremacy of
the English navy. It had been repeatedly demonstrated
previously in lesser battles that British ships and sailors
were superior to those of France, but in the great triumph at the Nile the navy of Great Britain gained a
complete ascendancy. It gave inspiration to the entire
naval service and imbued officers and men with a new
spirit that made England's ships and Nelson's name
feared and respected all the world over.

Scarcely had his wound healed when Nelson hastened to Naples and gave himself up afresh to the

domination of Lady Hamilton. The French were moving upon Naples, and this astute woman strenuously advocated the flight of the King and Queen. Owing to her relations with Nelson she had little difficulty in persuading him to receive the royal family together with herself and her husband on board his flagship and convey them, on the night of December 21st, in safety to Palermo, Sicily. In the meantime a Republic had been proclaimed in Naples, and Lady Hamilton instilled into Nelson's mind the hatred which she herself, as well as the King and Queen, possessed for the Republicans. At her solicitation Nelson assembled eighteen vessels and, accompanied by the woman who had begun to play an important rôle in his life, he sailed for Naples and entered the bay with his whole fleet under full sail, June 25, 1799. On his arrival, however, he found that the revolution had been put down and Naples occupied by the army of Cardinal Rufo, who had remained loyal to the court. The cardinal had entered into a treaty of capitulation which had been ratified by a representative of England, but the revengeful woman who stood beside Nelson on the bridge of his flagship would hear of no treaty. She demanded a full measure of satisfaction for her friend the Queen, and coerced Nelson into disregarding the treaty. The result of which instituted a reign of terror in which a massacre of forty thousand citizens followed before the vengeance of the Queen was satisfied. More painful even than this action of Nelson's in granting a horrifying license of treachery was his treatment of a former friend and companion in arms, Caraccioli, Admiral of the Neapolitan navy. Caraccioli had attended the King to Palermo as a faithful adherent, but after the revolution was accomplished he returned to Naples with the full permission of his Sovereign to save his estates from confiscation. The new Government, against his own desires, created him Commander-in-Chief of the naval forces. During the negotiations for surrender his friends, foreseeing the vengeance of the Queen, aided him to escape, but he was arrested and brought back. Here transpired the darkest act in Nelson's life. His abject slavery to Lady Hamilton, who had already caused this brave and truly heroic man to bring disgrace upon himself and the Nation he had so often meritoriously served, now induced him to lend himself to judicial murder. Caraccioli was delivered over to the English squadron on the demand of Nelson, who merely repeated the demand of Lady Hamilton. Further obeying her desires, Nelson charged a court-martial with the task of condemning the wretched Caraccioli. The members of the court-martial, after a vain effort to seek clemency in his behalf, sentenced the prisoner to perpetual banishment, but Nelson himself, at the dictation of the woman he so shamelessly served, changed the reading of the warrant to death instead of banishment. The execution was to take place in a few hours, and Nelson shut himself in his cabin with the woman who was responsible for this inglorious page in his history and refused to listen to all intercessors. Caraccioli, bound and fettered like a criminal, was taken aboard his own flagship, the Minerva, and there ignominiously hanged to the yardarm after Nelson, as a final act of cruelty, had refused him even the boon of being shot instead of strangled. For these disgraceful services Nelson was created Duke of Bronte by the King of Naples and given a revenue in proportion to his rank.

Returning to England during the winter of 1800, Nelson was received with the greatest honors. The

Government and the corporation of London bestowed
on him presents of great value and addresses of thanks,
and the whole Nation hailed him as a savior.   Lady
Hamilton accompanied him, but to all else except the
greatness of his services to his country the English
Nation was blind.

Nelson separated from his wife, making no effort
to screen himself from his guilt.   He secured a
house in the country at Merton, and there lived
for a time in quiet.   He was soon again, however,
called upon to perform a service for England.   Early
in 1801 a British fleet was fitted out to move against
Denmark, which headed the northern courts in a
renewal of the armed neutrality of 1780.   This fleet was
placed in charge of Sir Peter Parker for the reason that
negotiations were to be attempted before the harsher
arguments of force were resorted to.   Nelson was
placed second in command, and his duty began where
that of Parker ended.   Diplomatic efforts failed, and
April 7th the British warships cast anchor around the
capital of Denmark.   All arrangements for a desperate
resistance had been completed.   The city was protected
by formidable batteries and a heavily armed fleet protected by a shoal, similar in a manner to the situation
at Aboukir, formed a strong addition to the defense
of the Danish capital.   On May 2nd Nelson made the
attack.   He was at a disadvantage in having to deal
with both forts and ships simultaneously, and in forcing
his way inside the shoal lost three of his ships by ground-
ing.   The Danish fleet was practically destroyed, but
Nelson's ships had also suffered severely, and the land
batteries were still effective.   His attitude, however,
was so threatening against the city that a truce was
formed, which resulted in a peaceful agreement.   In

1803 Nelson was appointed to the Mediterranean squadron, and for two years his unceasing vigilance kept the French fleets penned up in harbors while Napoleon was waiting for them to appear in the British Channel to aid in his great project of invading England. Nelson, at the expiration of this period, returned to England to seek a few months of repose at Merton. He had, however, enjoyed this privilege but a few days when the information came that the fleet of Villeneuve, which Nelson had so long and fruitlessly sought, had put in to Cadiz to refit. The supreme moment of Nelson's career was at hand. Eagerly he prepared for the duty before him. He expressed the greatest confidence in his ability to completely annihilate the combined French and Spanish fleet, and seemed only to long for the opportunity of meeting them. Yet it was with a premonition of death that he left Lady Hamilton and his sisters at Merton. In his private diary, dated September 14, 1805, appears the following: "At half past ten, drove from dear, dear Merton, where I left all which I hold dear in this world, to go and serve my King and country. May the great God, before whom I bend, enable me to fulfill the expectations of my country; and if it be His good pleasure that I should return, my thanks will never cease being offered up to His throne of mercy. If, on the other hand, it is His good providence to cut short my days upon earth, I bow with the greatest submission, full of confidence in the hope that He will protect those so dear to me that I may leave behind. His will be done. Amen. Amen. Amen." There are numerous other evidences that the image of death was before his mind from this time forward until it actually came, as he expected. Lamartine relates that at the moment of departure from England, Nelson sent for the custodian of his effects in London and directed him to engrave his name and a short expressive epitaph on the coffin constructed from the mainmast of the French three-decker, L'Orient, which had been presented to him after the victory at Aboukir. "I may want it on my return," was his prophetic remark. His embarkation on the Victory at Portsmouth was the occasion of a triumphal testimonial on the part of his countrymen. Thousands escorted and cheered him. On October 2nd Nelson arrived before Cadiz and learned, to his great satisfaction, that Villeneuve's fleet was still there. Nelson did all he could to encourage the sailing of the French fleet by keeping his squadrons out of sight of land and depending upon reports of the enemy's movements from his scouting frigates. Nelson is variously reported by historians to have had thirty-three or thirty-four sail, while the combined fleet under Villeneuve is given by some authorities as exactly equal in number to that of Nelson. Lamartine, however, asserts that the French and Spanish fleet was composed of forty-two men-of-war and eight frigates. The orders of Nelson for the expected battle were brief and simple. They were in pursuance of his usual course, to break the opposing line and engage in detached groups. Just as the sun was peeping above the horizon on the morning of October 20th, Villeneuve's fleet started out of Cadiz and Nelson received frequent reports from his frigates of the course being pursued by the enemy. The movements of the French fleet seemed undecided, and it was evident that Villeneuve, whose final departure from Cadiz was the result of accusations of cowardice by Napoleon, was not eager to meet the British in spite of the imposing array with which he was attended. All day Nelson waited in vain for the enemy to reach the open sea. Before dawn the following morning Nelson was informed that the enemy was still at sea and inclining northward. With his squadron he set off obliquely in the same direction. When the sun came up it revealed the combined fleets about eight leagues distant. As the British ships were crowding toward the enemy in two columns, one led by Nelson in the Victory and the other by Collingwood in the Royal Sovereign, Nelson descended to his cabin and gave another evidence of his singular piety by inscribing upon his journal the following prayer: "May the great God, whom I worship, grant to my country, and for the benefit of Europe in general, a great and glorious victory; and may no misconduct in anyone tarnish it; and may humanity, after victory, be the predominant feature in the British fleet. For myself, individually, I commit my life to Him who made me, and may His blessing light upon my endeavors for serving my country faithfully. To Him I resign myself, and the just cause which is intrusted to me to defend. Amen. Amen. Amen." At this moment, also, the thoughts of the warrior returned to her who had exercised such a dominant influence in his life, and whom he never again expected to see, for the prayer in his private journal is followed by a request to his country in these words:

"October the 21st, 1805, in sight of the combined fleets of France and Spain, distance about ten miles.

"Whereas, the eminent services of Emma Hamilton, widow of the Right Honorable Sir William Hamilton, have been of the very greatest service to our King and country, to my knowledge, without her receiving any reward from either our King or country—first, that she obtained the King of Spain's letter, in 1796, to his brother, the King of Naples, acquainting him of his intentions to declare war against England, from which letter the ministry sent out orders to then Sir John Jervis to strike a stroke, if opportunity offered, against either the arsenal of Spain or her fleets. That neither of these was done is not the fault of Lady Hamilton. The opportunity might have been offered. Secondly, the British fleet under my command could never have returned the second time to Egypt, had not Lady Hamilton's influence with the Queen of Naples caused letters to be written to the Governor of Syracuse that he was to encourage the fleet being supplied with everything, should they put into any port in Sicily. We put into Syracuse, and received every supply, went to Egypt, and destroyed the French fleet. Could I have rewarded those services, I would not now call upon my country, but as that has not been in my power, I leave Emma, Lady Hamilton, therefor, a legacy to my King and country, that they will give her an ample provision to maintain her rank in life. I also leave to the beneficence of my country my adopted daughter, Horatia Nelson Thompson, and I desire she will use in future the name of Nelson only. These are the only favors I ask of my King and country at this moment when I am going to fight their battle. May God bless my King and country and all those whom I hold dear. My relations it is needless to mention; they will, of course, be amply provided for.   NELSON AND BRONTE."

Nelson called upon Captain Henry Blackwood, of the Euryalus, and Captain T. M. Hardy, of the Victory, to sign the document as witnesses.

On returning to the quarterdeck Nelson appeared calm and serious, instead of displaying the usual fiery spirit to which the officers who stood about him had been accustomed. Nelson was equally confident that

the battle which was now to be fought meant victory
for his country and death for himself. The fleet was
now bearing rapidly down upon the enemy, and Nelson
displayed from the masthead of the Victory the famous
signal, "England expects that every man will do his
duty." From every ship this signal was responded to
with enthusiastic cheers. It was now time for the captains of the various vessels to repair to their own ships,
and Captain Blackwood clasped Nelson's hand and
assured him of victory. That the presentiment of death
still clung to Nelson is seen by his reply. "Adieu,
Blackwood," he said, "I shall never see you again."

Within a few minutes later, Admiral Collingwood's
flagship, the Royal Sovereign, broke the enemy's line
and soon the Victory passed into a storm of lead poured
from the French ships. Scott, the secretary of Nelson,
fell at the commander's feet at the first shower of shot
and a second later a chain shot killed eight men on the
quarterdeck. Through the midst of this deadly hail the
Victory proceeded, reserving her fire for closer quarters.
She now became the target for the formidable French
Redoutable, the Bucentaur, and the Spanish Santissima
Trinidad of 150 guns, the greatest warship the world
had up to that time seen. The Redoutable was chosen
as the adversary of the Victory and having exchanged
broadsides, the two ships closed with a tremendous
shock, and the crews of each prepared to board the
other. The battle had quickly become general, and
terrific carnage was wrought on both sides. Some distance away, ten sail of the combined fleet had been stationed as a reserve squadron. In the confusion which
had already been brought about among the French and
Spanish ships, Villeneuve repeatedly signaled the reserve
ships for aid, but they seemed paralyzed and made no

move to enter the engagement.   In the meantime a
terrific struggle was in progress between the Victory
and Redoutable, whose commander, Captain Lucas,
proved a brave and unyielding foe.   Dense clouds of
smoke hovered over the scene of combat and sharpshooters in the rigging and tops poured an incessant
and deadly fire upon the decks of the enemy, while each
kept up a furious cannonade.   Villeneuve had soon after
the engagement began by accident got the bowsprit of
his vessel entangled in the stern gallery of the Santissima
Trinidad, and was unable to extricate it.   In this condition he was attacked by the British ships with the most
disasterous effects.   Hundreds of the officers and crew
were killed and finally, with his ship shot to pieces, and
every gun out of service, Villenueve was compelled to
surrender.   The Santissima Trinidad, deserted by her
companion battle-ships, struck her colors after four
hours of the most valiant resistance.   In the meantime a
succession of single combats had resulted in some cases
with terrific slaughter.   The Fougueux was commanded
successively by three officers, who fell one after the
other, surrendering only when 400 dead strewed her
decks.   The Achille was the last of Villeneuve's fleet to
resist.   Her crew continued to deal destruction upon
the British ships even after her decks had taken fire, and
as no effort was made to extinguish the flames, the ship
blew up with a terrific detonation, and in that moment
sent into eternity 500 men.

The battle between the Victory and the Redoutable
had, owing to the fact that their position was such that
neither could use its broadsides with effect, resolved
itself into a fire of musketry on both sides.   The French
riflemen picked off the British officers who were distin-
guishable by their decorations.   Nelson wore upon his

uniform the stars for orders with which he had been decorated by his own and other governments. These
ornaments made him a conspicuous mark. Before the
battle some of his officers had discussed with each other
the advisability of suggesting to Nelson the removal of
these ornaments. This was not done, however, for the
reason that on a former similar occasion when this had
been suggested, he replied, "No, no, in honor I gained
and in honor I will die with them." On the Victory
200 were picked off by the French riflemen. Nelson
was standing in the midst of his fallen officers and men
when a musket-shot from the Redoutable struck him
between the shoulder and the neck. He fell face foremost upon the deck. As he raised himself to one knee
he calmly spoke to Captain Hardy, "I am killed, my
friend," he said, "the French have done for Nelson at
last." "I hope not," replied Hardy. "Hope nothing,"
replied Nelson, "the ball has pierced my spine."

As he was being carried below he noticed that the
tiller ropes had been shot away and gave orders to
replace them. Such was his indomitable interest in his
ship and the battle. He was placed on a cot in one of
the midshipmen's berths and the surgeon at once pronounced the wound mortal. Knowing that his last
hour had come, Nelson ordered the surgeons to pay no
attention to him, but employ themselves where their aid
would be of benefit. The dying commander inquired
with great frequency regarding the progress of the
battle. When he heard the cheers of the crew of the
Victory as from time to time the ships of the enemy
struck, his features lighted up and his eye flashed with
delight. At last Hardy came to announce an undisputed victory. Nelson's mind during his last moments
was concerned with his country and with the fatal love

which had caused the only blemishes on his glorious career. He requested Hardy to watch over Lady Hamilton. "Embrace me, Hardy," said he, and as Hardy bent over him and kissed his cheek, he said, "Thank God, I have done my duty." It was with these words on his lips that the noble and undaunted warrior died. The joy in England over the greatest naval triumph the Nation had ever achieved was saddened by grief over the death of Nelson. His remains were brought to England. The crew of the Victory carried the body of their commander to his last resting place in the vaults of St. Peter's Cathedral, and the whole Nation mourned. Monuments to his memory and greatness were raised in nearly every city of the Kingdom, and there were none to recall the two great errors of the warrior's life. Nor did the King and the country, to whom he appealed on behalf of Lady Hamilton, take cognizance of his request and thereby commemorate his fault. Twenty years after the death of Nelson, there died an unknown woman in an obscure section of Calais. She died in poverty, and had to be buried by public charity. The papers which she left behind disclosed that she was Lady Hamilton.

NAPOLEON I

1769-1821

"THE MAN OF DESTINY"

No character in the world's history has been more bitterly assailed than that of Napoleon, nor has any been accorded greater admiration or more fulsome praise. In the hands of some historians, even his best deeds and those incidents of his life which tend to show his noblest traits, have been unqualifiedly condemned and ascribed to sinister motives, while on the other hand the darkest chapters of his career have by ardent admirers been so adroitly painted as to add luster to his fame. Neither side of his character can obscure the other. The good and bad in him seem to have predominated by turns. The point in which he was always consistent was his insatiable ambition. To satisfy this he allowed nothing to stand in the way. To obtain a desired result, he did not hesitate to sacrifice numberless lives and the best blood of nations, yet he could weep on viewing the carnage after that result had been obtained. Born in obscurity, he arose, first gradually, then with tremendous strides, until he reached the zenith of fame. For a quarter of a century he deluged Europe with blood and woe, trod paths of glory unprecedented since the days of Alexander, attained an eminence of almost unparalleled power, from which he was hurled by the combined efforts of his enemies, arose again triumphant and serene, only to be once more denounced and banished, and to die a broken-hearted exile and a captive. Yet, after his death, the Nation which had cast him off wept that he was no more,

and honored his remains by bringing them to the capital
to rest in a tomb of unequaled magnificence. Throughout Napoleon's career, one fact stands undisputed and
unassailable—his genius and ability as a warrior. His
courage never failed him. Reverses did not daunt him,
nor did the most formidable obstacles dismay him. He
fought and suffered with his soldiers, and they laid down
their lives when called upon, with a fervor that passes
understanding. Never were troops more devoted to
their leader than were the soldiers of Napoleon. This
fervor began with the battle of the Bridge of Lodi, where
the veterans of the army nicknamed him, "the Little
Corporal." It was here, too, according to Napoleon's
own statement, that he first felt the spark of great ambition glowing within him. "Neither the quelling of the
sections," he says, "nor the victory of Montenotte, induced me to think myself a superior character. It was
not till after the terrible passage of the Bridge of Lodi
that the idea shot across my mind that I might become
a decisive actor in the political arena. Then arose, for
the first time, the spark of great ambition." He had
caught his first glimpse of his "star of Destiny," and with
mystic mein unfalteringly followed it. He never lost
sight of it until at last it set behind the flame-streaked,
smoke-crowned field of Waterloo.

There has been some dispute concerning the date of
Napoleon's birth, but the general acceptance is that he
came into the world August 15, 1769. This is the date
which appears upon the records of the military school at
Brienne, which he entered in 1779. The claim has been
made that he was born in 1768, and that a false date was
given in order that he might be admitted to the school,
which accepted none over ten years of age. He came
of the family of Bonaparte, or, as it was frequently writ-

ten, de Buenaparte. This family was of ancient Tuscan
origin, and one branch of it had settled in the Island of
Corsica during the early part of the Sixteenth Century.
Charles Marie de Buenaparte was of noble descent, and
a man of affairs in Corsica. He married Letitia Ram-
olino, at the town of Ajaccio, two months after the island
had been subdued by the French and added to French
territory. There was nothing extraordinary in the early
boyhood of Napoleon to attract attention. In 1779 he
accompanied his father, who was chosen as Representative from the Island of Corsica to the court of Louis XVI.
In this year admission was obtained for the boy to enter
the military school at Brienne. Here his position became somewhat humiliating, both from the fact that he
was regarded as an Italian, and for the reason that his
means were small compared with those of most of the
other pupils at the institution. It is related that Napoleon devoted himself to study, and that although he
was far from bright in some branches, it was noticeable
that in all of those matters which are necessary to a soldier's knowledge, he advanced rapidly. He remained at
the school at Brienne for five years, and it was during
his last year, according to all accounts, that he erected
snow forts and engaged with his companions in mimic
battle. In 1784 he became one of the three students
annually selected from among the cadets to enter the
Royal Military School at Paris. In February of the
following year Napoleon's father died, and the lad sincerely mourned the death of his parent. In September,
1785, one year after entering the Royal School, he stood
his examination and received his first commission, that
of Lieutenant of Artillery. During the next few years he
was stationed with his regiment at Valence, Lyons, Paris,
Auxonne, and other towns, and had an opportunity of

NAPOLEON I.

Painting by P. Delaroche

meeting with a varied class of people, and obtaining that general knowledge which is to be acquired only by travel and contact with the inhabitants of different sections of the country.   During these years also he had leave on a number of occasions to visit his home at Ajaccio, remaining there several months each time.   These leaves were granted on account of sickness.   At this time he devoted himself to a considerable extent to literature, such as he knew it, and his productions, while they cannot be said to have any particular merit, are remarkable enough as the work of a boy.   Bourrienne, who afterward became the private secretary of Napoleon, relates that they were together in Paris on the 20th of June, 1793, that memorable day when mobs surged wildly through the streets of the Capital, surrounded the Tuileries, and demanded the life of the King.   Watching the passion-inspired masses, Napoleon turned to Bourrienne, with the remark, "What madness, he should have blown four or five hundred of them into the air, and the rest would have taken to their heels."   Napoleon even went so far in his pity for this miserable monarch, that he wrote him a letter and offered to command the troops which should put an end to the disorderly rabble.   But the obscure officer, as he then was, received no reply, and it was but a few months later that the monarch was executed in front of his palace, while the mobs howled in a delirium of joy.   When the Revolution broke out in France, General Paoli, who had for years exercised a dictatorship over Corsica, but had been forced to flee, was received back with honor by the National Assembly after the Revolution of 1789, and restored to his former position in Corsica.   But in 1792 he fell under the anathema of the Assembly, and he was ordered to appear before the convention to give an account of himself and

Corsica. He refused, and when troops under Salicetti came to remove him from office, the Corsicans rallied around him and prepared for resistance. Napoleon was at this time at the parental abode in Ajaccio, and was offered flattering terms by Paoli, whose side he had taken in the previous Revolution. But Napoleon declined, and offered his services to Salicetti instead. Soon the undisguised hatred of Napoleon for Jacobin excesses laid him open to suspicion, and he was sent to Paris for trial. He was acquitted in triumph. Ajaccio was the only town in Corsica which had not by this time declared against France, and against Ajaccio Paoli and his followers marched. Napoleon's mother and the others of the family fled from the island and safely reached Marseilles, though in a destitute condition. In France itself there had been a reaction against Jacobinism, and Marseilles was chief among the rebellious cities. At Toulon the monarchist fugitives had gathered by thousands, seeking protection under the guns of the Spanish and British fleets. The fleets were invited to garrison the city, and the invitation was promptly accepted and the town well fortified. The revolutionary leaders sent forward two armies to capture Toulon. After three months of disasters to the besieging armies, Napoleon came upon the field with a commission to take charge of the artillery. With his train of 200 guns he made the final assault December 19, 1793, reduced the works of the enemy, and made it possible for the soldiers to invade the town and wreck vengeance upon the garrison and inhabitants. The streets of Toulon ran with blood, and the tri-color waved over the shattered ramparts. Despite the attempt of jealous rivals to conceal the facts, Napoleon was given due credit for the victory, and he was appointed to undertake the defense of the entire coast of

France along the Mediterranean.   Within a few weeks
he had accomplished the tremendous task and rejoined
the army at Nice.   For his services he was promoted to
Brigadier-General of Artillery.   Soon General Dumer-
bion was leading the armies to conquest.   The Maritime
Alps was gained, and the way prepared for pushing into
Italy.   While the Generals under whom Napoleon
fought at this time were willing enough that he should
take the brunt of the battle, and while they usually consulted him, and followed his councils, he still remained
comparatively obscure, his superiors taking to themselves all the glory.   He did, however, shine sufficiently
to make others jealous.   Albetti and Salicetti plotted
against him.   He was relieved of his command, and soon
afterward placed under arrest at the instigation of his
enemies.   They had no charges which could hold
against him, and he was released after a brief imprison-
ment.   Headley asserts that the injustice attempted
against Napoleon is clearly shown by an effort on the
part of his enemies to have him reduced in rank.   He
handed in his resignation and went to Marseilles to visit
his mother and family.   While there he became engaged
to Eugenie Desiree Clery, the daughter of a merchant.
Poverty alone kept him at this time from marrying, and
the engagement was broken off.   She subsequently
became the wife of Bernadotte, and was Queen of
Sweden.   In May of 1795, Napoleon went to Paris.
This period, so graphically described by himself, was the
darkest of his youth.   He was penniless, and at the same
time had to endure the thought that his mother was in
need.   He was actually contemplating suicide, he relates,
when, by good fortune, he met one of the very few of his
schoolmates with whom he had been closely united—
Demasis, who was so struck with Napoleon's gloomy

appearance, that he questioned him and learned the truth, with the result that he pressed $6,000 in gold upon him. Afterward Napoleon repaid him ten-fold in money, and gave him a high position. Evidence of his despondency is seen in a letter written June 25, 1795, in which he says, "Life is a flimsy dream." Exactly one month later he writes to his brother Joseph that he has received an appointment with the army of the West, but sickness detains him. August 20 he informs his brother that he is attached to the topographical board of the Committee of Public Safety, and that for the asking he can be sent to Turkey as General of Artillery. Two weeks later he writes that the Committee does not want him to leave France, and that he is to be reappointed to the artillery. By some of its acts the Convention was making myriads of enemies. The act which evoked the greatest bitterness was one by which the Convention should be renewed periodically, but only to the extent of one-third of its membership. In this move the Parisians saw a selfish tenacity to bring about continuity of power. The disaffected sections or wards created an insurrectionist Assembly, and this was arbitrarily suppressed by the Convention by force of arms. This roused the insurrectionists to a fiery pitch. The National Guard joined in the move, and the forces were preparing to march on the Tuileries. Menou had charge of the small body of the Convention's troops. He proved himself incapable, was arrested and imprisoned, and Barras, a politician, was given the command. "I have the man you want," announced Barras to the Convention, "a little Corsican officer, who will not stand upon ceremony." It was almost midnight, and the members of the Convention, pale and momentarily in peril, grasped at the straw, and calling Napoleon before them, gave him full power to act.   He planted cannon at the cross streets and bridges, and with his troops, numbering 5,000, waited for the attack by 40,000, most of them soldiers of the National Guard.   October 5 the insurgent hosts advanced, expecting an easy victory.   A few musket shots were exchanged and then the cannon, loaded with grape, swept the insurgent columns with a hail of death.   Again and again they poured forth upon the panic-stricken insurgents, and soon the streets were filled with slain and wounded.   The spark of rebellion was quenched with blood.   It was the work of one hour.   Calmly he returned to the Convention, which unanimously declared that his energy had saved the Republic, and made him Commander of the Army of the Interior.   He was thus at once placed in a position of the greatest power, military and political.   This step also, according to the generally accepted record of the affair, brought him into contact with Josephine, who played such an important part in his life and in the history of France.*   The story goes that among the arms captured during the search of the sections was a sword that had been worn by Viscount Beauharnais, who had fallen a victim to the guillotine.   Eugene, his son, came to beg the return of the sword, and Napoleon granted his request.   Josephine, the lad's mother, then twenty-eight years of age, called to thank Napoleon in person for his kindness. Their acquaintance resulted in marriage, March 9, 1796. Her family was one of the highest social standing in Paris, and Napoleon profited highly by the marriage from a social standpoint.   Twelve days after the marriage, Napoleon, having been appointed Commander-in-Chief of the army of Italy, turned, as Headley says, "from the ravishing tones of love" to the "sweeter notes of

* See Volume "Famous Women."

fame's shrill trumpet." He found the army in Italy in
a desperate condition. It numbered 50,000 men, poorly
fed and clad, lacking in cavalry, and surrounded on every
side by formidable foes. His first address to his new
army electrified the discouraged and discontented soldiers. "You are hungry and naked," he said, "the Republic owes you much, but she has not the means to pay
her debts. I am come to lead you into the most fertile
plains the sun beholds. Rich provinces, opulent towns,
all shall be at your disposal. Soldiers, with such a
prospect before you, can you fail in courage and con-
stancy?" The three objects of the expedition which
Napoleon was now about to undertake were; first, to
compel the King of Sardinia, who, although he had lost
Savoy and Nice, still maintained a formidable army on
the frontiers of Piedmont, to sever his alliance with Austria; secondly, to compel Austria to withdraw her heavy
armies from the French frontier on the Rhine. This was
to be accomplished by an invasion into Austria's Italian
provinces, and if possible to stir up the Italian subjects of
the Austrian crown to revolt and throw off the yoke.
The third object was to bring the Vatican to terms, owing
to the fact that it was suspected by the French Directory
that the Church was secretly encouraging the Royalists.
Napoleon lost little time in preparation. He reached
Nice, March 27, and the campaign opened April 10.
Beaulieu, the Austrian General, had taken every precau-
tion. He had arranged his great force to cover Genoa,
and guard the passes of the Alps. He held a strong position at Voltri, ten miles from Genoa, and another large
force under D'Argenteau, occupied Montenotte, a
summit further west. Colli, with the Sardinian troops,
was stationed at Ceva. The array was an imposing one.
All of these troops were tried and seasoned, and the Gen-

erals were renowned for skill. But Napoleon had plans
of his own, not only in regard to the manner in which he
would attack the enemy, but also in regard to the manner
in which he would cross the frowning Alps. He followed
along the chain close to the shores of the Mediterranean,
through March storms and April rains, to a point where
the ridges sink almost to a plain, and then moved rapidly
and silently upon Montenotte. The night of April 11
was unusually dark and stormy, yet all through the night
the army of Napoleon pushed steadily forward through
torrents of rain, over miry roads, across swollen streams,
and finally as day was about to dawn, the various divisions took up their positions around the camp of the
enemy. Within an hour the order to attack was given,
and the wet and weary troopers fell upon the unsuspecting Austrians, causing them to precipitously take to
flight, leaving of their number 3,000 dead and wounded
upon the field. The defeated army tried to rally at Dego,
joining forces with Beaulieu. He was dislodged, and
3,000 of his soldiers taken prisoners. At Millesimo 1,500
Sardinians surrendered. At Ceva he fought the Sardinians under Colli. The enemy retreated, but he again
fell upon them and won a complete victory. With the
enemy scattered and flying in all directions, Napoleon
rapidly marched upon Turin, the capital of Sardinia, and
dictated his own terms. Within the space of one month
the young General had fought three great battles, had
killed, wounded, or captured 25,000 men, and taken 80
guns and 21 standards, and that with an army inferior in
numbers and equipment as compared with the enemy.
By the terms of peace, the King of Sardinia gave up three
great fortresses in the Alps, and abandoned his coalition
with Austria. His army was now a victorious host, and
the promises he had made relative to finding plenty of all

things needed for their comfort proved true. The troops, therefore, had already begun to exhibit that devotion and loyalty which was so often in after years demonstrated by those who served under Napoleon. His gaze was now turned upon Lombardy. By skillful maneuvering he caused the Austrians to believe that he desired to cross the river at Valenza, and while the enemy was preparing for him at that point, he was rapidly and under cover of night marching to a point eight miles distant. The distance was made in thirty-six hours, and the entire army crossed the Po in ferry boats without the loss of a single man, and in the face of two large reconnoitering parties of the enemy. This was May 7, and four days later was fought the memorable battle of Lodi. The Adda River was here spanned by a large wooden bridge. Beaulieu had prepared to make a desperate resistance. He had posted strong bodies of troops in the town of Lodi, and with his main army waited on the opposite side, after posting thirty cannon so as to completely sweep the bridge. No more daring task was ever undertaken in warfare than this feat of taking an army across the bridge of Lodi. The outposts of Napoleon's army drove the Austrians before them out of the town and across the bridge only to be met with a deadly storm from the batteries. Napoleon's first care was to plant cannon to offset those of the enemy. With his own hands he pointed and aimed guns, and in the meantime he had sent a detachment to ford the river some distance away, with orders to attack the Austrian flank. At the moment when the attack was made Napoleon gave the word and columns of grenadiers, led by Lannes, Lallemagne, and Berthier, swept forward. For a moment the hail of shot checked them, but the next, rallied by the officers, and urged by Napoleon himself, they swarmed across the structure and were upon the Austrian gunners, bayoneting them at their posts. Lannes, that gallant fighter and self-elected body guard of Napoleon's, was the first to cross the bridge. Following his giant form, and second to cross, was the diminutive figure of Napoleon. Four days more and Napoleon entered Milan, the capital of Lombardy, in triumph. This was May 15, 1796. The citadel alone had not surrendered to the victor. After resting a week Napoleon set forward to pursue the Austrian General. He left a force to blockade the citadel, and with the balance of his army, he marched upon Mantua, "the citadel of Italy." Here Beaulieu had strongly entrenched his army, with Mantua to the left and Peschiera, a Venetian fortress which he had taken, on the right. At this juncture the Directory, fearing that Napoleon's power and glory was growing too fast, proposed to divide the command, letting half of the army go against the Austrians, while Napoleon, with the other half, could proceed against the Papal dominions. Their plans were met by a simple and absolute refusal on the part of the young Corsican. At this time also an insurrection arose in Lombardy as a result of heavy taxes imposed by the French. Napoleon pitilessly turned upon them, and without mercy slew all who were concerned in the outbreak. Advancing now upon the Austrians, he again deceived Beaulieu, their General. Napoleon crossed the River Mincio at a point where he was not expected, and laid siege to Mantua. It was occupied by 15,000 Austrians. July 29, General Wurmser at the head of an Austrian force, variously estimated at from 50,000 to 80,000 men, advanced to the relief of Mantua. Several engagements were fought, the principal one being at Bassano, where a sanguinary conflict took place, which resulted in tremendous losses to the Austrians,

6,000 of whom laid down their arms. September 13th occurred the battle of St. George, a suburb of Mantua, and Wurmser once more suffered defeat, and with the balance of his army retreated into the fortress, making the total number of Austrians blockaded there 26,000. Austria now proceeded to raise another army to relieve Mantua. Alvinzi advanced at the head of 50,000 men, most of whom, however, were raw recruits. The Austrians arrived near the middle of November, and for three days battles raged with varying success, Alvinzi being finally compelled to retire. During these three days of terrible fighting around Arcola, beginning September 15th, Napoleon lost 8,000 men, and the slaughter of the enemy is stated to have been much greater. Austria pushed forward reinforcements to Alvinzi, and in January, 1797, he again found himself strong enough to make an attempt at driving Napoleon from Mantua. With 60,000 men he advanced as far as Rivoli, and here on the heights a desperately contested battle was carried on, with the result that Napoleon added another to his growing list of brilliant victories. In the meantime, a second column of Austrians had advanced upon Mantua and this information reaching Napoleon, he determined to go to the assistance of the force he had left to keep up the blockade. After the battle of the 14th he marched all night and all of the next day, arrived at Mantua late on the 15th, and the next morning led in person a desperate assault to drive Wurmser, who was attempting to fight his way out, back again to his prison. The Austrian column under Provera, which had so unexpectedly appeared at Mantua, now found itself surrounded, and the commander and 5,000 men surrendered. Other detached bodies followed this example and Wurmser, bravely as he had held out against disease and starvation, was compelled to surrender and evacuate Mantua. Napoleon admired Wurmser's obstinate courage, and allowed him to proceed unmolested to Austria with an escort of 700 of his soldiers. The Directory protested, but Napoleon replied that his act was done in justice to a brave man and the dignity of France. Lombardy was now under the banner of the Republic, and the whole Nation rang with praises of the military genius and bravery of Napoleon.

In June of 1796, when about to take up the siege of Mantua, Napoleon had made a hasty incursion into the Papal dominions, extorted from the Pope £1,500,000 sterling, and he now once more turned his eyes in that direction. The Papal troops to the number of 40,000 had been congregated in anticipation of this very event, and in spite of the manner in which the Austrians were defeated, the Generals of the Vatican troops determined to resist Napoleon's advance. The first opposing force he met was that of Cardinal Burea. It required about one hour for Napoleon's troops to effectually scatter this branch of the Papal army. He triumphantly entered Faenza, and then Ancona, and on February 10th marched into Loretto and seized the treasure. He made no attempt to interfere with the religion, although urged by the Directory to treat the hierarchy of Rome with the utmost severity. February 19th, after seven days of negotiations, a treaty was signed with the Pope by which Avignon was formally ceded to France. All that now remained unsubdued in Northern Italy was Venice. Napoleon urged an alliance with France, but the Government demanded neutrality and it was granted. One result of the campaign against the Pope was the gain for France of hundreds of statues and a collection of paintings of the old masters, which were sent to Paris to be placed in the National Museum.

Up to this time Napoleon's army had fought no fewer than fourteen pitched battles, had taken part in seventy actions, captured over 100,000 prisoners, 2,000 heavy guns, over 500 field pieces, and besides maintaining itself without cost to the Republic, had sent to Paris millions in money, and valuable treasure of other description, such as paintings, statuary, and priceless manuscripts. Napoleon was now about to begin his sixth campaign. He turned toward Vienna, the Capital of Austria. To give the details of this campaign would be practically a repetition of the previous one against Austria. The Austrians, under Archduke Charles, again operated on a double basis, one division on the frontier of Tyrol, and the other under the Archduke on the Friulese. Napoleon marched against the Archduke, and sent Joubert with an army against the Austrians in Tyrol. March 12th Napoleon's army attacked and defeated the Austrians, who retreated with the French in full pursuit. Gradisca was stormed, and 5,000 prisoners taken. Through Trieste and Fiume and across the mountain passes, the thinning ranks of the Austrians fled before the victorious French. In the meantime General Laudon had gained some successes in Tyrol, and the Venetians, notwithstanding that they had solemnly pledged themselves to neutrality, had committed acts of violence against the French soldiers. This led to an attempt to disarm them, and the consequence was several insurrections, in which many hundreds of the French were massacred. Just before this came to the ears of Napoleon, the court of Vienna had ordered Archduke Charles to bring the war to an end, and in April, 1797,

negotiations were begun at Leoben. Having specified
the terms of the treaty, and without waiting for its conclusion, Napoleon marched upon the treacherous Venetians. They begged for mercy. "French blood has
been treacherously shed," replied Napoleon. "If you
could offer me the treasures of Peru; if you cover your
whole dominion with gold, the atonement would be
insufficient; the Lion of St. Mark must bite the dust."
Venice offered no resistance, and Napoleon satisfied his
anger by taking five ships of war, 3,000,000 francs in
gold, besides paintings and manuscripts, organized a
democratic form of government, and made a treaty with
terms to suit himself. He also here discovered in Venice
proof of criminal negotiations between General Pichegru
on the Rhine with the Bourbons. He sent the facts to
Paris, and Pichegru was replaced by General Hoche.
Pichegru returned to Paris and became the President of
the Five Hundred. At this crisis the Directory sent for
Napoleon, and he dispatched Augereau to Paris, and
the latter with his troops, on September 4, 1797, arrested
the undesirable representatives, and Pichegru with 150
others were exiled.

After arranging his affairs in Italy, Napoleon installed
himself at the castle of Montebello, near Milan, and was
there joined by Josephine. After months of negotiations between France and Austria, the treaty was finally
concluded and signed at Campo-Formio, October 3,
1797. By this treaty the Emperor yielded Flanders and
the boundary of the Rhine, as well as the fortress of
Mentz, to France. The several new republics of Lombardy were united under the name of the Cisalpine
Republic. To indemnify Austria for the loss of Lombardy, Napoleon did not hesitate to cede the city itself
and the Italian provinces to the Emperor, while the

Ionian Islands and Dalmatia were retained under French Sovereignty.   November 17th Napoleon left Milan and Italy, and paid a brief visit to Rastatt, where the Congress of the German powers had been assembled, and then proceeded to Paris, where he arrived December 5th.   The Directory was unhappy and jealous.   Napoleon neither asked their advice, accepted their suggestions, nor respected their desires.   His plan was his own secret, and every move was with a view to the future, which he seemed to see with a clear vision.   January 2, 1798, Napoleon appeared before the court of Luxembourg with the treaty of Campo-Formio.   The multitude received him with the wildest demonstrations of enthusiasm.   Here he made his first speech.   He had often before or after battles addressed his soldiers in stirring words, but this was his first address before the French public.   He was introduced by Talleyrand, and when he concluded his brief but vigorous and brilliant discourse the assembled concourse wildly shouted, "Vive Napoleon, Conqueror of Italy, Pacificator of Europe, and Savior of France."   He was elected a member of the Institute, the distinguished literary establishment of the Capital, in place of Carnot, who had been exiled.   He assumed the dress of a citizen instead of the uniform of a General.   There was nothing of ostentation about him.   He was economical, and while he might have amassed millions, he was comparatively poor. In spite of this the Directory was jealous and suspicious. They well knew his power and influence.   They knew that the soldiery returning from Italy had sung and said through every town and village that it was time to get rid of the lawyers and make the "Little Corporal" King.   When the motion was made in the Chambers to grant to Napoleon the estate of Chambord, it was lost, and this petty jealousy became more than ever conspicuous and significant to Napoleon, who secretly despised their authority.

The succeeding great scene in the Napoleonic drama was the proposed invasion of England, but Napoleon, after thorough investigation, said to Bourrienne, "It would be too hazardous. I will not undertake it. I will not risk on such a stake our beautiful France." His next thought was to inflict indirectly upon England a blow by a campaign in Egypt. The expedition was sanctioned by the Directory, who perhaps thought that in this dangerous climate they might forever be rid of Napoleon. The French army and magnificent fleet was assembled at Toulon, and among the invaders was a large corps of scientists and connoisseurs, who were to select the choicest antiquarian treasures of Egypt for the embellishment of the French Capital. He received his appointment April 12, 1798, but it was not until May 29th that he set sail. The reason for this delay is obvious. When Napoleon arrived at Toulon a squadron of English ships under Nelson was cruising in sight of the port. On the evening of May 19th a violent gale drove the English ships to sea, and so disabled some of them that Nelson was compelled to put into Sardinian ports to repair them. Napoleon instantly ordered the troops to embark. His force consisted of 40,000 picked soldiers, and he had stimulated their eagerness by promising that each of them were to receive seven acres of land. He did not give the location of the land, but the soldiers knew him for a General who kept his promises. June 9th Napoleon reached Malta, and, being refused admission to the harbor for more than four of his ships, under the treaties which bound the Island, he attacked, and after a cannonade of two days, the place

capitulated. In writing of this incident to his brother
Joseph, he called it the strongest place in Europe. Nelson, in the meantime, was searching the coasts of Egypt
for the fleet of Napoleon, but the latter eluded him.
July 1st Napoleon reached Alexandria, and disembarked
his troops during a gale. Many of his soldiers sank to
eternal sleep during that disembarkation. He had before him the task of conquering 2,500,000 people—
Turks, Copts, Arabs, and the fierce Mamelukes.
Alexandria was soon subdued with terrific slaughter,
and Napoleon raised the tri-color over the city's
crumbling walls. Leaving 3,000 men to hold the
city, he began on July 8th that terrible march across
the burning desert toward Cairo. After a skirmish
at Chebreiss, in which many of the enemy were
slain, the main army of the Mamelukes, under Mourad
Bey, was met with in sight of the pyramids. With wild
cries the savage hosts advanced gallantly upon the
French. "Soldiers," said Napoleon, "from the summit
of yonder pyramids forty ages look down upon you."
Then the battle began. The Mamelukes lost 2,000
killed, and in their flight hundreds were drowned in the
Nile. The French lost about a score killed and six score
wounded. On July 24th Cairo capitulated. All of
Lower Egypt was in the hands of Napoleon. In a letter
written immediately after this he expresses his desire to
return to France, but only a week after his arrival at
Cairo came the battle of Aboukir in which the French
fleet was totally destroyed by Nelson's squadron.
Although his designs had thus received a death-blow,
Napoleon, when the news of the disaster to his fleet
reached him, merely sighed and remarked, "To France
the Fates have decreed the empire of the land—to England, the sea." Napoleon remained in Cairo during the

winter, and gave himself up to planning canals to connect the Mediterranean with the Red Sea. He also devoted much time to making laws and regulating internal affairs in Egypt. In February, with an army of 12,-000, he marched into Syria, forced El-Arish to capitulate, then took Gaza, the ancient city of the Philistines, and advanced upon Jaffa, the Joppa of the Bible, arriving before its walls March 3d. The place was taken by assault, and 3,000 of its defenders were slain with arms in their hands, while thousands of others were massacred by the infuriated French soldiers, who for three hours continued to kill and pillage until stopped by their officers. Upward of 2,000 who were taken prisoners in one building were at Napoleon's orders taken out on the sands, formed into squares and shot down until not a living soul remained. For this wholesale slaughter Napoleon has been severely condemned, but his side of the incident is that these were part of the garrison which capitulated at El-Arish, and were liberated on giving their pledge to refrain from again taking up arms against the French. Napoleon now turned to Acre, renowned in the annals of the Crusades. March 19th the attack upon Acre began, but the task was hopeless from the first. The siege guns, while being transported by sea from Alexandria, fell into the hands of an English fleet under Sir Sidney Smith. After spending a month before Acre the battle of Mount Tabor took place. Kleber had been sent to cut off the arrival of 30,000 Turks from the mountains of Samaria, intended to reinforce Acre. Kleber was all but beaten when Napoleon, with fresh battalions, came to the rescue, and the Turks were signally defeated. After another month before Acre Napoleon gave up the effort. Disease was carrying off many of his troops, and on the awful march back to Jaffa hundreds lay down on the sands never again to rise. During this march his last horse was given up to the hospital train, and he walked beside his soldiers, cheering and comforting them. The army reached Jaffa May 24th, and by the middle of June Napoleon was back in Cairo. In July he learned through intercepted messages that a force of 18,000 Turks had landed before Alexandria, and that the fleets of Russia, Turkey, and England were in the bay. Leaving Dessaix in command at Cairo, with the bulk of the army he made forced marches and reached Alexandria July 25th. The following day the most sanguinary battle of the Egyptian campaign was fought. In spite of the cannonading from the ships, the infantry under Napoleon and the invincible cavalry under Murat swept upon the Turks, and in the hand to hand struggle which followed 12,000 perished and 6,000 were taken prisoners. In August, after he had returned to Cairo, he received from Sir Sidney Smith a number of papers, which showed the disasters France had suffered during his absence, and this determined him to hasten back to France. He left Egypt in charge of Kleber, and, accompanied by his favorite Generals, reached France October 9, 1799. Napoleon did not find the France that he had left. Italy had practically been lost. On every border of the Republic the enemy hung, waiting for a favorable opportunity. Among the people there was alarm and discontent. Royalty was at conflict with extreme Republicanism, and between the two the Directory seemed to have lost both dignity and power. Napoleon took up his quarters in his old house in the Rue de la Victoire. He was conscious of the fact that the people were with him, but he had powerful enemies. Before he could hope to assume the reins of Government the Directory must be

crushed, and the Council of the Ancients and that of
the Five Hundred must be disposed of. In the Directory, besides the Royalists, Barras represented the
Jacobins and Sieyès, the moderates or Republicans.
Both of the latter sought to form an alliance with
Napoleon, who favored the position of Sieyès as best
suited to forward his designs. Napoleon's brother
Lucien was President of the Council of the Five Hundred, and had the benefit of the coaching of the shrewd
Talleyrand. November 8th the evidences of civil com-
motion became more distinct than ever. The dragoons,
the officers of the national guard, and those of the garrison, had requested an interview with Napoleon, and he
had named the following morning to receive them. At
6 o'clock on the morning of November 9th military
bands led the way to Napoleon's humble home, and
thousands of the populace gathered there. The Council of the Ancients assembled at 7 o'clock at the
Tuileries. They decided that bold measures were
required to save the Republic. They passed two
motions, one to hold their sittings at the chateau of
St. Cloud outside of the Capital, and the other to give
Napoleon supreme command of the military forces in
and around Paris. The tidings were borne to Napoleon,
and he hurried to the Tuileries to accept the charge.
In the meantime the Directory suddenly awakened to
the fact that a crisis was at hand. The following day
Napoleon again addressed the Council of Ancients, and
at the conclusion the majority cheered him. But a
different reception awaited him in the Council of the
Five Hundred. They were shouting, "Down with the
Dictator" and "Long live the Constitution." Lucien
Bonaparte and the moderates of the Council in vain
attempted to restore order. In the midst of the excite-

ment, Napoleon entered, accompanied by four grenadiers. The grenadiers remained near the doors, while
Napoleon approached into the center of the Council.
A storm of protest arose. "Outlawry," they cried;
"Drawn swords in the sanctuary of the laws," "Let him
be proclaimed a traitor." Members rushed upon him.
One of them, Arena, aimed a dagger at his throat. He
was rescued by the grenadiers, and coming into the open
air announced to his soldiers, "I offered them fame, and
they met me with daggers." In the meantime the com-
motion in the Council increased. A sentence of outlawry was demanded against him. In vain his brother
Lucien insisted upon the right to speak in behalf of his
brother. Being refused, he indignantly flung off his
insignia of office and left the place. Going out to the
soldiery, he mounted a horse, and, as President of the
Council, pronounced it dissolved, and ordered Napoleon
to carry out the decree with force. A detachment of
grenadiers entered the hall and drove the members out
at the points of bayonets. Then Lucien Bonaparte collected the moderate members of the Council, and these,
sitting as an assembly, came to an understanding with
the Council of Ancients whereby both bodies adjourned
to the middle of the following February. The whole
authority of State, meantime, was deposed in a Provisional Consulate. The Consuls named were Napoleon,
Sieyès, and Ducos. Napoleon went home, embraced
Josephine and said, "To-morrow we sleep in the palace
of the Luxembourg." The next morning he met with
the Consuls, and his display of versatility and superiority of knowledge of the affairs of the Government was
such that Sieyès, on returning to his house, remarked
to Talleyrand and others who had assembled there,
"Gentlemen, I perceive that you have got a master.

Bonaparte can do, and will do, everything himself."
The Consulate as originally organized did not last long.
Through the promulgation of a new constitution,
December 14th, Napoleon became Chief Consul, Camba-
ceres Second Consul, and Lebrun Third Consul.
Napoleon was approaching dangerously near to a
throne.   The First Consul under the constitution
was practically regent.   He had absolute control of
every department.   The Conservative Senate, the Tri-
bunate, and the Legislative Senate, which were created
by the same constitution, were rather his assistants than
a safeguard.   There was no real check upon his authority.   Toward the end of the year he moved into the
Tuileries, and the splendor of his establishment there
was little less magnificent than maintained by monarchs.
He was called First Consul, and the Tuileries was given
the more Republican name of Government Palace, but
in fact he was King, and the Government Palace was
his court.   About this time Napoleon wrote a personal
letter to King George III, of England, proposing peace
between the two Nations.   Lord Grènville, England's
Secretary of State, in reply wrote to Talleyrand that the
King saw nothing in the new Government "which tend
to make foreign powers regard it as either more stable,
or more trustworthy, than the transitory forms it had
supplanted."   January 7th, three days after receiving
this letter, Napoleon issued an edict creating an army
of reserve, comprising the veterans and strengthened
the service by 30,000 recruits.   The preparations for a
mighty struggle now went forward with amazing rapidity.   On April 24th the campaign was begun.   The army
under Moreau crossed the Rhine at several points into
Germany, and met with flattering successes.   An army
under General Massena had advanced into Italy.   It

was not expected that Napoleon himself would take the field, but on May 9th he appeared suddenly at Geneva and took command of the army of reserve under Berthier. At this time Massena was struggling vainly against the superior forces of Melas in Italy, and a few days later Napoleon, with his army in three divisions, crossed the Alps. Massena had been besieged in Genoa since April 21st, but Napoleon, instead of going to his relief, as was expected, marched upon Milan and took possession of the city and the whole line of the Po and the Ticino. He then rapidly marched to Alessandria, which was occupied by Melas and the Austrians. Napoleon appeared before the town May 13th, and the following day the Austrians marched out and proceeded to Marengo. The battle of Marengo which followed appeared for a brief space to be an Austrian victory, and in fact Melas had retired to his tent to write dispatches telling of his success when a fortunate charge of Kellerman's cavalry and the appearance of Dessaix, who had just returned from Egypt, with 6,000 men, turned the tide of battle and resulted in a crushing defeat for the Austrians. The concluding and decisive battle of the campaign was, however, won on December 3d by Moreau, who signally defeated 70,000 Austrians under Archduke Charles, and placed the Austrian Capital at the mercy of the French. Negotiations then began, and the treaty of Luneville, February 9, 1801, was the result. England had now no ally in Europe, while France had secured the friendship of Denmark and Russia, and had made a treaty with the United States. Peace negotiations between England and France were finally concluded at Amiens March 27, 1802. In August of that year, to signalize the national regard for Napoleon in bringing about the pacification of Europe, the people of France voted on

the question, "Shall Napoleon be First Consul for life."
Naturally he was elected by an overwhelming majority.
The year 1803 had scarcely been ushered in before fresh
signs of trouble between France and England began to
be visible. By the treaty of Amiens, England was to
yield up possession of Malta, but refused to comply with
the agreement. English newspapers assailed the character of Napoleon, and he protested, only to be coolly
informed that his only redress was in the English courts.
He finally did bring action against a royalist Frenchman
who had settled in England, and was publishing a French
paper in London. The editor was found guilty of libel,
but his counsel, Sir James Mackintosh, delivered a tirade
against the character of Napoleon, which was calculated
to injure him much more than had the newspapers.
England's refusal to give up Malta was based on an
interview between Napoleon and Lord Whitworth in
which Napoleon said: "Every gale that blows from England is burdened with enmity; your Government coun-
tenances Georges, Pichegru, and other infamous men
who have sworn to assassinate me. Your journals slander me, and the redress I am offered is but adding
mockery to insult. I could make myself master of
Egypt to-morrow, if I pleased. Egypt, indeed, must,
sooner or later, belong to France, but I have no wish
to go to war for such a trivial object." The war was
declared by England, May 15th. Before the proclamation reached Paris, according to the claims made by
Napoleon, the English were already capturing French
ships, and as a retaliatory measure he ordered the arrest
of all English citizens in France. Napoleon sent troops
into Hanover, the patrimonial possession of the King of
England, and within ten days the French had captured
16,000 prisoners, taken 400 cannon and 30,000 muskets

and 3,500 fine horses. By these successes Napoleon managed to maintain his armies without expense to France, and besides crippled England's commerce with many important points on the continent. In the meantime he was busy with his scheme of invasion. Troops numbering 160,000 were mustered in camps along the French and Dutch coasts. Soult, Ney, Davoust, and Victor were the Generals selected to lead these armies. But England had 500 ships of war blockading ports and destroying shipping, and along her coasts were scattered camps of troops. Napoleon watched and waited for an opportunity to cross the channel in his flat-bottomed boats, either during such a calm that the English ships would be unable to move, or immediately after a storm, when they would be far out at sea. Early in 1804 a conspiracy against Napoleon was discovered. Count d'Artois was its leader, and carried on his operations from London. Pichegru and Moreau were involved, as were many others. Napoleon also suspected the complicity of the Duke d'Enghein, who lived at Ettenheim on German territory. Notwithstanding this, Napoleon sent dragoons to seize him, had him instantly tried in the night and shot at 2 o'clock in the morning. For this act Napoleon was everywhere severely condemned. Many of the conspirators against him were executed and others were exiled or imprisoned. One month after the execution of the Duke, it was proposed to make Napoleon Emperor. Carnot opposed it, but he was practically alone, and on May 18, 1804, the Senate unanimously passed the decree. He was given the right to name his successor. Congratulations came from all the Rulers of Europe except England, Russia, and Sweden. Napoleon desired to leave nothing undone that should make his power certain, and therefore sent for Pope

Pius VII to come to Paris and crown him. The Pope consented, and Napoleon was crowned December 2, 1804. Titles, dress, and manners quickly became those of Royalty. Ten years before, Napoleon was a captain in the army of the Republic. Originally a Corsican, he hated the French, yet became a republican and adopted the Nation as his own. And now, that he had assumed a crown and held a monarch's scepter, he received homage from the same multitude that had but recently cried itself hoarse with "Vive la Republique." He was now invited to accept the iron crown of Charlemagne, worn by the Lombard Kings, and proceeded to Milan, where he was crowned May 26, 1805. His title then became Emperor of the French and King of Italy. While at Milan, Napoleon received the first intimation that a coalition was forming against him. England, Russia, and Sweden had entered into a league with the avowed purposes of restoring the independence of Holland and Switzerland; to free the north of Germany from the presence of French troops; to procure the restoration of Piedmont to the King of Sardinia; and, finally, the evacuation of Italy by Napoleon. Until, by the attainment of these objects, the sway of France should be reduced to limits compatible with the independence of other European States, no peace was to be signed by any of the contracting Powers. Austria did not at first venture into the coalition, but on learning of Napoleon's crowning at Milan, at once threw 80,000 troops into Bavaria, the ally of France, and tried to compel the Elector to join the coalition. In the meantime Napoleon was hastening from Milan to Paris, and arrived there in the latter part of July, 1805. An army was hastily sent forward and by strategy surrounded the Austrians, who capitulated without conditions of any kind. Meanwhile the

Czar of Russia with 116,000 troops had advanced as far
as Moravia. England sent 30,000 troops into Hanover
to press upon the enemy from that quarter. Napoleon
was joined by Ney's forces after their success in the
Tyrol, by Murat, who had watched the retreat to Bohemia, and also by Augereau with fresh reserves from
France. Then began the march upon the German capital.
November 7 Francis fled from the unprotected city, and
November 13, Napoleon entered and seized the supplies
and arms stored there in great quantities. Instead of
remaining in Vienna and giving the enemy an opportunity to further concentrate their forces, Napoleon
marched forward and met the allied army, December 2,
on the field of Austerlitz. When the sun rose that winter morning the confident Russians and the finely drilled
Austrians advanced upon the French with no misgiv-
ings of defeat. The first onset was made upon Napoleon's right, which he had made to appear extremely
weak, while really he had a formidable force, both of
horse and foot concealed behind the convent of Ray-
gern, some distance to the rear of the French right.
The Russians fell into the trap and were suddenly over-
whelmed. The move left a gap in the Russian center,
into which Soult at once plunged, and soon the tide of
slaughter was carried to every part of the allied armies.
During the rout that followed one whole division of
Russians was crossing a frozen lake, when the French
artillery fired round shot at the ice and broke it up,
engulfing, it is said, 6,000 men. In a letter written the
following day Napoleon says he fancies that he can still
hear the cries of the wretches, "whom it was impossible
to save." This is a peculiar passage, inasmuch as eye-
witnesses have related that the firing upon the ice was
done at Napoleon's express orders, with the sole pur-

pose of drowning the Russians. In this battle the Russians lost 20,000 and the Austrians 6,000. Napoleon took 40,000 prisoners, including 40 Generals. His own loss Napoleon gives as 900 slain, with double that number wounded. In this same letter, he states that his health is good, notwithstanding that he has "slept in the open air for a week." The morning after the battle, Francis of Austria met Napoleon, and after a two hours' conference, it was agreed that the Russians might withdraw after a pledge not to again resume hostilities against the French. A treaty with Austria was signed December 15 at Presburg, and one with Prussia at Vienna December 27. The opening months of 1806 were occupied in efforts on the part of Napoleon to reaching some definite understanding with England and Russia. The Confederation of the Rhine was also formed, in which some of the smaller German States came under the protectorate of France. The negotiations with Russia and England failed, and now suddenly a new coalition was formed in which Prussia took the place formerly occupied by Austria. A Prussian army of 200,000 took the field, invaded Saxony, and compelled that State to become an ally. Napoleon pursued the same line of tactics used against the Austrians the previous year. He sent his armies to cut off the rear of the Prussians, and then sent a proposal of peace to the King. Receiving no reply, decisive steps were taken. In a fierce battle at Saalfield, the Prussians under Prince Louis were defeated. Naumburg and its magazine was blown up, and the Prince received a mortal wound. October 14, the contending armies met in decisive conflict at Jena and Auerstadt, and 20,000 Prussians were killed or taken prisoners. Napoleon then took up the march to Berlin and entered the town October 27.

With a remnant of his army the King of Prussia fled to the frontier of Poland, and there met Alexander of Russia advancing with an army to come to his assistance. The campaign of the winter which followed was a terrible one for the French troops. Through bitter cold and driving snowstorms, they marched 400 miles to Warsaw and invested the city, November 28. The next great battle of this campaign was on the field of Eylau, February 7, 1807. Each side lost heavily, and while the Russians retired to Königsberg, Napoleon retreated to the Vistula. Offers of peace by Napoleon were rejected. After remaining in winter quarters upon the Vistula, in the spring he received supplies and reinforcements from France. With 300,000 men he renewed the campaign. May 26 the town of Dantzic capitulated after a siege of 51 days. June 14, the anniversary of Marengo, the deciding battle was fought opposite the town of Friedland. The Russians were so completely beaten that the Czar began to think of peace, and on June 25 the two rulers met on a raft moored in the River Niemen, near the town of Tilsit. They had a long conversation, to which no person was a witness; both established themselves in Tilsit and lived there as old friends for three weeks, until peace was signed July 8, 1807. Prussia was compelled to accept harsh terms, but Russia was treated like a friend instead of an enemy. Napoleon returned to Paris July 27, and was received with the greatest enthusiasm. In 1808, Napoleon, having come to the conclusion that Portugal and Spain were necessary to him, dispatched Junot to Lisbon with an army, which arrived there November 30. The royal family fled aboard ships and sailed for Brazil. In the same year, French troops were poured into Spain and placed under command of Murat, who took up his march to Madrid. King Charles abdicated, and Ferdinand, the heir apparent, was placed upon the throne, but Napoleon soon induced him to also abdicate, and made Joseph Bonaparte, already King of Naples, ruler of Spain. Soon, however, the entire Nation revolted. King Joseph was compelled to flee for his life, and French garrisons were overcome and massacred. Napoleon, with several formidable armies, at once entered Spain, and the enemy faded away before his advance as the dew before the morning sun. Success followed success, until on December 4, after a stern resistance, Spain capitulated. Leaving Soult to wipe out the last vestiges of the insurrection, Napoleon, with the utmost speed, hurried back to Paris. The reason for this sudden move was that he had received information that Austria and England, taking advantage of his absence, were about to invade France from the north. He reached the capital January 22, and in the meantime Joseph once more ascended the throne. Austria took the leadership in the war of 1809 by declaring hostilities April 6. Napoleon hastened to Strasburg. April 13 he moved against Archduke Charles, whose army was composed of 180,000 men. April 20 a fierce battle was fought at Abensburg, and the following day a battle at Landshut, in which the Austrians lost 9,000 men, thirty guns and all their stores. The Archduke concentrated his forces and gave battle to the French at Eckmuhl. The conflict lasted from 2 in the afternoon until dark, and the Austrians were driven from the field with terrible losses. Charles retreated to Ratisbon, where he made a last stand, and was again defeated. He then retreated into Bohemia, and Napoleon again entered Vienna, May 13. The final battle was fought at Wagram July 6. Five days later an armistice was signed at Znaim. The treaty with Austria

was finally signed October 14 at Schonbrunn, and by
this act Austria lost 45,000 square miles of territory and
4,000,000 population. On his return to Paris, Napoleon
for the first time broached to Josephine the necessity
of divorce. They were childless, and Napoleon pointed
out the desire of the whole Nation that he should have
an heir, and it was necessary besides that he should by
marriage connect himself with one of the great reigning powers and thus establish the security of France. It
was a cruel and crushing blow to the devoted and gentle
Josephine, and Napoleon suffered as well, but he placed
his destiny and France beside the love of Josephine, and
locked his heart against his own inclinations. The
formal separation took place December 15. March 10,
1810, Berthier, representing Napoleon, received at
Vienna the hand of Princess Marie Louise as the bride
of Napoleon. She was 18, he was 40. March 20, 1811,
she bore a son, and another of Napoleon's ambitions had
been gratified. Negotiations with England, looking
toward peace, however, failed utterly. That Nation
refused to recognize Joseph as King of Spain, and the
open hostility between the two Nations continued.
Russia also suddenly became the enemy of France.
England's influence and pressure from abroad and his
own nobility caused Czar Alexander, in spite of the
treaty of Tilsit, to declare war against France in April,
1812. With 600,000 French, Italian, and German troops
Napoleon now began the wonderful invasion of Russia.
June 24 his forces began crossing the Niemen, and four
days later he entered Vilna, the capital of Russian
Poland, which had been evacuated at his approach.
While waiting for supplies, Napoleon attempted to open
negotiations with Alexander, but his offers were
rejected. It was not until July 16 that he left Vilna.

As he proceeded the Russian plan of defense was made plain to him. The country had been laid entirely waste. Not a vestige of anything that could serve an army remained. Villages were burned and supplies destroyed, the people proceeding with the Russian army and becoming a part of it. The hostile armies met September 7 near the village of Borodino. It was a victory for Napoleon, although he lost 30,000 men. The loss of the Russians was 50,000. September 14 the armies of Napoleon entered Moscow. The great city was found to be practically deserted. On the night of the day of occupation fires started in various parts of town. They were with difficulty extinguished. The following day and evening fresh fires broke out and spread in every direction until the whole city was destroyed. Twice between this time and the retreat, Napoleon attempted to open negotiations with Alexander, but was met with silence. Autumn came, and on October 13, three weeks earlier than at any previous recorded period, snow fell and struck terror to the hearts of the soldiers. Famine and disease had wrought havoc among the troops. On October 18 the army left Moscow and proceeded southward. During the march, bands of Cossacks hung on the outskirts, and whenever opportunity offered, cut off detached companies or plundered baggage. History does not contain so pitiful or so disastrous a retreat as this. Smolensk was reached November 9. On that terrible march 90,000 soldiers died. It was not until December 6 that a bare remnant of the magnificent army which had advanced into Russia reached Vilna, more dead than alive. The campaign had cost Napoleon half a million lives. He hastened to France to again organize an army. Nearly every family in France mourned some friend or relative lost in Russia, yet the

magic of Napoleon's name caused them to again enter
cheerfully upon the work. Arsenals were kept busy, supplies were raised, and soldiers flocked by the thousands
to his standard. Within a few weeks he had an army
of 350,000 men. But at this time the populace of Prussia began to show signs of rising to throw off the hated
yoke inflicted by Napoleon. Six years had elapsed since
Jena, and Prussia had recovered from the blow. All
of the German States except Saxony entered into a
coalition against the French. England furnished gold,
and Sweden sent 35,000 men. Spain had not yet been
pacified, and Napoleon's troops there were kept busy.
Alexander marched from Russia with an army and
joined the allies. April 15, 1813, Napoleon started out
with his army of youthful and fresh enthusiasts. The
first clash was on May 2, near Lutzen. A large force
of the allied armies fell upon the French, and the battle
was waged for eight hours. At the end of that time
Napoleon was left victor of the field, but his own losses
had been so great that he could not afford to pursue
the enemy. May 21 and 22 the second sanguinary conflict of this campaign was fought near Bautzen. Napoleon lost 15,000 men, the allies, 10,000. The army of
the allies then retreated into upper Silesia and Napoleon
advanced to Breslau. Austria at this point offered to
mediate, and an armistice was declared. At this crisis
came news from Spain of the defeat of the French there,
the Duke of Wellington having won several victories.
August 10, Austria signed the alliance, offensive and
defensive, with Russia and Prussia, and the war against
Napoleon from this quarter was renewed. Austria sent
100,000 men into the field, bringing the total number of
the allied troops close to 500,000. Napoleon was posted
at Dresden, where his magazine was located. On Aug-

ust 25 the allied armies began to bombard Dresden. After two days of fighting the allies retreated, but the strength of Napoleon was all but exhausted. Now the King of Bavaria was forced to join the allies, and the King of Westphalia was forced by a revolution to flee for his life. Troubles were fast gathering around Napoleon. He had 100,000 troops with which to contend against five times that number. Already his star was leaving the glorious zenith and approaching a dismal horizon. France responded to an urgent appeal by forwarding 160,000 conscripts, and Napoleon now proposed to march on Berlin and compel the enemy to defend their cities. But his Generals opposed the enterprise. He then marched to Leipsic to make a final stand. The allied armies soon confronted him, and on the morning of September 16, at daybreak, a battle began which continued from dawn to dark for three successive days, when Napoleon finally determined to retreat. He marched his troops through the town and began the crossing of the two bridges which span the Pleisse. One of the bridges broke down, and the task of getting all the army across one bridge was hopeless. When daylight came and the enemy discovered the move made by Napoleon, an assault was made upon the town. The soldier who had been stationed to blow up the bridge when all had crossed, in the confusion started his train too soon and killed many of his comrades. This act also caused 25,000 troops who had not yet crossed the bridge to fall prisoners to the allies. Napoleon's total loss was 50,000. He continued his retreat to Paris, where he arrived November 5. Wellington had driven the French out of Spain and was already on French soil. The situation was now desperate. On every side France was threatened with invasion. January 25, 1814, Napoleon, having raised fresh armies, again proceeded to the front. Two days later and only 100 miles from Paris, he met a force of Blücher's Cossacks. The French were victorious and the next day attacked the castle of Brienne, occupied by 60,000 Russians. Napoleon's force numbered but 20,000. He gained a victory, but his enemies were crowding him on every side. He was now willing to negotiate for peace, and that, too, on the humbling terms that France should give up the territory taken from other Nations and return to its original limits. But during February, with two armies marching upon Paris, Napoleon moved with such rapidity that in nine days he gained seven victories, made nine marches in the depth of winter, and drove out or frightened away two armies, each larger than his own. His wonderful success during this brief period led Napoleon to believe that his star was again in the ascendancy, and when again the negotiations for peace were opened he refused to sign an armistice on the terms previously proposed. Napoleon now marched northward against Blücher, and on March 7 gave him battle at Craonne. The Prussians could not withstand the attacks of the French, and retired to the stronghold of Laon. Here on March 10 Napoleon marched up the mist-covered slopes to receive a resistless storm of iron hail from behind the terrace walls, which sheltered the entrenched foe. Napoleon was compelled to retire, and the following day retreated to Chavignon, leaving behind him on those bloody heights, 10,000 men and 30 cannon. He began to strengthen his position at Soissons, when the tidings came to him that Rheims had been captured by St. Priest, a French emigrant, with a corps of Russians. After a hurried march Napoleon attacked at midnight and retook the place, St. Priest being among the killed. But the end was fast approaching. Napoleon, like a lion at bay, knew not which way to turn or which of his enemies to attack first. There was always the danger that while engaged with one foe, others might march upon Paris. He finally determined to remain in the rear of the invading armies and by the terror of his name and by marching and countermarching and repeated attacks, distract their attention from Paris and cause them to turn back upon him until he could receive succor from his garrisons on the Rhine. Generals Marmont and Mortier were meanwhile to dispute the advance of the enemy. In Paris terror and confusion reigned. The enemy steadily advanced, each day drawing nearer to the Capital. Marmont and Mortier bravely but fruitlessly resisted up to the very walls of Paris. March 30 was a day of death and ruin. From the heights a constant cannonade was poured into the streets, and officers who came out with flags of truce to beg for a cessation of hostilities were shot on their approach. At 5 o'clock in the afternoon the capitulation was signed. When Napoleon arrived he found himself too late. After the first desperate resolve to still push into Paris, he calmly sent Caulaincourt there to accept such terms as might be offered, and retired to the old castle of Fontainebleau and quietly sought his bed and rest. At that moment the triumphal procession of the allies was moving through the Paris boulevards, 50,000 troops of many Nations, surrounding the victorious monarchs and princes. From the mighty throng of excited Frenchmen arose the shouts of acclamation which always greets the victor. But many groups were silent, and many hearts were filled with grief. The allied Sovereigns demanded the abdication of Napoleon, and this he penned April 4 and sent to them. It contained no conditions whatever in behalf of Napoleon, and Alexander of Russia expressed surprise at this, and at the meeting of the Sovereigns proposed that Napoleon retain his title with the sovereignty of the Island of Elba. The allies consented and fixed upon Napoleon a pension of 6,000,000 francs annually, to be paid by France. April 11 Napoleon signed his acceptance of the terms offered, on April 20 bade farewell to the Old Guard, and departed, accompanied by four commissioners, representing each of the four great Powers which had brought about his downfall, to the harbor of Fréjus, where on the 28th he embarked on the British frigate Undaunted, and was carried to Elba. He landed at the solitary island May 3, 1814, under a salute from the battery at Porto Ferrajo. The allied Powers placed upon the throne of France, Louis XVIII, brother of the slain monarch. He had been an exile in England. Everything having to the minds of the Sovereigns been satisfactorily arranged, the French prisoners of war, between 200,000 and 300,000 of them, were released from German fortresses and, returning to France, found everything changed. On learning what had happened, their invariable answer was, "It would not have taken place if we had been here." February 27, 1815, without the slightest intimation of the startling events that were about to take place reaching the outside world, Napoleon embarked from Elba with the thousand soldiers who had accompanied him there, and on March 1 reached Cannes. As soon as he touched French soil, soldiers began flocking to his standard. From city to city the swelling and irresistible tide rolled on toward Paris, and on the evening of March 20, Napoleon entered Paris and was borne on the shoulders of Parisians to the Tuileries, from which the aged and gouty Louis had but a few hours previously fled. The world was electrified, and once again the great Nations began to prepare for war. It was in vain that Napoleon attempted to negotiate, showing as his reasons for returning that the promises made him had not been kept. His pension had not been paid, his wife and his son were detained in Austria, and finally, the Nation desired him to once again assume the scepter. But the Powers had determined that he must be utterly crushed, and preparation went forward, with the result that in two months all was in readiness for the final fatal struggle. With daylight, June 12, Napoleon left Paris to join his army and march against his enemies. Two days later he reviewed at Avesnes all his available troops, numbering 135,000 men. He was pitted against Blücher with 100,000 men and Wellington with 76,000. For a few days there was considerable maneuvering, some skirmishes, a few minor battles, and two of importance, Quatre Bras and Ligny, until finally, June 18, 1815, came the shock which was felt around the world, the battle of Waterloo. At the outset neither of the armies had their full forces upon the field. Blücher was some distance away from Wellington's army, and a splendid division of Napoleon's force under Grouchy was in pursuit of a division of Prussians. At 11 o'clock the engagement began. Slowly it extended as one division after another entered into the conflict, until across the wide plain for nearly two miles, the fearful struggle raged. At a moment when Wellington's columns began to waver, Blücher came upon the field with 60,000 men and Napoleon sent his last troops, the Old Guard, into the fray. Grouchy and his troops, had they arrived at this juncture, might have changed the whole future history of Europe. Finally, at 4 o'clock, the battle ended. The

French army was no more. In fragments it was flying for safety, pursued by relentless Prussians. Napoleon seeing that all was lost hastened to Paris. Wellington and Blücher lost about 22,000 men, Napoleon over 30,000. June 22 Napoleon wrote his second abdication and sent it to the Chambers. This was the end of Napoleon's "hundred days." He decided to embark for the United States, and for that purpose went to Rochefort, only to be informed that English warships were watching every vessel to see that he did not escape. Finally, after various means of escape had been tried, he determined to claim the protection of England, and July 15 was received aboard the Bellerophon. But England did not receive him as a guest. Instead he was made a prisoner and transported to the Island of St. Helena, where he landed October 16. In this desolate and cheerless spot he was surrounded by sentinels and guards, whose duty it was to see that he did not again escape. For five years he was a prisoner at St. Helena, and died there, May 5, 1821, of cancer of the stomach, from which he had suffered for several years. His body was dressed as in life and he was buried in a quiet spot which he had himself selected. In 1840 the remains of Napoleon were, by permission of the English Government, removed to France. From the mouth of the Seine to Paris a funeral cortege was formed of twelve steamers. The banks of the stream were crowded with spectators, and all Paris participated in the services over Napoleon's ashes, which, according to his early wishes, at last found a place of repose "on the banks of the Seine," though in a magnificent catafalque in the Church of the Invalides.

WELLINGTON
1769-1852

THE GREATEST MAN OF A GREAT AGE

Disraeli, who delivered the eulogium at the funeral services over the Duke of Wellington, pronounced him, "the greatest man of a great age." The British Nation, which owed him much, echoed the sentiment, for among all the great men of the Kingdom, it could boast of none, who in the combined capacity of warrior and statesman, was his equal. Arthur Wellesley, Duke of Wellington, was the third son of Garrett, second Earl of Mornington. His mother was Anne, the daughter of Arthur Hill, Viscount Dungannon. Strangely enough, the exact date and even the place of his birth, cannot be stated with absolute certainty. It was, however, one of the last days of April or the first day of May, 1769, and his birthplace was either in Merrion street, Dublin, or at Dungan Castle in the County of Meath. The family from which Wellington sprung was one of great antiquity, his ancestors having originally settled in Rutlandshire. His father was a man of extensive acquaintance and endowed with a hospitable disposition, had no inclination for public affairs, but devoted most of his time to the study and practice of music. This fondness for music and failure to interest himself in the affairs of his estate, was responsible for the fact that when he died at his house in Kensington, on May 22, 1781, his large family was not well provided for, his property being encumbered to a considerable extent.

Wellington's earlier education was begun at Eton as
was that of his elder brother, Viscount Wellesley, who
later completed his course at Oxford. Wellington was
placed under the tuition of Rev. H. Mitchell, A.M., vicar
of Brighton, and was later sent to the military academy
at Angers. In his previous studies he had given little
promise of developing into the brilliant statesman and
a military genius whose destiny it was to accomplish
the overthrow of Napoleon Bonaparte's gigantic
schemes of conquest. At Angers, however, he became
fairly proficient in the work laid out for him and it early
became evident that the prospect of a career at arms
inspired him to give his best efforts in this direction.
Not long after, Lord Mornington, Wellington's senior
brother, had attained his majority, he was elected a
representative of the royal borough of New Windsor
and was named one of the commissioners for Indian
affairs. This appointment subsequently made it possible for him to aid his younger brother toward the goal of
fame. Wellington obtained his first commission in
March, 1787, entering the army as an ensign in the
Seventy-third Regiment. His advance was rapid and
after having served with various regiments, was, in 1793,
gazetted major of the Thirty-third Foot. In September
of the same year, upon the retirement of Lieutenant-
Colonel Yorke, he secured that position. Wellington
had in the meantime become a member of the Irish Parliament. He was first returned to the Parliament in the
summer of 1790 from the borough of Trim, whose patronage belonged to the house of Mornington. He sat
for the borough in 1791, 1792, and 1793. His appearance at this time is described as a ruddy-faced, juvenile
looking youth. He wore a scarlet uniform with large
epaulettes and was extremely popular among men of

DUKE OF WELLINGTON

Painting by Thomas Lawrence

his age and rank. As a speaker he was already possessed of a fluent delivery and his remarks were always terse and directly to the point. As an attache of the Irish court, having been appointed to the staff of the Earl of Westmoreland, Wellington found himself compelled to make larger expenditures than he could well afford, in order that he might maintain the dignity of his station. At this time a wealthy tradesman generously advanced him the required amount, and it was not many years before he was able to repay the debt and at the same time acknowledge his gratitude by appointing the tradesman to a position of honor. Wellington's career in Parliament was interrupted by a call to active military service. The republican army of France had been making rapid progress, and storm clouds were beginning to appear on the horizon of European political affairs. England concluded that aid given the Bourbon party of France might serve to check the alarming spread of republicanism. As Lieutenant-Colonel of the Thirty-third, Wellington embarked in June, 1794, at Cork and in the following month arrived at Ostend. Here Lord Moore soon arrived with additional troops. The armies of the coalition had been driven off French soil and were trying to maintain their positions in Austrian Flanders. The Austrian and Hanoverian commanders had suffered successive defeats, however, and the result of these reverses was to cause the Duke of York to retreat to Antwerp. Lord Moore decided to evacuate Ostend and hasten to his relief. It was at Antwerp that Wellington first saw an army in the field. The campaign in Flanders was brief and unsatisfactory and at its close, Wellington was selected by Sir David Dundas to cover the retreat of the army. This movement, filled with peril and of a nature to try the stoutest heart, was accomplished in the midst of the rigors of a severe winter and the manner in which the rear-guard fulfilled its mission raised the young Lieutenant-Colonel high in the estimation of his superiors.   In 1796, Wellington's regiment was ordered to India, and landed at Calcutta in February of 1797.   In May of the following year, his brother, Lord Mornington, afterward Marquis of Wellesley, arrived at Calcutta, having been made Governor-General.   At this time Tippoo Saib, Sultan of the Mysore, was preparing to make war in an effort to recover the territory he had lost by the treaty of 1792. The new Governor-General took effective measures to suppress him, after first having attempted pacific methods.   The British army, including native allies numbered 40,000 men, while Tippoo Saib had an available force of 76,000 fighting men.   War was declared February 22, 1799.   The Thirty-third Regiment was attached to a subsidiary force of the Nizam of Ducon, the most formidable ally of the British.   Under orders of General Harris, Wellington was given command of this division and the march upon Seringapatam began.   In the first engagement with Tippoo he was defeated, with a loss of 1,500 men and in a second battle the division commanded by Wellington defeated a force of 2,000 of the rebel's best cavalry.   Tippoo retreated to Seringapatam and the British appeared before the city April 3d. Three days later in an assault upon the works, Wellington was wounded in the knee and narrowly escaped falling into the hands of his savage enemies.   It was not until May 4 that the city was captured, Tippoo Saib having been slain.   Wellington was then made Military Governor of Mysore.   This experience in settling and administering affairs in the conquered territory was of great value to him.   His position was by no means a secure one, the frontiers of Mysore being constantly harassed by native tribes, one of the most desperate of the marauding bands being led by a chief called Doondiah. So vigorously did Wellington take up the pursuit after this native bandit and his followers that Doondiah sought refuge in the neighboring territory of Mahratta. Wellington, with his troops, pursued the fugitive through the Mahratta territory and completely put him to rout. During his campaign in this territory he acquired a knowledge of the country and the people, which proved invaluable to him later on when the Mahratta War broke out. In the meantime, however, his career in India threatened to come to an end. He received orders in December, 1800, to take command of a body of troops for service in Ceylon. Later, a change was made whereby the destination of the troops was changed to Egypt, and in consequence Wellington was notified that he would be made second in command to General Baird, instead of at the head of the expedition, as at first ordered. He felt deeply aggrieved at this, but so earnest was he for the success of the expedition that without having received any instructions to do so, and at the risk of being severely censured, he removed the troops from Trincomalee, where they had been waiting embarkation for Ceylon, to Bombay, feeling convinced that if the troops were to be of any value for service in Egypt, they would have to be provisioned in Bombay without further delay. In justifying himself in this action before his superiors, Wellington displayed a remarkable acquaintance with the necessities of an invasion of Egypt. His expected trip to Egypt was canceled by an attack of fever on the eve of departure, and when he recovered he was ordered back to Mysore. In the meantime, Holkar and other native chiefs had made war against the Mahratta territory and

the Peshwa had fled to the coast. The potentate laid his
case before the Indian Government and a treaty was
effected with him by which his territory was to be restored. This apparently formidable task fell to Wellington, who, to the surprise of all, accomplished it without
being compelled to strike a blow or defend himself
against one. With his troops he left Seringapatam,
March 12, 1803, and crossed into Mahratta. He started
for Poona, the capital, 600 miles distant, and his progress
through the territory was a succession of triumphs. His
extraordinary success on this occasion was the result of
his tact, firmness, good judgment, and thorough understanding of the characters with whom he had to deal.
When sixty miles from Poona he learned that a rival of
the Peshwa, Amrut Rao, was about to consign the town
to the flames. Without losing a moment, at the head
of his cavalry he pressed on and reached Poona on the
afternoon of April 20, in time to save it from destruction.
The Peshwa was restored to his power and became a
faithful ally to the British. Wellington was now made
Governor-General over all of the states and tribes of that
section of India. His most troublesome adversary was
Sindhia, one of the chieftains who had put the Peshwa to
flight. Failing to arrive at a peaceful understanding
with Sindhia, Wellington declared war on him on
August 6, 1803. He marched northward, captured
Ahmadnager on August 11, crossed the Godavery, and
on September 23 came upon the combined forces of
Sindhia and the Rajah of Berar. The enemy occupied a
strong position, and in point of numbers were greatly
superior to Wellington's force, but without hesitation he
valiantly attacked the natives and defeated them, though
not until after a most desperate battle had been fought,
in which 2,500 men were slain. The victory resulted in

the capture of 100 cannon.   This battle, which is known
as the battle of Assaye, was the most sanguinary engagement in which Wellington had thus far participated, but
fate had decreed that he should be the leader on another
bloody field, in comparison with which, the battle of
Assaye could scarcely be ranked as a skirmish.   The war
against Sindhia and the Rajah of Berar was concluded by
a second and decisive victory at Argaum on September
29.   Wellington was not yet thirty-five years of age, and
yet he had already gained an enviable reputation, not
only for bravery and skill upon the field of battle, but also
as a master diplomat in dealing with the cunning and
often treacherous potentates of India.   At this time he
presented a striking appearance.   He was of middle
height, muscular, and straight, and his distinguished air
would anywhere attract attention.   He sailed for England on March 10, 1804.   His merit as a commanding
officer was now fully established, and the King and
Parliament thanked him for his splendid achievements in
the Indian campaigns.   In 1805 he was made Colonel of
the Thirty-Third Regiment, and the following year was
returned to Parliament from the borough of Rye.   On
April 10, 1806, Wellington married Katherine Paken-
ham, daughter of Edward Michael, second Earl of Long-
ford.   Two sons were the issue of this marriage, Arthur,
born in 1807, and Charles, born in the following year.

The administration of the Earl of Mornington, his
illustrious brother, was attacked in the House of Commons, and Wellington made such a vigorous defense of
his brother that the House gave a vote of thanks to the
Earl, instead of criticising his actions in India.   In 1807
Wellington was appointed Chief Secretary for Ireland.
From August 29 of this year, he aided Lord Cathcart in
bringing about the surrender of the Danish forces at

Copenhagen and by the terms of the treaty agreed upon, the Danish fleet was delivered over to the British Government.   The object of this move was to prevent the squadron from falling into the hands of Napoleon.   In February, 1808, Wellington again received the thanks of Parliament, and in April of that year he was promoted to the rank of Lieutenant-General.   He was then placed in command of a detachment of the army, detailed to aid in resisting the aggressions of the French in Spain and Portugal.   With his forces he embarked for Spain in July.   August 2 he landed his troops at Mondego Bay, and issued a proclamation to the Portuguese explaining his mission.   The peninsula was almost completely in the possession of the French.   Saborde, with a force of 6,000 French troops, was attacked at Rolica, August 17, and forced to retreat.   The battle of Rolica resulted in the killing or wounding of 1,200 of the 5,000 men engaged.   On the 19th and 20th insts. reinforcements arrived, which increased the army of Wellington to 16,000 men.   A battle was precipitated the following day at Vimeiro, in which the attacking force of 14,000 French were driven back in great confusion, with a loss of 36 officers and 594 men, killed and wounded.   In the midst of this engagement he was superseded in command by Sir Henry Burrard, and vainly endeavored to induce the new commander to follow up the victory with pursuit.   Wellington returned to England and once more took his seat in the House of Commons.   Sir John Moore, who succeeded to the command of the army in Spain, after a disasterous retreat, engaged the French at Corunna, was victorious, but lost his life just as the battle was won and his army hastened to the ships.   In spite of the bitter attacks made upon his military record about this time, Wellington was again made Com-

mander-in-Chief of the forces in the Spanish Peninsula.
Resigning his position as Secretary to Ireland, he sailed
for Spain, April 16, 1809.   In addition to his own he
was given a large force of Spanish and Portuguese
troops, and at once began a movement toward the enemy.
Oporto, which had been captured by Marshal Soult, was
attacked and retaken, the French being driven out.
Baggage, booty, and artillery were left behind, and fell
into the hands of the victor.   He now bent his energies
toward bringing about an engagement with Marshal Victor, whose forces consisted of 53,000 men.   Wellington's
army consisted of 22,000 British troops and Spanish
allies to the number of 56,000.   At Talavera the army of
Victor was encountered on July 27.   The battle opened
with an attack by the French light infantry, and soon
the engagement became general.   The fighting continued into the night, and at daylight the following morning it was resumed.   For a time the French were forced
back, but rallied, and in a desperate charge swept back
the German hussars, who were among the English allies.
This advantage was but momentary.   The Germans reformed and fell upon the French with resistless fury.   At
6 o'clock on the second day of the battle the French fell
back under the repeated onslaughts of the British and
allied troops, and ceased to resist.   The losses to the
French, according to their own figures, were 7,389 men,
killed, wounded, and prisoners.   The British forces lost
5,423.   After this battle, despite the fact that he had
been victorious, Wellington found himself placed in an
extremely critical condition.   His troops, composed to
a large extent of raw material, were poorly fed and poorly
equipped.   Hundreds of horses were unfit for service or
had been killed in battle.   In addition to these discouraging conditions, his requests for aid from his own Gov-

ernment were received with cold indifference. His
enemies were still making accusations against him, and
maintained that he had accomplished nothing of importance in the peninsula. Spain's promise to supply
the British with provisions was not kept. Under these
circumstances Wellington decided to withdraw from the
country, asserting that a half starved army was worse
than no army at all. Finally, however, he came to the
conclusion that he would henceforth confine his attentions to the protection of Lisbon. On September 16,
1809, Wellington received the gratifying intelligence
that he had been raised to the peerage, with the titles of
Baron Douro of Wellesley, Viscount Wellington of Talavera and Wellington. He now spent several months in
strengthening his position in Portugal. He surmised
that in the spring Napoleon would throw a tremendous
force into the Spanish Peninsula, and strongly fortified
the mountain passes to the north of Lisbon, and left no
point open to easy invasion between the Tagus and the
ocean. His expectations proved to be correct. Marshal Massena had taken the place of Soult. He was the
most distinguished of all the Generals in the Austrian
campaign, and as summer drew near, he approached
Portugal with an army of 70,000 men. Like his pre-
decessor, he hoped to obtain the crown of Portugal by
wresting the territory from the British. At the same
time Napoleon, in order to crush all opposition in Spain,
dispatched a tremendous force into that country. Wellington's plan was to retire further and further toward
the coast in the hope that the French would follow. He
figured that they would have an extremely difficult task
to perform in the event that they should be compelled to
retreat through the hostile territory. The French did
exactly what he had anticipated. They attacked Ciudad

Rodrigo, and, much to the surprise and disgust of the
Spaniards, Wellington firmly refused to lend the beleaguered city any assistance, which he might have done
had such a movement accorded with the plans he had
mapped out.   Rodrigo therefore fell, and after the investment of Coa in the middle of August, the invasion of
Portugal was really begun.   Massena captured Almeida
and pushed forward, declaring he would drive the English into the sea within a few weeks.   In the meantime
Wellington was strengthening his position about Busaco.
Upon the arrival of the French, the British, to the number of 25,000, were immediately attacked, and succeeded
in repulsing the French.   Massena had lost about 6,000
men in killed, wounded, and prisoners.   After administering this check to the onward march of the invaders,
Wellington withdrew to Lisbon, and there massed an
army of 100,000 men, including the allies.   At this time
Massena, with his army, were seeking in vain for a way
through the mountains, which Wellington had so carefully fortified during the fall and winter.

The natural strength of the English position was considerably increased by the military labors of the leader.
Inside the fortifications Wellington's army was enjoying
health and plenty, while outside Massena's soldiers were
striving to endure conditions akin to starvation.   Under
these circumstances it did not require much time for
Massena to come to the conclusion that discretion demanded his departure.   He retired with his entire army.
Wellington now took the offensive and was soon in full
pursuit of the French.   From this time, October, 1810,
until the following May, there was a series of engagements between the two armies.   At Albuera, May 16, a
battle was fought which resulted in a victory for the
English.   In this engagement the allies lost 3,500 men

out of 7,000. The French lost 9,500 men. Soon after this battle Badajoz was besieged, but the attempt to take this city failed. All the efforts of the French to maintain themselves in Portugal proved unsuccessful. Wellington took Rodrigo and invested Badajoz a second time. It was not until another and still more determined effort had been made, however, that the stronghold finally fell into the hands of the English. The victors lost 5,000 men, killed and wounded, and took 4,000 prisoners. Wellington moved on to Madrid, where he was received with enthusiastic demonstration by the people. Before reaching the capital he had fought the battle of Salamanca—a decisive victory for the British and a severe blow to the French. The English General continued to assume the offensive in his campaign against the French armies in Spain. His siege of Burgos proved a failure in September, 1812, and the allied army retreated to Agueda. In the following year, after a reorganization of his army, Wellington departed from Portugal. He followed Joseph Bonaparte to Vitoria, and on June 21 he utterly routed the French near that city. Joseph Bonaparte conducted an inglorious retreat, having lost about 7,000. The French armies retreated to the Pyrenees, still hunted by the English, and finally passed over the mountain range and out of Spain. Wellington had finally brought his victorious forces in sight of France. On June 21 the French army in Spain had been practically annihilated, but on July 21 Soult found himself in command of a force 80,000 strong. The English began a siege of San Sebastian, but the project was abandoned after determined efforts to take the place by storm, and from this time until August 1, Wellington was engaged in what are called the Battles of the Pyrenees. In the various combats here Soult, lost 8,000 men, but Wellington's military ability was tried to the utmost to maintain the advantage he had secured during the previous years.

After these operations the siege of San Sebastian was once more resumed. A fleet of transports from England brought necessary engines and equipment to the British. On September 8, after a vigorous assault by the allies, the stronghold was captured. One of the dark chapters in the history of the peninsular campaigns is that describing the sack of the captured city. Officers attempted to restrain the victors, but in spite of their efforts the soldiers committed the most serious excesses. The fall of Pampeluna was now the only object sought by Wellington before he should march against the entrenched camps of the French. This stronghold was surrendered October 31. The English army next made the famous passage of the Bidassoa, and the advance into France was begun. Soult, with 30,000 men, attacked the English on the Heights of St. Pierre, but was repulsed. During the early months of 1814 Bayonne was invested and taken, the English army crossed the Adour, gave battle at Orthez, and caused the French to retreat. Bordeaux was entered, and Soult added once more defeat to his growing list at Toulouse.

While Napoleon's lieutenants were losing ground thus rapidly in the south of France, Bonaparte himself was undertaking a defense of the approaches to his Capital. One million men had been collected in Europe for the purpose of overthrowing the Emperor, and he found himself more narrowly confined from day to day.

Lamartine describes the situation as follows:

"Wellington had descended from the Pyrenees on the south, with the best troops of Spain and Portugal. The armies of Marshal Soult and Marshal Suchet had retired rapidly on France to defend their native soil against the invasion of two long-provoked nations. Bubna and Bellegarde, two Austrian Generals, at the head of 100,000 men, held Prince Eugene, Napoleon's Viceroy, in check on the Milanese territory, and crossed the Alps to debouch at Lyons by the gorge of Savoy. Bernadotte, the modern Coriolanus, had sold himself to the coalition at the price of the crown of Sweden. Against Belgium and the Rhine he conducted a force of 120,000 men, consisting of all the second rate nations of the North. Prince Schwartzenburg, generalissimo of the coalition, and Blücher, the Prussian General, crossed the Rhine on the 31st day of December and directed about 200,000 men of all nations to the foot of the Vosges. Four columns of 400,000 combatants penetrated Germany by four roads to recruit with inexhaustible reinforcements the van of the armies already entered upon the soil of France. The sovereigns themselves (the Emperors of Russia and Austria and the Kings of Prussia and of Sweden), marched with their troops. Against these masses, recruited by patriotism, Napoleon could only bring the exhausted and broken-up remains of his once splendid armies."

The allied army concentrated forces at Chalons on March 22, and thence marched on Paris. The city was occupied by some 15,000 troops under Marmont, but on the evening of March 30, after a short combat, the capital capitulated. On the following day it was occupied by the allies. March 31 Napoleon brought his army within ten miles of Paris, but finding it in the hands of his enemies, he hastily retreated, and began to muster all his available forces at Fontainebleau. Hostilities ceased throughout Europe. Wellington was made Ambassador at the court of France, and arrived in Paris May 4.

He was elevated to a Dukedom.   After visiting Madrid in order to avert an impending crisis in Spanish affairs, the Duke rejoined the army at Bordeaux on June 10. The armies were disbanded as peace had been signed by the allied powers, and on June 23 Wellington reached Dover.   He was received after an absence of five years with expressive demonstrations in his honor.   He had left England trembling at the success of Napoleon and the alarming spread of Republicanism.   In person he received the thanks of the House of Lords, and a similar honor was accorded him by the House of Commons.   An annuity of £10,000 was unanimously voted him, and a former grant of £200,000 pounds was increased to £300,-000.   Several of his distinguished associates were also substantially rewarded.   Wellington did not remain in England long, leaving to assume his duties at Paris, and arriving in that capital August 22.   In the meantime Napoleon had been assigned to the small Island of Elba as his future Kingdom and retreat.   Numbers of retired officers and soldiers who had fought under Napoleon's banners were scattered throughout France.   Later events proved these disbanded military men still clung with remarkable devotion to the cause of their fallen leader.   This was the condition in France when the year 1815 opened.   Elba was so near the scene of Napoleon's extended campaigns, that it was an easy matter for him to maintain communication with his partisans.   Napoleon left Elba and landed at Cannes on March 1 with 1,200 troops.   This movement called forth a declaration of Austrian, Spanish, French, British, Portuguese, Russian, Prussian, and Swedish plenipotentiaries denouncing the ex-Emperor as an enemy and a disturber of the world's peace.   Napoleon increased his forces with remarkable rapidity, and became more aggressive as the days passed. In the face of the approaching crisis, the Duke of Wellington was appointed Commander-in-Chief of the army of the Netherlands. The man whose inordinate ambition had caused Europe to tremble, found himself opposed by an allied force, notably, united in a common purpose; that of finally wresting from him the last vestige of his regained strength.

His forces altogether had been estimated at about 150,000 men. The allied armies included British, Germans, and Hanoverians, numbered 74,000 men. The Duke's headquarters were at Brussels. The Prussian army of 115,000 men was concentrated on the Meuse. The French army, 150,000 strong, was commanded by Marshal Grouchy. The first battle between fragments of these forces was fought at Ligny on June 14. Napoleon attacked the Prussian outposts, and forced them to retreat. After this engagement Wellington's corps were united at Quatre Bras on the road from Charleroi to Brussels. On June 15 Napoleon attacked a brigade of Wellington's army at Frasne and forced it also to retreat. Another attack was made by Marshal Ney, near Quatre Bras, upon the forces under Blücher. In the engagement the British and their allies sustained a loss of 3,750. The assault failed, but Blücher fell back to unite with the fourth corps. On June 17 Napoleon's and Wellington's armies were ready for combat, but the former had defeated Marshal Grouchy and Blücher had still failed to join Wellington. On the 18th the British line was formed. Napoleon gazed upon the simple arrangement of the British troops with satisfaction, and disposed his own forces accordingly. After the battle started both Wellington and the Emperor were in its midst. The French directed the first attack shortly before 11 o'clock on the old storehouse of Hougoumont. The first assault did not succeed in dislodging the allies, and was followed by another. Blow after blow fell upon the defense of Hougoumont during the remainder of the day, but the place held its own until the last furious attacks were made upon Wellington's left. Picton commanded the British here. Drouet led his columns of French up to within forty yards of the English. His forward sections were confused by a well directed volley of musketry. Picton ordered a charge. At that moment he fell mortally wounded, but his command was carried out, and the French infantry was disorganized and routed. Napoleon's division under D'Erton moved against the farmhouse of La Haye Sainte, but was compelled to retreat with considerable loss. The position was finally taken, however, and its defenders were put to death. Napoleon attempted to wear out the English at other points, but his advances terminated in defeat and loss. Wellington drew upon his reserves. His battalions were fearfully depleted, however, and the "Stories of Waterloo" tells us that he "almost despaired. He calculated, and justly, that he had an army which would perish where it stood; but when he saw the devastation caused by the incessant attacks of an enemy, who appeared determined to succeed, is it surprising that his watch was frequently consulted and that he prayed for night or Blücher." Blücher's coming was finally heralded by the rumble of moving artillery. Wellington took courage, but Napoleon was similarly effected by the intelligence that fresh troops were approaching. He believed this to be his corps under Marshal Grouchy, with which he expected to make a final and overpowering attack. He learned his error when the Prussians appeared, and threw back his left wing. The Imperial Guard was hurled against the British infantry, but fell back repulsed, and the pursuit which at once ensued, served to utterly rout them. A second column of the guards were thrown against the infantry, but they, too, were compelled to flee in hopeless disorder. Before the French could rally, Wellington ordered and put into execution a general attack, and in the end, Napoleon's magnificent army of the previous day was completely shattered. Maxwell places the French loss in killed, wounded, prisoners, and soldiers, who, in dismay, fled to their homes, at 40,000. The same authority places the loss of the allies at 23,000. Wellington proceeded to Paris, while the remnant of the French forces collected at Laon. On July 8 he had the satisfaction of seeing Louis XVIII reënter Paris. On June 22 Napoleon had formally abdicated, and a few weeks later was a captive on the Island of St. Helena. Wellington left Paris for London on June 29, 1816. On the evening before his departure an attempt was made to blow up the building in which he was giving a grand entertainment to men of prominence in Paris. In the fall of 1816 Wellington returned to Paris, and resumed his duties as plenipotentiary to the court of Louis XVIII. He materially aided the Government in settling claims of the powers against France. A second attempt was made to assassinate him on February 11, 1818, when Marie Andre Cantillon, a subaltern officer, discharged a pistol at him as he was entering his hotel. On this occasion Wellington received the congratulations of the allied sovereigns on his escape. The armies of occupation in France broke up November 1, 1819. In December of that year Wellington was made Master-General of Ordnance in England. The following year he took his seat in the House of Lords. In December he became Governor of Plymouth, and on February 19 was appointed Colonel-in-Chief of the Rifle Brigade. In 1827 he was made General Commander-in-Chief and Colonel of the First Grenadier Guards. In the meantime he was devoting himself to the performance of public duties, and interesting himself more extensively in politics than he had previously done. In February, 1828, he became Premier to King George IV. After the death of that monarch in 1830, Wellington's popularity greatly declined. He was bitterly assailed for his opposition to the "reform bill," the feeling being so bitter as to lead, at least on one occasion, to personal violence. In 1834 Wellington was elected Chancellor of the University of Oxford. In 1842 he became General Commander-in-Chief, a position which he had once resigned. One of the most notable affairs of state with which he had to deal during his Premiership under King George IV, was the movement for Catholic emancipation. It was hoped and expected by the Protestant party that Wellington would steadfastly resist this. But convinced that the time had come when it must be granted, as was usual with him, he subordinated party spirit and personal interest for what he considered the interest of the Nation. His Ministry, therefore, in spite of all opposition, presented in 1829 a bill for the relief of Catholics. Although he amply explained and justified his course, he at once became the object of much bitter calumny, and in one instance these aspersions became so annoying that Wellington issued a challenge to the Earl of Winchelsea, one of the loudest of his traducers. In spite of the violent opposition with which the public often received Wellington's position on matters of great importance to the Nation, there were none who sincerely doubted his conscientiousness and the splendor of his military career could not but command respect and admiration. The last act of any considerable importance, politically, with which Wellington

was connected, was the appointment of the Earl of Derby
as Premier upon his suggestion. Wellington was remarkably active to the very last day of his life. His
death came suddenly at Walmer, September 14, 1852,
being the result of a stroke of apoplexy. He was buried
under the dome of St. Paul's, and in the chapel of the
cathedral stands a monument erected to his memory.

OLIVER HAZARD PERRY
1785-1819

"WE HAVE MET THE ENEMY AND THEY ARE OURS"

When the gallant Decatur was informed of the untimely death of his friend and fellow officer, Commodore Perry, he solemnly remarked: "The American Navy has lost its brightest ornament." It was not the fate of this brave naval hero to fall gloriously in battle, defending the flag of his country, but the laurel was still fresh upon the young victor's brow, when, on his thirty-fourth birthday, he quietly passed away, the victim of disease. He met death as he had often braved it, calmly, courageously, and undismayed. "Few persons," he said, according to Dr. M. Morgan, who attended him in his last hours, "have greater inducements to make them wish to live than I, but I am perfectly ready to go if it pleases the Almighty to take me; 'the debt of nature must be paid.'" Since the death of Washington, twenty years before, no event in the mortality records of the Nation caused such universal sorrow as the passing of this noble and intrepid soul. His career was one of genuine merit and brilliancy, the result of his own exertions and achievements. His was a dauntless spirit, which difficulties could not discourage nor dangers appall. His intense patriotism and zeal in his profession, coupled with cool daring and devotion to duty, gained for his name immortal renown. Brave, skillful, resolute, magnanimous, his example, so illustrious, will always remain

347

an inspiration to future heroes of the American navy and impel to deeds of glory and valor.

Oliver Hazard Perry, the son of Christopher Raymond Perry and Sarah Alexander Perry, was born August 23, 1785, at South Kingston, situated opposite the town of Newport on the Narragansett in Washington County and State of Rhode Island. His paternal ancestor in the fifth generation was Edmund Perry, who was born in Devonshire, England, about 1630. He was a man of education and refinement and one of those, who, as a result of religious persecution in his native land, emigrated to Massachusetts and settled in Plymouth about thirty years after the founding of that colony. But religious intolerance existed in the new colony to almost as great an extent as in the old world, and this fact induced the seeker for peace to remove to Rhode Island and settle in the beautiful promontory overlooking Narragansett Bay. Here, among the Indians, he found a spot where he might worship God according to the dictates of his own conscience. Mackenzie, in his life of Commodore Perry, calls attention to the fact that a civilized descendant of these very Indians served under Perry on Lake Erie, and fell fighting for his country aboard the Lawrence. Freeman Perry, great-grandson of Edmund Perry and grandfather of the future naval hero, was born in 1732, and his third son, Christopher, the father of Oliver Hazard, was born December 4, 1761. Although a mere lad when the Revolution broke out, he served through nearly the whole war, and then entered before the mast in a privateer commanded by Captain Reed, and from thenceforward continued to devote himself to the sea in various capacities and arose at the age of twenty-three to the command of a merchantman. It was at this time that he married Sarah

Alexander, a young woman of high character and liberal education. Oliver Hazard was their first child and his chief characteristics of earliest years were, an uncommon beauty and a sweetness of disposition which was the subject of remark. His first tuition was given by his mother, and he was able to read at a very tender age. The greater part of his boyhood education, however, was gained at the school of a venerable Scotchman, named Kelly, at Tower Hill, distant about four miles from the Perry homestead. Christopher Perry, meanwhile, pursued his calling as commander of merchant vessels and made several cruises to South America. His family having increased to four children, and desiring to give them the advantages of a better education than could be obtained near home, he removed to Newport. Here Oliver was placed under the instruction of a Mr. Frazer, an excellent teacher in the ordinary branches and in mathematics and their application to navigation and nautical astronomy as well. To these sciences, Oliver readily applied himself, and it was the boast of Mr. Frazer that his scholar, Perry, was the best navigator in Rhode Island. Near the close of the year 1797, Captain Perry abandoned the sea-faring profession and established himself at the small village of Westerly. About this time the relations of this Government with France began to be somewhat strained. France expected our aid in the war against England, and the French representative in the United States went so far as to grant commissions for the fitting out of privateers in America against England. American merchant vessels not infrequently became the prey of French cruisers. These conditions induced the United States to make provision for increases of the navy in 1798, and Captain Perry was one of the first to apply for a command of one of the new craft. This being satisfactorily arranged, he went to Warren to superintend the construction of his ship. He was accompanied by his wife, and during this time Oliver was left to take charge of the household and look after his brothers and sisters. When Captain Perry received a commission as post-captain in the navy, Oliver implored him to be allowed to enter the navy also, and the ambitious lad was made midshipman aboard his father's ship, the General Greene. He reported for duty in April, 1799, and this was the beginning of his glorious naval career. His first cruise was to Cuba, the Greene being employed in convoying American merchant vessels in that vicinity. Yellow fever among the crew compelled the Greene to return to Newport in July, but she resumed her station early in the autumn. Civil war was at this time raging in St. Domingo. Rigaud, a mulatto chieftain, aimed at establishing an independent government in opposition to General Toussaint, who operated under the name of the French Republic. Rigaud, with a number of armed barges, was operating a predatory warfare along the coast, and in many instances his acts amounted to piracy. American commerce had suffered from his depredations, and the American Consul-General at St. Domingo requested that the Greene take the side of Toussaint against Rigaud. Having the Government's approval to the plan, Capt. Perry started out after the craft of Rigaud and on February 9, 1800, discovered some of Rigaud's cruisers under the protection of three forts on the coast. The Greene at once stood in, and in thirty minutes silenced the forts and was preparing to take possession of the vessels when a French frigate appeared and the Greene gave chase, for while aiding Toussaint in St. Domingo, America was at war with

France on the seas. Shortly after this incident the General Greene proceeded to Jaquemel, which was the stronghold of Rigaud and which was being besieged from the land by Toussaint. The fire of the Greene upon the fortifications compelled the garrison of 5,000 to surrender the town to Toussaint. In May following, while the Greene was giving convoy to an American vessel bound for Havana, a British battleship signaled the merchant vessel to heave to, and fired a shot. Capt. Perry signaled the brig to proceed, and when the British warship sent a boat to board the merchant, he threw a shot in front of it, and although the Britisher protested, the boarding of the brig was not permitted. This stand was taken in spite of the fact that the British ship was one of seventy-four guns and tremendously superior to the Greene. These incidents are of interest only as showing the school in which the future naval hero was receiving his earliest training in his chosen profession. He was in the meantime studious and had attained a degree of knowledge far beyond his years. Toward the close of the year 1800, Tripoli, Tunis, and Algiers were making trouble with the American commerce in the Mediterranean, the Bashaw of Tripoli having gone so far as to demand a money present from the United States, threatening to begin hostilities against the commerce of the Nation unless it was forthcoming. An American squadron was sent against the Barbarians in 1801, and another the following year. This second squadron was composed of the Chesapeake, Constellation, New York, Adams, and John Adams, frigates, and the schooner Enterprise. Perry again embarked as midshipman after a year of idleness. He was assigned to the Adams, Capt. Hugh G. Campbell, a brave and valuable officer, who came to regard young Perry with a sincere regard, and the friendship which sprang up between them continued until death. It became the tedious task of the Adams to watch two Tripolitan vessels in the harbor at Gibraltar. During this service, Perry's seventeenth birthday was made memorable by his promotion to an acting lieutenancy. In May the squadron assembled at Malta and soon after sailed for Tripoli. On approaching the city, a number of small merchant vessels were discovered trying to make the harbor under convoy of several gunboats. Chase was given but the vessels succeeded in making a smaller harbor adjoining the city, where they were hastily unloaded and drawn upon the beach. A stone building on shore was quickly fortified and filled with troops from the town, while the gunboats escaped along shore and got under protection of the batteries. The following day an expedition from the American squadron started for shore under Lieutenant David Porter with the perilous mission of destroying the vessels on the beach. The tars pulled in against a heavy musketry fire from Moors and Arabs, fired the shipping, and returned to their ships in the midst of the enemy's fire. In this brief expedition twelve Americans were either killed or wounded. After a year of blockading and cruising along the coasts of Tunis, Algiers, and Tripoli, the Adams returned to the United States, arriving at Newport in November, 1803. Young Perry now devoted himself to the study of mathematics and astronomy. He at this time displayed during his leisure hours a taste for society and was exceedingly fond of music, being himself a performer on the flute. His only extravagance was that of hiring horses, as he was fond of riding and never let an opportunity escape to gratify it. Aside from this he is said to have been an excellent hand at billiards and a skillful fencer. These were his tastes and occupations as he was approaching manhood. During this time Commodore Preble was in command of the Mediterranean squadron and carried on a succession of brilliant campaigns against the enemies of American commerce. The news of Preble's exploits awakened the spirit of enthusiasm in the young officers who were at home inactive, and Perry was among the first to make strenuous efforts to be ordered to join the squadron. His opportunity came when Congress ordered several additional vessels to the Mediterranean, among them the Constellation, which was given to Captain Campbell, and aboard which Perry naturally secured his berth as lieutenant. The Constellation arrived at Tripoli in September, 1804, but Commodore Preble had been superseded by Commodore Barron, and Perry and other young officers who had come with high hopes of having opportunities to distinguish themselves were highly disappointed at the peaceful course pursued by the Commodore. Perry was for a time given command of the schooner Nautillus, and some time later, when Commodore Rodgers had relieved Commodore Barron, Perry was ordered to the Commodore's flagship, having by his appearance, manners, and conversation, attracted the attention of his superior, who was favorably impressed with the young lieutenant. That his opinion of Perry was not shaken during the succeeding months is shown by the fact that when toward the end of the summer of 1806, after having satisfactorily settled affairs with the Barbary powers, Commodore Rodgers prepared to return home, and for that purpose transferred his flag to the Essex, he took Perry with him to that ship, which reached the United States in October. Once more on shore, Perry resumed his studies, and in January, 1807, first met Elizabeth Champlin Mason, then a beautiful

girl of sixteen, to whom Perry's heart went out and who
later became his wife. This was the period of gunboat
and embargo policy, and Perry had been detailed to
superintend the construction of seventeen gunboats at
Newport. He completed his work by June, and it is
further to his credit that the Navy Department selected
him to command this large detachment of gunboats.
With his flotilla he proceeded to New York to protect
the harbor and adjacent waters from the encroachments
of French and English belligerents.   The wars being
carried on at this time by other Nations had thrown the
bulk of the maritime carrying trade into the hands of the
American merchant marine, and this awakened the jealousy of both France and England, each Nation being,
moreover, desirous of depriving the other of the advantages which each was deriving from the American trade,
our merchant vessels became the prey of both, and the
timid policy pursued by America at this time in regard
to the navy left the merchant marine practically without
protection, and in addition helped to ruin it by declaring
the embargo in 1807, as already stated. To maintain the
embargo, more gunboats were now ordered built, and
Perry, having so satisfactorily carried out his first orders
in that line, was again detailed to this service, which
occupied him from February, 1808, to April, 1809. He
was then appointed to succeed Lieutenant Jacob Jones
on board the schooner Revenge of fourteen guns,
attached to the squadron of Commodore Rodgers. After
cruising during the summer and winter with this squadron, Perry was in April, 1810, ordered to Washington
for the purpose of placing the Revenge under extensive
repairs. The work was quickly completed, and on May 20
he started for Charleston. The log-book shows an incident during this trip which is briefly and concisely stated

by Perry in the following words: "At ten thirty, John-son Dickson, marine, fell overboard. Rounded to, out boat, brought him safe on board." In July of this year, Perry was ordered to proceed to Amelia Island in Spanish waters to seize a ship named Angel and flying the British flag. The order was executed on a warrant which showed that the ship was really an American named Diana, owned by Americans and having been unlawfully detained by her master, who was an Englishman. The disputed ship was lying under the batteries of the British gunbrig Plumper and schooner Jupiter, but notwithstanding this, Perry boldly sailed in, took possession of the Diana, and carried her out from under the British guns. Soon after this the Revenge fell in with a British sloop-of-war, and the Englishman demanded that the commander of the Revenge come aboard the sloop and explain the nature of his vessel. Instead of complying, Perry distinctly refused, and, being no match for the British sloop from a point of guns, he quietly but quickly ordered his crew of ninety men armed with pistols, cutlasses and battleaxes, determining, if fired upon, to sweep down upon the Britisher and board her when the vessels came in contact. Fortunately the commander of the sloop was a prudent man, and the clash was averted. But it was these kind of acts that enlisted the admiration and loyalty of the men who served under him and filled them with confidence, not only in his ability, but in themselves. The log-book gives evidence of the attention bestowed by Perry to make his vessel formidable in every way. His crew was drilled to the very highest efficiency in gun practice and firing, floating targets being used, the men in this way encountering the swell of the ocean and practically the same difficulties as though they were engaged in a

real encounter. In December of 1810 Perry was ordered
to survey the coast between Newport and New London
and prepare a chart of its anchorages and headlands.
While engaged in this work, the Revenge was wrecked
on the night of January 11, through the fault of a pilot.
A court of inquiry was ordered and Perry was completely exonerated from any blame in the matter. The
Secretary of the Navy, writing to Commodore Rodgers
in regard to the affair, says: "With respect to Lieutenant Perry, I can only say, that my confidence in him
has not been in any degree diminished by his conduct
on the occasion."

Some months after this, Perry obtained a furlough
and in May was married to Miss Mason, and spent his
honeymoon visiting various parts of New England.
During this time the relations between the United States
and Great Britain, instead of improving, had gradually
become more and more strained. Not only did England continue to despoil our commerce, but her cruisers
impressed American seamen under the pretext that they
were Englishmen, and forcibly compelled them to serve
on British ships. Finally popular indignation rose to
such a pitch that in June, 1812, war was declared against
England. In anticipation of this event, Perry hurried
to Washington and presented himself for active service.
He was promised the first vacancy in conformity with
his rank, and in the meantime was made master commandant and placed in charge of a flotilla of twelve gunboats for the protection of the harbor of Newport and
adjacent waters. Perry was given permission to make
his own selections for commanders of the gunboats, and
he did not make one bad appointment. His total force
numbered about two hundred officers and men. This
service, which failed to bring him into contact with the

OLIVER HAZARD PERRY 357

enemy, was not to his liking, and in November he renewed his solicitations to be given duty of a more effective character. Finding no opportunity for a place on the ocean, Perry looked in another direction, as is shown by the following extract from a letter written by him at this time to the Secretary of the Navy and presented by his friend, W. S. Rodgers. It reads: "I have instructed my friend, Mr. W. S. Rodgers, to wait on you with a tender of my services to the Lakes. There are fifty or sixty men under my command that are remarkably active and strong, capable of performing any service. In the hope that I should have the honor of commanding them whenever they should meet the enemy, I have taken unwearied pains in preparing them for such an event. I beg, therefore, sir, that we may be employed in some way in which we can be serviceable to our country."

At the same time he offered his services to Commodore I. Chauncey, who had command of the lakes. Perry's persistance at this time for an opportunity "to meet the enemy" is remarkable. Having learned that the Government is about to increase the navy by several line-of-battle ships, frigates, and sloops, he writes anxiously to Captain Morris and hints, "I despair of getting to sea very shortly, unless I should be fortunate to get the Hornet." Then again he devoted himself to the task of obtaining accurate information as to the shipbuilding capabilities of his own State. He submitted the result in tabular form, showing the quantity of suitable ship-timber, mines of iron ore, numbers of smelting forges, trip-hammers, ship carpenters, joiners, rope and sail makers, and other artisans engaged in the construction of a ship. Incidentally he mentions the fact that a number of mechanics are out of employment, and would

work for low wages. In January, 1813, Lieutenant
Allen was given command of the brig Argus. Perry
stood at the head of the line for the first vacant command,
and considered that he had been unjustly treated. He
wrote to the Secretary of the Navy protesting, and also
to Congressman J. B. Howell, soliciting his aid to have
the matter righted, explaining that he possesses an "ardent desire to meet the enemies of my country." February 1, 1813, he received a letter from Commodore Chauncey, who states that he has made application to the
Secretary of the Navy to have Perry ordered to the lakes
for services. In the letter the Commodore pays Perry
the following compliment: "You are the very person
that I want for a particular service, in which you may
gain reputation for yourself and honor for your country."
A few days later he received word from his friend Rodgers that the Commodore's request had been granted,
and that he was to be ordered to Lake Erie with a detachment of the best men at Newport. His mission was to
be to build two heavy brigs on the lake to meet the force
which England was already mobilizing there. February
17th Perry was elated to receive orders to proceed to
Sackett's Harbor with all the best men in his command. That same day he sent fifty men on their way
to the rendezvous, two days later another fifty, and
on February 21st a third installment of fifty men.
His object in thus dividing them was to increase
their chances of securing lodging and conveyance
along the route. The following day Perry himself,
having turned over his flotilla to his next in command, started for Sackett's Harbor. He arrived
at his destination March 3, and although he was anxious
to begin with his work on the squadron on Lake Erie, he
was detained by the Commodore until March 16, owing

to the fact that an attack was expected on Sackett's Harbor, with the purpose of destroying the shipping.   Finally he received the necessary orders, and proceeded to Lake Erie, arriving at Buffalo March 24, and continuing his journey toward Erie in a sleigh on the ice.   He arrived at the village of Erie March 27.   Here he found that the keels of two twenty-gun brigs had been laid, and three gunboats were in course of construction, but to his astonishment he discovered that none of the guns with which the ships were to be equipped had arrived, and also that there was not a musket or a cartridge in the village with which to defend the property against attack. The work was progressing slowly, as fifty carpenters who had been sent from Philadelphia four weeks before had not yet arrived.   Perry's own men had been left at Sackett's Harbor, and so he at once sent a messenger to Buffalo after forty seamen and muskets and cartridges. An idea of the arduous nature of the task which confronted him may be gathered from the fact that nearly everything needed had to be brought a distance of 500 miles through a thinly settled country, with extremely poor transportation accommodations.   For the iron work on these ships, 1,000 pounds of iron was brought from Buffalo, and the balance was picked up in the shape of scraps of all sorts in the neighboring smithies.   After many delays and the most strenuous exertions, the three gunboats were finally launched and equipped, and the brigs were well along toward completion.   At this time an incident took place in Perry's career which amply demonstrated that his desire to see action was no empty boast.   When at Sackett's Harbor he had been informed by Commodore Chauncey that an attack was soon to be made upon Fort George, and the young captain had then extracted a promise from the Commodore that he would send for him and allow him to take part in the attack unless other duty prevented. On the evening of May 23, Perry received the welcome tidings that Chauncey had proceeded to Niagara, and that the attack would be made in a day or two. It was after sunset when he received this information, yet he determined to set out at once. In a four-oared open boat, the night dark and squally, and buffeted by headwinds, Perry, with his little crew, reached Buffalo the following night, and then proceeded again by boat, part of the time within musket-shot of the enemy's lines. At Strawberry Point he was warned that forty men occupied Grand Island for the purpose of intercepting boats, and he was compelled to proceed with more caution. Arrived at Sclosser, a terrific downpour of rain began. He was unable to secure a horse, and proceeded on foot for two and a half miles, when the storm became so violent that he took shelter in a farmhouse. In the meantime his men had captured a horse on the town commons and rigged up a bridle from a rope, and borrowed a saddle that was without stirrup, girth, or crupper. The sailors pursued him with this sorry animal, came up with him, and proudly presented the steed. He then pushed forward through the rain and arrived at camp the evening of May 25. The following morning Perry was given command of 500 marines and seamen and general charge of the debarkation of the troops that were to storm Fort George. That he performed his share in the conflict, which resulted in the capture of the fort, is shown by the official report of Commodore Chauncey, who, in relating the services of Perry, says: "He was present at every point where he could be useful, under showers of musketry, but fortunately escaped unhurt." After the fall of the fort, the British evacuated the whole frontier along the Niagara,

and this made it possible to move five small vessels which
had been detained at Black Rock, into Lake Erie.   It
was an arduous task, oxen and men being employed to
drag the vessels against the strong current of the Niagara, but it was finally accomplished under the direction
of Perry.   June 14 he sailed with this little squadron from
Buffalo for Erie.   At that moment the British had a
force on Lake Erie fully six times as formidable as that
which Perry was conducting, and the greatest vigilance
and tact was necessary to get past the enemy.   As Perry
was entering the harbor of Erie in safety on the evening
of June 18, the British flotilla hove in sight, showing how
narrow was his escape.   Following this, sickness fell
upon his men, and out of the 110 which he had at this
time, but thirty were fit for service.   It was with the
greatest difficulty that he was able to get more men sent
on to him.   His own excellent men sent from Newport
had been for the most part detained with Commodore
Chauncey, who appreciated their ability and wished to
retain them on his ships.   The fate of General Harrison
and his army, which was at this time engaged in trying to
regain possession of the territory of Michigan, depended
practically upon the success of the American squadron
upon Lake Erie, and while several orders were sent to
Perry urging haste, no men were sent to him, and he had
recruited a force of soldiers, boys, and negroes, and
finally, on July 30, with meager reinforcements, he mustered 300 officers and men, many of them debilitated and
sick.   This was the force he had to man two twenty-gun
brigs and eight smaller vessels of a total of fifteen guns.
Commodore Barclay, in command of the British squadron, a man of experience, who had fought under Nelson
at Trafalgar, had in the meantime been reinforced with
a new and formidable ship, the Detroit,   With the ma-

terial at hand, poor as it was, Perry worked indefatigably, exercising the men at the guns and making them as near perfect as possible in every branch of the work that was to be required of them. He had named the brig which he himself was to command, the Lawrence, in memory of that noble soul whose last words, "Don't give up the ship," had sent a thrill through every heroic heart. The other brig was named the Niagara. Before daylight on the morning of August 6 Perry started out with his squadron in search of the enemy. After cruising about for twenty-four hours he returned to the anchorage at Erie. Hambleton in his journal at this time says of Perry: "His officers are few and inexperienced, and we are short of seamen. His repeated and urgent requests for men having been treated with the most mortifying neglect, he declines making another." On August 10 Lieutenant Elliott, with several officers and eighty-nine seamen, arrived. This addition to his forces electrified Perry, and he was more eager than ever to seek the enemy and bring about an engagement. On August 12 the squadron got under way, sailing in double column. The right was led by the Lawrence, Captain Perry, followed by the Porcupine, Caledonis, Ohio, and Ariel. The left was led by the Niagara, Lieutenant Elliott, followed by the Trippe, Tigress, Somers, and Scorpion. On August 19, the squadron arrived off Sandusky, and after a conference with General Harrison, who was not yet ready to advance with his army, Perry sailed on a reconnoitering expedition, and discovered the British squadron at anchor within Bar Point. Large numbers of the men being attacked with bilious fever, he anchored his ships in Put-in-Bay. On the last day of the month Perry received from General Harrison nearly one hundred men to act as marines with the squadron and this brought the total of his force up to 490 souls. A few days later he learned from some citizens who arrived at Sandusky from Malden, that the British squadron was about to sail. Perry also at this time learned pretty accurately the strength of the enemy. The fleet consisted of the new Detroit, 19 guns; Queen Charlotte, 17 guns; Lady Prevost, schooner, 13 guns; Hunter, brig, 10 guns; Little Belt, sloop, 3 guns; Chippeway, schooner, one long gun. This made a total of 63 guns, 35 of which were long. The total strength of the crews was 502 men and officers, of which 150 of the seamen were from the Royal navy. Of the American squadron, mounting 54 guns, only the Lawrence and the Niagara could be considered as men-of-war, and owing to the large number of long guns of the enemy, the American ships would be at a great disadvantage in any but a close encounter. Perry was now confident that an engagement would be brought on, and summoned his officers on board the Lawrence. He explained to them his views in whatever contingency might arise. He gave it as his intention to bring the enemy to close quarters, and his final emphatic injunction was given in the words of Nelson: "If you lay your enemy close alongside, you cannot be out of your place." Perry now produced a battleflag, the hoisting of which on the Lawrence was to be the signal to commence action. It was a large blue flag and bore in white letters, the words "Don't give up the ship." At sunrise on the morning of September 10 the British squadron was discovered standing toward Put-in-Bay. Perry at once ordered the squadron to get under way, and in a few minutes the ships began beating out of the harbor. Several of the group of the Bass Islands interposed between the two squadrons, and Perry made an effort to get

around to windward of the islands in order to get a leading breeze to run down upon the enemy. The wind,
however, was unsteady, and several hours were spent
in repeated tacking. As 10 o'clock approached Perry
became impatient and ordered the squadron to run to
the leeward of the islands. Sailing-Master Taylor
remarked that they would then have to attack from the
leeward. "I don't care," replied Perry, "to windward
or to leeward, they shall fight to-day." At that very
moment, however, the wind suddenly shifted and they
were enabled to carry out the original intention. It was
a perfect autumn day and the British squadron as it hove
to, with its red ensigns fluttering gently in the breeze,
and formed in line of battle, presented a formidable
appearance. The sick list of the American squadron
contained 116 names, and many of the guns were short-
handed. The rival fleets were still some miles distant
when Perry, mounting a gun-slide, produced his battleflag, and, calling up the crew, told its meaning and asked
them whether he should hoist it. His answer was a
resounding cheer, and the signal was sent to the masthead. The crews of the other ships cheered and many
of the sick crawled out of their bunks and took their
stations to do their share in defending their flag and
country. Perry went from gun to gun and had a word
of cheer for each crew, and everywhere the men
responded in a manner which showed how much confidence they had in their young commander. Suddenly
from the British squadron came the ringing notes of a
bugle, followed by cheers from the various crews. It
was now close to noon and the opposing squadrons had
approached to within a mile and a half of each other.
The Detroit opened the engagement with a single shot
at the Lawrence, but it failed to take effect. Five min-

utes later the long guns of the British began to thunder. The few long guns on the American ships replied. The Lawrence and some of the other vessels steadily bore down upon the English ships and although the Lawrence, which was receiving the concentrated fire of the enemy, was suffering to a considerable extent, the resolute advance was continued until within 350 yards of the enemy, when a rapid and destructive fire was opened on the Detroit. The Scorpion and Ariel sustained the Lawrence in the unequal task she had undertaken. The commander of the Caledonia had followed the Lawrence closely and gallantly closed with the Hunter of the British squadron. But the Niagara remained at a distance, keeping up a long and ineffectual fire. Half an hour after the battle commenced, the Queen Charlotte, which the Niagara had been ordered to attack, came up astern of the Detroit and opened a terrific fire upon the Lawrence. Overwhelming as was the force thus directed against her, she continued to maintain the contest for two hours. By this time her condition was terrible. The sails were torn asunder, the rigging shattered and one by one the guns were dismounted until but one remained that could be fired. The men fell on every hand. Of 100 men who entered the engagement, 22 had been killed outright and 61 wounded. Perry undauntedly continued to work his single remaining gun, sending now and again as man after man dropped, for another and another hand from among those who were removing the wounded. Some of the wounded, hearing how few able men remained to fight, crawled on deck and offered their services. Finally Perry himself, with the aid of Hambleton, his purser, and Breese, the chaplain, were serving the solitary gun, but at length it, too, was disabled. Throughout this terrible ordeal, from first to last, according to the accounts of those who were present, Perry appeared collected, undismayed, and even cheerful. Having nothing further with which to make resistance, Perry looked over the remnant of his crew and found but eighteen persons not disabled by wounds, aside from his little brother, then twelve years of age, who served in the capacity of powder carrier. Repeatedly during the engagement, Perry's attention had been called to the strange conduct of the Niagara, which lay far to windward and had made no effort to come to the relief of the Lawrence. But one chance remained and Perry was not slow to take advantage of it. Turning the command of the Lawrence over to his first lieutenant, the brave Yarnell, Perry ordered a boat to convey him to the Niagara. "If a victory is to be gained, I'll gain it," was his confident remark as he went down the gangway. While Perry stood erect in the boat on his way to the Niagara, then half a mile distant, the British made every effort to sink the craft carrying the intrepid commander. The few survivors on the Lawrence watched his progress with pain, and when they saw him safely reach the Niagara, the devoted little band gave a cheer. The Lawrence was still the center of the enemy's fire, apparently with the determination of sinking her. To save the wounded, Yarnell hauled down the colors and a tremendous cheer went up from the British ships. But their victory was destined to be short-lived. Having taken control of the Niagara and sent her commander, Elliott, astern to order up the gunboats, Perry once more bore down upon the British. In maneuvering to receive the Niagara, the Queen Charlotte and the Detroit got foul and their rigging became entangled. At this moment the Niagara passed slowly under the bows of the Detroit and poured a destructive shower of grape and canister into both vessels, at the same time raking the Lady Provost with the larboard guns. The marines on the Niagara picked off the men on the decks. Taking spirit at this renewed action by the Niagara, the other vessels of Perry's squadron closed in and fought with such precision and effect that the British soon gave up all resistance. The Queen Charlotte struck first, and the Detroit at once followed the example. The Hunter and Lady Provost struck their colors a minute later. Within half an hour after Perry took command of the Niagara, the victory had been completely won. Commodore Barclay and many of the British officers had been wounded, and the decks of their ships presented scenes of indescribable carnage. The killed of the British squadron had been thrown overboard as they fell, but according to Commodore Barclay the number was forty-one. His wounded numbered ninety-four. The aggregate losses of the Americans amounted to twenty-seven killed and ninety-six wounded, of which, as stated, twenty-two were killed on the Lawrence and sixty-one wounded. Perry had won a dazzling victory, captured six splendid prizes, and taken 308 prisoners. He now sent the famous message to General Harrison, "We have met the enemy, and they are ours. Two ships, two brigs, one schooner, and one sloop." And then, at 4 o'clock, one hour after the great achievement had been accomplished, the young commander of twenty-seven years sat down and with mingled piety and modesty penned a brief note to the Secretary of the Navy, saying that it had "pleased the Almighty to give to the arms of the United States a signal victory," and that the British squadron had surrendered after "a sharp conflict." The wounded of the British, as well as the Americans, were given the very best of care, the prisoners were humanely treated, and Perry secured for Commodore Barclay a parole which enabled that officer to return to England. Perry's victory was of the greatest importance in that it led to the evacuation of Detroit, and the relinquishment of the whole territory of Michigan by the British, and facilitated the overthrow of that power in Upper Canada and on all the lakes. Perry's magnanimity was shown in the official report of the engagement, in which he not only neglected to reveal the peculiar conduct of Elliott, but accords him credit for having kept the Niagara out of the fight. Elliott later on attempted to secure for himself the glory of the victory, and circulated disparaging reports about Captain Perry, for which he was later court-martialed.

After the battle Perry returned to Put-in-Bay, and, having landed his wounded, reorganized his squadrons and transported the army of General Harrison across to Canada. They found the town of Malden evacuated, and met with no resistance worthy of the name anywhere along the coast. The British army under General Proctor, and the Indians under the famous Chief Tecumseh, were retreating, and when Harrison determined to pursue, Perry left his ships in command of Elliott and became an aid to General Harrison. In this capacity he took part in the battle of the Thames against the British and Indians, which resulted in the utter defeat of the enemy. On October 7th Perry returned to the United States, being soon after followed to Detroit by the army under Harrison. All resistance had disappeared in that section of Canada, and both the army and the navy now waited to learn from the Government what further work there was to be done. It was at Detroit that Perry was first made aware of the glory which had attached to his name as a result of his victory. He was lauded in the newspapers, and the people fairly worshiped him. From the Secretary of the Navy he received a most flattering congratulation. His name was on every lip, and demonstrations of joy at his success were everywhere given. Soon after he was notified that he had been promoted to post-captain, and was granted leave of absence to visit his relatives.

Perry's journey across the country toward his home was a continual series of ovations. Public receptions were tendered him, illuminations were held in his honor, schools took holidays, and everywhere he was praised and honored from the small villages to the large cities through which he passed. Mayors and high officials came to meet him and urge upon him their hospitality, dinners were given, he was toasted, cheered and wept over, and accepted it all with grace and modesty. The universal feeling was one of blended respect, admiration, and gratified national pride. November 18, 1813, Perry reached Newport. The town was decked in the national colors, the shipping in the harbor was in gala attire, the church bells rang, and salutes were fired from Fort Wolcott, and from the flotilla. Having buried himself for a brief space in the bosom of his family, which consisted of his wife and two boys, he asked leave early in January to visit the Capital in order to look after the adjudication of his prizes. The request was granted in the most flattering terms. Congress had already passed a vote of thanks, and followed it up by presenting him with a jeweled sword, a gold medal and $5,000 in money. Congress also in substantial manner rewarded every officer and sailor who had fought under him on that memorable day in September on Lake Erie. Perry reached the National Capital late in January. He was invited to a seat on the floor of the Senate, an honor seldom bestowed, and was publicly entertained by the leading citizens of the Nation.   During the balance of the year Perry was employed in preparing a flying squadron to prey upon the commerce and coasts of England, but peace was signed between the two Nations at Ghent in December, 1814, and it was determined to send Perry to the Mediterranean to punish or come to terms, as the case might warrant, with the Dey of Algiers, whose ships had ruthlessly preyed on American commerce during the war.   Perry at this time had command of the first-class frigate Java, which had but recently been launched in Baltimore.   In addition, however, he was engaged in the construction of three other ships, which were also to be under his command.   Congress declared war against Algiers immediately after the ratification of peace with England, and as Perry's ships were far from complete, Decatur was sent to the Mediterranean and, after capturing some of the enemy's shipping, concluded a treaty which made further force in that vicinity unnecessary.   Toward the end of the year 1815, however, the Dey of Algiers had become dissatisfied with the treaty he had concluded with Decatur, and, American commerce again becoming endangered, Perry was ordered to proceed to the Mediterranean in the Java.   Departing from Newport, January 21, 1816, he joined the squadron of Commodore Shaw at Port Mahon, March 7th, after a boisterous voyage across the Atlantic. The whole squadron arrived at Algiers April 8th.   There they found a British fleet lined up before the batteries and demanding a treaty similar to that made with the United States.   Negotiations were carried on for months, and it was not until November, after the arrival of Commodore Chauncey, that a new treaty was agreed upon between the Dey and a commission, of which Captain Perry was a member. Two months prior to this time an incident took place which forms the only instance in his career which is open to censure. This was his trouble with John Heath, captain of the marines on board the Java. Perry had on several occasions been treated by Heath in what he considered an insolent manner, and at last, becoming provoked beyond endurance Perry struck Heath a blow. Each brought charges against the other, and the court-martial which sat in December of that year, pronounced both guilty, and both were leniently punished, the sentence being private reprimand by the Commander-in-Chief. January 12, 1817, the Java left the squadron to carry the new treaty with Algiers to the United States, and reached Newport March 3d. The wounded feelings of Captain Heath had not been healed, and he challenged Perry to a duel. The report, becoming public, caused the greatest excitement. The meeting finally took place October 19, 1818, on the Jersey shore of the Hudson. Heath fired at Perry and missed him, and Perry declined to return the fire, whereupon Heath declared himself satisfied. Perry spent the winter of the year 1818 at Newport with his family, and was not again called upon for active service until April, 1819, when he was requested by the Government to undertake a trip to Venezuela, then in a state of revolt against Spain, to seek reparation for the seizure of some property belonging to Americans. He unhesitatingly accepted the service, and with the sloop John Adams and the schooner Nonsuch left in June for South America. At the mouth of the Orinoco the John Adams was left, while Perry proceeded up the river in the Nonsuch and reached Angostura July 26th, and at once began negotiations with Vice-President Zea,

Bolivar being absent with the army at the time. August 15th, having in the main accomplished the purpose of his mission, Perry started down the river. On the morning of the 18th, having reached the mouth of the river, Perry was taken ill, and the symptoms of yellow fever left no doubt as to the nature of the disease. He grew rapidly worse and died on August 23d, his birthday, near Port Spain. The following afternoon the body was solemnly carried ashore, attended by 120 seamen in boats, rowing with measured stroke, while minute guns were fired from the Adams. The Governor of Trinidad, and other officials, attended the funeral services, and with every mark of sympathy and grief the remains of the gallant young commander was lowered into the grave. The whole Nation mourned his untimely demise, and President Monroe in his first succeeding annual message referred to Perry's death as a national calamity. Congress provided for his family, and later had the remains brought to Newport and there interred.

His great victory on Lake Erie will always remain one of the most illustrious incidents of the Nation's history, and despite efforts that were made during his life to rob him of the honors due him, posterity will forever cherish and respect the name of Oliver Hazard Perry.

VON MOLTKE

1800-1891

CENTRAL FIGURE OF THE FRANCO-PRUSSIAN WAR

Helmuth Karl Bernhard von Moltke, one of the ablest military strategists of modern times, was born at Parchim, a little village in Mecklinburg, on October 26, 1800. Baron Fritz von Moltke, his father, belonged to one of the oldest families in the German Empire. His mother was the daughter of Financial Councilor Paschen, a wealthy merchant of Hamburg. As a child, Helmuth lived at Lüebeck. In that city the future general first encountered the soldiers of France. After Napoleon had become Emperor, defeated the allied armies of Russia, Prussia, and Austria, Blücher withdrew to Lüebeck and 60,000 French troops pursued him. The city was sacked, and in the devastation which followed Baron Moltke's house and property suffered like those of thousands of other residents of the city. It practically ruined Baron Moltke and left him a poor man. With his fortune gone, the question of the education of his children became a serious matter. Helmuth, when eleven years of age, was taken in charge by General Lorenz, who prepared him for the military academy at Copenhagen. In the fall of 1811 Helmuth and his brother became pupils of that institution. Their father was unable to pay their expenses and they were enrolled as free State pupils. The discipline at the school was of the utmost rigor and young Moltke was thus early taught to endure hardships without complaining. In

1866, in writing of this period of his life, he says, "without friends or relatives in a strange city, we passed a joyless childhood. The discipline was severe, even hard and even to-day, when my judgment has become impartial in regard to it, I must say that it was too hard and too severe. We were obliged, however, to accustom ourselves to deprivations of all kinds at an early age. That was the only saving feature of our stay." Moltke remained in the academy seven years. He mastered the Danish language, and the school records, still preserved, show him to have been a good pupil and a diligent student. His final examination was passed with credit in 1818. It was necessary for him to serve as a page in the Court of Denmark for one year after completing his academical course, in order to repay the King for the money expended on his education. Following his service in the court, Moltke, in 1819, was made a lieutenant in the Oldenburg Infantry. At the time he received his first commission he was a tall slender youth, possessed of a great deal of energy and industrious and faithful to his duty. In 1822, he resigned his commission in the army of Denmark and was appointed second lieutenant in the Eighth Prussian Regiment of Infantry. After a year had elapsed, he was sent to the Academy of War in Berlin. He was poor, but employed all of his earnings in obtaining extra lessons in French and English. It was during his course at Berlin that a desire for travel in foreign countries was aroused in Moltke. He graduated and was assigned to the topographical department of the army. From the date when he finished the academy work at Berlin until 1835 von Moltke followed the daily routine of a Prussian soldier. In 1835 he went to Turkey with the intention of remaining abroad a few months. His stay, however, lengthened into four years, as he was requested by the Sultan to enter the Turkish service. Although comparatively young and with the most brilliant period of his career still before him, the soldier was called upon to aid in applying the Prussian system of military organization to Turkey. In writing of his life in the Prussian army, Moltke states that there was nothing to record but dates and dates again. In the Turkish army, however, his career was full of incidents and adventure. He traveled about in Asia Minor and participated in the campaign against Mehemed Ali. His particular knowledge of military science along certain lines was here brought into constant play. The Sultan traveled through Romelia and Bulgaria and Moltke served as his escort. He prepared an extensive study of the Turkish army, drew plans of Constantinople and the Dardenelles and surveyed both banks of the Bosphorus. His inspection of the armies, construction of bridges, aqueducts and palaces, proved of much value to the Sultan, and the ruler bestowed many marks of honor upon the Prussian soldier. He was fond of sketching and of writing of matters which came under his observation, and amused the women and children in the streets of Constantinople by drawing their likenesses. During all of this time, however, his stay in the Orient was under the orders of his Sovereign and he was securing complete and highly valuable information as to the strategic operation and the direction of vast armies which was to stand him in good stead in serving his Fatherland. Finally he returned to Prussia, and the military duties there awaiting him. In 1841 Moltke married Marie Burt, daughter of John Heytinger Burt, an Englishman. Appointed Adjutant of Prince Henry of Prussia in 1845, Moltke accompanied his chief to Rome. He had further opportunities for topographical studies around Rome and the Campagna, and did not fail to take advantage of them. Prince Henry died, and after a sojourn of less than a year in Italy, Moltke returned to Prussia. He prepared the "Contorni di Roma," which are regarded as authoritive. His next assignment took him to Coblenz, when he was again placed on the general staff. His advancement was rapid, and in 1855 he was made Adjutant to the Crown Prince. He traveled through England, Scotland, Russia, and France. It was not until he had reached the age of fifty-seven years that Moltke's really active service for Prussia began. In 1857, King Frederick William IV, who afterward abdicated, turned the throne and the affairs of state over to his brother, Prince William. General von Manteuffel was summoned to a position in the Cabinet and Moltke succeeded him as chief of the general staff. Three years later, as a result of events that had transpired in the meantime, it devolved upon Moltke to make the necessary preparations for a war with France. Much difficulty had been experienced in the unification of Germany on account of the jealousy between Prussia and Austria, each Nation insisting that it should be the nucleus about which an Empire was to be formed. When, in 1849, there was a revolt in Hungary, Prussia had attempted to unite Germany, leaving out Austria. Prussia was joined by a number of States. Austria made a similar attempt and was also aided by a powerful alliance of States. Disputes over territory arose and civil war was with difficulty averted. A temporary confederation was again finally established. In 1859 Austria made war against Sardinia and attempted to draw Prussia into the struggle, but without success. In 1861, upon the death of King Frederick William IV, Prince William took the

GENERAL VON MOLTKE

Painting by F. Lenbach

title of William I, and Otto von Bismarck became his Prime Minister and Minister of Foreign Affairs. The confederate relations of Austria and Prussia were unsatisfactory, but the jealousy was kept in abeyance through a dispute with Denmark over the Duchies of Schleswig and Holstein. Before a French war could be undertaken, therefore, it became necessary to dispose of the issue with Denmark. Moltke directed the movements in the campaigns and to him is conceded the credit of the favorable results for Germany. Prussia and Austria joined forces against the common enemy. The united armies crossed the Eider in February, 1864, and drove the Danes back from Danewirk. The fortress of Duppel was taken, and after continued defeat and loss, Denmark consented to relinquish her claims upon the Duchies of Schleswig, Holstein, and Lanenberg in favor of Austria and Prussia. After the close of this war, Austria and Prussia became involved in a dispute over the spoils—the three Duchies named. Each insisted that the other should not have possession of the disputed territory. Although this affair was finally adjusted in an amicable manner, other difficulties arose which sustained the jealousy and friction between the two countries. In June, 1866, Italy joined with Prussia in declaring war against Austria, and the "Six Weeks' War" was commenced. Prussia's allies were defeated at Custozza. An important engagement took place at Königgrätz between the Prussians and Austrians, in which the latter were badly defeated. General Benedick, in command of the Austrian army, having lost 40,000 in previous battles, had retreated to Königgrätz on June 30th. The movement of the Austrian army had been concealed from Moltke and King William for some time. Then two Prussian armies were dispatched by different routes, and the attack was made on July 3d. The Austrians could not withstand the fire from the Prussian needle guns, and after fighting almost all day the Austrians were compelled to retreat. Throughout this engagement Moltke had been in the saddle for fourteen hours, having, during that time, been without food, except for a piece of sausage which had been given to him by a soldier. Thus Moltke demonstrated that he was, even though sixty-six years of age, capable of enduring hardship as well as the most active of his men. Austria's might had been broken, and Bismarck saw the opportunity of establishing greater Prussian power. In July, 1870, Napoleon III of France declared war against Germany, and Moltke was again placed in the position of director of the military movements. It had probably been Napoleon's hope that the Germans of the south, if they did not become active allies of the French, would at least remain neutral during the conflict. But the States, north and south, once more united against a common enemy, and 1,000,000 men were soon in the field under the King of Prussia. The French crossed the frontier announcing that they would dictate peace at Berlin. The first battle of importance after this invasion commenced took place August 4, 1870, at Weissenburg. The French were defeated, and the next combat was fought at Worth, on French territory. The French army was under command of Marshal MacMahon, and again suffered defeat. Moltke says the German loss in this battle, which took place August 6th, was 489 officers and 10,000 men. The Germans captured 200 French officers and 9,000 prisoners. The total loss of the French, according to Moltke, was so great and the demoralization so complete as to make the troops unmanageable. On

August 14th the battle of Colombey-Nouilly was fought. It resulted in a victory for the German arms, although they lost 5,000 men in the engagement, while the French lost but 3,600. The greatest cavalry combat of the war was fought near Mars-La-Tour, August 16th, and each of the contending forces lost 16,000 men. The right wing of the French army was now compelled to abandon all offensive movements. Moltke brought his strategic ability into play in the plans for the subsequent campaign. August 18th the French were again defeated near Gravelotte. St. Privat was taken with 2,000 prisoners, and Amanvillers was burned. The German loss in these engagements amounted to 20,584 men and the French loss 13,000 men in killed, wounded, and prisoners. On August 30th two large divisions of the contending forces met at Beaumont and the French suffered a severe defeat, having 1,800 killed and losing 3,000 in prisoners, as well as almost all of their baggage, treasure, and ammunition. Two days later the memorable battle of Sedan was fought. The French made a gallant but vain resistance, and after a bitter struggle, hemmed in on every hand by the victorious Germans, Napoleon delivered his sword to King William. General von Wimpffen arranged the surrender of the French army with General Moltke. The German military director insisted upon the disarmament and detention of the entire French army, and on the morning of Sept. 2d capitulation was signed upon these terms. This victory cost the German armies 8,500 men and 460 officers. The French lost 17,000 men killed, 21,000 taken prisoners during the action, and 83,000 surrendered. Moltke says of Sedan: "The trophies taken at Sedan consisted of three standards, 419 field pieces, and 139 guns, 66,000 stands of arms, over 1,000 baggage wagons, and 6,000 horses fit for service. With the surrender of this army, imperialism in France was extinct." After Sedan two of the German armies marched upon the French capital, which was invested September 19th. Six army corps were drawn up in front of the city on a line of eleven miles. The French proposed an armistice, but rejected the conditions made by the Germans. The third German army had occupied the country to the south and southeast, and other forces were stationed on the north and northeast. The French were repeatedly beaten in attempts to break through this line of investments. A new French army was organized, with the purpose of relieving Paris, but at this juncture a fresh disaster befell the French. Metz, in possession of Marshal Bazaine, was surrounded by German forces and compelled to surrender on October 27th. During the siege of seventy-two days, Moltke says, "the Germans had lost 240 officers and 5,500 men in killed and wounded. Six thousand French officers and 167,000 men were taken prisoners, besides 20,000 sick who could not be at once removed, making about 200,000 in all. Fifty-six Imperial eagles, 622 field, and 2,876 fortress guns, 72 mitrailleuses, and 260,000 small arms fell into the hands of the Germans." Early in January of the following year the French made the final attempt to break through the German lines and escape from Paris. They were driven back with heavy loss, and finally, on January 28th the capital surrendered. On May 10, 1871, the final treaty of peace was signed by representatives of France and Germany. By this Treaty of Frankfort, France was compelled to give up to the Germans the provinces of Alsace and Lorraine and to pay an indemnity of 5,000,-000,000 francs. Moltke returned to Prussia and to United Germany. While he had been directing the movements of armies against the French, the unification of the various States had been accomplished. In November, 1870, treaties had been made with the South German States. In December the German sovereigns had proposed that the President of the Confederation should be given the title of the German Emperor. King William had accordingly been solemnly proclaimed Emperor of Germany, January 18, 1871. The war which the German States waged in common had done much to make coalition possible. Moltke was received by his Emperor and by his countrymen with may marks of distinguished gratitude and honor. He became the leading military official in the Empire. His closing years were of more or less active service for his country. He purchased the estate of Creisau and took great pleasure in beautifying the parks about his castle and in the companionship of the members of his own family. He took considerable exercise even after he had passed the number of years usually allotted to men. His reserved nature led him to indulge in such pastimes as whist in preference to society. He was a lover of children and spent much of his time with his great-nephews and great-nieces. On the ninetieth anniversary of his birth the German Nation celebrated the event. April 24, 1891, he breathed his last at Berlin. Several important additions to historical literature came from Moltke's pen, among them being the "Letters from Turkey," and the "Campaign in Turkey," the "Italian Campaign of 1859," and the "History of the Franco-Prussian War."

GARIBALDI

1807-1882

THE LIBERATOR OF ITALY

Giuseppe Garibaldi was a patriot. During his entire eventful career he proved himself a devoted lover of liberty, the enemy of oppression, a hater of tyranny, whether governmental, political, or religious. His enemies have made him out an atheist and a blasphemer. But Garibaldi, according to his own assertions, was not such. "I believe in God," he said; "I am of the religion of Christ, not of the religion of the Popes. I do not admit any intermediary between God and man. Priests have thrust themselves in, in order to make a shop of religion."

His life was in many respects Quixotic, eccentric, and erratic. Yet he was consistent. He was strong in his principles, and adhered to them with a tenacity that was remarkable. From his youth he exhibited marked talents as a warrior of the guerilla order, and among this class he has not a peer in modern times. His career in two hemispheres, as a fighter on land and sea, repeatedly demonstrates him a really heroic type. Romantic episodes are not wanting among the events which succeeded one another with startling rapidity throughout his life. His intense hatred of the church of Rome served to make him many enemies, but in his native land he is known as the liberator of Italy, and his memory is cherished by prince and peasant alike with pride and reverence.

Garibaldi imbibed his bitterness against the Roman

Church as a natural result of his connection with the revolutionary society of Mazzini, which, like the reform party of the period, opposed the temporal power exercised by the Pope, and the right of the Papal power to act with arbitrary violence and inflict sufferings on the citizens of provinces presided over by cruel and oppressive Cardinals. The fact also that the Papal power was upheld by hated Austria with her troops added to the popular feeling against the Church. In this atmosphere Garibaldi became saturated, and none were more fierce against the Papacy. He wrote and preached that so long as the Pope held temporal power there was no hope of freedom for Italy.

Giuseppe Garibaldi was born at Nice in 1807, whether on July 19th, as recorded by some historians, or on July 4th, which is the generally accepted date, matters little. His father was a sea captain, who came from a long line of soldiers and sailors, all renowned for courage and patriotism. The family originally hailed from Chiavari, Genoa, where the name can be traced back for centuries. His childhood was spent upon the shores of the Mediterranean, and, according to J. Theodore Bent's history of his life, he was, as a boy, contemplative and fond of solitude, yet a wild youth and guilty of many an escapade. Like his father and forefathers, he showed a natural inclination for the sea, and early began a life of adventure.

At the age of twenty-one he made his first voyage. During this trip, according to his own narrative written for Cassell's Magazine, the ship was three times attacked and plundered by Greek pirates. With his mates he reached Constantinople in a destitute condition. Letters written by him about this time do not show that he entertained any particular resentment against the pirates who had robbed him, but against the Government. which permitted its citizens to be thus despoiled. During this period also, it appears, the affection for national liberty, which afterward became the dominating principle of his life, was kindled. The turn which his mind was taking can be gathered from the following scrap of a diary written at Constantinople: "Those noble victims of Greek brigandage, and those who fall a prey every day to Italian brigandage, must be added to the huge column of debts which European despotism forever contracts with humanity."

Under these circumstances it is easy to understand how, in 1834, Garibaldi associated himself in a movement then under way in Italy under the direction of Mazzini against the ruling powers. The revolt was general and widespread. For small offenses citizens had died under the lash in the public squares. Executions and prosecutions, both at Naples and in the pontifical States, were frequent. Even the Government of Charles Albert, up to that time the most liberal Sovereign in Italy, was tyrannical and arbitrary. The first extensive plot of Mazzini, in which Garibaldi was involved, failed miserably. The plan was to occupy the village of St. Julien, and there set up the flag of revolt. The scheme was betrayed, and the plotters were forced to flee for their lives. Garibaldi, after many privations, succeeded in reaching his birthplace, an outlaw. From there he fled to Marseilles and began the life of an exile, a life he was destined to continue for fourteen years, during which time his career was one of marvelous adventures among the Republics of South America, which doubtless served to fit him in a great measure for the tremendous struggles he was afterward to undertake on behalf of his native land.

During a brief period after reaching Marseilles, Gari-

G. GARIBALDI

Painting by Ossani

baldi continued to make voyages in the Mediterranean on board French merchant ships. He saw no hope for renewing the struggle on behalf of his country, and embarked on the brig Nantonnier of Nantes for Rio Janeiro, in 1836. At this town, aided by several of his countrymen, who, like himself, were exiles for political intrigues, he purchased a small vessel and established himself in the coasting trade. He continued in this business for nine months with but poor success. At this time the province of Rio Grande proclaimed itself a Republic and openly rebelled against the authority of the Emperor of Brazil.

In the opening skirmishes of this insurrection a number of Italians, who had espoused the cause of the rebellion, were taken prisoners, loaded with chains and brought to Brazil. Garibaldi witnessed their arrival, and the sight of his countrymen suffering in the cause of liberty inspired him to enter the struggle. He transformed his ship into a vessel of war, and called it, for the sake of old associations, the Mazzini. His services were gladly accepted, and with but sixteen companions he set out under the Republican flag of Rio Grande to make war against the Empire of Brazil. During the first days of their voyage they captured a large ship owned by an Austrian merchant who had settled in Brazil. Their second encounter was not so successful. While attempting to enter the port of Montevideo they were attacked by two armed Brazilian ships, and Garibaldi was severely wounded, and some of his men slain. The crew crowded on all sail and escaped to the harbor of Gualequay, where they regarded themselves as safe. But the flag of Rio Grande was not recognized, and the crew of the Mazzini and their leader were consigned to prison.

Garibaldi slowly recovered from his wound, and was

given his liberty on parole. On learning, however, that his captors intended to send him to Bajada and deliver him up to the Brazilians, he considered himself free from any obligation, and made his escape. After wandering about in the forests for three days, he was found by soldiers, who had been sent to search for him. For this escapade he was terribly punished, being hung up by the wrists and tortured in an effort to compel him to impart information regarding the plans of the insurgents. He was then imprisoned for two months, after which he was set at liberty. Returning to Rio, he took part in several land battles against the Brazilians, and was then given command of three small vessels furnished by the incipient Republic. With these ships he carried on a persistent and aggressive warfare, capturing prizes, and often landing, and, with his crews, invading the enemy's country, only to retreat to his ships on the appearance of superior numbers, to renew the attack at some other point. It was here that Garibaldi acquired that skill in hasty maneuvers which was to stand him in good stead in after years in the Tyrol, and in his campaigns in Sicily. During this eventful period of his life Garibaldi became a splendid shot, an adroit swordsman, and an expert horseman.

It was in the midst of these campaigns that he met and fell in love with the far famed Anita. Although married, she did not hesitate to leave her husband to become the partner of Garibaldi. Of this event Ricciardi says: "He took Anita Rivieras in pretty much the same manner that he did Palermo."

It was only a day or two after he had carried away the beautiful Creole that the Brazilian fleet came upon Garibaldi determined to crush him. In the battle that followed Anita stood by the side of her adopted spouse and fired the first gun at the enemy. After a desperate conflict the imperial squadron withdrew when the Garibaldians were at the point of giving up. For six years Garibaldi faithfully served the Republic of Rio Grande in its struggle for independence, when the war degenerated into a conflict of individual ambition, for which he had no heart. During all of this time Anita faithfully remained by his side, helping to fight his battles, nursing him when wounded, and bearing him besides a son, which was born September 16, 1840. Prior to his departure for Italy, in the spring of 1848, two other children had been added to his family.

The struggle against Austria was then beginning, and Garibaldi presented himself to the Minister of War at Turin to offer his arm in Italy's service. His name was already well known, and he had an enviable reputation for valor and daring, but his connection with Mazzini and the revolutionary movement of fourteen years previous had not been forgotten. He was sent to the headquarters of the King at Roverbello, and was there received courteously by Charles Albert, who, however, did not definitely accept his proposals, but referred him back to the Secretary of War. The King could not forget that he had been a rebel against him, nor had Garibaldi forgotten that the King had forced him into exile. Impatient at the uncertain treatment accorded him, he without further ado hastened to Milan, where the provisional Government was preparing a defense against the Austrians, and was enthusiastically received. He was empowered to raise volunteers for the protection of Burgamo, and soon found himself at the head of several thousand volunteers. A few weeks later he was called upon to protect Milan itself from the Austrians, for the army of Charles Albert had been out-maneuvered and defeated at every point by Radetzky, and had been compelled to fall back upon Milan. But the Milanese received Charles Albert and his army with curses, and the agents of Mazzini made it so uncomfortable for the King that he was compelled to flee for his life. Following this, on August 9, 1848, Charles Albert came to terms with the Austrians and agreed to surrender Milan. In the meantime Garibaldi, by forced marches, had reached Monza, but twelve miles from the Capital, and here he was informed of the armistice, and ordered to evacuate Lombardy. Not having had an opportunity to strike a single blow against the enemy, Garibaldi refused to recognize the armistice, and declared the King to be a traitor.

For a time he succeeded in animating his troops with this spirit, and he determined to fight to the last. But he was harassed on every side, and his army, after forced marches, reached Luino greatly reduced in numbers, destitute of provisions, and completely worn out by fatigue and sickness. Garibaldi himself became a victim of typhus, and for a time his life was despaired of. After recovering, he went to rejoin his family at Nice, and, after a brief period of repose, proceeded to Genoa, where he received from Charles Albert, who had repented of his treatment, an offer of a high rank in the Sardinian army. But Garibaldi had been aroused to a high pitch of enthusiasm by reports that valiant resistance was being made against the Austrians at Venice under Daniele Manin, and he determined to again throw his lot with the revolutionists instead of enjoying a position of dignity in the Piedmontese army.

Accompanied by 250 volunteers, he started for Venice, and on reaching Ravenna he was apprised of the stirring events at that moment transpiring in Rome.

Pope Pius IX had retracted his liberal policy, Rossi had been assassinated, the Pope had fled to Gaeta, and Rome was in a state of siege. From his youth the eternal city had been the goal of his ambition, and now with a following of but 1,500 men, which had flocked to his standard, he abandoned his march toward Venice, and bent his course toward Rome.

With his little band he threw himself into the thick of the conflict, and when the task of defending Rome was given up as hopeless, and the French entered as victors, Garibaldi did not surrender, but with 5,000 troops withdrew in the direction of Tivoli. He escaped the pursuit of the Austrians, and led his army into Tuscany, hoping to awaken a revolutionary movement there. But Tuscany had suffered severely from insurrection, and preferred peace under a foreign rule. Garibaldi and his army, now reduced to half of the number that had left Rome with him, sought refuge at San Marino. The Austrians were in hot pursuit, and soon had the city surrounded, waiting for the Garibaldians to issue forth. Through the interposition of the local authorities, terms were made with the Austrian commander, Gortschowsky, which included a safe conduct for Garibaldi and his officers on condition that they would go to America.

Unwilling to accept these conditions, Garibaldi, accompanied by Anita and a few faithful followers, contrived to escape during the night, and made his way, after the greatest hardships, to the shores of the Adriatic. At the port of Cesenatico he secured from fishermen thirteen boats, and with his company embarked for Venice. It was a furious night, and, in spite of their desperate efforts, they did not succeed in getting out of the port until daybreak, just as the Austrians were entering the town. Sails were spread, and on the following morning four of the boats which contained Garibaldi and his immediate followers reached the mouth of the Po. The other nine had been discovered by the Austrians, many of the crews were slain, and the remainder surrendered. During this voyage the faithful Anita had suffered terribly, and was borne by Garibaldi to an adjoining cornfield, where, in the midst of dangers from Austrian scouts, he watched her life slowly ebbing away. Later in the day he contrived to have her conveyed, after many dangers from pursuing Austrians, to a cottage on the estate of the friendly Marquis Guiccioli. Here, just after being placed upon a couch, the faithful woman breathed her last in Garibaldi's arms. In the meantime nine of his followers had been captured and instantly executed.

Thoroughly disheartened, grief-stricken by his great bereavement, and realizing that all hope was at an end, Garibaldi tore himself away from the side of his dead mate, and, after wandering for thirty-five days in disguise, encountering many perils, half starved, and accompanied by but one friend, he arrived safely at Genoa.

He then went to Tunis, and later to Gibraltar, but at both places he was refused permission to remain. He crossed to Tangiers, and, after a stay of several weeks, embarked for Liverpool, and from there proceeded to New York. This was in the year 1851. He remained in New York until 1853, when he was given command of an Italian ship bound for China, thence to Italy, and then to return to New York. He made the round trip successfully, reaching New York again in 1856. During this voyage he explored the desolate island of Caprera, where he bought a tract of land, which afterward became his home. On leaving the United States he went directly to his new-made home, and there lived peace-fully until 1859. In the winter of that year the climax was reached of the intertwining of French and Italian politics, under the manipulation of Cavour, the Italian Minister. Garibaldi knew nothing of the portentous agreements that were being entered into—agreements that meant war with Austria, the formation of the King-dom of Italy from the Alps to the Adriatic, and the ces-sion of Nice and Savoy.

Garibaldi was summoned to Turin and asked by Cavour to take command of the Chasseurs of the Alps. This was the beginning of one of his most celebrated cam-paigns, which made him the idol of Italy and won for him the admiration of Europe. By the end of the fol-lowing April he was in command of three regiments of infantry. When these volunteers entered Lombardy they were joined by large additions of Milanese. Aus-tria demanded that these troops be dismissed. Cavour declined to comply and Austria began hostilities. On the 6th of May Garibaldi left Biella for Casale, and two days later engaged in several skirmishes with the Aus-trians. Then the jealousy of the older Generals in the army began to manifest itself by throwing obstacles in his way. These facts were made known to Victor Emmanuel, who straightway granted Garibaldi permis-sion to make war when and where he pleased. Less than five hours after receiving this permission he had begun the series of brilliant exploits which continued through the campaign, and served, owing to their reck-lessness and effrontery, to dumbfound and confuse the Austrians.

Night and day during the succeeding weeks he kept up continued skirmishes with the Austrians in the moun-tains and on the plains. Volunteers flocked to his ranks,

and on May 23d his army entered Varese during a heavy
storm, momentarily expecting an attack from the Austrians. Two days later General Urban, with an Austrian army of 5,000, began bombarding the town; but
in the face of the determined resistance made by the Garibaldians, was compelled to retreat. The Austrians
encamped at San Fermo, leaving Garibaldi in some per-
plexity regarding their future movements. At this
juncture he received information which led him to believe that the object of the Austrians was to cut off his
approach to Como. In spite of the fact that he was outnumbered nearly three to one, he determined to attack.
With fixed bayonets his brave troops went to the assault,
captured San Fermo after a desperate contest, and
pursued the Austrians through the town of Como,
scattering them in great disorder along the road to
Monza. The Garibaldians in this engagement secured
large quantities of ammunition and supplies. After fortifying the place, Garibaldi, with the majority of his
troops, hastened to Varese, which Urban was preparing
to attack. He had demanded a war indemnity of 2,000,-
000 francs, threatening on refusal to sack the town. At
dawn Garibaldi, by rapid maneuvers, had reached a desirable but dangerous position. He was practically in a
trap, and in the first attack of the Austrians suffered
severely. He began the erection of palisades, and at the
same time dispatched a telegram to the allied army
asking for reinforcements. He knew full well that there
were no allies in the vicinity, and that his dispatch would
fall into the hands of the Austrians. This proved true.
The Austrians felt certain that Garibaldi was waiting for
reinforcements which would never come, and that
eventually he must surrender. That night he made a
great display of bivouac fires, and marched his men up

and down before them. During the midst of a storm he quietly marched his army away through ravines and by-paths, and at dawn was back in Como, having completely outwitted his adversary.

Throughout the summer Garibaldi continued making headway, defeating or outgeneraling the Austrians at every turn until July, when an armistice was declared. With his volunteers he was at this time encamped at Lovere, where he remained awaiting developments. When, on July 15th, the Peace of Villafranca was announced Garibaldi and his men were filled with anger, and would have disregarded the treaty but for an imperial order from Victor Emmanuel. He then resigned his commission, and returned to his peaceful abode at Caprera.

In the year 1860 Garibaldi's surprising expedition to Sicily and Naples was made. The revolutionary movements in other sections of Italy had found a responsive thrill in the hearts of the oppressed Sicilians. They had suffered atrocities of every description at the hands of Maniscalco and Salzano, who had been made rulers by Francis II. This state of affairs attracted the attention and awakened the sympathy of the Garibaldian party. On the night of the 5th of May, 1860, Garibaldi, at the head of 1,000 volunteers, set sail from Genoa. Just before his departure he sent a message to the King, announcing his project. With his troops he landed at Marsala May 11th, and his appearance electrified the people of that town. Neapolitan cruisers were already upon his track, and within two hours after he had disembarked his two ships had been destroyed by the Neapolitan fleet. Garibaldi immediately issued two proclamations, one to the people of Sicily, the other to the Neapolitan army. The first informed the Sicilians that he had come to liberate them. He called them to arms, and appealed to them to show the world how a country can become freed from its oppressors by the powerful will of a united people. In the second he asked the soldiers of the Neapolitan army to fight side by side with him against the enemies of Italy. Almost immediately a corps of Sicilians of 1,200 men was organized. Garibaldi led his troops to Salemi, where he was enthusiastically received by the citizens. He declared himself dictator, and proclaimed the royal Government suspended. He made a general levy upon citizens between the ages of seventeen and fifty, and volunteers poured into his ranks by the hundreds. Wherever the Garibaldian army went it was received with open arms. By rapid movements he completely deceived the Neapolitans, and while Naples was being informed that his army had been scattered and routed, Garibaldi was almost at the gates of Palermo. He first encountered the royal army at Calatafimi, and the battle lasted three hours. For a time success was doubtful, but the Neapolitans were finally repulsed with heavy losses. Garibaldi arrived at Palermo at 3 o'clock in the morning of May 27th, and before the authorities had recovered from their surprise the guard at the Termini gate had been overpowered and the insurgents were streaming into the city. Residents rushed half dressed from their houses in a frenzy of joy to welcome their deliverer. Barricades against the royal troops were built in the streets out of vehicles, merchandise, and furniture of every description, which were freely supplied by the citizens. Even women and children aided in the work. Everywhere fighting was in progress, and after four hours' of desperate work the royal army was dislodged from all points except the castle and the royal palace. For two days Palermo continued to be the scene of a bloody conflict, acts of terrible cruelty being committed. The royal troops pillaged, burned, and massacred wherever they gained an entrance, while the inhabitants aided the Garibaldians and fought with the ferocity of long-suppressed hatred. Finally, on May 30th, through the efforts of the English Consul, Garibaldi had a meeting with Lanza, the commander of the royal troops, and a truce of twenty-four hours was agreed upon. Before the expiration of this time instructions arrived from Naples ordering the Neapolitans to evacuate Palermo.

A great victory had been won, but it had cost Garibaldi many of his bravest men. During the fighting Garibaldi performed many deeds of heroic daring, once being surrounded by four dragoons who, with uplifted swords, demanded his surrender. Garibaldi fearlessly drew his sword, and in turn demanded the surrender of his adversaries. Had not some of his men at this moment come to his assistance his life would have certainly paid the forfeit of his valor. From Palermo Garibaldi made a rapid advance upon Messina. As the battle of Calatafimi had been the opening wedge for his entering into Palermo, so the battle of Milazzo opened the way for him to Messina. For hours after commencing the attack upon this point the Garibaldians failed to make any headway, and it was only by one of Garibaldi's masterly guerrilla movements that the day was won. With two aides and only fifty men he made a detour, and managed to turn the right of the defending line, thus outflanking the Neapolitans and forcing them to beat a hasty retreat to their fortress which, however, was so persistently attacked by the Neapolitan warship, Veloce, which had joined Garibaldi's side, that the royal troops were compelled to capitulate. This hard-fought battle completed the conquest of Sicily, and Garibaldi and his army entered Messina to be received with the same enthusiasm that had been exhibited at Palermo.

Having rested his army for a month, and leaving the administration of Sicily in the hands of a subdictator, Garibaldi proceeded to carry out the second part of the great project he had undertaken. He embarked his army and landed on the Calabrian Coast, where he found the inhabitants eager to coöperate with him to overthrow the much-hated dynasty of the Spanish Bourbons. On this expedition Garibaldi took with him a little more than 4,000 troops. The successes of Sicily were repeated, and on August 21st the defenders of the city of Reggio capitulated, leaving in the hands of the victorious Garibaldians all their arms, ammunition, and supplies. Thus a foothold had been gained on the mainland, and Garibaldi hastily summoned reinforcements from Messina and instituted that victorious campaign which a few weeks later found him within the walls of the city of Naples itself.

Garibaldi's march from Reggio to Naples was a succession of triumphs. The Bourbon soldiers were so disheartened at the defeats they had sustained that they were ready to lay down their arms at the mere mention of the conqueror's name. At Villa San Giovani 12,000 Neapolitan soldiers consented to unconditional surrender, although confronted by only a few hundred volunteers. At Soveria, a few days later, the victor, with about fifty men, accepted the surrender of 1,200 Neapolitans. The nearer he approached to Naples, the greater his welcome seemed to become. Not a hand was raised against him or his followers. Salerno was evacuated without a blow. On September 7th Garibaldi, with a few followers, left Salerno by train for Naples.

King Francis had been practically deserted by his army,
his advisers had already begun making overtures to the
conquering Garibaldi, and so, almost alone, the miserable young monarch sailed from Naples to Gaeta, where
he hoped to make a last struggle for supremacy.   Meanwhile the train carrying Garibaldi was met at every station by wild crowds, who came to cheer their hero and
liberator.   When he entered Naples, according to Bent's
narrative, the troops of King Francis threw up their
caps and shouted, "Viva Garibaldi."

He was hailed as Dictator, and idolized and feted by
the populace.   In the meantime the agents of Cavour
were busy with plans to dissuade him from proceeding
with his project of marching upon Rome.   At the same
time King Francis was rallying what remained of his
forces around Gaeta, prepared to make a last stand on the
banks of the Volturno.   At this moment, also, Victor
Emmanuel was hastening with an army toward the
Neapolitan frontier to block the expected onward move
of Garibaldi toward Rome.   On October 1st, the last
battle in the Sicilian campaigns was fought at Volturno.
Garibaldi's army of 37,000 was opposed by that of King
Francis, numbering about 40,000.   The Garibaldian
advance line of 11,000 was being hard pressed, and was
retreating before the Neapolitans when the arrival of
5,000 reserves turned the tide of battle, and the Neapolitan forces were completely routed.

When Victor Emmanuel crossed the Neapolitan
frontier with his army, he was met by Garibaldi, who
came to deliver up his dictatorship to his Sovereign.   He
had already caused the citizens of Naples and Sicily to
vote upon the question of annexation to Piedmont, and
they favored it unanimously.   On November 7th Victor
Emmanuel entered Naples by the side of the red-shirted

Garibaldi and was proclaimed King. Almost his first act toward the man who had placed him there was to sternly forbid him to make any effort upon Rome, and Garibaldi sorrowfully took leave of his volunteers and once again returned to Caprera, having refused all offers of honors and emoluments from the Government.

The year 1861 was ushered in peacefully enough, but Garibaldi soon grew restless among his quiet surroundings. He remained closely in touch with political events and the affairs of the Government. Rome, the loadstone of his life, was constantly uppermost in his mind. There were also other matters which disturbed and fretted him. His beloved Southern army had not received the recognition he had craved for it. In the interests of diplomacy, it was urged, such an army could not be maintained on the Roman frontier. Diplomacy, however, had no part in Garibaldi's makeup, and his hatred of the Papacy and the priesthood grew more bitter every day. When, therefore, he was offered a seat in Parliament, he gladly accepted it as an opportunity to force his grievances upon the Government. When, in April of 1861, he appeared in the Assembly at Turin, it was not as a deputy of peace. He was attired in the red shirt, and wore the broad-brimmed hat that had served as his attire in the campaigns. The scene in the Assembly was a tempestuous and memorable one, Garibaldi indignantly and passionately attacking the policy of the Government as represented by Cavour. The latter favored and was pursuing a waiting policy as regarded Rome; while Garibaldi was for no other policy but action. These two were reconciled before the session closed, and Garibaldi again returned to Caprera. During the spring of 1862, the impatience of the people, fostered by the Garibaldi party, grew more than ever perceptible for the overthrow of the temporal power of the Pope, and the establishing in Rome the capital of the Kingdom of Italy. Cavour had died, and his place was filled by the crafty Ratazzi. The historian, Bent, does not hesitate to pronounce against Ratazzi as the author of a trap into which Garibaldi was easily led. Apparently having the silent consent of the Government, and certainly so believing, Garibaldi placed himself at the head of an expedition to move against Rome. He was afforded every opportunity to organize his volunteers, and the King, although openly proclaiming against the enterprise, placed no obstacle in his way, until, after camping for the night on the now famous hill of Aspromonte, the Garibaldians at dawn found themselves surrounded by royal troops. Both sides afterward disclaimed responsibility for the sharp conflict which followed. Garibaldi was ordering his men not to fire, when he was struck by two balls from Royalist rifles. His troops were disarmed, and he was taken to Spezia, and after several months of suffering was able to return to his island home. The affair was a sad blot on the reign of Victor Emmanuel, concerning which many explanations have been offered, but the whole truth of which will perhaps never be known.

Following an unusually long period of peace, Italy again began war against Austria, and in July of 1866, Garibaldi was invited to take command of the volunteers. Without hesitation, he accepted, and in the short campaign which followed, in which, however, twenty battles were fought, and at the end of which the Garibaldians had advanced almost to the walls of Trieste, he exhibited the same valor, skill, and daring which had marked the fighting of his younger days. During one of these engagements he was wounded in the thigh, but remained out of his saddle only a few days. Peace was brought about through the intervention of foreign powers, and Garibaldi, disgusted, but uncomplaining, wended his way home to wait for the next opportunity to take up arms against his enemies. He had not long to wait.

The year 1867 dawned upon Italy and found her, for the first time in centuries, free from foreign rule. By the peace concluded the previous year, the Venetian territory had been ceded to Italy, and the Austrians had departed to their own country. France had withdrawn her troops from Rome under the pledge that the Pope was to be left in undisturbed possession. The time was ripe, and all the conditions seemed favorable for another of those revolutionary movements which had continually stirred Italy. Garibaldi at once came to the front. In February he toured the country, calling the patriots to arms. Organizations, having for their object the establishment of the Roman Republic, sprung up on every hand. When, in September, Garibaldi set out for the Roman frontier, volunteers were everywhere awaiting to join him. For months the Government had been watching these preparations, but determined to act only when Garibaldi was on his way to the scene of action. On arriving at Sinalunga, he was arrested and hastily transferred to the citadel at Alessandria. Here he was well treated, and after a few days was liberated and taken to his home at Caprera, while several warships were detailed to watch the island and prevent him from leaving it. The arrest of Garibaldi did not still the rising storm. Volunteers continued to cross the frontier, and began carrying on a guerrilla warfare against the Papal troops. While this was going on, Garibaldi, in spite of the watch kept over him, managed to escape, and in seven days reached Florence, where he was given an ovation. He then proceeded toward Rome, the Government making no further effort to hinder him. He placed himself at the head of the volunteers, and took up a position at Monte Rotondo, twelve miles from Rome. The pledge with France had been broken, and French troops were landed at Rome, October 30th. Together with the Papal forces, they marched against the Garibaldians, and after some promiscuous fighting, came the battle of Mentana on November 3d. The soldiers of Garibaldi fought with courage and desperation against the disciplined French legions and the Papal troops, but were terribly defeated. Over 600 of the volunteers were killed or wounded, and about 1,600 were taken prisoners. Garibaldi was in the thickest of the fight, but after the blow his army had suffered, nothing remained for him but to retreat. He started for Florence, but at Montevarchi was made a prisoner by the orders of the Government and conveyed to Varignano fortress in Spezia. Soon afterward the King permitted him to retire to Caprera. So far as Italy was concerned his campaigns were forever ended. In 1870, soon after the breaking out of the Franco-Prussian War, Garibaldi, though not much more than a wreck of his former self, offered his services to France. After some hesitation they were accepted. He was given command of several brigades of raw volunteers, and with them performed valuable service, though not to be compared with the brilliant exploits of his previous campaigns. During the armistice of February, 1871, he resigned his command and returned to Italy to receive once more the plaudits of an idolizing multitude. In the meantime, Rome, which he had failed to conquer, had been won to Italy with scarcely a blow, and thither he went in 1875, having been elected to Parliament. He was received with the wildest acclamations. Feeble, bent, and scarcely able to walk without assistance, the old warrior was still the idol of the people. His advent was feared yet desired. But there was nothing further to fear. His fighting days were past, at least as far as the sword was concerned. With the pen he continued to battle for reforms, and besides completed several books, romantically describing his campaigns.

Giuseppe Garibaldi breathed his last on Friday, June 2, 1882, at Caprera. To the end, he remained firm in the principles which had dominated his life. He loved liberty, his country, and his countrymen. When his heart ceased to beat, the whole Nation mourned. In the midst of a furious storm his remains were consigned to the grave on the island where he had passed his only peaceful days. The island was afterward purchased by the Government, and is held sacred to his memory.

ROBERT EDWARD LEE
1807-1870

HERO OF A LOST CAUSE

Wolseley, the English General, regarded Robert E. Lee the greatest of American generals. Lee was neither an enthusiast or fanatic. He believed when he took up the sword in hostility against the Federal Government that he was doing his duty and he was willing to abide by the consequences, be what they might. He was a kind-hearted, dignified, and Christian gentleman. His bravery was unquestioned. From the very outset of his military career, which began under General Scott in the Mexican War, he displayed that zeal and intrepidity which won for him praise and promotion. His high character and self-sacrifice in the interest of the cause which he believed to be just, gained the sincere admiration of even his former foes, while the calm dignity with which he met adversity and submitted to the inevitable, aroused Northern sympathy and Southern pride. "In person," says McCabe, "General Lee was strikingly handsome. He was tall in stature and possessed one of the most perfectly proportioned figures the writer ever saw. He was so perfectly proportioned and so graceful in motion that walking seemed to be no exertion to him. His features were handsome and his expression commanding, yet kind and winning. In his manner he was quiet and modest, but thoroughly self-possessed. His whole bearing seemed to me to merit the expression of 'antique heroism' applied to him by a foreign writer.

He was courteous and kind to all, and at the height of his power the humblest private in his army approached him with an absolute certainty of a cordial reception. He was devotedly loved by his friends, and personally he had no enemies. He was strong in his friendships, and slow to condemn any one. In the midst of the fierce passions of war, his moderation was most remarkable. He was absolutely free from bitterness of feeling, and always spoke of his adversaries with kindness and respect. He possessed the most perfect command over his temper, and it is said that he was never seen angry. An oath never passed his lips, and he used neither tobacco nor liquors." Lee made a long, desperate, and brilliant, but unequal, struggle and viewed as a master of defensive warfare, ranks second to no warrior in the world.

Robert Edward Lee descended from a race of statesmen and warriors. The ancestry of the family, established through Richard Lee, an Englishman of the Cavalier stock, who emigrated to America and settled in Virginia while that colony still paid allegiance to Charles I of England; has been traced back to the Fourteenth Century to Johns de Lee. Richard Lee of the County of Shropshire, England, came to the new world as secretary of the Virginia colony and member of the King's privy council. His descendant, Robert E. Lee, was born January 19, 1807, at Stratford, Westmoreland County, Virginia. His father was Colonel Henry Lee, who won distinction during the Revolutionary War and who was subsequently Governor of Virginia. The latter was the son of Richard Lee, whose paternal grandfather, of the same name, was the founder of the family in America. Robert Lee's mother was Matilda Lee, a daughter of Philip Ludwell Lee, and a sister of Richard

Henry Lee, who in 1776 offered in the Continental Congress the famous resolution which was the precursor to the Declaration of Independence. Robert Lee was born in the old homestead which had served the family from generation to generation. His boyhood life was passed in Northern Neck, part of the time amid scenes of war in 1814. While the second war with England was in progress British ships were ravaging Virginia coast cities. He was at that time seven years old, and the stirring events happening so near his home left an indellible impression upon his young mind. At the age of eighteen he entered the military academy at West Point. He was a model student, and one of exemplary habits, as is attested by the fact that during his entire course of four years he never received a demerit for misconduct, an unusual thing in the annals of the institution. July 4, 1829, he graduated from the academy with highest honors, and became by brevet a second lieutenant in the corps of topographical engineers. For several years he was engaged with work in connection with the Atlantic coast defenses. When he had been three years in the service, the young lieutenant was married to Miss Mary Custis, the daughter of George Washington Parke Custis and granddaughter of Martha Washington. Seven children, three sons and four daughters, resulted from this union. In after years during the struggle between the North and South, the first and second of these sons, George Washington Custis and William Henry Fitzhugh Lee, were Major-Generals in the Confederate army, while the third son, Robert Edward Lee, Jr., entered the service as a private and was later promoted to a staff appointment. Soon after his marriage, young Lieutenant Lee was appointed assistant astronomer for the demarkation of the boundary line between Ohio and

Michigan, and subsequently, in 1836, the war department, pleased with the young officer's efficiency, bestowed upon him the rank of first lieutenant. Later he was appointed captain of engineers. In 1844 he became a member of the board of visitors at West Point, and the next year was selected as member of the board of engineers of the military academy. At the outbreak of the Mexican War, Captain Lee was confronted with the prospect of his initiation into the grim reality of war, and his first experience in the making of history, upon whose pages his name was destined to appear so conspicuously, under circumstances then undreamed of, came at Vera Cruz. Lee was assigned to the Central Army in the invasion of Mexico as chief engineer, which position he held under General Scott, throughout the whole campaign. He assumed his duties with the army March 10, 1847. On that day the work of investing the City of Vera Cruz was commenced, and it devolved upon Captain Lee to enact the important rôle of adviser to his superiors in the matter of engineering the siege which terminated in a few days with the surrender of the town and castle. That this speedy result was in a measure due to Lee's advice and instrumentality is acknowledged by General Scott in his memoirs, in which he says, "I am compelled to make special mention of Captain Lee. This officer greatly distinguished himself at the siege of Vera Cruz." During the days that followed, while the American army was marching against the City of Mexico, Lee gave further signal proof of his courage and skill by reconnoisances which proved of great value to his superiors. His vigilance and thorough attainments in military engineering enabled the American forces to avoid many dangerous traps set by their adversaries along the road to the capital, which had been strongly fortified. In recognition of his services, Scott had appointed Lee a member of his personal staff. While the movement toward the City of Mexico was in progress, a fierce battle was fought at Cerro Gordo, April 18th. The success that attended the Americans at this point was largely due to Lee, who, with a reconnoitering party discovered a way through a deep and tortuous mountain passage by which light artillery batteries could be mounted on the heights of Cerro Gordo in such a manner as to place the forces of the enemy posted there at the mercy of Scott. The accomplishment of this feat and the resultant defeat of the defenders of the place was rewarded by breveting him as a major. It is related that during one of his perilous scouting expeditions, Lee found himself within the ranks of the enemy. Unwittingly he had gone too far and had a narrow escape from being discovered. He concealed himself under a fallen tree and remained there while Mexican soldiers passed in dangerous proximity. He was compelled to remain in his hiding place until darkness fell when his safe escape became possible. Again at Churubusco and at Contreras he distinguished himself and as a consequence once more received promotion, this time being advanced to brevet lieutenant-colonel. Lee, conducting Ransom's Brigade, had been detached from Scott's forces to assist Cadwallader's Brigade in the attack on Contreras. At 3 o'clock in the morning of August 19th while the actual attack was being made by Cadwallader's troops from a point of vantage, Lee contrived an ingenious move which threw the enemy off its guard and enabled Cadwallader to effect the capture of the town in seventeen minutes. Lee led Ransom's Brigade across a deep ravine in front to distract the enemy, but after crossing, turned the intended feint to good effect by advancing within range of the enemy's works and pouring a destructive volley into the opposing ranks. After the battle at Molinos del Rey and Churubusco, preliminary to the siege of the City of Mexico, in which Lee conducted himself with characteristic gallantry, he came with Scott upon the field of Chapultepec. Here, while the city was being invested, he was wounded September 13th, but remained by the side of General Scott until, weak from loss of blood and exhausted from the loss of two nights' sleep at the batteries, he fainted and was carried to the rear. Referring to Lee's military science and bravery, which had contributed to the series of American victories, even to the fall of the capital city, General Scott wrote: "Lee is the greatest military genius in America."

On returning North Colonel Lee was appointed Superintendent of West Point Academy, September 1, 1852, and for the next three years devoted himself to the duties devolving upon him in his new capacity. April 1, 1855, to accept the Lieutenant-Colonelcy of the Second Cavalry Regiment, having received his commission with the full rank, Lee resigned from West Point. The same year his regiment was dispatched to Texas to put down Indian uprisings, and for the next four years Lee was engaged in dangerous and arduous contention with the hostile aborigines. He returned on leave of absence to Washington in 1859 in time to take command of the body of militia, which, on the 18th of October routed John Brown and his band of fellow conspirators from their stronghold at Harper's Ferry. This was the insignificant prelude to the War of the Rebellion.

Lee had returned to Texas, and was there in the early part of 1861, when the great crisis was approaching. He had carefully watched with varying emotions the political

ROBERT E. LEE

horoscope of the country, but had shared no part in its evolutions. Had Virginia remained with the Union Lee must have remained also, for next to his State his country was his dearest idol. But when Virginia seceded, though the Lieutenant-Generalship of the Federal army might have been his; though it cost the severing of ties with the Union army, cemented by twenty-five years of continuous service, marking a distinguished career—when the test came—he stood with his State. As he replied to Montgomery Blair, who was authorized to offer him command of the Federal army if he should stay with the Union: "Mr. Blair, I look upon secession as Anarchy. If I owned 4,000,000 slaves in the South I would sacrifice them all to the Union; but how can I draw my sword upon Virginia, my native State?" When implored by his friend, General Scott, not to desert the North, he declared, "I am compelled to. I cannot consult my own feelings in this matter."

The resignation from the Federal service was forthcoming, April 20, 1861. It was written from Arlington, Va., whither Lee had gone, and accompanying it a letter to General Scott, in which he said: "Save in defense of my State I never desire again to draw my sword." The resignation was at once accepted, and three days later his commission as commander of all the forces in Virginia was confirmed by the State Legislature. General Lee immediately undertook the work of organizing and mobilizing the State volunteer troops.

Recruiting went on all over the State, and Lee soon found himself in command of a large force. The first engagement of the war was at Great Bethel, June 10, 1861. While of small importance, it still served to inspire the people of the South with confidence and enthusiasm, for in this battle, 1,800 infantry and six

pieces of artillery, poorly entrenched, defeated a body of
5,000 troops well supplied with artillery.   It was the first
test of strength between the combatants, and had success
attended the Southern arms at the same ratio for one
year, the result of the war would have been exactly
opposite to what it was.   One of the first moves of General Lee was to send troops to Western Virginia, where
the enemy were mobilizing so rapidly along the Ohio
River that, unless action was taken to counterbalance
the movement, that portion of the State would speedily
become irretrievably Federal.   About 5,000 infantry, a
few hundred cavalry, and several batteries of artillery
were assembled at Beverley before July 1st, and the command was given to Brigadier-General R. S. Garnett,
who had been serving as General Lee's Adjutant-General.
Soon afterward this force was defeated by Federal troops
under McClellan, and Garnett himself was killed.   This
disaster was preceded by smaller defeats, and followed by
a series of others.   On September 10th Brigadier-General Floyd was badly beaten at Carnifex Ferry by Rosecrans, who had succeeded McClellan in Western Virginia, and General Lee was ordered to take command of
the army in that region.   He took with him reinforcements which, added to Garnett's troops, gave him an
army of 16,000 men.   By August 10th Lee had reached
the neighborhood of Cheat Mountain, and found that
formidable position strongly fortified, and therefore determined to employ strategy in dislodging the enemy.
Part of the Federal army held the post known as Elk
Water, the rest held the pass at the second of the three
summits of the mountain.   Lee arranged for a combined
attack upon the enemy at both these positions.   The
weather was extremely cold, and the difficulties of the
troops in reaching the positions assigned to them were

great. Elk Water was surrounded, and Colonel Rust,
who had gained a position in the rear of the fortifications
on Cheat Mountain, was to give the signal for the combined attack, but found the enemy's works stronger than
had been reported, and abandoned his part of the general
plan.   Rust's failure rendered the attack on Elk Water
useless, and Lee withdrew all his troops.   For this he
was severely criticised, but it was plain that the capture
of Elk Water would have availed nothing, while Cheat
Mountain was left to the Federals.   Leaving a small
force to watch the Federals, Lee hastened with 15,000
men to the relief of Floyd and Wise, against whom the
combined forces of Rosecrans and Cox were advancing.
The adversaries met at Sewell Mountain and remained
confronting each other for nearly two weeks, each expecting the other to attack.   Finally, October 6th, Rosecrans broke camp in the night and retreated westward.
Owing to the terrible condition of the roads no attempt
at pursuit was made.   Three days before this, 4,000
Federals moved out from Cheat Mountain, and attacked
General Henry R. Jackson, who had been left by Lee
with 2,500 men to hold the Federals in check.   So advantageously had General Lee posted this force that the
Federals were repulsed with 260 killed and wounded,
while the Confederates lost but 6 killed and 31 wounded.
This conflict, known as the battle of Green Brier, closed
the campaign in Western Virginia.   Lee was now
directed to proceed to Charleston and take command of
the Coast Department.   Fort Hatteras and the works in
Port Royal Harbor had been captured by the Federals,
and the interior was threatened.   Without the aid of a
navy it was impossible to dislodge the enemy from the
positions they had occupied, but Lee during the winter
fortified exposed points along the coast.   How skillfully

he performed this task was subsequently demonstrated by the futile efforts of the Federals to make any headway in this quarter. By the spring of 1862 the Confederate cause had suffered in so many directions that dissatisfaction against the military authorities was engendered. It was desired that the military affairs of the Confederacy should be no longer conducted by a civilian, but by a soldier, and in response to the general demand the Confederate Congress fixed upon General Lee as the man for the place. President Davis procured the passage of an act creating the office of Commanding-General, and promptly appointed Lee to the position. Lee entered upon his new duties March 13, 1862. Davis' action created some surprise, but his course was amply vindicated by the increased vigor which Lee infused into all the military movements of the Confederacy. Lee retained this position but a few months, when he was called to a more active field of usefulness than that of directing the movements of the armies at long range from Richmond. James D. McCabe, Jr., in his exhaustive work on the life and campaigns of Lee, holds that the victory of Manassas was the greatest misfortune that could have befallen the South, as it gave the Confederates a mistaken idea that the North had received a mortal wound. This delusion was disastrous in its effects, and owing to the general impression that the war was already practically won it became difficult to secure fresh volunteers, and soon defeats began to follow one another with alarming regularity. The Peninsular campaign had for three months, beginning with March, 1862, proven a series of disappointments to the Confederate authorities, when, in view of the critical condition of affairs, President Davis determined to place General Lee at the head of the army of Northern Virginia. Though still retaining his position as Commanding General, he was ordered to enter upon this new task without delay, which he did June 3, 1862. His first and most immediate care was to put the army in condition for an effective campaign. By June 20th he had brought the strength of the army of Northern Virginia up to 70,000 men. Lee was fully impressed with the danger of allowing McClellan to approach Richmond, and it was in accordance with this that he issued his orders for the campaign on June 24th. Jackson had succeeded in preventing a conjunction of the forces of McClellan and McDowell, and had rendered Shields and Fremont useless for the balance of the campaign, and Lee now determined to bring Jackson to the Chickahominy to be ready for the struggle in defense of the Southern capital. At the same time the report was caused to reach the Federals that Jackson was preparing for a new campaign, thus inducing the troops intended to reinforce McClellan to remain in Northern Virginia. While these preparations of the Southern forces were going on McClellan was eagerly watching for some sign which might disclose their intentions. He finally decided, on June 25th, to advance. The attack was made on the Confederate position on the Williamsburg road, but the assault was repulsed, and the Southern line remained unbroken. McClellan's army, in the face of the tactics employed by Lee, had gradually changed from an army of invasion, superior in numbers, to an army acting on the defensive and expecting attack. On June 27th the Federal line was located on a range of hills extending from Chickahominy to Cold Harbor, and behind Powhite Creek, a small marshy stream, running through a densely wooded country. The right rested in the rear of Cold Harbor, and was posted in the woods and clearings. The left rested on a wooded bluff rising abruptly from a deep ravine, leading to the Chickahominy. General Lee's great plan had now been perfected, each of the divisions, having occupied the positions assigned to them. At half past 2 o'clock the attack began at Cold Harbor, and soon the whole Confederate line, being advanced, assailed the Federal position in repeated fierce charges. Again and again they were beaten back, only to renew the struggle with greater ardor. As the afternoon was drawing to a close no perceptible impression had yet been made by the Confederates, and the indications were that the day was to be a victorious one for the Federals. At a critical juncture the army of Jackson arrived, and the attack was once more renewed along the whole line. Without going into details of the savage conflict which now ensued, the key point of the enemy's line was finally broken by Hood's brigade, upon which General Lee threw forward his entire force, and swept the enemy with irresistible fury to the Chickahominy. Darkness was already falling when the Confederates halted on the ground they had so gallantly captured. That night General Lee sent the news of the victory to President Davis, and concluded with the words: "We sleep on the field, and shall renew the contest in the morning." The losses on both sides had been heavy. According to the best reports the Union forces lost nearly 7,000 men, and the Southern army about 8,000. The following day the Federal army began a retreat, with Confederate divisions in pursuit. On June 30th, during the pursuit, General Lee, with Longstreet's division, fought a sharp battle on Frazier's farm, which resulted in another victory for the Confederates, who captured many prisoners, fourteen pieces of artillery, and several stands of small arms. It was now General Lee's desire to bring on a general battle with

McClellan, and July 1st found the entire Confederate army encamped on the battle-field of Frazier's farm. It was no longer possible to prevent McClellan from reaching the James River, for the advance guard was already there; the artillery and baggage trains were in the rear of Malvern hill, and communication had been established with the gunboats. The Federal army was concentrated in a strong position, with the left and center on Malvern hill. In front of this position was open ground, varying in width from a quarter to half a mile. Advancing to the attack, and before reaching this open ground, the Confederates had to traverse a wooded and swampy country, upon which the Federal batteries and the gunboats from the river kept up an incessant fire. It was near the close of the afternoon before the entire Confederate line was formed for the attack. This was one of the most fiercely contested battles of the war, and fortune seemed to favor first one side and then the other, until night mercifully descended and stopped the slaughter. By morning McClellan had withdrawn his forces, and was on the road to Harrison's landing and Westover. The Confederate loss at Malvern Hill was 5,000, and that of the Federals is said to have been even greater. General Lee at once dispatched the cavalry in pursuit of McClellan, and the gallant General Stuart pressed vigorously upon the enemy's rear. Skirmishes were frequent, and a number of prisoners were captured. For several days each side maneuvered in the expectation of another battle, until July 8th, when General Lee decided to return to the vicinity of Richmond. Practically, the campaign was a success for the South. The siege of Richmond had been raised, and the enemy driven from the strong positions they had occupied. During this campaign 19,533 men were killed, wounded, or disappeared. McClellan reported the Federal loss at 1,582 killed, 7,709 wounded, and 5,958 missing. In an eloquent address Lee thanked his troops for their heroic conduct in the Peninsular campaign. In order to keep McClellan stationary, or if possible to cause him to withdraw, Lee sent forty-three guns to Coggin's Point, opposite Harrison's landing, and the expedition reached its place late on the night of July 21st. The Federal shipping lay within a mile of the Southern shore, and the glimmering lights on the ships and on the shore, where the Federal camp lay in profound slumber, offered excellent marks for the Confederate gunners. The bombardment began at midnight. The fire was returned by the gunboats, and the duel continued until the Confederates had exhausted their ammunition, when they withdrew. The next day McClellan sent a force across the river and occupied Coggin's Point. By August 5th they again occupied Malvern, and General Lee, with the divisions of Longstreet and McLaws, and that of Ripley, at once moved against the intrepid foe. After some skirmishing, McClellan again withdrew. The evacuation of Harrison's landing was commenced August 16th, and was finished two days later. Satisfied that McClellan was going for good, General Lee marched upon the Rapidan.

At this time General Pope had just taken charge of the newly created Federal army of Virginia, and among the many general orders issued by him, he says in one of them, "I have come from the West, where we have always seen the backs of our enemies—from an army whose business it has been to seek the adversary, whose policy has been attack and not defence." Yet within a few weeks General Lee compelled the boastful Pope to perform the very act which, according to his proclamation, was so repugnant to him. Pope was sadly beaten at Cedar Run by Jackson's army August 8th, and eight days later Lee arrived at Gordonsville and joined General Longstreet. The army at once began an advance on the Rapidan. Lee personally made a reconnoissance of the enemy's lines, and decided to lose no time in attacking. But Pope became alarmed, and sought safety beyond the Rappahannock. Under Lee's direction, Jackson and Stuart continued to harry his forces and seize his wagon trains. On August 30th the second battle of Manassas was fought, and proved one of Lee's most signal victories.

The last battle of Lee's campaign in Northern Virginia was the conflict of Ox Hill, near Germantown, on September 1st. The Federal army had taken up a strong position, but when the attack came at 5 o'clock in the afternoon, in the midst of a shower, the resistless charges of the Confederates could not be withstood, and after withdrawing that night, Pope, on the following day, retreated with his whole army to Alexandria and thence to Washington. The Confederate loss in this campaign from the Rappahannock to the Potomac was, in all branches of the army, 9,112. The Federal losses, according to McCabe, exceeded 30,000, including eight Generals, and over 2,000 prisoners. This was the end of a brilliant campaign, worthy in every respect of the illustrious soldier who conducted it. Lee now determined to invade Maryland. There were many indications that Maryland would have joined in the rebellion had not the strong hand of the Federal Government quickly disarmed the State. By September 7th the entire army had crossed the Potomac, and found lodgment in the enemy's country, and on the same day arrived at Frederick. The army was received as a host of friends and in return the citizens were treated with the greatest consideration by the soldiers. Lee issued a proclamation, offering to help the State throw off the yoke of the Federal Government, and also opened recruiting offices. Results were not, however, flattering. September 10th General Jackson was detached by Lee to capture Harper's Ferry and Martinsburg, a task which was successfully carried out. It was not Lee's plan in entering Maryland to march upon either Baltimore or Washington, but to draw McClellan away to the Cumberland Valley. His plan was, in part, successful. The army of McClellan and Pope was consolidated under McClellan, and he started from Washington, September 5th, with 87,000 men. On the 10th Lee left Frederick, passed South Mountain, and marched toward Boonsboro. Two days later McClellan entered Frederick, drove out the Confederate cavalry, which had been left there to watch the enemy, and on the following day had the good luck to find the confidential order of the campaign, issued by Lee to D. H. Hill. The document had in some manner been lost, and had been picked up and turned over to McClellan, to whom it was of inestimable value, giving him as it did the greatest advantage one commander can have over another—that of accurately knowing the plans of the enemy. McClellan's first move was to attack Hill's division at South Mountain, at the same time being able, owing to his knowledge of Lee's plan, to move against and defeat other detachments of the Confederates. When South Mountain became untenable after a battle, which involved heavy losses on both sides, the troops hastened to join Lee at Sharpsburg, where he was now concentrating his army. McClellan advanced on Sharpsburg, and found the Confederates in position on the west bank of Antietam Creek. Lee's army composed at this time about 33,000 men, with which he was to oppose the recently equipped army of over 80,000 of the enemy.

The battle began at 4 o'clock on the afternoon of September 16th, continued until dark, and was resumed with greater vigor the following morning. By 4 o'clock in the afternoon the Federal forces had broken the Confederate center and crossed the creek, when the sudden arrival of A. P. Hill's division checked, and at dusk drove back the troops of McClellan and recovered the lost ground, so that the day closed as it had begun, except for over 20,000 killed and wounded soldiers scattered over the field, of which the Confederates had lost about 8,000. During the following day both armies remained inactive, Lee not being strong enough to assume the offensive, and McClellan waiting for fresh troops, which were on the way from Washington. On the night of the 18th, having nothing to gain by remaining, Lee decided to retire into Virginia. The crossing of the Potomac was made by the entire army without mishap. A correspondent of the New York Tribune expressed the disappointment of McClellan over the masterly retreat which Lee had effected as follows: "He leaves us the debris of his late camps, two disabled pieces of artillery, a few hundred stragglers, 2,000 wounded, and as many unburied dead. Not a sound field-piece, caisson, ambulance, or wagon; not a tent, box of stores, or a pound of ammunition. He takes with him the supplies gathered in Maryland, and the rich spoils of Harper's Ferry." General Porter was sent in pursuit of the Confederates, but succeeded only in meeting a small force under Pendleton, which he scattered, capturing four pieces of artillery. When Lee learned of it he sent A. P. Hill back with a division, and on the 20th drove the Federals into the river, almost annihilating Porter's command. McClellan remained north of the Potomac, and Lee withdrew to the vicinity of Winchester. During the several

weeks of rest which followed McClellan prepared for
another attempt against the Southern capital. Lee had
also reorganized his army, and had received reinforcements to the number of 30,000, when hostilities again
opened in October. The army of McClellan now numbered 110,000 men. McClellan hesitated whether to
move directly upon Lee by way of the Shenandoah Valley or to enter Virginia east of the Blue Ridge, and en-
deavor to place his great force between Lee and Richmond. He finally decided upon the latter course. As
soon as McClellan set out on this project, Lee put his
army in motion. On November 7th McClellan was suddenly, through political animosity, removed from command, and the army of the Potomac was given to Burnside. The Federal army was at this time at Warrentown,
and on November 15th Burnside began the march on
Fredericksburg. By the 20th the entire army was before the town, but Lee who had early surmised the plans
of the enemy, had reinforced the town, and with his whole
army occupied the heights back of the city. Burnside's
plan was to cross the Rappahannock for the attack on
Fredericksburg on five pontoon bridges. The work of
building the floating bridge was commenced after midnight December 11th. It was detected and stopped by
Southern sharpshooters. Although there were no Confederate troops in Fredericksburg itself, Burnside now
began to bombard the town across the river, in spite of
the fact that he had given no notice and that it was filled
with women and children. On the 13th, having gotten
some regiments across the river in boats, the bridges were
completed and the attack on the Confederate positions
began. From noon until dark the battle raged, and six
desperate assaults were made upon the heights, but without success. The entire Federal army was employed in

the assaults, while but 25,000 of Lee's troops were engaged, the balance of the army being spectators.   The
casualties of that terrible day were: Federal losses,
12,321 killed, wounded, or missing; Confederate losses
were 4,201 killed, and a few prisoners.   On the night of
the 15th, during a storm, Burnside recrossed the river
and retired, having failed in his effort against Fredericksburg.   Soon after this Lee's army went into winter
quarters along the Rappahannock from Fredericksburg
to Port Royal.   January 19th Burnside made another
attempt upon the army around Fredericksburg.   A violent storm and the formidable preparations made by Lee
to receive him, caused Burnside to abandon the plan.
March 30, 1863, Lee announced to the Government that
the spring campaign had opened, and that he might have
the army on the move at any day.   Hooker had now
succeeded Burnside in command of the army of the Potomac.   Lee was convinced that Hooker would attack him
as soon as the roads became passable.   This danger
found him in a weak condition, for Longstreet, with
24,000 men, had been taken from him and sent south of
the James River, leaving Lee less than 50,000 men.   He
urgently demanded reinforcements or the return of
Longstreet, but was not heeded.   Lee made the best
dispositions possible, and waited for the enemy.   On the
night of April 30th, when nearing the enemy's lines,
Hooker was in high spirits, and exclaimed in talking
with his officers: "The Rebel army is now the legitimate
property of the Army of the Potomac.   They may as well
pack up their haversacks and make for Richmond.   I
shall be after them."   Just beyond Chancellorsville was
a ridge of considerable value to either army, owing to its
elevation.   On the morning of May 1st, Hooker attempted to occupy this ridge, which was defended by a

weak Confederate force.   He was all but victorious when
General Jackson, with several brigades, arrived and saved
the day.   Hooker retired to Chancellorsville, and General Lee immediately decided to attack him.   This great
battle, in which the gallant General Jackson received his
death-wounds was fought May 2d and 3d, and at 10
o'clock on the latter date the Confederate flag floated
over Chancellorsville.   Hooker soon after vanished with
his army as had his predecessors.   While the army of
Northern Virginia had thus been successful, the Confederate armies in the West and Southwest had been steadily
beaten.   Lee at this juncture again prepared to invade
the North.   The movement began in June, and the first
clash came June 9th at Beverley's ford, and simultaneously at Kelley's ford.   In both the Confederates were
successful.   Having crossed the Potomac, Lee arrived
June 29th at Middleton, only to learn that the Federal
army was about to move over the mountains to assail his
communications.   This necessitated new dispositions,
which brought about the wonderful and sanguinary
battle of Gettysburg, July 1st, 2d, and 3d, and was the
only real disaster that had thus far overtaken Lee's army.
The Confederates lost 20,000, and the Federals 23,000.
On the night of July 4th Lee began to retreat.   July 7th
his army was on the banks of the swollen Potomac.   He
was compelled to wait until the 13th, when the river was
fordable.   Having retired to Culpepper, Lee having no
hope of being able to resume operations during the fall,
granted furloughs on an extensive scale, and the withdrawal of Longstreet's corps for duty in Tennessee left
the army in September in a defensive state.   As Meade's
army advanced into Northern Virginia, Lee took up a
strong position on the Rapidan.   Skirmishes and minor
combats were of daily occurrence, but Lee skillfully

avoided a general battle with Meade, his forces being too small to give any hope of success. He went into winter quarters behind the Rapidan, the right wing resting on Morton's ford, and the left was strongly intrenched along the left bank of Mine Run Creek. The lower fords of the Rapidan were left uncovered. On learning this Meade determined to make another effort to destroy Lee and his army. An examination of Lee's lines, however, convinced him that they were impregnable, and the effort was abandoned. The army remained in winter quarters until the opening of the momentous campaign of 1864, which was to decide the great struggle. Longstreet's corps returned May 1st, but even including this, Lee's army numbered less than 50,000 men, and the facts that he could secure no reinforcements and would doubtless soon be called upon to confront the great army of General Grant, who had now been given full command of the Federal armies, caused the Southern Commander no little anxiety. It was evident that the concluding struggle of the war would be made in Virginia. The first great battle of the campaign was that of the Wilderness, the story of which, together with the other battles of this memorable campaign, is told in the narrative of Grant. Through all of the obstacles and vicissitudes that beset him, Lee patiently and valiantly held on, although poorly supported during much of the time by those whose cause he fought. New Years day of 1865 witnessed a sad and pitiful spectacle in the devoted army of General Lee. On every hand he was threatened with ruin, and with him the cause of the South. Food was scarce, the army was literally starving, and disease and death lurked everywhere. The last effort to rally the waning confidence of the people was the elevation of Lee to Commander-in-Chief of all the armies of the Confederacy. Lee was practically the only man in the South in whom the populace had not lost faith. But the time for both hope and faith was passing. Grant was daily drawing more and more closely the coils which he had cast about the South. The surrender of Richmond and Petersburg necessarily served as a prelude to the surrender of Lee. Retreating after the fall of Richmond, which was evacuated April 2d, after the desperate fighting and the great sacrifice of blood that had been made to save it, Lee was pursued and assailed from every side; he was finally completely hemmed in at Farmville, April 7th, when Grant at once opened negotiations for the surrender of the Confederate army. It was effected April 9th, when Lee signed the final agreement at the village of Appomattox Court House. This was the end of the war. Peace was restored, Lee, the last mainstay of the Southern cause, had been vanquished, but he had fought valiantly, and in accordance with his conscience. He maintained to the last moment that he was still capable of resisting, but surrendered in the interest of peace.

After the surrender Lee remained quietly at his home in Richmond, where he was visited by thousands, who called to express their admiration of his abilities as a warrior. Federal officers passing North after the war called on him to shake his hand, and they were received with dignified kindness. On October 12, 1870, at Lexington, General Lee died after a brief illness, which came upon him suddenly in the form of nervous prostration. Not only the South, but the whole Nation mourned his death, for his ability and worth was everywhere recognized.

WILLIAM TECUMSEH SHERMAN

Photo from life

WILLIAM TECUMSEH SHERMAN

1820-1891

"TRUE AND HONEST"

No better brief summary, perhaps, of the character and true greatness of General Sherman, can be found than the message of President Harrison to Congress on the event of the venerable warrior's death. Harrison had served as an officer in Sherman's army in Georgia, and cherished the love and respect for Sherman that was shared by every loyal soldier who ever served under him. The message in part said: "The death of William Tecumseh Sherman is an event that will bring sorrow to the heart of every patriotic citizen. No living American was so loved and venerated as he. To look upon his face, to hear his name, was to have one's love of country intensified. He served his country not for fame, not out of a sense of professional duty, but for the love of the flag and of the beneficent civil institutions of which it was the emblem. He was an ideal soldier, and shared to the fullest the esprit de corps of the army; but he cherished the civil institutions organized under the Constitution, and was a soldier only that these might be perpetuated in undiminished usefulness and honor. He was in nothing an imitator. A profound student of military science and precedent, he drew from them principles and suggestions, and so adapted them to novel conditions that his campaigns will continue to be the profitable study of the military profession through the world. His general nature made him comrade to every soldier of the great Union army. His career was complete; his honors were

full.   He had received from the Government the highest
rank known to our military establishment, and from the
people unstinted gratitude and love."   Sherman was the
soul of simplicity, and his candor was renowned.   He
asserted of himself that he had no natural military genius,
but other geniuses, military and otherwise, have viewed
his career with a coldly critical gaze, and have differed
with his modest estimate.   Not only did he possess to
the very highest degree the true military genius, but also
those other qualifications which go to make up the perfect soldier as a leader of soldiers; courage, determination, coolness, sound judgment and, above all, that
attribute which inspired to a marvelous degree the confidence and enthusiasm of men and officers alike.

William Tecumseh Sherman was born at Lancaster,
Ohio, February 8, 1820.   He descended from an illustrious family, whose antecedents came to America from
England as early as 1634.   He was the sixth of eleven
children of Judge Charles R. Sherman and Mary Hoyt,
the daughter of an influential family.   Their marriage
took place in Norwalk, Conn., in 1810, and a year later
they followed the tide of emigration to Ohio, where the
young lawyer built up a practice and was subsequently
elevated to the Ohio Supreme Court Bench.   He died
in June, 1829, leaving his family in straitened circumstances.   William T. Sherman was nine years of age at
the time of the death of his father.   To relieve the mother
of the care of all of her children, William was adopted into
the family of Thomas Ewing, a well-to-do lawyer and
friend of the lad's father.   Young Sherman was brought
up as one of the Ewing family, and after the election of
Ewing as United States Senator, he, in 1836, appointed
his foster-son to a cadetship at West Point Military
Academy.   During the four years of his stay at the

academy he devoted himself to his studies, showing a
decided inclination for military engineering and surveying. In June, 1840, he graduated with high honors,
standing near the head of his class. His commission as
second lieutenant attached him to the Third Artillery,
stationed at Fort Pierce, Florida, to preserve order
among the Seminole Indians. It not infrequently happened that the Indians in groups or bands roved away
from their reservation, and it became necessary to find
them and bring them back. In this work Sherman received his first lessons in actual fighting, as the Indians
at times resisted, and bloodshed resulted. Beyond these
incidents affairs were dull at Fort Pierce, and the young
lieutenant was anxious to see camp life on the Western
frontier, as appears from letters received from him at this
time. November 30, 1841, he was promoted to first
lieutenant, and was transferred to St. Augustine. The
following February he was again transferred, this time
to Fort Morgan, Mobile Bay, and in June he was ordered
to Fort Moultrie at Charleston, South Carolina. At
about this time there occurred in Sherman's life an incident which years afterward served to influence the destiny
of the Nation. This was an expedition which he made
through the upper part of Georgia and Alabama, while
detailed on special work in connection with his military
duties. He here became thoroughly acquainted with
the topography of the country, in which many years after
he was destined to lead one of the greatest campaigns in
American history. In April, 1846, Sherman was detailed
to Governor's Island, New York, and a little later to the
recruiting station at Pittsburg, Pennsylvania. Soon
after this he was authorized to open a recruiting station
at Zanesville, Ohio. When the news of the battles of
Palo Alto and Resaca de la Palma reached him, Sherman

could restrain his enthusiasm no longer, and applied to the Adjutant-General at Washington to be ordered to the front. Without waiting for a reply he left his office in charge of a corporal, and hurried to Cincinnati and presented himself to Colonel Fanning, a veteran, with the request that he be sent to the front at once. Instead of having his desire gratified the veteran scored him for deserting his post, and advised him to hasten back with all possible speed. Returning to Pittsburg, he found orders assigning him to Company F, then under orders for California. With other officers, he sailed aboard the "Lexington" around Cape Horn and reached the bay of Monterey, January 26, 1847, the voyage having occupied 198 days. Months of idleness followed. The Californians seemed to have not the remotest intentions of going to war, and the dull routine for garrison life was broken by hunting trips and social duties. Lieutenant Sherman was an interested witness to the wild scramble which followed the discovery of gold in California. He did not himself escape the gold fever, but after a fruitless prospecting tour was content to return to Monterey and earn money by surveying boom town and mining property. The money thus acquired was invested in real estate at Sacremento. Soon came the information that the war with Mexico was over, and that peace had been signed. This gave him the desire to return East. In January, 1850, he gained the required permission, and as the bearer of dispatches safely made the trip by way of Panama. During all the years from the time he was adopted into the family of Mr. Ewing, Sherman had carried with him the memory of Ellen Boyle Ewing, daughter of his benefactor, and from the time he went to West Point, a correspondence was kept up between them. From playmates at Lancaster the childhood affection had developed into lasting devotion, and immediately on his return to the East, Sherman proceeded to Washington and was married to Miss Ewing, whose father at this time held the office of Secretary of the Interior. The marriage took place May 1st. Sherman served during the next three years at St. Louis and New Orleans, and in September, 1853, having resigned his position in the army, he again returned to California and engaged in business there. Six years later he returned East and took up the practice of law in Kansas, for a time lived on a farm there, then removed to Louisiana, where, in the summer of 1859 he became the head of the Louisiana "Seminary of Learning and Military Academy," a State institution located at Alexandria. He occupied this position until February, 1861, when Louisiana signified her intention of joining the secession. Sherman then resigned and went to Washington. His brother, John Sherman, was already one of the great Republican leaders, and through him, William Sherman secured a personal interview with President Lincoln, and offered his services in the event of war, which was at that moment regarded in the North as only a remote possibility. The apparent indifference to the true state of affairs disgusted Sherman, the soldier, and he left Washington for Lancaster and from there went to St. Louis and became president of a street railway company. He tried to settle down to business, but found it impossible. The very air was surcharged with war. Early in April he was offered the chief clerkship in the War Department at Washington with the certainty of soon becoming Assistant Secretary of War. In a sarcastic letter he declined to accept the position, and it was predicted that Sherman would join the sedition. A little later he was tempted by an offer of the Brigadier-Generalship and command of the Military Department of Missouri. Sherman replied that he had already offered his services to the Nation, that his offer had been declined, and that he now had business affairs which required his attention. The attack on Sumter at last aroused the North. Lincoln called for 75,000 volunteers for three months. "You might as well try to put out the flames of a burning house with a squirt gun," was Sherman's comment on this move. In May, Sherman yielded to the solicitations of his friends and accepted the Colonelcy of the Thirteenth Regular Infantry Regiment. He began active duty at Washington, June 20, 1861. A little later he was placed in command of five regiments, composing the third brigade of the first division of McDowell's army corps, though retaining the rank of Colonel. He took command of these troops at Fort Corcoran early in July. Under General Tyler the division moved to the front about the middle of the month, engaged in a skirmish at Centreville, July 18th, and three days later took part in the battle of Bull Run. Though Sherman had seen thirteen years of army life, this was his first experience at real war. The part he took in that memorable battle of July 21st, however, was such as to secure for him the rank of Brigadier-General of Volunteers. In the battle mentioned, Sherman led his command into action early in the afternoon, and with such determination was the charge made that the enemy was driven back for a mile. Then the retreating troops made a stand, and so valiantly resisted that defeat was turned into victory. Some of the Federal regiments took to flight, and a precipitous retreat of the whole army began. Sherman's troops, in spite of his threats and exhortations, joined in the flight, and the retreat to Centreville was spoken of in Sherman's report as "disorderly in the extreme." Under General Tyler's orders the retreat was continued to the Potomac, and the forward movement, which had set out with an "On to Richmond" enthusiasm, found itself at noon on the next day after Bull Run back at Fort Corcoran. Here, according to Sherman's own report, he found a miscellaneous crowd crossing the aqueduct and ferries and "conceiving this to be demoralization," says the report, "I at once commanded the guard to be increased and all persons attempting to pass over to be stopped. This produced the effect desired. Men sought their proper companies and comparative order was restored." That Sherman's brigade was in the thick of the battle of Bull Run is evidenced by the fact that he lost 111 killed, 205 wounded, and 293 missing. He now devoted himself to reorganization, as it was expected that the Rebels would follow up the advantage they had gained by pursuit and attack. In the ranks of the Northern troops much dissatisfaction prevailed, and incipient mutinies sprung up everywhere. When this sentiment made itself apparent in Sherman's ranks, he promptly and sternly suppressed it. One day Sherman, always a rigid disciplinarian, was approached by a mutinous captain of the Sixty-Ninth New York Regiment, who announced his intention of leaving his post of duty. Sherman quietly turned upon the man and in that determined tone, which was one of his characteristics, said: "If you attempt to leave without orders, I will shoot you like a dog." The mutinous captain did not dare leave, but a few days later, when President Lincoln visited the troops, he complained to the President of the threat made by Sherman. Lincoln seriously replied, "Well, if I were you and he threatened to shoot, I would be mighty careful, for Sherman looks like a man who would do just what he says." On August 24th his commission as Brigadier-General having been issued, Sherman received an order transferring him to the Army of the Cumberland, where he was given command of a brigade under General Robert Anderson. Sherman had aroused the disapprobation of McClellan by characterizing the battle of Bull Run as the best planned but worst fought battle of the campaign, and therefore was highly pleased at the transfer. Anderson established headquarters at Louisville, and began the work of organizing his army against the threatened invasion by two Rebel forces under Johnston and Crittenden, which were advancing from Tennessee. As senior Brigadier-General the active work fell to Sherman, and when Anderson resigned on October 8th, the command of the Army of the Cumberland fell to Sherman. Soon after this, a visit by Secretary of War Simon Cameron to Sherman's headquarters set into circulation a rumor which for a time clouded Sherman's career with a cruel slander. Cameron asked Sherman how many troops he needed, and told him to speak frankly, assuring him that the interview was confidential. At this time McClellan had 100,000 men to operate on a line sixty miles long, and Fremont in Missouri had a similar number for a line 100 miles long. Sherman had but 18,000 men to hold a line 300 miles in length. Under these circumstances the reply of Sherman to the question of Cameron was, "60,000 now and 200,000 before we are done." His demands were regarded as preposterous, and soon after, while the matter was being discussed in the War Office, the remark was made, "Sherman must be crazy, he wants 200,000 men in Kentucky." This was overheard by a correspondent, and appeared in one of the New York papers. The report spread, and was, as usual, exaggerated, until half the country firmly believed that the Army of the Cumberland was in command of an insane man.

But the "madman's" prophesy came true. Within six
months there were 60,000 Union soldiers in Kentucky,
and before the war closed there were 200,000. November 12th Sherman was relieved of his command and sent
to St. Louis, where Fremont had been succeeded by
Halleck. The latter placed Sherman in command of an
instruction camp, but later, when Grant began the brilliant campaign against Forts Henry and Donelson, Sherman was dispatched to Paducah to gather troops from
Ohio and Indiana for the purpose of reinforcing Grant.
From this time forth sprang up a friendship between
Grant and Sherman, which came to be of the most cordial
nature. Each had the most unbounded admiration for
the military genius of the other, and throughout the war,
as Grant mounted step by step to the highest military
command of the Nation, Sherman followed, but one step
behind, and when Grant became President, Sherman
reached the eminence toward which his modest ambition
had directed him, but which he would have scorned to
dispute with Grant, for reasons of pure personal friendship. March 10, 1862, Sherman, in command of four
brigades, which he had organized, was ordered to join
General Smith, preliminary to the occupation of Pittsburg Landing, where the battle of Shiloh was fought,
Sunday, April 6th. This great struggle was the hardest
in Sherman's career. He himself regarded the battle as
the most severe of the war. Sherman held the most
important point in that terrible conflict, and Grant's hope
of success hung upon one thing, that he would be able
to hold out against the enemy until nightfall, when Buell
was due to arrive with reinforcements. For the victory at
Shiloh General Grant has accorded to Sherman all the
credit. Grant often related how, during the day, as he
wavered between hope and despair, he rode up and down

the lines calculating the chances of success, he was always
cheered by the sight of Sherman's division, which held
the key to the position. It always inspired him with
renewed courage to exchange a few words with Sherman,
who, he felt confident, would hold his position whatever
might happen to the balance of the army. Although
Sherman's ranks were composed to a large extent of
raw recruits, who had never before been under fire, the
daring and courage of their leader so inspired them that
they fought like veterans and received the incessant
showers of deadly fire without a murmur. Sherman was
twice wounded during the battle, once through the hand
and once in the shoulder. Another bullet passed
through his hat, and several horses were shot under him.
Yet he never faltered, and it is not difficult to realize how,
with such a commander, the men who served under him
became an army of victors. Sherman relates in his
Memoirs of the inspiring effect the victory at Shiloh had
upon him. The newspapers, who had proclaimed him
insane, now gave him credit for a military skill and daring
that none had dreamed of. Yet after the repulse at
Chickasaw Bayou the insanity story was once more revived. He could now, however, afford to laugh at it.
He had gained the confidence and respect of his superiors, and the whole Nation respected and applauded
his prowess. Chickasaw was part of the early attempts
of Grant upon Vicksburg, and although the defeat of
Sherman on this occasion was a severe blow, it was succeeded by a most brilliant campaign, which fully retrieved
what had been lost, and ended in the downfall of the
Gibraltar of the Mississippi. In this campaign Sherman played a most conspicuous and important part. Although he opposed the plan of Grant and tried to induce
his chief to change it, he nevertheless entered upon his

share with an energy and zealousness which was, in itself, half of the success achieved. During eighteen days of forced marching and almost continual fighting, and forty-nine days of siege, he never removed his clothes to sleep. Sherman led the advance in the final assault upon Vicksburg, and, following its fall, the battle of Chattanooga, in November, 1863, when Sherman's troops were joyfully greeted by the Army of the Cumberland as "Grant's Gophers," in allusion to the sapping and mining done by them at Vicksburg. Here Rosecrans was surrounded by the victorious foe, who occupied Missionary Ridge and Lookout Mountain. The history of the Civil War contains no more dazzling exploit than the assaults and captures of these great strongholds in which Sherman was, next to Grant, the central figure. Without having had a moment's rest after the arduous task at Chattanooga the commands of Sherman and Howard were dispatched to the relief of Burnside at Knoxville, and having encountered the enemy at Loudon and put him to flight, learned, to their relief, that Knoxville was safe, and returned through the mirey roads to Chattanooga. In his report of the campaign Sherman says nothing of his own sufferings or the hardships that he was always willing to share with his troops, but speaks of them in the following language: "In reviewing the facts, I must do justice to my command for the patience, cheerfulness, and courage which the officers and men have displayed throughout, in battle, on the march, and in camp. For long periods, without regular rations or supplies of any kind, they have marched through and over rocks, sometimes barefooted, without a murmur, without a moment's rest. After a march of over 400 miles, without stop for three successive nights, we crossed the Tennessee, fought our part of the battle of Chattanooga, pursued the enemy out of Tennessee, and then turned more than 100 miles north, and compelled Longstreet to raise the siege of Knoxville, which gave so much anxiety to the whole country." In February of 1864, Sherman conducted the campaign across the State of Mississippi from east to west, which is known in history as the Meridian raid. With more than 25,000 troops he penetrated the enemy's country and foraged successfully for men and animals throughout the entire march. It was a shining example of what could be accomplished by an army without a base of supplies, and its success was so great that it suggested to Sherman another similar march on a larger scale. It was, in fact, a prelude to the great March to the Sea. Following the promotion of Grant to the command of all the Union forces, Sherman naturally succeeded to the leadership of the four armies of the Cumberland, the Tennessee, the Ohio, and the Trans-Mississippi. This great change, which marked the beginning of the end, took place March 4, 1864. An example of the true friendship that existed between Grant and Sherman, and the characteristic modesty of both, is shown by the correspondence between them at this time, when Grant attained the high position of Lieutenant-General. Instinctively he turned first to Sherman in his hour of triumph, and wrote: "Dear Sherman—I want to express my thanks to you and McPherson, as the men to whom, above all others, I feel indebted for whatever I have had of success. How far your advice and assistance have been of help to me you know. How far your execution of whatever has been given you to do, entitles you to the reward I am receiving, you cannot know as well as I. I feel all the gratitude this letter would express, giving it the most flattering construction. The word 'you' I use in the

plural, intending it for McPherson also.   I should write
to him, and will some day, but starting in the morning, I
do not know that I will find time just now."   The reply
of Sherman to this letter was no less generous and
modest.   He refers to Grant as the legitimate successor
of Washington, and says in part, "I believe you are as
brave, patriotic, and just as the great prototype, Washington—as unselfish, kindhearted, and honest as a man
should be—but the chief characteristic is the simple faith
in success you have always manifested, which I can liken
to nothing else than the faith a Christian has in the
Savior.   This faith gave you the victory at Shiloh and
Vicksburg.   Also when you have completed your best
preparations, you go into battle without hesitation, as
at Chattanooga—no doubts—no reserve; and I tell you,
it was this that made us act with confidence. I knew
that, wherever I was, that you thought of me, and if
I got in a tight place you would help me out, if alive.
My only point of doubts was, in your knowledge of grand
strategy, and of books of science and history; but, I confess, your common sense seems to have supplied all
these."   Sherman had now about 100,000 men after
allowing for the garrisons, which he would have to supply.   With this force he proposed to strike a deadly blow
at the Confederacy.   With deliberation and care he
prepared for his campaign upon Atlanta.   April 27th, his
formidable force was assembled at Chattanooga, and the
next day Sherman established his headquarters there.
On May 6th the march to Atlanta began, and on the
following day a large force of the enemy was met and
routed at Dalton.   From that moment battles formed a
daily part of the march of 100 days.   When Atlanta fell
and Hood escaped from the grasp that was stretched out
after him, and went into Alabama, Sherman disdained

pursuing, but decided instead upon the most daring project of his career—to strike for Richmond, and get in the rear of the army of Lee. To protect Nashville against a possible attack of Hood, he sent Thomas with two corps, and then, after destroying his own communications, started from Atlanta to the sea with a force of 60,000 troops. The distance was 300 miles, through the country of the enemy. He was confident that he would be able to feed his army during this long march. If the country through which he had to pass should for some reason fail him, he had 12,000 horses and mules which would keep the troops from starvation. Sherman issued a set of orders for the march, which stand as a marvel for brevity and conciseness, and took in every possible contingency that might arise during the march. His correspondence with Grant in regard to his great project ended November 2d, when Grant simply telegraphed, "Go on then, as you proposed." On November 12th Sherman received a last message from Thomas at Nashville, and sent a reply. Then the wire of the last instrument was cut and a few moments later a burning bridge over which the telegraph wires were strung fell with a crash. Sherman was now absolutely and completely isolated from the North. The inhabitants had been ordered out of the city, and when the last train load had disappeared the rails were torn up for miles and the city was given to the torch. On March 27, 1865, the great march had come to an end, and Grant and Sherman met at City Point for a conference. Sherman had already received letters from Grant and Lincoln complimenting him in the most flattering terms for his success, and his arrival at City Point was marked by a salute from the guns of Porter's fleet. Later the Generals met Lincoln on board the River Queen, and the final plans for the crushing of the Confederacy were laid. The Atlanta campaign followed by the March to the Sea, and the movement through the Carolinas practically gave the death blow to the Southern cause. When Lee surrendered to Grant he did so from dire necessity, for he had no place to turn with his army. Thus the credit for bringing the war to a close must stand divided between Grant and Sherman. But even in this great hour of victory, Sherman could not escape without the bitter flings which had been thrown at him from time to time. He was accused in connection with the surrender of Johnston in North Carolina, of every crime from stupidity to treason. Sherman's terms were simply that the soldiers return home and obey the laws, pledging them that they would not be molested so long as they did not take up arms. He also pledged that the States would be allowed to carry on their civil governments as previously. These terms Sherman knew to have coincided with Lincoln's sentiments, but Lincoln had been assassinated and President Johnson, who succeeded him, was full of bitterness against the South. After the close of the war and the great review in Washington, Sherman was placed at the head of the Military Division of the Mississippi, later called the Military Division of the Missouri, with headquarters at St. Louis. He had charge of protecting the construction of the Pacific Railroad, then being constructed west from the Missouri. When Grant became President, Sherman rose to the full rank of General of all the armies, and he fulfilled the duties of that high position in fact as well as name. He visited every military post in the country, with two exceptions, and by telegraph directed the movements of troops in the far West from his headquarters at Washington. It was affirmed that no living man was so conversant with the

topography, geography, and resources of every section
of the United States as General Sherman. He was a
great traveler, and spent his vacations among the mountains and deserts of the West on horseback in preference
to watering resorts or the society of city life. In 1871
and 1872 he spent a year in foreign lands. In 1877 Sherman spent 115 days visiting the Indian country and the
Northwest. During this time he traveled nearly 10,000
miles. His description of this trip shows him to be a
forceful and graphic writer, even more than his descrip-
tions of battle-fields. Sherman's home was blessed with
eight children, and the first great misfortune in his domestic life was the death of his son, Willie, who died of
typhoid fever at Memphis, October 3, 1863. He was
with his father in the campaign of the Mississippi, and
was a favorite with the troops, who made him an honor-
ary sergeant of the Thirteenth. Mrs. Sherman died in
New York, November 28, 1888, after a long illness.
February 14, 1891, the famous warrior passed away.
He had taken a cold some days previously, which fastened itself upon his lungs, and caused his rapid decline.
Only a gentle sigh escaped the veteran's lips as his spirit
took flight. An imposing military funeral was held in
New York, and the remains were carried by special train,
accompanied by a guard of honor, to St. Louis, which for
many years had been the home of the General. At every
station along the long journey bands of music played
solemn dirges and crowds gathered to show their respect
for the departed hero. Arrived at St. Louis, a funeral
procession was formed, composed of the regular troops,
State and municipal officers, and great numbers of friends
of the deceased. He was buried beside the graves of his
wife and two of his children. His son, Rev. Thomas E.
Sherman, performed the last religious services over the

flag-covered casket.   A company of troops fired a fare-well salute of three volleys, followed by an answering roar from the artillery.   Then a solitary bugler stepped forward and sounded taps over the grave of the distinguished soldier, and the solemn and impressive ceremonies came to an end.   According to his own wish, the monument over his grave contains no inscription beyond his name, the dates of his birth and death and the simple epitaph, "True and Honest."

ULYSSES SIMPSON GRANT
1822-1885

"LET US HAVE PEACE"

President Lincoln, when asked to name the greatest
of American Generals, unhesitatingly replied, "U. S.
Grant." The calm determination which made Grant
remain before Vicksburg for months without even mildly
resenting the ridicule which was being heaped upon him,
and the firm resolution that never failed to carry out a
project once fixed upon, only partly explains the great
success and remarkable career of Grant as a warrior.
Many of his biographers have given credit to these qualities alone, but even a cursory glance at his achievements
cannot fail to demonstrate that, in addition to courage
and unfaltering persistency, he was endowed with such
far-reaching judgment and skill both in the planning and
execution of great projects as cannot be said to have
been surpassed by any of the most notable commanders
of the world. From obscure and unpromising boyhood
he advanced by merit alone to an eminence attained by
but few American citizens. Through it all he remained
the same modest, unassuming character as when he
worked in his youth in his father's tannery. In every
difficulty and under the most discouraging and perilous
conditions that imperturbable calm, which was a characteristic of the man, was never broken. There is no
instance recorded in which Grant ever showed anger, nor
has there ever been any denial of the assertion that he
never used a profane word. His accomplishments as a

ULYSSES SIMPSON GRANT 443

soldier in meeting and overcoming obstacles of apparently insurmountable proportions is little short of marvelous. In addition to other qualities which made him great as a soldier, was the confidence and loyalty which he inspired in his troops by his own example. He was quick to see a fault, but quicker to pardon offense. He never forgot to thank his soldiers for the part they had taken in bringing about victory, and his addresses to his troops read like the stirring addresses of Napoleon. The grateful Nation which he had served, remembered and honored him both before and after his death. Twice he was chosen President of the United States, and was offered a third term. Congress created for him a rank of distinction which no other American ever received, and when his brilliant career ended a whole Nation bent with grief. His name and fame will live long after the magnificent marble tomb in which he sleeps has crumbled and become a thing of the past.

Ulysses Simpson Grant was born April 27, 1822, at Point Pleasant, Clermont County, Ohio. His ancestry is Scotch, and the first member of the family appears to have been Matthew Grant, who emigrated from the Old World and settled in New England in 1630. At the close of the Revolutionary War, Noah Grant, sixth in descent from Matthew, removed to Westmoreland County, Pennsylvania, and was there married. In 1797 Jesse Root Grant was born, and two years later the parents removed to Ohio. In 1805 the lad was left an orphan, and was received into the family of Judge George Tod. Later he was apprenticed to learn the tanner's trade, and upon attaining legal age, he set up in business for himself, first at Ravenna, and finally at Point Pleasant, Ohio. In June, 1821, he married Hannah Simpson, daughter of John Simpson, who two years previously had moved to Ohio from Montgomery County, Pennsylvania, where the family had been known for several generations. Ulysses Grant was the first fruit of this marriage. The child was christened Hiram Ulysses Grant, and it was not until he entered West Point as a cadet that fate caused the initials of the Nation to fasten themselves upon the future warrior. It came about through the mistake of the Congressman who secured young Grant's appointment, and sent in the name of the cadet as Ulysses S. Grant. Subsequent efforts to have the error corrected upon the records of the academy failed, and Grant adopted the name. One year after the birth of their child the parents removed to Georgetown. They were poor, and while the father taught the lad industry and frugality, the mother instilled into his mind the Christian principles of truth and honesty. This early training remained indelibly stamped upon Grant throughout his whole life. It is asserted that at no period in his life was Grant ever heard to utter a profane word. His first occupation was that of hauling firewood from distant parts of the farm with his father's team. He was then but eight years of age. Four years later, his father having obtained a contract to build the Brown County Jail, the lad of twelve was set to hauling the logs of which the structure was to be built. As an example of the ingenuity displayed by him at this early age, it is related that he loaded these logs upon the wagon without any assistance by backing his wagon up to a tree-trunk which had been cut and lay aslant in such a way that one end was on the ground, while the other was elevated, and then, with the aid of a log-chain and the use of his team, he drew the heavy logs up the slanting trunk and into the wagon. Many other incidents are related of his boyhood, tending to show that he was even then possessed of the pluck and determination which was later displayed when the fate of a Nation was at stake. Until he was seventeen years of age young Grant continued to work at all sorts of manual labor about the farm and around the tannery of his father in the pioneer settlement of Georgetown. But neither mind or body became stunted for lack of parental care. His parents instructed him carefully to the extent of their own ability, and for the balance of his early education he had to depend upon the "subscription schools" of Georgetown. Work and study were thus intermingled, and while the body grew to hardy proportions to withstand the hardships of campaigns upon the field, the mind was prepared in rough but strong rudiments for the mental requirements which the future was to demand of him. Young Grant was fond of agricultural pursuits, but averse to the tannery, and his father failed to enlist his sympathies in that business to any extent. Both father and son were anxious that he should secure an education, but the means of the family, which now consisted of eight children, were limited, and West Point came to be looked upon as the only hope. Application was made, fortunately with success, and Grant arrived at West Point June 3, 1839. Dr. Henry Coppée, who was at West Point at this time, describes him as a plain, common-sense, straightforward youth of quiet disposition, respected by all, and extremely popular in the small circle of those whom he called friends. Nearly all cadets had nick-names, and that bestowed upon Grant was, "Uncle Sam," on account of the initials of his name. It is related that he was an excellent horseman, but exhibited little enthusiasm in any of the branches of study, with the exception of mathematics as applied to mechanics and military engineering. General James H. Stokes, a classmate of

Grant's, says that the "smart" set looked upon Grant as "countrified." He was rather slouchy in his air, and unsoldierly in his appearance. As a rider he had no superior at the academy. General James B. Fry, who arrived at West Point as a cadet in June, 1843, relates that he entered the riding hall as the members of the graduating class were being given their final mounted exercises. The board of visitors and a large number of spectators, both ladies and gentlemen, were present. H. R. Hershberger, the riding master, placed the leaping bar at a height of 6 feet 5 inches, and called, "Cadet Grant." Out from the ranks of the class, which was formed in line through the center of the hall, dashed a slender youth on a splendid horse and galloped down to the end of the hall. As he turned and came down toward the bar the animal increased his pace and a splendid picture was presented as horse and rider gathered themselves for the effort. The bar was cleared perfectly and gracefully, while the spectators gazed with astonished admiration. "Cadet Grant," says Fry, "remained a living image in my memory." This feat has no equal in military annals. Grant graduated from West Point in June, 1843, as brevet second lieutenant in the Fourth United States Infantry. His service with the army began the following month at Jefferson Barracks, St. Louis, where his regiment was stationed. The following summer the regiment was ordered to Nachitoches, La. Texas was at this time fighting for independence, and war with Mexico was momentarily expected. The bill annexing Texas was signed March 1, 1845. The Fourth expected to be at once ordered to Mexico, but no movement came until July, and then only as far as New Orleans. In September the regiment proceeded to Corpus Christi, Texas, where General Zachary Taylor's army

of occupation was located.   Shortly after the arrival of
the Fourth Regiment Taylor's force of 3,000 men crossed
the Rio Grande and began to intrench itself before the
Mexican town of Matamoras.   Here began the war with
Mexico.   Lieutenant Grant's first taste of battle was at
Palo Alto, where a large force of Mexicans was met.   It
was mainly an artillery duel, and Grant's conduct in this,
his first fight, was admirable.   In a skirmish at Resaca de
la Palma, the following day, Grant led a charge, which
resulted in the capture of a Mexican Colonel and several
other prisoners.   One incident of the Mexican War in
which Grant's horsemanship came into play took place
at Monterey.   The Third and Fourth Regiments had
succeeded in advancing to within a short distance of the
plaza of the town where the Mexican troops were concentrated, and were under fire from troops posted on
the roofs of houses, when suddenly the ammunition of the
Americans gave out.   A volunteer was called for to
return to General Twiggs for a fresh supply, and Grant
promptly responded, and ran the perilous gauntlet in
safety.   That evening the Mexicans surrendered.   General Winfield Scott now became the ranking officer of
the armies in Mexico, and throughout all of the battles
under this General, Grant distinguished himself by his
bravery, energy, and activity.   He served as quartermaster during the march into the interior, and as such
was exempt from active duty in the field, but every
time his regiment went into action Grant occupied his
post at the front.   At Chapultepec, in September, 1846,
he was in the front rank of skirmishers which led the
attack.   One of his distinguishing acts during this battle
gained for him favorable mention from three of his
superior officers.   He discovered a church which commanded the rear of the gate to San Cosme.   With a

mountain howitzer and a few soldiers he broke into the church, mounted the howitzer in the steeple, and opened a disastrous fire upon the defenders of the gate. For this act of ingenuity and bravery he received the brevet of Captain, which was awarded in 1849, though not confirmed until the following year. As the Americans were entering the city on September 14th Lieutenant Sidney Smith was killed. His death advanced Grant to the grade of first lieutenant. After the close of the war with Mexico Grant returned with his regiment to the United States, and in August, 1848, was married to Miss Julia Dent, of St. Louis, a sister of one of his West Point classmates. For a brief time Grant was stationed at Sackett's Harbor, New York, and was then ordered to Detroit, where he passed two years in the ordinary duties of the garrison. Subsequently the regiment was ordered to California, a portion of it being detached for duty in Oregon. Grant's rank as captain had been confirmed, and July 5, 1853, he was given command of a company stationed at Humboldt Bay, California. Having served there through the winter and spring, he became disgusted with his life of inactivity and the cheerless surroundings, and resigned. He then settled upon a farm near St. Louis, but finding it neither pleasant nor profitable, and his health failing somewhat, he tried the real estate business in St. Louis, but soon gave it up, and became a clerk in the leather establishment which his father had set up at Galena, Ill., and which was being conducted by two of his younger brothers. In 1860 Abraham Lincoln was elected President, and this was followed immediately by the secession of the Southern States. Grant immediately gave up all thought of leather and returned to the sword. Upon the President's call for troops, patriotic meetings were held, in which he was a leading spirit. A company

ULYSSES S. GRANT

Photo from life

of volunteers was raised, of which Grant was given charge. He was then called upon by Governor Yates, who had learned through a friend of Grant's military career, to assist the Adjutant-General of the State in mustering in the State's quota of troops. Grant had already offered his services to the general Government, but no notice was taken of it. He went to Cincinnati and tried to get on the staff of McClellan, but failed. Governor Yates then commissioned him Colonel of the Twenty-First Illinois Volunteers. James Grant Wilson, in his story of the life of Grant, relates that long afterward Governor Yates raised his right hand and exclaimed: "It was the most glorious day of my life when I signed that commission." On August 7, 1861, Grant was commissioned Brigadier-General, and was sent to southern Missouri, which was threatened by the Confederates. The district of southeastern Missouri was placed under his command September 1st, and included portions on the borders of Kentucky and Tennessee. His headquarters were at Cairo, the importance of which, strategetically, Grant immediately realized. Kentucky claimed to be neutral and forbade the establishment of military posts within her boundaries. This position, however, was not maintained against the South, and Grant, seeing the importance of the location of Paducah, sent a detachment and occupied it without even consulting his superiors. Early in November Grant was directed by Fremont to make demonstrations in the vicinity of Columbus, where the enemy was located in great strength. On November 5th a second dispatch came from Fremont, saying that Polk, in command at Columbus, was sending reinforcements into southwestern Missouri, and that it was of vital importance to check the further incursion into Missouri by making feints against Columbus and Belmont. November 6th Grant began his move against the enemy with 3,100 men on transports, attended by two gunboats, dropped down the river and made a pretense of landing on the Kentucky shore. During the night he learned that large bodies of the enemy were crossing from Columbus to Belmont, and although he had been ordered only to make demonstrations, he now determined to attack, and the troops were marched toward the Confederate encampment at Belmont. The whole force was deployed as skirmishers, and at 9 o'clock the attack began. Grant himself led an impetuous charge, captured the camp, together with several hundred prisoners, artillery, baggage, and stores, and drove the enemy to their transports. He then ordered the complete destruction of the encampment, and with the prisoners and captured artillery, started for his own transports. In the meantime large reinforcements had come from Columbus, and a panic was almost raised by a report, quickly spread, that they had been surrounded by the Rebels. A young officer dashed excitedly up to Grant and gave this startling information. "Well," said Grant, with that quiet demeanor so often afterward observed under most trying circumstances, "if that is true, we must cut our way out as we cut our way in." It was true, but Grant's conduct was so confident and inspiring that his officers valiantly led the troops to a second attack, and reached the transports in safety. The troops reëmbarked and returned to Cairo. Grant's loss amounted to 85 killed, 300 wounded, and about 100 missing. The loss to the enemy was, all told, 642. Compared to subsequent engagements, in which Grant was the master spirit, this brief campaign was insignificant, yet it was characteristic of the man, and served as an indication of what was to come. It also gave

Grant that estimation in the eyes of his soldiers which from that moment never waned. On his return to Cairo Grant briefly, but eloquently, thanked his soldiers for their courageous conduct. A few days later Fremont was superseded by General Halleck in the Western Department, and Grant's territory was enlarged to include all of southern Illinois, that part of Kentucky west of the Cumberland River, and the southern section of Missouri. During the winter he greatly increased his forces, organized and disciplined his army, and made every preparation to respond to any demand that might be made upon him. From reports that he had received, Grant was confident that Fort Henry on the Tennessee River, which had been called the Gibraltar of America, could be easily taken. The movement took place February 6, 1862. The plan was to be a combined naval and land attack, with Foote in command of the gunboats. While Grant with his army was struggling over the muddy roads in the direction of Fort Henry, Foote had already arrived, and after a brief bombardment, compelled the surrender of the enemy. Grant took possession and was ordered by Halleck, who had previously believed the place impregnable, to hold on to the position and strengthen it. Grant, however, had already turned his eyes toward Fort Donelson, on the Cumberland River, twelve miles distant. It was the key to Nashville, and he determined to reduce it. Leaving a force to hold Fort Henry, he marched with 15,000 men across the country, while Foote carried six regiments on his gunboats and went around to aid in the attack from the water front. The Rebel works were of great strength, being located on steep hills and protected naturally by gullies and ravines, while additional obstructions had been provided in the shape of large trees, which had been felled and so placed as to make an advance through their tangled branches seem impossible. It commanded both the river and the interior, mounted sixty-five cannon, and was held by 20,000 men. Grant's army appeared before the fort February 12th, and Foote having arrived, the attack began. After a short, determined contest, however, the fleet was disabled and driven off. Grant determined to closely invest the place, until Foote could repair his losses. A great semi-circle was formed around the works, and the Rebel commanders realized that they must take immediate action against the enemy or be starved into submission. The main force poured out of the fort against Grant's right wing. Smaller forces made feints against the center and left of the besieging army. At this time Grant was away consulting with Foote. On his way back to the army he was met by a courier, and, putting spurs to his horse, galloped forward and into the vortex of the battle. At the moment of his arrival a scene of confusion met his gaze. Thousands of fugitives were rushing about panic-stricken. The right had struggled long and heroically against the overwhelming Confederate forces, but was now being cut to pieces and scattered. His arrival was none too soon. In an instant he saw clearly what was to be done. Galloping to the left, commanded by Smith, he ordered an immediate attack on the Rebel works. He knew that this must be the enemy's weakest point. A braver charge was never made, and at dusk a portion of the outside works were captured. The weather had for days been extremely cold, and now a driving snowstorm added to the misery of the troops. Many were frozen to death during those terrible days before Donelson. The next morning a flag of truce was flung out by the Rebels. Floyd, who was in supreme command of the Fort, and Pillow, next in command, had, during the night, turned everything over to Brigadier-General Buckner, and had made their escape to Nashville. Buckner sent a communication to Grant, requesting an armistice until noon and the appointment of commissioners to agree upon terms of capitulation. But Grant was not a man of formalities. Without a second's hesitation, he dispatched the famous reply, "No other terms than unconditional and immediate surrender can be accepted. I propose to move immediately upon your works." The surrender was at once effected. Over 17,000 small arms, 65 guns, and 15,000 prisoners was the result of the victory. It was the most important that had been gained, and February 16, 1862, became a memorable date in the war. All over the North church bells rang, guns thundered, and Grant's name was upon every lip. With the fall of Donelson, Nashville, Bowling Green, and Columbus were evacuated by the Confederates. With one strong blow Grant had broken down the whole line of the enemy's defense from the Mississippi to the Alleghany Mountains, and forced it beyond the State of Kentucky. General Halleck tried to rob Grant of the credit for this victory, but the greatness of the exploit was recognized at Washington, and the Secretary of War recommended Grant for the rank of Major-General. Just after this Grant proceeded to Nashville to consult with General Buell without first having asked Halleck's permission, and the latter's jealousy was so aroused that, by false reports to Washington, he was empowered to turn Grant's command over to General Smith for an advance into Tennessee, while Grant was ordered to remain in charge of the garrison at Fort Henry. As a consequence of this many false and injurious rumors concerning Grant were put in circulation, one of them being that, during the capture of Fort Donelson, Grant was drunk on the flagship of Foote's fleet. But the people were with Grant, and Halleck, finding that he could not injure his popularity, restored him to his command. This was on March 13th, and Grant joined the army at Savannah, nine miles below Pittsburg Landing. His directions were to act on the defensive until the arrival of Buell with 40,000 troops from Columbia, about ninety miles away. For three weeks the army lay waiting, while the Confederates, under Johnston, were daily gaining stength. On learning of the approach of Buell, Johnston decided to strike Grant's army before Buell's arrival. On April 6th, the Confederates attacked in full force. Grant was breakfasting at Savannah when the battle opened, and, surmising what was taking place, he dispatched a courier to hurry Buell along and another to Wallace, whose division was at Crump's Landing, five miles away. He then pushed to the front and found the divisions of Sherman and McClernand magnificently battling against great odds. The situation was desperate. Grant moved about from point to point, calmly smoking a cigar and urging the men to hold their ground until the arrival of reinforcements. But as the hours passed and the ranks grew thinner and thinner, nothing was heard either from Buell or Wallace. Finally, late in the afternoon, Buell arrived, but accompanied only by a few staff officers, having left his army far in the rear. Buell regarded the day as lost, but Grant doggedly asserted that, "I don't despair of whipping them yet." At last darkness came, and the fighting ceased. A terrific storm broke on the exhausted troops. Instead of seeking shelter Grant went from one commander to another giving instructions for the attack, which he had determined to make the following morning. At midnight he stretched himself upon the ground, resting his head

against a stump, and with the rain beating down upon
him and drenching him to the skin, he composedly went
to sleep, sharing the sufferings and hardships of the common soldier. The following morning the battle was
resumed. It continued unabated through the day, the
Confederates gradually yielding before the Union troops.
Colonel Badeau relates an incident which took place near
the close of the day. Grant was watching a stubborn
fight at the edge of a wood between his own troops and
those of the enemy. He saw that his troops were beginning to give way, and, glancing about, saw the First
Ohio Regiment marching toward a distant part of the
field. He placed himself at their head and led the charge
to relieve the wavering ranks, which were at this moment
retreating before the enemy. The charge was successful and the Confederates were swept from one of the last
important positions in the battle of Shiloh; or, as it is
sometimes called, Pittsburg Landing. Grant's total loss
in this terrible conflict was 12,217, that of the enemy
11,000. Johnston had fallen during the battle and was
succeeded by Beauregard. The great losses of the Federal army in this battle caused a great outcry against
Grant. Congressman and Governors demanded his removal, but so extreme a step was not taken. Halleck,
however, now placed himself at the head of the army,
with Grant nominally second in command. His position
was practically one of disgrace and humiliation. He
made, however, no defense and uttered no complaint.
Having reorganized the army, it took Halleck six weeks
to advance fifteen miles. Grant had been criticised for
not throwing up intrenchments, but Halleck practically
"dug his way to Corinth." When he arrived there the
enemy had vanished, leaving an empty town and a few
wooden guns. A pursuit was barren of result, and,

finally, after further pursuing his system of throwing up intrenchments and waiting in vain for attacks, Halleck was called to Washington.   On leaving, he offered the command of the Army of the Tennessee to Colonel Allen, a quartermaster, who declined it.   This again gave Grant the command of the army, and he fortified Corinth in such a way that it could be held by a small force. October 3d, the Rebel forces advanced against Corinth, 40,000 strong, and though defended by but 19,000, the enemy was repulsed with great loss.   A grand expedition against Vicksburg was now planned, and Grant's department, being enlarged to cover the Mississippi to this place, he concentrated his army and arrived at Young's Point January 29, 1863.   Vicksburg was deemed impregnable.   It occupied the bluffs commanding the river, and was surrounded by a net work of swamps, bayous, and rivers, the largest of the latter being the Yazoo, flowing from the east and entering the Mississippi nine miles above Vicksburg.   On Haines' Bluff there were heavy batteries, and all along from there to Vicksburg, a distance of eleven miles, and thence to Warrenton, six miles below Vicksburg, the high lands were covered with batteries and rifle pits.   The only approach was through the swamps and marshes.   The great problem which now confronted Grant was to secure a foothold on the high land east of the Mississippi.   The herculean task which Grant now entered upon, the suffering and privation which he and his army endured for months, the failures and successes, the brilliant campaign, which resulted in the capture of Jackson, the capital of Mississippi, would require a separate volume if all of the elaborate plans of attack and difficulties encountered in the general plan upon Vicksburg were to be enumerated in detail.   Finally, on May 19th, with three corps in position from the Mississippi below to the Yazoo above Vicksburg, he had the place completely invested. Colonel Badeau, the military biographer of Grant, says of this great exploit, "After long months of toiling and waiting—after repeated failures, till the enemy laughed in derision at Grant's futile obstinacy, he had at last, by one of the most brilliant military movements on record, succeeded in flinging his strong arms around the Gibraltar of the Mississippi. From the perseverance he had shown from the outset, from the tireless energy with which he had worked undeviatingly toward that single point; from the tremendous blows he had dealt the foe, as he bore swiftly down upon it, he had astonished his own army and paralyzed that of his adversaries." Not the least remarkable part of the movement against Vicksburg was the famous twenty days' campaign preceding the establishment of his base at Chickasaw Landing, which gave him the final grip upon the doomed city. This is summed up by Colonel Badeau as follows: "In that time Grant had marched more than 200 miles, beaten two armies in five several battles, captured twenty-seven heavy cannon, sixty-one pieces of field artillery, taken 26,500 prisoners, and killed and wounded at least 6,000 Rebels more. He had forced the evacuation of Grand Gulf, seized the capital of the State, destroyed the railroads of Jackson for a distance of more than thirty miles, and invested the principal Rebel stronghold on the Mississippi River. Separating forces twice as numerous as his own, he had beaten first, at Port Gibson, a portion of Pemberton's army; then, at Raymond and Jackson, the troops under Johnston's immediate command; and again, at Champion Hill and the Big Black River, the whole force that Pemberton dared take outside the works at Vicksburg. Starting without teams, and with an average of two days' rations in haversacks, he had picked up wagons in the country, and subsisted principally on forage and rations that he found on the road.   Only five days' rations had been issued in twenty days.   His losses were 698 killed, 3,407 wounded, and 30 missing—in all 4,335."

At 2 o'clock on the afternoon of May 19th a general assault was made all along against the Rebel line. Everywhere was the assault repulsed.   On the 22d a second and more determined attempt was made, supported by Admiral Porter, with all his guns from the river.   All day the earth shook with the thunder of cannonading, the terrible assault covering miles of space, where storming columns dashed against the hostile works to be cut down by a desolating fire of canister and grape.   Still no impression was made upon the formidable works of the enemy.   Days and weeks passed. Gradually the work of sapping and mining proceeded and trenches were pushed forward on every side.   Meanwhile the sharpshooters kept up incessant firing to prevent interference with the work.   At last, on the 25th of June, the day fixed for the explosion of the mines arrived. The fuse was ignited, and was followed by a spectacle grand and terrible.   The surrounding country shook, as if with the shock of an earthquake.   Debris of every kind was thrown hundreds of feet into the air.   At the same moment the artillery opened all along the line.   Into the crater made by the explosion sprang a column of troops which had been held in readiness for that purpose.   A fierce struggle took place and the enemy retired to an interior line.   The assault continued until darkness all along the lines.   July 1st another mine was sprung, and another abyss formed and occupied.   On July 3d Pemberton proposed an armistice to arrange terms of capitulation. At 3 o'clock that afternoon Grant and Pemberton met on a grassy slope just outside the fortifications. Each dismounted, advanced on foot, and the two shook hands. Pemberton asked Grant what terms he proposed. Grant replied that only unconditional surrender of city and garrison would be accepted. Pemberton haughtily replied that under those circumstances hostilities might as well be immediately resumed. "Very well," replied Grant, and the two turned and parted. General Bowen, however, who accompanied Pemberton, proposed a further discussion. Pemberton eagerly pressed for terms that would somewhat soften his humiliation. Finally terms were agreed upon for the surrender of the city and the paroles of officers and men upon laying down their arms. The following morning, the Fourth of July, the garrison marched out by regiments, stacked their arms, gave up their colors, and marched back into the city, to remain prisoners of war until paroled. On Saturday, July 11th, everything having been completed, the weaponless army marched forth. Four days later Port Hudson fell, thus opening the Mississippi throughout its entire length. In a letter written by President Lincoln, July 13, 1863, to General Grant, he acknowledges the great service done to the country, admits that he regarded Grant's plans in the attempt on Vicksburg a mistake and concludes, "You were right and I was wrong." The campaign of Vicksburg cost Grant in killed and wounded and missing 8,873 men, while the loss to the enemy was 56,000 troops, besides vast stores of war material and public property.

For three months following the fall of Vicksburg, Grant and his army remained practically idle, many of his troops being sent to reinforce movements in other sections of the country. But events were hurrying

Grant forward to the high position which he was destined to reach. On the last day of September, Halleck, having become fully alive to the perilous state of affairs in the Cumberland department, telegraphed Grant requesting him to proceed to Nashville to take charge of the movement of troops of which Rosecrans was in pressing need. Grant went to Cairo, and there received a telegram directing him to go to Louisville with his staff. He started the same day, and at Indianapolis was met by the Secretary of War himself, with an order consolidating the three departments of Ohio, Cumberland, and his own into one, to be called the military division of the Mississippi. Grant was placed at the head of this division, with full power to plan and execute his campaigns without interference from any one. Grant's first act after assuming this authority was to place Thomas in command of the Army of the Cumberland instead of Rosecrans, and his first message to Thomas was, "Hold Chattanooga at all hazards." Thomas promptly responded, "I will hold it till we starve." Grant himself soon joined Thomas at Chattanooga. The army was in a half-starved condition. Bragg, with a large force of Confederates, held the river between Chattanooga and Bridgeport—the terminus of the railroad from Nashville—so that the only means of getting supplies was over the Cumberland Mountains, a distance of sixty miles. The heights all around Chattanooga on every side were occupied by the Rebel armies and fortifications. Grant's first care was to provide means for the feeding of the troops. This was accomplished by clearing the enemy out of Lookout Valley and opening the river as far as Bridgeport, which left but nine miles of land transportation for supplies. Grant's next move was to drive the enemy from the threatening heights. Before this could be attempted, Sherman must arrive from Memphis—400 miles away. Grant ordered Sherman to disregard his previous orders to repair the railroad as he proceeded, and to drop everything and hurry forward. Sherman reached Chattanooga November 15th. Grant rapidly matured his plans, and on November 25th, the several divisions having gained during the preceding days the various strategic positions assigned to them, made those unsurpassed charges up the precipitous sides of Lookout Mountain and Missionary Ridge and gained glorious victories in the face of the most desperate resistance. The trophies of the day were 6,000 prisoners and forty cannon. The next day Bragg was in full flight with the victors in hot pursuit. It continued for two days, and was stopped at Grant's order only for the purpose of sending relief to Burnside at Knoxville, which was besieged by the army of Longstreet. On the approach of the reinforcements Longstreet withdrew and rapidly retreated eastward. This ended one of the most brilliant campaigns conducted by Grant or any other commander. He had in a brief period driven 45,000 men from positions that were considered impregnable, relieved all East Tennessee and firmly established a base for further operations in the interior. He received from President Lincoln a telegram expressing the most profound admiration and gratitude. On December 17th, Congress voted a resolution of thanks to Grant and his soldiers, and a gold medal was struck in his honor. On February 29, 1864, Congress passed a bill which revived the grade of Lieutenant-General, and promptly confirmed the nomination of Grant to the high position, never before occupied except by two men, Washington and Scott. Grant was ordered by the President to report at Washington, and arrived there March 4th. His arrival was the signal for wildest demonstrations of enthusiasm, and he was lionized to the fullest gratification but greatly to his own annoyance, expressed by this simple soul in the remark, "I hope soon to get away from Washington, for I am tired of this show business."

Grant had no faith in the many visionary schemes which were propounded and fostered to bring the rebellion to an end. He was certain that it would not end until the military power of one or the other was broken. Atlanta and Richmond now became the two points toward which he turned his thoughts, and he determined to assail the two great armies of the South, that of Lee on the Rapidan and Johnston at Dalton, with all the strength at his command. To Meade, the commander of the Army of the Potomac, his simple order was, "Where Lee goes, go after him." When spring came, the public expected a great movement to begin and it came, although not so quickly as had been expected. Grant had carefully gone over all the problems that confronted him, and finally gave the signal which set three great armies, composed of more than a quarter of a million men in motion. The army of Lee was stretched for miles along the Rapidan and held all the fords. On the morning of May 4th the mighty host which was to sweep him to destruction began to move. Grant was desirous of getting between Lee and Richmond, and for this purpose sent his army across the Potomac. He did not desire to battle in that vast wilderness now occupied by Lee, but it was the plan of the latter to bring about this very result. The fighting in the Wilderness began on the morning of May 5th. To Grant it was a surprise. The conditions of campaigning in the Wilderness and the battle of this day is well summed up in Swinton's "Army of the Potomac," in these words: "The woods of the Wilderness have not the ordinary features of a forest. The region rests on a belt of mineral rocks, and for above a hundred years extensive mining has been carried on. To feed the mines, the timber of the country for many miles around had been cut down, and in place there had arisen a dense undergrowth and low-limbed and scraggy pines, scrub oaks, and hazel. It is a region of gloom and the shadow of death. Maneuvering here was out of the question, and only Indian tactics told. The troops could only receive directions by a point of the compass, for not only were the lines of battle entirely hidden from the sight of the commander, but no officer could see ten files on each side of him. Artillery was wholly ruled out of use, the massive concentration of 300 guns stood silent. Cavalry was still more useless. But in that horrid thicket there lurked 200,000 men, and through it lurid fires played; and though no array of battle could be seen, there came out of it the crackle and roll of musketry, like the noisy boiling of some hell-cauldron, that told the dread story of death. Such was the battle of the Wilderness." The fighting ceased only with the fall of darkness, and the next morning found the army of Grant no further advanced than when the battle began. In fact, some ground had been lost. But Grant determined to continue the deadly contest. Longstreet arrived with a fresh army in the night, and although he recoiled at the first resistless rush of the Federals, the Texans made so gallant a charge that Grant's troops were compelled to fall back. For seven miles over the uneven ground and in dark ravines the slaughter continued for another day. The third day both armies were too exhausted to fight, and that night Grant tried to march around Lee at Spottsylvania. Lee knew of the march within an hour and sent troops by a shorter route to intercept his foe. For days the fighting continued, until, on June 12th, finding himself unable to break through the enemy's lines, Grant, under cover of darkness, struck across the country to the James River, and crossed it. In this disastrous campaign, Grant had lost nearly 60,000 men and had thus far accomplished nothing. The losses of Lee, it is asserted, did not exceed 10,000. But Grant was now beginning to make himself felt in the vicinity of Petersburg and Richmond, and through the fall and winter his operations were everywhere meeting with flattering success. March 24, 1865, the final great movement began. On April 2d Petersburg fell. It was the last straw, and Lee at once advised the Confederate President to evacuate Richmond. In the meantime the fighting in front of that city had reached its limits. The Confederates could no longer continue the struggle to save the Capital. On the morning of April 3d the advance of the Federal army entered the city and the Stars and Stripes was hoisted over the Capitol, while Grant continued to press after the conquered foe. The pursuit continued until the 9th, when Lee found himself practically hemmed in on all sides at Appomattox. On that morning he requested an interview regarding terms of surrender, which Grant had two days previously advised him to do. The two great soldiers met and clasped hands in the house of Wilmer McLean at Appomattox. They had served together in the Mexican War, and remembered each other. Grant sat down and wrote out the terms of surrender, and Lee, after reading the document and discussing the details to some extent, signed the agreement. To all intents and purposes this ended the war. It was followed April 26th by the surrender of Johnston to Sherman. Mobile had fallen

April 11th, and the other Southern armies surrendered gradually, the last being on May 26th. Grant visited Washington, where a grand review, the most imposing this country has ever witnessed, was held. In New York, Chicago, and everywhere where Grant appeared he met with great and spontaneous ovations, not the least of them being the town of Galena, Ill., which was the point from which he had started for the war. Numerous swords were presented to him, and gifts of every description were showered upon him by States, municipalities, and private individuals who admired his skill and success. In July, 1866, Congress created the title of General, never before in existence in America, and conferred it upon Grant. In 1868 Grant was nominated for President and elected by the almost unanimous vote of the Nation. After serving his first term he was reëlected. During his service as President, Grant proved himself no less a statesman than he had been a warrior. A third term as President was offered him, but he firmly refused to accept it. He now had the opportunity to gratify a desire which had clung to him from youth, to see the Old World and its wonders. He set sail from Philadelphia May 17, 1877, accompanied by Mrs. Grant and his youngest son. He visited nearly every Nation upon the earth, and was everywhere accorded the highest honors. His return to the United States was the signal for another series of ovations such as has been accorded to few citizens of this Nation. Early in the year 1884, General Grant began to be troubled with the illness which proved his last. It was cancer of the tongue, and from the first there was no hope that he could be cured. His closing days were given up to preparing his autobiography, in which he wished to be strictly accurate in the smallest matters.

Facing the last enemy, the gallant soldier remained as undismayed as had been his habit on the field of battle. He died peacefully on the morning of Thursday, July 23, 1885. His death was felt the world over, and expressions of regret and sympathy came from every quarter of the globe. His mortal remains lie under a magnificent monument in Riverside Park in the City of New York. Cut into the enduring marble of his tomb are the memorable words he uttered at the first convention which nominated him for the Presidency: "Let us have peace."

THOMAS JONATHAN JACKSON
1824-1863

"DO YOUR DUTY AND LEAVE THE REST TO GOD"

As a warrior, General Thomas Jonathan Jackson, better known to fame as "Stonewall" Jackson, has frequently been compared to Napoleon. In the characters of these two men as warriors, there is indeed a great similarity. The wonderful marches and the rapidity with which movements in strategy were carried out by Jackson were never surpassed by Napoleon. The clear vision of military plans which Napoleon possessed to so remarkable a degree was also a distinguishing characteristic of Stonewall Jackson. The confidence and loyalty of soldiers for their leader was never shown by the French troops of the "Little Corporal" to a more pronounced extent than was that of the Southern soldiers to "Old Jack." Like Napoleon, too, Jackson was on terms of friendly familiarity with the common trooper under his command. While Jackson was not a strict disciplinarian, no man ever drew the line of duty closer, and none ever performed it more faithfully. These traits, together with his calm and never-failing courage, his confidence and cool daring, and the aggressive spirit which at all times predominated his movements in the campaigns, accounts for the devotion with which his men followed their intrepid leader against many a forlorn hope and turned the tide of more than one desperate conflict. Stonewall Jackson's genius as a soldier was excelled only by his gallantry and indomitable bravery. He was throughout a consistent and practical Christian, and solemnly attributed to the Almighty every victory, while defeats were accepted with a calm resignation as part of the plan of the Creator. Jackson died as he had lived, a warrior and a Christian. General Lee, in announcing the death of Jackson to the army, wrote: "The daring, skill, and energy of this great and good soldier, by a decree of all-wise Providence, are now lost to us. But while we mourn his death, we feel that his spirit lives, and will inspire the whole army with his indomitable courage and unshaken confidence in God as our hope and strength."

The first of the Jacksons of Virginia came to America in 1748. This was John Jackson, of London, England, a youth of Scotch-Irish descent. Aboard the same vessel which brought Jackson to America was Elizabeth Cummins, a stately Saxon beauty, also bound for the new colonies in America. Shortly after their arrival they were married in Maryland, and soon moved to Western Virginia, and still later crossed the Alleghany Mountains and settled upon the Buckhannon River with other intrepid pioneers, who saw more of Indians than of white people. Among their children was Edward, who made his home in Lewis County; became a member of the Legislature, and was county surveyor. Jonathan, the son of Edward Jackson, settled in the town of Clarksburg, Harrison County, Va., where he practiced law, and was married to Julia Neale, daughter of Thomas Neale. It was at Clarksburg that Thomas Jonathan Jackson was born January 21, 1824, being the youngest of four children. In 1827 the father died, and three years later the mother married a second time, so that at six years of age Thomas was sent to live with relatives that were better able to provide for him than his mother and stepfather, who were very poor. Thomas finally came to live with Cummings E. Jackson, an uncle, near Weston, and here he remained, working on the farm and attending school long enough to acquire an ordinary English education. At sixteen years of age Thomas was so well thought of that the Justices of the County Court of Lewis County elected him constable, and while serving in this capacity he learned that there was a vacancy at West Point, and through the aid of Colonel J. M. Bennett he was admitted as a cadet in July, 1842. As a student the progress of Jackson was slow during the first year, but by close application he improved during the second year, and in the two succeeding years made great advances. He is described at this time as an awkward, absent-minded young man, who, although he was the subject of jest at times among his fellows, had really won many friendships among them because of his determination and energy in struggling to master an education without having had the necessary preparatory training from childhood. At this time no one would suspect him of possessing even a spark of military genius. Jackson graduated and received the appointment of brevet second-lieutenant of artillery, July 1, 1846. It was an auspicious moment. The United States was at war with Mexico, and the young graduate was assigned to the First Regiment of United States Artillery, then serving in Mexico under General Taylor. It was not until the spring of the following year that his regiment had an opportunity for active service. His first experience with war was in the attack and capture of Vera Cruz. After the fall of the city, Jackson became attached to the battery of Captain Magruder, a dashing and intrepid officer. In the battle of Churubusco, Captain Magruder's first lieutenant was killed, and this advanced Jackson to a position next in command to the Captain. In his official report, Captain Magruder says: "In a few moments, Lieutenant Jackson, commanding the second section of the battery, who had opened fire upon the enemy's works from a position on the right, hearing our fire still further in front, advanced in handsome style, and, being assigned by me to the post which had been so gallanty filled by Lieutenant Johnstone, kept up the fire with great briskness and effect. His conduct was equally conspicuous during the whole day, and I cannot too highly commend him to the Major-General's favorable consideration." For his splendid behavior in this battle Jackson was promoted to the brevet rank of captain. In the storming of the Castle of Chapultepec, Jackson is again mentioned in most flattering terms by his captain, who says: "If devotion, industry, talent, and gallantry are the highest qualities of a soldier, then he is entitled to the distinction which their profession confers." This was September 13, 1847, and it earned for the enthusiastic young soldier the brevet rank of major. It was the day of the fall of the City of Mexico, and the bravery of Jackson brought praise from many of the officers about him. The war with Mexico having come to an end, he was stationed for two years at Fort Hamilton, and was then ordered to Fort Meade, Florida. He remained but a short time, as the climate was so injurious to his health that he was compelled to return. Early in the year 1851 he sought the position of Professor of Natural and Experimental Philosophy at the Virginia Military Institute, and entered upon his duties September 1, 1851. This period of his life is marked by two events of interest; the first his marriage, and the second his profession of religion. The Military Institute was located near the town of Lexington, and Jackson became a member of the Presbyterian Church of that place. He attended with military regularity, and on November 22d made a public profession of faith. August 4, 1853, Jackson was married to Elinor Junkin, daughter of Rev. Dr. George Junkin, president of Washington College. She died fourteen months after the marriage, and a few years later, July 16, 1857, he married Mary Anna Morrison, daughter of Rev. R. H. Morrison, of Lincoln County, North Carolina. He was ever a devoted husband, of which bears witness the volume published by his wife, giving a large share of his correspondence with her during the Civil War and up to the time of his death. Jackson was in earnest about everything. He possessed a strong will, and although he has been referred to by some as a fatalist, this feature of his character consisted in his religious belief that God had created for him a mission in life, and that until he had accomplished it, no harm could come to him. This feeling was, however, strong in him before he professed religion, for it is a well-authenticated fact that during the Mexican campaign, on one occasion when the firing became so hot that his men took to shelter, Jackson walked quietly up and down by his battery and shouted to his men to return, and while shot was whistling all around him, confidently remarked, "See, they don't hit me." In the year 1858 Jackson made a journey to Europe and remained there several months. In the fall of 1859 the memorable John Brown raid took place at Harper's Ferry. Brown attempted to raise an insurrection among the negroes, and seized the Government stores, but was surrounded and captured. Among the troops ordered on duty to prevent a lynching of Brown were the cadets and their officers, and Jackson in the letter describing the execution of Brown deplores his refusal to see a minister, and expresses anguish that the victim must appear before the judgment throne unrepentant.

When in 1861 the war clouds broke as a result of the secession of several of the Southern States, Virginia for a time hung in the balance, uncertain what course to pursue. April 14, 1861, President Lincoln called for 75,000 men to enforce United States supremacy in those States which had seceded. This decided Virginia, and on April 17th the State joined the rebellion. It was expected that Federal troops would immediately be sent into Virginia, and the work of defense at once began. Col. Robert E. Lee, who had just resigned from the United States cavalry, was made Major-General of the troops in the State of Virginia. Steps were at once taken to secure the Fortress of Monroe and the Norfolk Navy Yard from falling into the hands of the Federal army. Major Jackson marched with his cadets to Camp Lee, at Richmond, where he began drilling new troops that were constantly flocking to the camp. While thus engaged he was nominated as Colonel by Governor Letcher. His appointment was immediately confirmed by the Convention, and he was ordered to proceed to Harper's Ferry to take charge of the troops which were being assembled there. He took command May 3, 1861. On May 23d General Joseph E. Johnston, a former officer of the United States army and a man of unquestioned ability, arrived, and took command of the entire force at that time mobilized. Jackson was then assigned to command a brigade of infantry, composed of four regiments of Virginians. At this time the newspapers of the North were predicting a brief and bloodless war. It was evident, however, that President Lincoln was not of this opinion, for on May 3d he called for 40,000 additional infantry volunteers, 18,000 seamen, and ten more regi-

"STONEWALL" JACKSON

ments for the regular army. This would give the Government a total of 150,000 troops. The plan of operation was to throw one strong column into the Mississippi valley, a second was to enter Kentucky and subdue the rebellion there, while a third was to march upon Richmond and stamp out the organization of the Confederacy in Virginia. At the same time all Southern ports were to be blockaded. The column for the invasion of Virginia it was intended to have move in detachments in four directions, converging upon Richmond, and after the capture of that city to quickly spread over the balance of the State and reduce it to submission. The Virginians were making strenuous efforts to meet the expected attack. Jackson was already beginning to achieve good results. He was rapidly molding his little army of volunteers into disciplined soldiers, and by his own example of tireless energy, imbuing them with that unyielding fortitude and magnificent courage which was destined to make the "Stonewall Brigade" famous in the annals of the Civil War. This brigade was composed to a large extent of very young men, many of them but fifteen years of age. Very few had ever experienced hardships of any kind. They had come from homes of luxury to enter upon a life which required their most heroic efforts, and yet it must be said that, unpromising as the material at first appeared, the result did not prove disappointing. The first opportunity afforded Jackson to test the courage and efficiency of his brigade did not come until July 2d. Jackson with his brigade had been dispatched on June 20th to the neighborhood of Martinsburg with orders to capture all of the Baltimore and Ohio rolling stock possible, to destroy the rest, and then to act in support of the cavalry under Stuart in the event of an advance by the enemy. Martinsburg was soon

reached, a number of locomotives were sent back to Winchester, forty engines and 300 cars were destroyed, and
Jackson then advanced to join Stuart. These two were
to act together against the invading force under Patterson.   On July 2d, General Patterson, at the head of
the Federal army, crossed the Potomac into Virginia.
Jackson immediately advanced to receive the attack. He
took with him only the Fifth Virginia and a battery of
four six-pounders, under Captain Pendleton.   The
infantry numbered 380 men.   Near the village of Falling
Waters they came upon the enemy, which consisted of
three brigades, aside from infantry and artillery.
Undaunted, Jackson ordered an advance, and the Federal troops hastily formed in line of battle, taking in a
barnyard and a farmhouse.   In spite of the heavy firing,
the attack of the Virginians was so fierce that the enemy
was compelled to retreat from the farmyard and across
the turnpike. Jackson with difficulty restrained his men
from taking up a pursuit, and fell back, whereupon the
Federal cavalry advanced to the attack.   Captain Pendleton, who was an Episcopal clergyman, had brought
up one of his six-pounders, and as the cavalry
approached, he gave the order, "Aim low, men; and may
the Lord have mercy on their souls."   The shot went
true and the cavalry wheeled in confusion. The lone
six-pounder was then, at General Jackson's orders,
turned upon the Federal artillery, and the firing continued for several hours, each side fearing to attack. To
prevent himself from being outflanked, Jackson was
finally compelled to retreat.   Each side lost but two
men and had a few wounded, and General Johnston, in
making his official report, refers to the engagement as
the "Affair of Falling Waters."   In the eyes of Jackson,
however, and those of his men, it was of far greater

importance, for he had been able to get an estimate of their nerve, and they had discovered that their leader was a man who would face death with them. A few days later, having returned to Winchester, Jackson received his commission as Brigadier-General, and at the same time an addition to his brigade by the arrival of the Thirty-third Virginia regiment.

At this time the Federal armies were preparing to strike a decisive blow against the main body of the Confederates at Manassas. In connection with this design, it was the purpose of General Patterson to hold the army of General Johnston in check while the main body of the Federal army, composed of 55,000 men under General McDowell, could advance upon Manassas to crush Beauregard without fear of interference. July 17th General Patterson was informed by telegraph that McDowell's army was at Fairfax Courthouse, only a few hours' march from Beauregard's position. This was the critical moment, and Patterson began a movement calculated to hold Johnston in the valley. An hour after midnight on the morning of July 18th the Federal troops had already begun action against the advance forces of the Confederates around Manassas. And at that moment General Johnston received an order from the Government at Richmond telling him to hasten to the aid of Beauregard. In order to accomplish this, it became necessary either to defeat the forces of General Patterson or to elude him. The latter was the course decided upon, and the Confederate forces skillfully outwitted the watching Federals, escaped through the rough pathway of Ashby's Gap, and determinedly set out toward Manassas. On the way a second message reached General Johnston from Beauregard, which said: "If you wish to help me, now is the time." The weary, half-famished soldiers were urged forward at a quickened pace. At Piedmont the fatigued infantry embarked on a train of the Manassas Gap Railroad, while the cavalry and artillery continued the march.

The majority of the troops arrived about noon, July 20th. Among the first was Jackson's brigade, and the assignment which he received found him with his 2,611 men occupying a position in the pine thickets in the very center of the Confederate line.   The battle of Manassas will always occupy a place among the celebrated conflicts of the world, and the fortunes of this memorable day was decided by the First brigade, whose gallant commander here first received the proud title of "Stonewall." It was the first great battle of the war. Opposed to the Federal army of 55,000 men, with nine regiments of cavalry, and twelve batteries of artillery, numbering 49 guns, was General Beauregard's force of 21,833 muskets, 29 pieces of smooth-bore artillery, and three companies of cavalry. By the arrival of General Johnston and General Holmes, this force was increased to 31,431 muskets, 55 guns, and 500 cavalry. These forces were posted behind earthworks along the watercourse known as Bull Run, and extended along the stream from Union Mills almost to Stone Bridge, a distance of eight miles.   Especially strong detachments were posted at the several fords. The center of the line rested at Mitchell's Ford, and at this point Jackson's brigade was stationed. An artillery battle on the 18th served as a prelude to the great struggle of the 21st. The fighting began early in the morning by a furious attack on the Confederate left. The Southerners fought with desperation, but were being pressed back by the overwhelming Federal line. A rapid and gallant advance by the regiments under General Bee checked for a time the onward rush. The limit of resistance was finally reached, and slowly but gradually the Federal troops pushed the enemy before them. Bee's battalion, badly shattered, finally broke and began a full retreat, while the Federals rushed forward with redoubled vigor and triumphant shouts upon the confused retreat, which was rapidly assuming the proportions of a rout. Bee frantically tried to rally his troops, but his efforts were unavailing. His voice was neither heard nor obeyed. At the moment when he was about to give up in despair a courier dashed up to inform him that reinforcements were approaching. Sweeping the field with a glance, Bee saw an array of glittering bayonets advancing in steady order. He galloped away to meet the rescuers, and in a moment was face to face with Jackson. "General," he cried, in bitterness, "they are beating us back." The stern features of Jackson betrayed no emotion as he replied, composedly: "Sir, we will give them the bayonet." The words acted like magic upon Bee. His own men were sweeping to the rear with the Federals in full pursuit, but the brigade of Jackson stood its ground, firmly and undismayed. The very sight was an inspiration. Bee plunged in among his men and shouted: "Look, there is Jackson standing like a stone wall. Let us determine to die here, and we will conquer." The detachments partially rallied and took up a position in support of Jackson. In an instant the fortune of the day had changed. The Federal forces suddenly found themselves confronted by the bayonets of Jackson's brigade, and the advance was checked. For hours afterward the battle raged. During that day Jackson's brigade made many a gallant charge, and his artillery caused havoc in the battalions of the enemy. Throughout it all Jackson remained as calm as though the bullets were not falling like hail and men dropping all about him. At one period, according to Cooke's narrative, one of the officers rode up to him and cried in excitement and alarm, "General, I think the day is going against us." The cool and brief retort of Jackson was, "If you think so, sir, you had better not say anything about it." Finally a bayonet charge by his brigade broke the Federal center, a position which he continued to hold against desperate odds until a general attack all along the line completed the work which Jackson and his men had so bravely begun. For the Northern army the day ended in a retreat which soon became a rout, and at last a precipitous flight, in which everything that would impede a hasty departure from the field was left behind and became spoil in the hands of the victors. Watching the panic when at its height, Jackson quietly remarked: "Give me 10,000 men and I will be in Washington to-night." The following day, in a letter to his wife, Jackson characteristically writes: "Whilst great credit is due to other parts of our great army, God made my brigade more instrumental than any other in repulsing the main attack."

For three days following the battle of Manassas Jackson waited and hoped for the order which should tell him to advance on Washington. "I have three days' rations," he said, "ready to advance. Why doesn't the order come?" The question has never been answered. Certain it is that Jackson here saw an opportunity which, if taken advantage of, by his superiors, might have brought about an entirely different termination of the war. During the succeeding months Jackson and his brigade remained inactive. In November he was promoted to the rank of Major-General, and was ordered to take charge of an army to be composed of detachments from various sections.   This army was officially styled the "Army of the Monongahela."   Jackson at once proceeded to Winchester.   He applied himself with great zeal to organizing and drilling the raw troops which formed part of his command.   His force numbered about 10,000.   Nearly a month after taking command, his old troops, the "Stonewall Brigade," became a part of his forces.   This was the result of a request on his part accompanied by explanations of plans he had laid for a forward movement against the enemy during the winter.   He proposed to clear Virginia of the enemy before spring, and he had even more extensive plans. They included a march into the North against Harrisburg, and finally against Philadelphia.   Jackson firmly believed that these operations, if properly carried out, would terminate the war before the summer of 1862. But his proposition did not find favor at Richmond. The Confederate authorities decided upon a defensive policy calculated to exhaust the patience and resources of the North.   Neither Jackson nor his troops remained idle during the winter; December 17th a part of the Stonewall Brigade marched to the Potomac, drove back the Northern troops posted there, and destroyed Dam No. 5 on the Chesapeake & Ohio Canal.   Jackson then prepared for a bold move against the Federal forces at Romney.   January 1, 1862, Jackson, with 9,000 troops, began a march, which on a lesser scale, might be compared to Napoleon's experience in Russia.   The weather, which was mild at the outset, became intensely cold. Snowstorms followed, and the men suffered terribly. The baggage wagons failed to keep up with the column, provisions became exhausted, and the soldiers, without blankets to cover them, hungry and fatigued, were obliged to sleep in the snow.   The advance met with

practically no resistance until Hancock was reached. At
Bath the Federals had retreated, leaving everything in
the hands of Jackson.   But at Hancock a stubborn
resistance was met with, and after two days of cannonading the effort to capture the town was abandoned. He
now turned to Romney, held by a force estimated at
from 6,000 to 12,000. The terrible weather continued,
men fell by scores in the line, horses perished, wagons
were wrecked, and the troops were almost seized with
a panic. In spite of all these difficulties, Jackson pushed
on to Romney, which was evacuated on his approach.
The object of his expedition had been accomplished, but
only through his perseverance. He left the place well
guarded, and, with his main body, returned to Winchester, having cleared two large counties of the enemy and
holding possession of an important site which the Federals had intended as a connecting link between the
East and West. General Loring and the troops that had
been left at Romney were dissatisfied at their assignment, and so effectually made their complaints to the
authorities at Richmond, that Loring received permission to withdraw from Romney. This evident lack of
confidence in his capacity made Jackson indignant, and
he promptly resigned his commission, but was prevailed
upon by friends to reconsider his hasty determination.

With the spring of 1862 the authorities at Washington began a determined campaign in Virginia, which
was intended as the decisive movement of the war.
Elaborate plans were laid for the converging of four
great armies upon the Confederate capital.   Two of
these, under Banks and Fremont, were to unite and drive
Jackson's forces out of the valley, cut the Confederate
communications, and sweep down toward Richmond.
The "campaign of the valley" was the greatest of Jack-

son's campaigns. Years afterward it was a proud distinction for any man to say that he had "fought with Jackson in the valley." It was not until February 26th that the Federals began to move. Major-General Banks, with 20,000 men, crossed the Potomac River at Harper's Ferry. General Lander was moving from above with a force of 11,000, and by the time he joined the columns of Banks the ranks of the latter had swollen to 35,000 troops, making a total of 46,000 men now posted in Jackson's front. Jackson had at his immediate disposal only about 4,000 men, but was expecting reinforcements, and, therefore, in his own words, "did not feel discouraged." He fully realized the advantages that would accrue to the Federal cause if the enemy succeeded in occupying the valley. On March 3d he wrote to a friend, "If this valley is lost, Virginia is lost." In the same letter he said: "My plan is to put on as bold a front as possible and use every means in my power to prevent an advance whilst our reorganization is going on." On the very day that this letter was written, Banks, with the main portion of his army, left Charlestown and marched to Martinsburg, from which an excellent road led straight upon Winchester, the headquarters of General Jackson. The expected collision came soon enough, and before any aid had come to the Confederates. On March 10th Banks moved upon Winchester, and on the following day was within six miles of the town. After a clash with Ashby's cavalry, which was compelled to fall back, Banks was surprised to find the enemy thrown forward in position to offer battle. This determined front induced him to make no further advance, but to wait for the arrival of his whole army. Jackson determined not to sacrifice his brave men and evacuated Winchester, taking care, however, to leave behind him not a vestige of anything that could be of use to the enemy. The next morning the Federals took possession, and also began a hot pursuit of Jackson. His army disputed every inch of the way, and it was a running battle from Winchester to Mount Jackson, a distance of 45 miles. Here the pursuit was discontinued. Banks massed his troops at Winchester, sent the majority across the Blue Ridge toward Fredericksburg, turned over the command to a subordinate, and went to Washington. Jackson was informed that but four regiments had been left at Winchester, and at once decided to regain his lost ground, a move which he expected would cause the return of the main army to the valley, and thus prevent it from interfering with the movements of the Confederates under General Johnston. Hastening forward, he fell upon the enemy near Kernstown, and it was not until a fierce battle had continued for some time that he discovered himself to be engaged with a force of 11,000. For two hours there was an incessant roar of musketry, officers and men fell on every hand, and still the Federals had failed to crush the indomitable troops of Jackson, who held their ground without flinching. The distance between the adversaries was short. About midway between the opposing lines ran a low but substantial stone wall, to gain the protecting advantage of which each side was gradually but cautiously advancing, keeping up a hot fire. Suddenly both lines broke into a mad rush to gain the stone wall. The Confederates reached it first, and their opponents were still some forty yards distant when the Southerners dropped on their knees, rested their guns on the wall, and poured a deadly fire into the Federal ranks. It was more than human nerve could withstand, and the Northerners broke and fled in wild confusion, leaving hundreds of dead and wounded on the field. The Stonewall Brigade did heroic work, coming at one time or another to the support of almost every part of the field. Finally, at sunset, and at the most critical moment in the battle, the supply of ammunition gave out, and General Garnett, who commanded the brigade, ordered his men to fall back in preference to seeing them shot down without power to return the enemy's fire. Seeing his favorite brigade thus retreating, Jackson galloped up and imperiously ordered a halt. "Beat the rally!" he ordered, grasping the drummer by the shoulder, while bullets sped all about them. The drum rolled and the disordered lines were reformed. But it was too late. The enemy had discovered and taken advantage of this one weak point. With wild cheers they pressed forward and bore back the Confederates. It was Jackson's first and last defeat, but was dearly paid for by the victors. Their loss, according to the reports given out soon afterward, was 418 killed. The Confederates had 80 killed and 342 wounded. Although beaten, Jackson had accomplished what he set out to do; for General Williams, who was leading the main body toward Fredericksburg, heard the roar of artillery, and, suspecting that the Confederates had been strongly reënforced, marched his immense force back into the valley. Jackson retreated slowly, while the enemy leisurely followed, and, after an occasional skirmish, crossed into Elk Run valley, and, on April 19th, took up a strong position near Swift Run Gap and faced the foe. Leaving General Ewell to confront Banks, Jackson proceeded to Staunton, and formed a junction with General Johnston, who with six regiments had advanced by forced marches to intercept the command of General Milroy, who was attempting to join Banks. May 7th four regiments of

Federal pickets were driven off Shenandoah Mountain and the Confederates advanced on the village of Mc-Dowell, where, after a desperate battle, the Northern troops were beaten. A few days later Jackson proceeded in the direction of Harrisonburg, held by General Banks. On Jackson's approach Banks fell back on Strasburg. Jackson now marched and countermarched through the valley, met Milroy's command May 17th, defeated it, and then resumed his march on Harrisonburg. How thoroughly concerned the Federal authorities were at this time with the movements of Jackson is shown by the dispatches of that period. Jackson continuously kept himself, not only in a position to harry the enemy, but also at a moment's notice to respond to any call for aid in the defense of Richmond. He never lost sight of his aim, which was to prevent a concerted attack upon the Confederate capital. That he was succeeding in this design is plainly evident from the following dispatch, sent May 21st by President Lincoln to General McDowell, then at Fredericksburg: "General Fremont has been ordered to move from Franklin on Harrisonburg to relieve General Banks and capture or destroy Jackson's or Ewell's forces. You are instructed, laying aside for the present the movement on Richmond, to put 20,000 men in motion at once for the Shenandoah, moving on the line or in advance of the Manassas Gap Railroad. Your object will be to capture the forces of Jackson and Ewell, either in coöperation with General Fremont, or alone." At this time Jackson was pursuing a daring and aggressive course. May 20th he joined forces with Ewell at Newmarket, while General Banks was fortifying himself at Strasburg. Jackson then made a swift march upon Front Royal, defeated the enemy May 23d, captured great quantities of stores and ammunition, and set out in pursuit of the fleeing Federals. During the day a section of rifled artillery, 700 prisoners, including 20 officers and large quantities of stores, had fallen into the hands of Jackson's army. The following morning the column was again in motion, this time toward Winchester. Near Middletown Jackson came upon the Federal cavalry in rapid retreat. An attack was at once made, the Federals routed, and 200 prisoners were captured, while the great body sought safety in flight. Banks had, in the meantime, ingloriously retreated from Strasburg to Winchester, and from there by rail to Harper's Ferry. Winchester fell under the combined attack of Jackson and Ewell on May 25th, and the victorious Confederates pressed vigorously after the vanquished foe to the very banks of the Potomac, capturing many prisoners, stores, and equipment of every character. But Federal garrisons still held Charlestown and Harper's Ferry, and to these Jackson now directed his attention. On May 28th, twenty minutes after the attack on Charlestown began, the Federal troops retreated and the Confederates entered and were received with the wildest demonstrations of joy by the inhabitants. The following day Jackson, with the main body of his army, was preparing to attack Harper's Ferry, when intelligence reached him that two great Federal armies were closing in upon his rear. Shields was approaching from Fredericksburg on his right, and Fremont from the south branch of the Potomac on his left. Their design was to concentrate a formidable force at Strasburg and cut off his retreat up the valley. His position was a hazardous one, and it was necessary to act with promptness and energy. He dispatched all of his troops to Winchester, and hurried there by special train. At Winchester was congregated the vast stores captured by him and valued at $300,000, and he had, besides, 2,300 prisoners. May 31st he sent the stores and prisoners up the valley and followed with the main body of his army. It was a race between the two armies, with Strasburg as the goal. Jackson reached it first and just in time, for the troops of General Fremont were already close by. After an attack upon Fremont's advance force, which resulted successfully, Jackson retreated toward the upper valley. The retreat resolved itself into a continuous series of skirmishes between the Federal vanguard and the Confederate rear. Finally, after passing Mount Jackson, the army crossed the bridge over the Shenandoah, burned it, and proceeded toward Richmond. At that moment General Shields, with a large Federal force, was advancing up the Luray valley to intercept Jackson at Port Republic, and Fremont's army had crossed the river and were again in pursuit of the Confederates. Jackson's plan was to keep the two Federal armies from uniting, and with this object in view he left General Ewell at Cross Keys to engage Fremont's army, while he proceeded to Port Republic to await the attack of Shields. It came June 7th, and the attacking force was repulsed with heavy loss. At about the same time the army of Fremont attacked the Confederates under Ewell at Cross Keys. The attack was unsuccessful, and Fremont was reported to have lost 2,000 in killed and wounded. Ewell was about to follow up the advantage he had gained by attacking his adversaries, when orders came for him to at once join Jackson at Port Republic. Shields, after being repulsed at Port Republic, had crossed the river and encamped. It was Jackson's design to unite his forces, fall upon Shields, and crush him at a single blow. At midnight Ewell's division left Cross Keys and joined

Jackson before daylight. A small force was left at Cross Keys in order to delude Fremont.

At sunrise Jackson attacked Shields, the battle being a most sanguinary one and resulting in the utter defeat of Shields and a panic-stricken retreat. Jackson captured 450 prisoners, a large quantity of small arms, and one piece of artillery. Immediately after the conflict, while the dead were being buried and the wounded removed, General Fremont and his force appeared on the opposite side of the river. He was furious at the manner in which he had been outwitted, but being unable to cross the river, he retired the next morning.

When the sun set June 9, 1862, the famous "valley campaign" had ended. In three months Jackson with his troops had covered 600 miles, fought four pitched battles, seven smaller engagements and skirmishes; had defeated four armies, captured seven pieces of artillery, 10,000 stands of arms, 4,000 prisoners, and an enormous quantity of stores. "The military results," says Cooke, "in their bearing upon the whole field contest had been very great. At an important crisis in the struggle Jackson had intervened with his small army and, by his skill, endurance, and enterprise, thrown the whole programme of the enemy into confusion. Their design of combining three heavy columns for an attack upon Richmond had been frustrated by his daring advance down the valley; all the campaign halted for the moment; and Fremont and McDowell were not only crippled for the time, but their dangerous adversary was in a condition to unite his forces with those of General Johnston, and make that sudden attack on Chickahominy which led to such important results."

During the next few days Jackson gave his men a well-earned rest, and for several succeeding days

marched and countermarched his army with the object
of deceiving the enemy into believing that the valley
was full of troops, and at the same time to divert attention from Richmond, where the real blow was now about
to be struck. General Robert E. Lee was now in command of the whole Confederate force in front of Richmond. His design was to make a general attack upon
the Federal lines. In this important undertaking he
needed the aid and services of General Jackson and his
army, and in order to help out the scheme of deception
practiced by Jackson, Lee sent reinforcements to the
number of 9,000 men to join him at Staunton.   This
having been done as a blind, the whole force under
Jackson rapidly countermarched and arrived at Ashland on the evening of June 25th, having in the meantime had a conference with General Lee. His directions
were to march with his own, Ewell's, and Whiting's divisions from Ashland to Mechanicsville in an attempt to
turn the enemy's right. At sunrise on the morning of
June 26th his army was on the move, and that afternoon,
after surmounting innumerable difficulties, Jackson was
opposite the right flank of the enemy at Mechanicsville.
The division of A. P. Hill had for some hours been in
position, waiting for the arrival of Jackson before beginning the attack. On being apprised of Jackson's
approach, Hill's division rushed upon the village, drove
out the enemy, and, without waiting until the attack of
Jackson could turn the enemy's flank, swept upon the
strong intrenchments. In spite of the valor of the onset,
the Confederates were repulsed, but remained all night
in front of the enemy's works. Thus began the seven
days' "battles around Richmond." The following morning Hill's division renewed the conflict, but the enemy,
discovering the approach of Jackson in their rear,

retreated along the Chickahominy toward Cold Harbor. Jackson was now ordered to proceed to Cold Harbor and fall upon the line of retreat. Not being acquainted with the country, Jackson took the wrong road, and, while he lost an hour by this mishap, it served in the end a good purpose, inasmuch as it brought him to his destination simultaneously with the arrival of General D. H. Hill, with whom he was instructed to coöperate. The battle was stubbornly fought, and for a time the brilliant charges of the Stonewall Brigade and D. H. Hill's command made no impression upon the foe. Jackson here showed greater excitement than he had ever before displayed upon a battlefield. Finally the enemy began to yield, and, with a spontaneous effort, the Confederates swept the Federal armies into the swamps and to the south side of the Chickahominy. On June 30th Jackson and his army captured a field hospital at Savage Station, containing 2,500 sick and wounded; other prisoners to the number of about 1,000 were also captured. July 1st Jackson and his troops took part in the desperate assault on Malvern Hill, which continued throughout the day, and ceased only on account of darkness and the exhausted condition of the troops. That night, during a discussion among the officers as to the probability of the next move of McClellan, the Federal General, Jackson remarked: "I think he will clear out in the morning." His prophecy came true, for at dawn it was discovered that the Federal army had vanished.

As a result of the disastrous outcome of General McClellan's campaign around Richmond, involving a change of war tactics on the part of the North, General John Pope was now placed in command of the Army of the Potomac. Pope advanced with his army through

Culpepper in the last days of July, without having met
an enemy. It was important, however, that his advance
should be checked, and for this purpose Jackson was
ordered toward Gordonsville to protect it from threatened assault. On August 2d the cavalry of the opposing armies clashed, the Confederates being compelled to
fall back. On the 9th Jackson's small army met Pope's
advance guard on Cedar Run, six miles from Culpepper
Courthouse. The Confederates were being over-
whelmed, when Jackson suddenly appeared, and, by his
presence, and the enthusiasm with which he inspired
the men, turned defeat into victory, which resulted in
a complete repulse of the Federal forces, over 400 prisoners being captured. This blow completely overthrew
the plans of Pope, and he refrained from any further
attempt to advance until fresh forces came to his aid.
Thus began the movement of the Confederates northward. The Federals were driven from Virginia, and
were finally compelled to concentrate all the available
strength possible in Maryland. The Confederates, and
not the Federals, were now the aggressors. On the
night of the 18th Pope's army retreated, and two days
later the whole Confederate army, Jackson having at
this time been joined by General Lee and his forces,
started in pursuit. While the wonderful marches made
at this time by Jackson's troops caused military men
to marvel, no battle of consequence was fought until
August 29th. The armies met near the scene of the first
battle of Manassas, and this battle has therefore become
known as the second battle of Manassas. In spite of
the repeated assaults of the Federals, the Confederates
stubbornly held their ground. The battle lasted three
successive days and ceased at 10 o'clock on the
night of the third day. During that night, in

the midst of a terrific rainstorm, the Federals retreated to the Heights of Centreville. The Confederate loss in this battle was 7,500, and that of the Federals even greater. The brunt of the battle fell upon
Jackson's corps, and his losses exceeded those of any
other division engaged. Recent Confederate successes emboldened Lee to invade Maryland. This move
caused consternation at Washington. Having penetrated as far as Frederick, Md., Lee ordered Jackson to
return to Virginia to dislodge the enemy at Martinsburg
and at Harper's Ferry. The Martinsburg garrison
evacuated the town upon Jackson's approach. Its citizens greeted him with astonishment and delight. On
the morning of September 13th Jackson's army
appeared before Harper's Ferry, and, after a bombardment on the following day, the occupants, on September
15th, surrendered. The victory gave Jackson 11,000
prisoners, 60 pieces of artillery, 13,000 stand of arms,
horses, wagons, and great quantities of military supplies.
In the meantime the forces of Lee had been compelled
by the approach of McClellan's grand army, to evacuate
Frederick, Md. The Federals pursued, and Lee determined to make a stand at Sharpsburg. To this point
Jackson was hastily summoned by a courier, who found
him at Harper's Ferry. The battle of Sharpsburg raged
for two days, the Confederates finally withdrawing into
Virginia in the face of overwhelming numbers. The
battle was fought September 16 and 17, 1862. Three
days later came the battle of Shepherdstown, in which
the Confederates, under Jackson, recaptured a number
of guns which they had lost. After a cessation of hostilities for several weeks, the two armies met again, this
time at Fredericksburg. The town was held by Federal
troops under Burnside. After a series of battles lasting

several days, Burnside quietly withdrew his forces during the stormy night of December 15th. The Federal
troops admitted a loss of 12,000 killed and wounded,
while the Confederate loss was 4,200. Out of this number 2,900 belonged to Jackson's corps. Following the
withdrawal of Burnside's troops from Fredericksburg,
hostilities ceased, and Jackson spent the winter peacefully in camp at Moss Neck. Spring found his corps
increased from 25,000 to 33,000 men, so diligently had
he employed the winter in recruiting. Early on the
morning of April 29th, the announcement was made
that Hooker, leading the Federal army, was crossing
the river. Jackson's corps was speedily rushed forward, when it was discovered that the crossing of the
enemy below Fredericksburg was merely a ruse to
engage attention while larger forces were crossing west
of Fredericksburg.   These forces proceeded toward
Chancellorsville, fifteen miles from Fredericksburg,
where Hooker was massing his army.   Jackson hastily
proceeded toward Chancellorsville, and on the afternoon
of the 2d sent a note to Lee, stating that the enemy had
made a stand at Chancellor's, two miles from Chancellorsville, and announced his intention of attacking.
That evening Jackson suddenly fell upon the enemy
and drove them before him, and, though checked for
a moment at the strong position of Melzi Chancellor's,
continued the rout through the forest and over the
uneven ground known as the "Wilderness," toward
Chancellorsville. Darkness had by this time come on
and the confusion was great. The lines of the various
divisions became mixed and disordered. While reform-
ing his lines for further pursuit, there came a sudden
lull in the fighting. At this time Jackson rode forward
to make a reconnoissance, and found Hooker with fresh

forces turned about and marching to face his foe. Jackson and a few members of his staff advanced along the turnpike for a short distance in the direction of the enemy, when suddenly there was a volley of musketry and the party turned and started for their own lines. As they advanced they were mistaken for Federal cavalry, and a body of Confederates opened fire upon them. General Jackson was thrice wounded. One ball passed through his right hand, another struck his left arm below the elbow, shattering the bone and severing the main artery, while a third struck the same arm above the elbow. Medical aid was hastily summoned, and, although the wounds caused him great pain, he made no complaint. He was carried for a distance by members of his staff, and then determined to walk. Finally, becoming so weak that he was unable to proceed further, he was placed upon a litter. All of this time they were under a heavy fire from the enemy. One of the men carrying him was shot, and the litter fell violently to the ground, causing Jackson for a time excruciating pain. A few hundred yards further on, Dr. McGuire appeared with an ambulance, and the General was taken to the field infirmary at the Wilderness Tavern. The left arm was amputated two inches below the shoulder. He complained that his right side had been injured in falling from the litter, and thought he had struck a stump or stone. No external evidence of injury, however, could be discovered. During the first few days he seemed to be recovering, but on the Thursday following was attacked with nausea and complained of great pain. Examination showed that pleuro-pneumonia had set in. His wife, who had already been sent for, arrived and remained at his bedside until he died. The end came peacefully on Sunday, May 10, 1863. Jackson faced

death as calmly on his bed of pain as he had on the field
of battle, and his last words, uttered distinctly and clearly
as the unconsciousness, from which there was to be no
awakening, began to fall upon him, showed how serene
was his mind and conscience.   These words were: "Let
us cross over the river and rest under the shade of the
trees."   His death was a severe blow to the cause for
which he had fought, and he was sincerely mourned by
the South.   His remains, according to his own request,
were buried at Lexington, after the highest marks of
honor and respect had been paid by the President, Cabinet, and officials of the Confederacy.